D0910294

ROCKEFELLER OF NEW YORK

Nelson A. Rockefeller. Photo by Bob Wands. Rockefeller Family Archives.

ROCKEFELLER OF NEW YORK

EXECUTIVE POWER IN THE STATEHOUSE

BY **ROBERT H. CONNERY**

AND **GERALD BENJAMIN**

CORNELL UNIVERSITY PRESS

ITHACA AND LONDON

First published 1979 by Cornell University Press.
Published in the United Kingdom by Cornell University Press Ltd.,
2-4 Brook Street, London W1Y 1AA.
Printed in the United States of America.

Library of Congress Cataloging in Publication Data
(For library cataloging purposes only)

Connery, Robert Howe, 1907–
  Rockefeller of New York.

  Includes index.
  1. Governors—New York (State)—Powers and duties. 2. Executive power—New York (State) 3. Rockefeller, Nelson Aldrich, 1908–1979 4. New York (State)—Politics and government—1951–   I. Benjamin, Gerald, joint author. II. Title.
JK3451.C66   353.9′747′032   78-23947
ISBN 0-8014-1188-2

Contents

Illustrations

Tables

Preface

Woodrow Wilson, in a lecture delivered at Columbia University in 1907, spoke frankly about the opportunities and limitations of the presidency. "The whole art of statesmanship," he said, "is the art of bringing the several parts of the government into effective cooperation for the accomplishment of particular common objects."[1] The future president had no doubt that in the American system of separation of powers, leadership is lodged in the executive, and that the frequent lack of it is a cardinal defect in our governmental process. A strong president can supply the needed leadership and "is at liberty, both in law and conscience, to be as big a man as he can."[2]

There is no question that Nelson Rockefeller would have heartily endorsed Wilson's views. Certainly he applied them while governor of New York. Rockefeller believed a successful governor was one who could bring the several parts of the state government into effective cooperation, and he sought to be as big a man as he could be.

This book explores in depth the means by which Rockefeller attempted to assert executive leadership in the statehouse, his problems, his successes, and his failures. During his long tenure as governor of the nation's most populous state, Rockefeller had ample opportunity to test the thesis that Woodrow Wilson so clearly set forth some seventy years ago.

Admittedly, New York is unique in some respects, not only in the magnitude of its urban population and its wealth but also in the power available to its chief executive—power much greater than that of his counterparts in most other states. The trend, however, is toward increased power for the governor in many of the nation's states. New York has been a forerunner, with the kind of chief executive that

11

is evolving in most states and that will be the norm in the decades ahead as state governments are pushed to assume a more active role in social and economic areas. To be effective in this expanded activity, powers divided between the executive and the legislative branches require that leadership be lodged somewhere. The governor is the logical choice for this role.

Nelson Rockefeller welcomed the tasks of leadership and attempted to solve the problems of the state as they appeared to him. He paid very little attention to ideology. It is difficult to evaluate an executive who chooses to be known as a problem solver. Ideologues, left and right, may be judged by the degree to which their positions on public policy conform to the general tenets of the world view they espouse. Pragmatists, however, are result-oriented. They need not be consistent, either across or within policy areas. Inconsistency across policy lines may easily be explained as an effort to make the best decision in a particular case. Within an area of policy, one may see a need to change course in order to try something new when a previous effort has failed. The very flexibility inherent in the problem-solving approach makes it exceedingly difficult to pin down the executive for an evaluative analysis.

It might be argued that Rockefeller, who chose to be an activist, pragmatic governor, should be judged on his own terms, that is, on the basis of whether his policies met their goals, whether they "succeeded." But this prescription for analysis is deceptively simple. Public policy emerges as the result of compromise. Policy goals are often unclear. Indeed, in both the design of policy and its implementation, each actor has his own goals, and often goals must be intentionally obscured if action is to be politically possible. Then there is the problem of measurement. Government, unlike business, has no bottom line. The problems—mental health, drug addiction, social welfare, urban housing, public transportation, and so on—are exceedingly complex. How is it known when, if ever, such problems are solved? Indexes of success and failure vary with the techniques used to measure them, and actors choose those measures that suit their needs.

Nor is the analysis of the motives of public officials any less complex. At best it is a chancy business. Certainly Rockefeller was ambitious for higher office, but personal ambition is one of the engines that drives a democratic system. We do not attempt to argue that Rockefeller as governor was devoid of personal and political motives. We do explore the effects of those motives on a complex process that was also influenced by other considerations—available alternatives, public needs, and policy priorities.

A critical analysis of policy is different from a questioning of motives. Certainly Rockefeller made errors in policy as governor. Perhaps his greatest error was a series of decisions on taxing and borrowing. But observers have tended to evaluate the programs of the entire Rockefeller administration on the basis of a few prominent examples. Emphasis on scattered decisions, however, may obscure rather than clarify the record. Only a careful, balanced, and detailed review of major public policy initiatives in New York between 1959 and 1973 can truly reveal Nelson Rockefeller's impact on the state, and in doing so suggest the extent and limits of executive power in state government in the United States today.

Decisions must be evaluated on the basis of the information available to the executive at the time of choice and the nature of the decision and implementation processes. Were available alternatives explored? Were resource constraints considered? At the same time, the long-term effect of decisions on New York State and its people cannot be ignored. Because Nelson Rockefeller served so long, the cumulative impact of his tenure was probably greater than that of any other man who ever served as governor. This analysis is properly concerned with the situation in which he found New York in 1958 and that in which he left it a decade and a half later.

It should be noted that this work is neither a biography of Nelson Rockefeller nor an exploration of his national political career. It explores his early years, before he became governor, only to the extent that his experiences influenced his actions in Albany. There are passing references to his vice-presidency, but this account ends, for all practical purposes, with the close of the Rockefeller governorship in 1973.

Research for this book began in 1969. While the public papers of Governor Rockefeller and his predecessors, containing their annual State of the State messages and a great variety of other documents, were a valuable source of information, our major sources were interviews with state, federal, and local officials, members of the governor's staff, journalists, and politicians of the major parties. We had free access to the Executive Chamber archives, which include the governor's correspondence. These files are voluminous (an accumulation of some seventy file-cabinet drawers a year) and offer much dross as well as insights into the way the state's business is conducted. The press was also a source of information, since it provided a running commentary on state problems and policies.

Interviews with our informants were largely unstructured; they dealt with the way the people being interviewed perceived their duties, their relations with other government agencies and the public, their major problems, and their suggestions for improvement. Journalists, politicians, and administrators were queried about the role of the governor in policy formation, his political tactics, and his personal characteristics. Governor Rockefeller and his immediate staff were interviewed many times. Neither the governor nor any of his staff, however, read the manuscript, although short passages were occasionally examined by state officials in the interest of factual accuracy.

We are grateful to a number of graduate students at Columbia University who during their summer vacations acted as research assistants. They compiled hundreds of pages of notes from interviews and public records. We would also like to thank our professional colleagues at Columbia and elsewhere who read various chapters of the manuscript. We owe an additional debt to a large number of public officials at every level of state government in New York and elsewhere who gave freely of their time and advice. Many of them are cited in the notes. Without their cooperation this work would not have been possible.

The librarians at Columbia University, the State University of New York at New Paltz, and the Legislative Reference Library in Albany assisted by making their extensive reference materials available. Joseph Ernst of the Rockefeller Family Archives Center in Pocantico Hills, New York, was especially helpful in obtaining photographs and other research materials. The help of Anne Cule in typing the manuscript was invaluable, as was the editorial assistance of William Farr.

While this book is thus the product of the joint endeavors of many people, we alone are responsible for the final manuscript, since we determined not only its conclusions but its form.

Robert H. Connery

New York City

Gerald Benjamin

New Paltz, New York

ROCKEFELLER OF NEW YORK

1

The Shaping of the New York Governorship

Nelson Rockefeller served as governor of New York for four consecutive terms covering fifteen years. He held office longer than any other New York governor in the past century, his tenure exceeded only by that of George Clinton in the late eighteenth century.[1] By the end of his last year in office, there were college seniors who could remember no other governor of the state in their lifetime. Indeed, many of these students attended colleges built by the state to accommodate them in accordance with projections made by Governor Rockefeller while they were still in kindergarten. Surely, like the Renaissance pope who outlived all of the cardinals who elected him and who had a medal struck with the motto "I created you, not you me," Rockefeller in many ways remade in his own image his state and the party that nominated him.

Because of the force of his decade-and-a-half presence at the pinnacle of state government, most contemporary treatments of New York seek to explain all of the political process in terms of Rockefeller's personal preferences and private motives.[2] The enormous wealth and prominence of the Rockefeller family contributed to this emphasis, as did the governor's activist style and well-known presidential ambition. But the phenomenon of the Rockefeller administration offers an opportunity to go beyond personal wealth and ambition, to explore two hardy perennial questions, two persistent and at times seemingly intractable problems in the study of state government: What freedom is there for an autonomous state policy in the American federal system? And within that range of freedom, whatever it may be, what scope is there for political leadership from the governor's office in determining the direction of policy choices? The two questions are related, but are at least analytically distinct. From them flows a third, one of transcendent importance: What are the limits of the ability of state government, and indeed of government in general, to find solutions to the societal problems that it approached so optimistically in the halcyon days of the 1960s?

The State in the Federal System

Nearly a century ago Woodrow Wilson wrote that "the question of the relations of the states to the federal government is the cardinal question of our constitutional system. At every turn of our national development we have been brought face to face with it, and no definition either of statesmen or of judges has ever quieted or decided it. It cannot, indeed, be settled by the opinion of any one generation, because it is a question of growth, and every successive stage of our political and economic development gives it a new aspect, makes it a new question."[3]

There is no doubt that the relation of the states to the national government is still the cardinal question of our constitutional system. In the paradoxical American federal system, which divides at the same time that it unites jurisdictions, state governments occupy a midway position. Laws, regulations, allocations of federal grants, supervision, and audits come down from Washington, binding the state. Counties, municipalities and organized private interests—commercial, philanthropic, and ideological—present Albany with demands that well up from their constituencies. These processes restrict choice and define the state agenda. So, for instance, any likely government of New York State, Republican or Democratic, must have built the Thruway or a similar superhighway, though not necessarily as a toll road with the name of former governor Thomas E. Dewey attached to it and not necessarily in the particular years when it was built. Similarly, any government in Albany in the past generation, like the governments in neighboring Connecticut and New Jersey, must have made and increased state grants-in-aid to local school districts. Are all major policy areas so constrained? Does any state, even the richest, have the will and the wherewithal to face, creatively and independently, the host of domestic problems now on America's agenda? Between the upper and nether millstones, how far could New York depart from the norm for state government?

The federal relationship in the American system has never been a simple one. Even in the earliest days of the republic, the national government was involved to some extent in policy areas generally considered preserves of the states, and as time passed, constitutional interpretation allowed growth in the scope and depth of the involvement.[4] This growth was not without pain. Much of the bitter debate that ultimately led to the Civil War was a failed attempt to find a firm definition of the division of power between the nation and the states.

In this century, technological changes with a national impact, such as the mass production of automobiles, generated demands on state government that ultimately could be met only through resources available at the national level. Similarly, the engulfing crisis of the Great Depression considerably extended the list of policy areas in which the states and the national government cooperated in seeking solutions to national problems tailored to local circumstances. And in those areas for which the states were not primarily responsible, the government in Washington added complexity to federalism by seeking direct relationships with cities and other local governments or by providing services directly to citizens.[5]

After the host of innovations in the 1930s, the two decades between America's entry into World War II and the coming of the Kennedy administration to Washington in 1961 saw little change in the shape of federalism. War management and foreign policy preoccupied the Democratic administrations before 1952, and though several studies and some new steps were taken by the Republicans under Eisenhower, they were usually in policy areas, such as highways, in which the relationships between the national and state governments were already well established.[6] In New York, as in many other states during this period, limited resources, cautious executive leadership, and a malapportioned state legislature ensured that efforts toward finding solutions to major social problems or tapping federal resources to do so would be minimal.

But as New York's newly elected governor, Nelson Rockefeller, took office in 1959, the most far-reaching changes in the federal system since the 1930s were in the offing. Scholars had already begun writing about a new role for the states, a redefinition of the federal–state relationship. They pointed out that, unlike most countries of the world, where major political decisions were made in a nation's capital, the United States had a flexible federal system that allowed the states to go beyond their traditional concerns and begin new programs in such areas as land-use control, the arts, public housing, urban development, and pollution abatement.[7] Then, under Presidents Kennedy and Johnson, federal programs were begun and funds poured into a vast number of new policy areas. Federal aid formulas made state involvement in these programs attractive, and if the states failed to act, there was always the possibility that they would again be bypassed. In addition, by the mid-1960s a different kind of national action, Supreme Court decisions mandating reapportionment of state legislatures, opened the way to increased state involvement in controversial social policy areas and thus to greater responsiveness to national initiatives.

A number of important issues emerged from the rapid and large-scale changes in federalism that occurred during the 1960s. Should grants be made as a result of competition among states and localities, or should they be distributed to all on the basis of formulas? How should program costs be shared between the nation and the states? Which level should control policy making? Under what circumstances should states, and even local governments, be bypassed by the national government in program implementation? Did federal programs distort state priorities? Did such programs cause states to overextend themselves fiscally? What of legislation passed on the national level that promised more than was ultimately delivered by the appropriations process? Could federal funding levels for aid programs be made predictable, so that states could accurately build them into their budgetary processes?

Nelson Rockefeller came to the New York governorship committed to the revitalization of state government. His activist, problem-solving style was evident from the first; it was not simply a response to the changing federal environment in which he found himself. But the context created by the domestic initiatives of the 1960s was one in which Rockefeller's already developed style could flourish. He sought to build a governorship in New York that could capitalize on every new opportunity offered by the changing federal system and ultimately, through lobbying in the national executive and legislative branches, to alter that system itself to meet the needs of the state. Rockefeller's successes and failures in this area are responsible for much of the shape of contemporary New York government and, because of the leadership role he assumed, had a great impact on state government elsewhere as well. Indeed, because of his activism, the study of the Rockefeller administration becomes an excellent means of gaining an understanding of the enormous changes in federalism during the governor's fifteen-year tenure and the manner in which those changes fundamentally altered state government in the United States.

To say all this, however, is not to argue that New York should be the focus of attention because its experience was somehow "typical" of that of state government during the years from 1959 to 1973. In fact, there is probably no "typical" state. It is interesting that the constitutional equality of the states in the federal system has shaped popular perceptions and has led observers to think that the category labeled "state" contains more or less equal entities. Yet there are almost as many social, economic, and geographic differences among the states as there are similarities. Some are fairly obvious. Rhode Island contains 1,214 square miles; Alaska, 586,412. Wyoming had a population of 362,000 in 1974; California, 20,876,000. In 1970 there were no metropolitan areas in Vermont, while nearby Massachusetts was 97.1 percent metropolitan. Other differences may be less apparent. Louisiana is rich in energy resources; Connecticut is energy poor. Maryland's 3,000 miles of tidal shoreline do not offer the same problems of resource development and environmental management as does landlocked Nebraska's plains.

The states differ widely not only in their objective circumstances but also in their political cultures.[8] Rates of voter participation in general elections vary widely among them. In Indiana, political parties are very strong. In California they are extraordinarily weak. New Jersey voters tolerate a relatively high level of political corruption, the people of Wisconsin almost none. Patronage is a way of life in Massachusetts, anathema in Minnesota. Two-party competition is close in Illinois, still almost nonexistent in some southern states.

There is a host of reasons—historical, demographic, social, and economic—for these differences among the states. The important point to remember is that they exist and that over time they have shaped the development of state governments and political institutions. Thus similar problems or policy areas are approached very differently in different contexts. There is, for example, great variety in the mix of state and local responsibilities among the states. In Hawaii almost everything, even elementary education, is administered from the state level. In New York the preference has been to leave the administration of as many programs as possible to the localities, with the state offering fiscal assistance and retaining an overseeing role. In the end, each state seems to get the government it wants and needs. The more populous states with developed economies tend to have executives and legislatures with greater powers and resources and bigger, stronger bureaucracies to deal with their more sophisticated environments.[9] And in each region pacesetters seem to emerge, states that set the standard for governance among their neighbors and sometimes for the entire nation.[10]

New York has been such a pacesetter. Labeled one of the "mega-states of America" by journalist Neal Peirce,[11] the Empire State ranks thirteenth in land area among the states, and until 1970 ranked first in population. If New York State had been an independent nation in 1959, when Rockefeller became governor, it would have been the twenty-fifth largest in population in the world. A state with a highly developed industrial economy and a strong agricultural base, New York is a place of contrasts. It has several major regional urban centers and one of the few world cities in the United States, New York City, which is the business, communications, and banking center of the nation and the world. Yet New York is also a rural state, with over 12 million acres of farmlands and, in the Adirondacks, one of the largest virgin forest preserves east of the Mississippi River. It is a state with extremes of affluence and poverty, in which the rich of Manhattan's Sutton Place live side by side with the poor of East Harlem. New York is also the state with the most diverse population in the nation.[12] In it, as publicists are fond of reminding visitors, you can find more Jews than in all of Israel, more Italians than in Naples or Milan, more Puerto Ricans than in San Juan, and more blacks than in the African nation of Liberia.

But to add to the complexity, New York's situation is not static. Throughout the period of the Rockefeller governorship the Empire State faced all the familiar problems of those northeastern and midwestern centers with already developed economies. Poor blacks and Puerto Ricans poured into the state's cities from the South and the West Indies in search of opportunity, at the same time that industries began to leave in search of locations that would offer lower costs and greater efficiency. The white middle-class population continued its exodus to the suburbs, leaving the urban centers bereft of indigenous leadership and with diminished tax bases from which to meet ever increasing demands for basic services. Social change translated into greater demands upon the city and state governments, but increasing taxes to meet these demands only served to exacerbate distinctive economic and demographic trends.

New York is interesting precisely because it is an atypical state, in both its resources and the problems it faces. As Nelson Rockefeller assumed the governorship, he took on the mantle of a governmental tradition of leadership among the states. New Yorkers knew they paid more taxes than the citizens of other states, perhaps because the size and complexity of their state demanded bigger government. New Yorkers had also come to expect more from their governor and state government in general. These expectations included what one scholar has called an "image of positive liberalism," a pattern of innovative and compassionate responses to major problems that provided a model for other states in the region and throughout the nation.[13]

The Premise of Gubernatorial Leadership

New York began with a strong executive. Historians like to point out that the dislike for the royal governors in the colonies led to a concentration of power in the legislature and to weak governors in the new states created during the War for Independence. New York State was a unique exception to this experience. There was no strong attack on executive power, and the first state constitution, adopted in 1777, gave George Clinton, the first governor, extensive powers. The constitution stated: "The supreme executive power and authority of this state shall be vested in a governor." He was to "take care that the laws are faithfully executed" and was empowered to "transact all necessary business with the officers of government." It was his responsibility to correspond with the Continental Congress and with other governors.

The governor was also commander in chief of the armed forces. He could grant pardons, convene the legislature on extraordinary occasions, inform the legislature on the condition of the state, and recommend matters for their consideration. The power to veto legislation and to appoint various state officers was not granted outright but placed under councils of which he was a member—the Council of Appointment and the Council of Revision.[14]

Most of the new state constitutions provided for the election of the governor by the state legislature. In New York State he was elected by the people, although with a restrictive franchise. One- or two-year terms were customary in most states. In New York the governor's term was three years. In most states the governor could not succeed himself; in New York he was eligible for reelection indefinitely. In fact, the first governor, George Clinton, served six consecutive three-year terms and seven years later was elected for a seventh term. Historian Allan Nevins called the three-year term and indefinite reeligibility an unheard-of act of generosity and characterized the New York governor's powers as "similar to those of the Crown Governor."[15] It has been argued that New York served as a model for the

United States presidency as designed by the constitutional convention in 1787.[16]

Notwithstanding the powers granted in the 1777 constitution, in New York, as elsewhere, the nineteenth-century governorship as an institution was subordinate in importance to the state legislature. In 1821 the term of the New York governor was reduced to two years, and although it returned to three in 1872, it was again reduced to two years in 1894. In the meantime the number of state officials elected directly by the people increased, and as the state took on new educational and business functions, a large number of boards and commissions were established, many of whose members served for terms considerably longer than that of the governor. By 1915 there were some 150 departments, boards, and commissions with responsibility so divided that it was all but impossible to discover where the real power lay. Indeed, no one seemed able to understand how the New York State government really worked.

Thus by the early twentieth century the need for reform was evident. The possibility of a return to the Hamiltonian notion of a strong executive became increasingly attractive. In 1915 the New York Bureau of Municipal Research, under the direction of Frederick Cleveland, who had been staff director of President Taft's Commission on Economy and Efficiency (1909–1911), was asked to prepare an appraisal of the governmental structure of New York State for the State Constitutional Convention Commission. The philosophy underlying this report, which profoundly influenced the reorganization of state governments elsewhere as well, was to make democratic control more effective through the short ballot and to reduce the number of elected offices while making overhead control of administration more efficient by increasing the power of the governor.[17]

The report recommended an increase in the governor's term from two to four years, the consolidation of state agencies into twenty departments under commissioners appointed by the governor and holding office at his pleasure, an executive department to serve as the governor's staff, an executive budget, and extension of the merit service to protect state employees from discharge for political reasons. The constitutional convention met in Albany in April 1915 under the chairmanship of Elihu Root. In his remarks opening the convention, Senator Root urged that the constitution be brought up to date and greatly reduced in length.[18] But the constitution that emerged was as long as its predecessor and was rejected by the voters when it was submitted in a referendum.

Alfred E. Smith, then a member of the legislature, played a significant role in the convention and gained the respect of leading Republicans as well as Democrats for his knowledge of state government. Smith embraced the major recommendations of the Cleveland study, although he found little support for them among rank-and-file convention members. The support came from such Republican leaders as Charles E. Hughes, Elihu Root, and John Lord O'Brian, who were unable to prevail over their fellow delegates.

In November 1918 Smith was elected governor by a plurality of almost 15,000 votes over Charles Whitman, who was serving his third term as governor. When Smith began his governorship, World War I had just ended and unemployment was spreading as many thousands of veterans returned. At the suggestion of Belle Moskowitz, one of his most trusted aides, Smith's first act was to appoint a reconstruction commission to work on postwar problems. Robert Moses was chief of staff for this commission.[19]

The commission reports covered a wide range of state fiscal, housing, and educational problems. Its most important recommendation called for a reorganization of the state government along the lines laid down in the Cleveland report and endorsed by Smith before he became governor. But Smith was defeated in 1920, and the legislature refused to pass the constitutional amendments necessary to reorganize the state government. Not until his reelection in 1922 and again in 1924 and 1926 did he succeed. Since a constitutional amendment required the approval of two successive legislatures and adoption by the voters in a referendum, the state departments were not finally consolidated until January 1, 1927, and the executive budget was not adopted until 1928.

Al Smith later called the reorganization of state government his greatest achievement. Certainly the changes he sponsored and fought for over a decade and a half provided the framework for the later strong governorships of Franklin D. Roosevelt, Herbert Lehman, and Thomas Dewey. All of these men were able to combine the formal powers given them by constitutional reform with the patronage and party leadership roles inherent in their offices to dominate state politics during their tenure.

New York was thus committed to the strong executive model of state government well before Nelson Rockefeller even considered seeking the governorship. The state began its life with a strong governor and was one of the first to accept the advice of twentieth-century reformers that the best route to modern democracy was a strong executive, in control of virtually all the functions of the state, who could then be called to account by the voters at election time. The legislature's meetings were too periodic, reformers argued, and its members too subject to the influence of special interests. Only the executive could command the information and resources to make the bureaucracy responsive and responsible.

Leadership Style

The powers of the governor, no matter how great, are an empty vessel, to be filled by the particular style of the person elected to the office. Research on leadership has shown that the effectiveness of a leader lies in his ability to motivate others to act within a given context, in a desired direction.[20] Techniques of leadership that may work in one set of circumstances may fail in others, and leaders must thus be sensitive to changing circumstances. There is no one "political man," no universal pattern of leadership.

Nevertheless, just as traditional analysts of government recommended the strengthening of formal executive powers (and continue to do so in those jurisdictions that still have weak executives), more recent writers have discerned an optimum leadership style. In his extraordinarily influential book *Presidential Power*, first published in 1960, Richard E. Neustadt argued for an activist executive, "a president who knows what power is and wants it."[21] In a later work, equally influential, James David Barber plumbed the characters of all presidents from Theodore Roosevelt to Richard Nixon. On the basis of his research, Barber isolated two key factors: the energy invested by the executive in his job ("Does he actively make his environment or is he passively made by it?") and his feelings about what he does ("Is his effort in life a burden to be endured or an opportunity for personal enjoyment?").[22] Of the four types yielded by these two categories, Barber found the active-positive presidents—FDR, Truman, and Kennedy—to be the most open to evidence, flexible, and able to lead successfully in a democratic environment.

The premium that analysts placed on activism in the executive was not confined to the national level. In the cities and the states, the search was for executives who could "make the system work" and "get things done." Television, with its need for photogenic leaders and stories that could be presented visually, served to enhance this emphasis. Activist mayors and governors, those who met the needs of the medium, became national figures.[23]

Nelson Rockefeller was clearly in Barber's active-positive mold. He sprang from an environment of enormous wealth and, though not raised permissively, once on his own was unaccustomed to being denied when he reached for a goal. He had the expectation, not uncommon among the very rich, that the environment could be altered to meet his needs. Solutions to problems could be found if enough material and intellectual resources could be brought to bear on them.

Rockefeller's early professional experiences reflected the development of this active-positive orientation. At an early age he held major corporate posts. As a director of Creole Petroleum Corporation in the 1930s, he successfully urged the reform of corporate activities in Latin America before the Standard Oil board. As the manager of Rockefeller Center, he aggressively cut prices in order to fill his father's empty buildings. The trade unions were kept happy because of Rockefeller's recognition of them, but other commercial renters compared Nelson's ruthless tactics to those of his grandfather, John D. Rockefeller. From his earliest days in business, Nelson Rockefeller was accustomed to being listened to and to doing what was necessary to get the job done.

Rockefeller's first major experience in government came in 1940, during Franklin D. Roosevelt's second term, when, just after the fall of France, he placed a memorandum on Latin American policy before Harry Hopkins, Roosevelt's closest adviser. Soon Rockefeller was on the staff of James Forrestal, another presidential aide, seeking to implement his plan of economic assistance to Latin America, designed to ward off the Nazi threat. Later he was to continue this work as a presidentially appointed coordinator of Latin American affairs.[24]

During his tenure as coordinator, Rockefeller was fortunate in having ready access to various influential members of the Roosevelt administration. Harry Hopkins, who had the president's ear, not only was Rockefeller's original sponsor but also advised him on how to win support for his program. Others knowledgeable in the ways of bureaucracy gave him good advice, which he heeded to his profit. Edwin M. ("Pa") Watson at the White House said: "If you want to see the President, don't raise problems without answers. He has enough problems on his desk already. Always be sure to have solutions ready, even if they are alternative solutions." He learned a great deal from Jesse Jones, with whom he worked closely, seeing him at least every Thursday afternoon at five o'clock. Jones once said to him, "When you go in to see the president, always have a memorandum ready explaining the course of action that you wish, which he can approve or disapprove, but be sure to get it in writing." After Roosevelt died, Rockefeller felt he was fortunate in having the president's written approval for a number of policies on which he wanted to act.[25]

In addition to the good offices of Hopkins, Pa Watson and Jesse Jones provided Rockefeller with access to Roosevelt. His propensity to bypass normal channels, however, ultimately got him into trouble. In November 1944, Edward Stettinius, Jr., the new secretary of state, appointed him assistant secretary for Latin America. Less than a year later, when James F. Byrnes succeeded Stettinius, one of his first actions was to request Rockefeller's resignation. In that brief period Rockefeller had managed to annoy high State Department officials and some of the press by two activities that in the long run proved sound.

The government of Juan Perón in Argentina not only was a dictatorship that disregarded civil rights and interfered in the governments of the neighboring countries but was also pro-Nazi. As a result, during the war years it was quarantined by the Allied powers and the other Latin American states. Shortly after Rockefeller became assistant secretary, he organized a conference of the Latin American powers in Mexico City with the approval of President Roosevelt. One of the results of this conference was an agreement that later became known as the Act of Chapultepec, which in turn led to the signing of an inter-American treaty of mutual defense by whose terms an attack on one country in the Western Hemisphere would be considered an attack on all and would require joint action against the aggressors. A regional agreement without Argentina would have had serious difficulties, and it was agreed at the Mexico City conference that if Argentina would democratize its government and declare war on the Axis powers, the quarantine would be lifted and diplomatic relations reestablished. These negotiations, which in large measure bypassed normal State Department channels, made Rockefeller no friends in the Foreign Service, or in the American press, which was bitterly anti-Perón.

The second incident concerned the drafting of the United Nations Charter at the San Francisco Conference. As the war drew to a close, the State Department was primarily concerned with the development of the United Nations. Rockefeller and his Latin American friends felt that a strong inter-American regional arrangement was of the utmost importance. The early draft of the UN Charter contained an article endorsed by the Soviet government that would permit military alliances among the member nations against former enemy states. No mention was made of the Western Hemisphere alliance. Rockefeller's efforts, exerted through Senator Arthur Vandenberg, led to the inclusion of Article 51 of the charter, specifically guaranteeing self-defense and recognizing the principles of the Monroe Doctrine and the Act of Chapultepec, and thus permitting the various Western Hemisphere agreements that came in the years that followed, including the Mutual Defense Pact of 1947.[26]

After his resignation as assistant secretary of state, Rockefeller returned to the family offices in New York City. He reentered public life seven years later when he joined the Eisenhower administration. As chairman of the president's Advisory Committee on Government Reorganization, he proposed, among other things, the creation of the Department of Health, Education, and Welfare (HEW). When the recommendation was implemented in 1953, he was appointed to serve as undersecretary of the new department and became the chief deputy to the secretary, Oveta Culp Hobby. At that time, heavy battalions in the Eisenhower administration (especially in the Treasury Department and the Bureau of the Budget) and in the GOP House leadership were trying to roll back the New Deal. For eighteen months Rockefeller was plunged into areas of domestic social policy that were highly controversial: aid to education and government health insurance. His efforts in these areas put him to the left of the Republican center of gravity and marked him as a liberal, a mark that stayed with him and became a permanent handicap in national politics among Republicans west of the Hudson.

It is thus not surprising that when the opportunity presented itself to return to the arena of foreign affairs, Rockefeller seized it. In December 1954 he resigned as undersecretary of HEW and became President Eisenhower's special assistant for foreign affairs. In this post he was to give "advice and assistance in the development of increased understanding and cooperation among all peoples," and, to facilitate his work, was mandated "to attend cabinet and other top level meetings."[27] Later the special assistant's job became a very important one under Kennedy, Johnson, and Nixon. Under Eisenhower, however, its duties were vague and its powers limited. This assignment was almost bound to bring him into conflict with the State Department as well as the Budget Bureau and the Treasury, as indeed it did.

With his many years of experience in the army, President Eisenhower was accustomed to a system in which the staff proposed a program and the chief acted on the basis of the proposal. He relied

Rockefeller with President Eisenhower (1955). Courtesy National Park Service.

heavily on major department heads. In foreign affairs he depended on Secretary of State John Foster Dulles (who had had a run-in with Rockefeller at San Francisco over the UN Charter in 1945), and in domestic affairs on Treasury Secretary George Humphrey and Budget Director Roland Hughes. These cabinet officers, along with Under Secretary of State Herbert Hoover, Jr., and John B. Hollister, director of the International Cooperation Administration, were committed to holding down government spending and felt that Rockefeller's influence with Eisenhower was harmful to their program. Nor did they approve of a special assistant in the White House dabbling in foreign affairs. On the other hand, Sherman Adams, who had been a governor and was a politician, was better able to understand what Rockefeller was talking about—that what was needed was to work out problems through personal contacts.

Eisenhower's reliance on the army staff system led him, in disputes between Rockefeller and his older department heads, to favor the latter. A major showdown came at the first summit conference in Geneva in 1955 to relieve Cold War tensions between the Soviet Union and the Western powers. In preparation for this meeting, Rockefeller arranged a seminar at Quantico, Virginia, the Marine Corps base near Washington, D.C. To this meeting he invited experts from colleges, private groups, and government. This technique, which Rockefeller had used earlier, was one that was to continue after he became governor of New York.

The major proposal that came out of the seminar was that the United States make a dramatic peace gesture at Geneva for an "open skies" plan that called for the international aerial inspection of all countries so as to prevent secret preparations for atomic warfare. Rockefeller wanted Eisenhower to take this position at Geneva, but Dulles strongly opposed it. Despite this opposition, Rockefeller approached the president three times with his idea. Finally Eisenhower said, "Damn it, Nelson. I told you that we are not going to do this and that we are simply going to identify the areas in dispute, as the secretary of state has stated."[28] When the Geneva meeting was held, Eisenhower's initial speech on the opening day merely defined the various issues in dispute between the East and the West. The speech aroused little interest and it soon appeared that little progress would be made without a fresh initiative.

Rockefeller, who was under wraps in Paris, was hurriedly summoned to Geneva and, with Harold Stassen, was given the job of drafting the open-skies plan for a new speech by the president. The proposal was enthusiastically received by the Western delegates, and even Soviet representatives had a few kind words for the proposal, although Khrushchev bitterly denounced the speech as insincere. Thus on three occasions during his Washington years Rockefeller had an impact on American foreign policies, but each time his recommendations ran counter to those of the State Department.

By December 1955, Rockefeller had had enough of bucking the major powers in the Eisenhower administration. He told the president that personal affairs made it necessary for him to resign as special assistant. Later he said, "After fifteen years in and out of federal appointive offices I came to the conclusion that decisions affecting our future as a nation, at home and abroad, were made by elected officials and not by appointed officials."[29]

Rockefeller learned several things from his Washington experience that later were of value to him as governor of New York. One was an understanding of the way in which legislative committees worked. Traditionally, junior bureaucrats get short shrift before congressional committees, whose members are conscious of their own importance. Frequently they are required to await the pleasure of the committee for an hour or two before being called upon to testify. For their part, congressmen and senators who have long served on a committee accumulate a good deal of knowledge about government activities in a particular area. Once or twice in early appearances Rockefeller was caught unprepared for questions posed by a committee member. Thereafter he took care to be thoroughly briefed on the subject upon which he was to give testimony. Senior congressmen could be abrupt in posing questions to a young man, even if—and perhaps because—he was a Rockefeller. Over the years he became quite skillful in presenting his testimony before congressional committees, relying heavily on visual aids, such as charts and graphs.[30] In the main, Rockefeller fared rather well, but he learned that he must carefully prepare his presentation and patiently argue his case. Later he applied these lessons in dealing with the New York State legislature.

Rockefeller's experience in various administrative posts gave him a keen appreciation of the importance of the organization. He learned the principles of management, although he later confessed that when he first went to Washington, he thought Franklin D. Roosevelt was a very inefficient manager.[31] Frequently the function of the new agencies that Roosevelt established overlapped with those of existing agencies. Years later Rockefeller realized that this was a method of getting people to do what Roosevelt wanted done in a program. Rockefeller concluded that "people can only change so much and bureaucrats soon get into a rut in the way in which they operate. The environment may change, but the bureaucrats won't move fast enough to meet new conditions. One way of handling this is to organize a new agency with new people."[32] As governor of New York, Rockefeller used this technique in creating the Department of Environmental Affairs, transferring functions from two older departments.

One lesson Rockefeller learned in Washington was the danger of putting too much power in the hands of a single subordinate. At one point, while he was coordinator for Latin America, his deputy with outside help worked out a scheme by which he could take control of economic affairs in Latin America away from Rockefeller. Rockefeller fired the deputy the same afternoon he heard about it.[33] This experience was probably the genesis of what was later called the "troika system" in New York State. Thereafter, as Jesse Jones suggested, Rockefeller always had three to five subordinates reporting directly to him, not one.

Despite these problems, his wartime post allowed Rockefeller to recruit several top assistants who were to become lifelong friends and associates. Among them were Wallace Harrison, an architect; John E. Lockwood, who became general counsel to the agency; Louise Boyer, a personal aide; and Frank Jamieson, who became director of the press section. Harrison, Jamieson, and Lockwood were the trio Rockefeller turned to most frequently in the years ahead.

An important by-product of his Washington experience was his acquaintanceship with a number of men who later occupied high federal office. In the 1940s Lyndon Johnson was a young congressman from Texas. He and Rockefeller, through their mutual affection for Sam Rayburn, began a friendship that continued until Johnson's death. Mike Mansfield was chairman of the House Committee on Foreign Affairs, before which Rockefeller testified on occasion as coordinator of Latin American affairs. Richard Nixon was vice-president at the time that Rockefeller served on President Eisenhower's White House staff. Rockefeller did not have many contacts with Nixon during that period, although he saw him at meetings of the cabinet and the National Security Council. He had also known him earlier, when Nixon was a congressman from California.

Besides these individuals, Rockefeller made a host of friends in Democratic as well as Republican circles. His experience both inside and outside of the government was cumulative. In early life he became interested in the educational and health activities of the Rockefeller Foundation. This knowledge was reinforced by his work as coordinator of Latin American affairs. His business experience was useful in Washington and broadened his knowledge of organization and management. In his relations with Congress and the president he had several setbacks and had to learn much in the rough school of practical politics. He had to work with many men from many walks of life, a valuable experience for a scion of a family of great wealth. He also became friendly with a number of young newspaper reporters in Washington, and these friendships continued over the years as they rose in the ranks of their profession.

On the other hand, he found that, while his name opened doors, even to the White House, it was not much protection in bureaucratic infighting. His wealth and contacts made it possible to develop imaginative proposals, but their acceptance depended on the decisions of other men. Even when his name brought access to high places, his style created jealousies and made enemies because he ignored proper channels. A brash young man with ideas, enthusiasm, and a good personality, he was a mediocre speaker. He was knocked around a bit in Washington and he learned from the experience.

Rockefeller's early experiences had revealed him to be an activist executive with a positive orientation toward problem solving. He had learned in Washington that the road to real political power did not lie through appointive office, but he had never carried a precinct, had never even sought election. He knew that if he were ever to reach the White House, he would have to return to his home state, New York, a state that in the twentieth century had been as much the mother of presidents as Virginia had been a century earlier. Indeed, he would return to New York, but Nelson Rockefeller did not intend to enter politics at the bottom.

The 1958 Election

There was no doubt that Nelson Rockefeller wanted to obtain elective office. The question was, which office? Should he run for a legislative post or for an executive one? Should he campaign for an office in New York City or in the state? He had spent most of his life in the city, but the odds against a Republican's obtaining the mayoralty of New York City were almost insurmountable. A legislative post either in Washington or in Albany, both of which were suggested by former governor Dewey, was unattractive to him. He argued that he was temperamentally more suited to an executive than a legislative post.

(Dewey, who urged Rockefeller to start at a lower rung on the political level, also offered to seek an appointment for him as postmaster in New York City. Rockefeller respectfully declined.)[34] Ultimately, Rockefeller realized that, of all these jobs, only the governorship was a sure stepping-stone to the presidency.

The incumbent governor of New York State, Averell Harriman, was a Democrat. But as a neophyte in state politics, Nelson Rockefeller would not easily win either the Republican gubernatorial nomination or the election. There were far more registered Democrats than Republicans in New York State, and Harriman, a respected figure with a national reputation, had all the advantages of incumbency. Moreover, since he was a rich man with many friends in the financial world, his reelection campaign in 1958 would be well financed. Although he could hardly have been characterized as an exciting governor, Harriman's policies had not created animosities among ethnic or economic groups that could be exploited by the party out of power. In a word, he looked like a hard candidate to beat.

L. Judson Morhouse, the state Republican chairman, was seeking a likely candidate for the 1958 gubernatorial nomination to face the incumbent Democrat. He first met Rockefeller in late 1955 at a party finance meeting.[35] Later wide-ranging conversations with Rockefeller led Morhouse to believe that he would make an effective candidate for the governorship in 1958. Rockefeller would be fifty years of age in that year. While he would certainly be old enough for responsible office, he had a youthful appeal, in contrast to Harriman, who would be sixty-seven years old. The situation had its advantages: Rockefeller's wealth would not be an electoral handicap because Harriman was also from a family of wealth. Indeed, Rockefeller's nomination would probably ensure an adequate Republican war chest. Moreover, Morhouse saw in Rockefeller a poised, intelligent, personable man who would make an effective candidate. On the other hand, Rockefeller was virtually unknown to the Republican county leaders, and several Republicans with long years of state party service yearned for the nomination.

An opportunity to improve Rockefeller's situation developed during the summer of 1956. The Democrats were eager to convene a state constitutional convention in the hope that reapportionment of the state legislature would add to the number of their seats. The state constitution required that the question of whether to hold such a convention be placed before the voters at the general election of 1957 and every twentieth year thereafter.[36] While the Republicans, who controlled both houses of the state legislature, were naturally opposed to the idea of reapportionment, they agreed to the creation of a bipartisan, fifteen-member Temporary State Commission on the Constitutional Convention. Five members were to be named by the speaker of the assembly, Oswald D. Heck, a Republican; five by the majority leader of the senate, Walter Mahoney, a Republican; and five by Harriman, the governor, who would also name the chairman. Rockefeller was named as one of the ten Republican members, and later when Harriman and the Republicans could not agree on an acceptable chairman, Morhouse suggested Rockefeller for the post. Harriman, who had known Rockefeller for many years, agreed, probably on the ground that Rockefeller did not have political ambitions.

It is ironic that two of Nelson Rockefeller's rivals for the Republican gubernatorial nomination, Heck and Mahoney, helped advance Rockefeller's aspirations. It is equally ironic that Harriman turned the spotlight on Rockefeller by this appointment. Late in 1957, at an off-the-record dinner for legislative correspondents in Albany, Governor Harriman jokingly told the diners that "there is a young man who sits among you tonight that would make the best Republican nominee for governor—Nelson Rockefeller."[37]

The commission post was critical for Rockefeller's rise to the governorship. It not only gave him visibility as an active participant in New York affairs but also provided him with an opportunity to familiarize himself with the operation of state government. Under Rockefeller, the commission held hearings around the state and commissioned studies on the background and functioning of the state constitution. In addition, while chairman of the commission, Rockefeller attracted to his staff two key men who were to serve him well in future political and administrative positions, George Hinman and Dr. William J. Ronan. Hinman, retained as commission counsel, was a Binghamton lawyer with a wide knowledge of upstate politics. In 1957 he introduced Rockefeller to William Hill, Broome County publisher and political leader, who was the patriarch of the Republican party upstate and the first county chairman to endorse Rockefeller. Ronan, who was dean of the School of Public Affairs and professor of public administration at New York University, became chief of staff to the commission. Both men continued for many years to be close associates of Rockefeller.

Helpful as the commission's chairmanship was, it still did not give Rockefeller a local political base from which to operate. The family home, Pocantico Hills, however, was located in Westchester County, a Republican stronghold just north of New York City. Westchester

County would be an ideal base, provided he could obtain the support of the county organization. This would not be an easy matter, however, as some were calling him "a New Deal Democrat in Republican clothing." By a fortunate set of circumstances, he won the backing of Malcolm Wilson, a state assemblyman from the county for twenty years, who was a respected spokesman for conservative Republicans upstate. Once the public opinion polls had convinced him of Rockefeller's potential as a candidate, Wilson agreed to become his campaign manager,[38] a decision that in turn led him to the lieutenant governorship and eventually made him Rockefeller's successor as governor in 1974. Wilson persuaded Rockefeller that identification with New York City would be fatal to his chances of securing upstate Republican support. His best chance of success rested on his stance as Westchester County's favorite son. With Wilson's aid, Rockefeller succeeded in winning the support of the county organization. As a further strategy, Wilson advised Rockefeller to delay announcing his candidacy as long as possible. While Rockefeller's position was officially uncertain, Wilson and Morhouse could urge county leaders not to commit themselves to other candidates.

Meanwhile, newspaper polls showed Harriman running far ahead of any possible Republican candidate. His lead had the effect of somewhat cooling the ardor of other Republican hopefuls. Rockefeller and Walter Mahoney gained ground over other candidates interested in the nomination,[39] but by June 1958 Rockefeller began to pull ahead of Mahoney in privately commissioned polls,[40] and Morhouse surreptitiously made these results available to county leaders. Finally, on June 30, Rockefeller announced his candidacy, but he still had a long way to go to obtain the nomination.

Here again Wilson's advice was effective. Rockefeller was unknown to county leaders, whereas his opponents had long-standing ties with them. Rockefeller was not at his best in reading formal speeches to large groups, partly because of a defect in his vision that affected his reading, causing him to transpose words. He was unusually successful, however, with small groups. So Wilson set up a series of luncheons and dinners with small groups of community leaders— young and old, men and women, many of whom had no party ties. Others, of course, were active in the Republican party. Then Rockefeller, his son Stephen, and Wilson toured the state in a station wagon. It is amusing to note that the station wagon could not possibly have held all of the Republican politicians who later claimed to have been on this trip.

As county leaders observed the reaction of these community

groups to Rockefeller's enthusiasm and charm, they gradually came to believe that he would make an effective candidate. By midsummer Rockefeller and Wilson had met with county leaders and informal groups in every part of the state except Erie County, which was Mahoney's home base. The fact that Harriman was still running ahead in the newspaper polls led to the withdrawal of several candidates for the nomination. When the well-managed Republican State Convention met in August, Rockefeller won the nomination by acclamation. His acceptance speech, probably one of the best he ever made, aroused tremendous enthusiasm among the convention delegates.[41]

The election campaign was an unexpected success.[42] Rockefeller's positions in regard to labor legislation, education, and rent control were considerably more liberal than one would expect of a Republican candidate, and appealed strongly to urban groups. In addition, when Frank Hogan, the Manhattan district attorney, supported by the Democratic organization, was nominated for the United States Senate over Thomas K. Finletter, the choice of party reformers, Rockefeller was able to identify Harriman with the Tammany organization, and thus "bossism" became a major issue. In the November election he led his ticket by a considerable margin and won by 573,000 votes. While the Republicans lost a few legislative seats, the loss would probably have been considerably more had Rockefeller not been the candidate for governor. Of this election Rockefeller said later, "I won it by a fluke since it appeared to be a Democratic year."[43]

Rockefeller's election in 1958 was a turning point. It placed an individual with an aggressive, problem-solving style in New York's constitutionally strong governorship at a time when state government generally was entering a period of enormous growth and change. The state constitution did not limit Rockefeller's reelection, and his incumbency was to survive three further elections. New York was the nation's richest state, better able than any other to apply internally generated resources to the solving of problems within its borders. A unique test case for the viability of state government was thus established. How effective could the activist executive style be at the state level, with all the limitations inherent in state government in a federal system? How far could the richest state go, driven by the engine of a strong, dominant, and ambitious governor, in meeting the major problems of the 1960s?

Nelson Rockefeller during his first term as governor, before a map of New York State (1961).

2

Party Leadership and Political Power

To observers of national politics during the three decades after World War II, New York seemed a Democratic bastion, but at the state level this period was one of Republican dominance. Republicans won all but two gubernatorial elections contested during this time, and, with the exception of the office of state comptroller, dominated all other statewide elected posts as well. In fact, one study demonstrated that, on the basis of a combined measure of party success in governorship and state legislative races, New York was the seventh most Republican state in the nation between 1959 and 1970.[1] Among the "megastates"—the ten identified by journalist Neal Peirce as being the most important politically, socially, and economically in the United States—New York was the most Republican in its internal politics and among the least competitive politically, ranking behind only Texas and Florida.[2]

Remarkably, this record of Republican success was achieved in the face of a consistent Democratic advantage in declared party preference among enrolled voters in the state. Between 1950 and 1970, in gubernatorial election years there were never more Republicans than Democrats in New York. The Democratic registration advantage over the Republicans varied widely during this period, dropping as low as 59,559 in 1958, the year of Governor Rockefeller's first election, and rising as high as 886,440 eight years later. As of 1970, the Democratic advantage was about 600,000 voters (see Table 1).[3]

How, then, were the Republicans able to retain control of the governorship? Several factors worked to their advantage. First, gubernatorial elections were held in off years. Like other states, New York showed a pattern of surge and decline in voter turnout, with the

Table 1. Democratic Enrollment Advantage in New York State in Gubernatorial Election Years, 1950–1970

Year	Enrolled Republicans	Enrolled Democrats	Democratic advantage
1950	2,160,920	2,619,727	458,807
1954	2,093,216	2,307,572	214,356
1958	2,603,718	2,663,277	59,559
1962	3,050,764	3,461,911	411,147
1966	2,878,615	3,755,055	876,440
1970	2,957,908	3,566,257	608,349

Source: *New York State Legislative Manual,* 1951–1971.

surge coming in presidential years and the decline in off or gubernatorial years. Thus, in the 1968 presidential election, 6,961,690 New Yorkers voted, or about 88 percent of those eligible, while in the 1970 election for governor 6,150,477 voted, or 78 percent of those eligible.

A further examination of the voting statistics demonstrates that those who turned out under the stimulus of the presidential contest tended to cast their ballots for the Democratic candidate. In New York, the surge of presidential years always gives an advantage to the Democrats, but proves an advantage to the Republicans only in years when they have an exceptionally strong presidential candidate. The off-year gubernatorial election helped keep the state government in Republican hands by sheltering it from the Democratic trend in national elections.

A second factor that helped define the political landscape of New York gubernatorial elections was the upstate–downstate split. In 1970, 58 percent of the enrolled Democrats in the state lived in New York City. In the fifty-seven counties outside the city, Democrats had an enrollment edge in only three: Albany, Erie (which includes the city of Buffalo), and Rockland. All other counties were dominated by the Republicans, even those containing major cities, such as Monroe (Rochester), Onondaga (Syracuse), and Broome (Binghamton).

The split was significant because New York City Democrats showed a decreasing ability to deliver the vote for their party's gubernatorial candidate. At its peak for a gubernatorial election in the last quarter century, the New York City Democratic party in 1954 provided Harriman with 1,260,426 votes, or about 78 percent of its enrolled numbers. In 1970, with 2,068, 116 Democratic voters on its rolls in the city, the same party could deliver only 920,875 votes for Arthur Goldberg, about 44 percent of the enrolled Democrats in the city. In contrast, in the upstate region between 1950 and 1958 the Republican party consistently delivered to its candidates more votes than it had enrolled voters, and in its *worst* gubernatorial year, 1966, the upstate Republican party provided Rockefeller with 77 percent of its enrolled strength, a figure that came close to the Democratic party's performance in its area of strength, New York City, in its best year (see Table 2).

Another key to Republican gubernatorial victory was the party's relative success in areas of Democratic strength. The vote for the GOP in New York City exceeded the number of voters enrolled in that party by an average of about 400,000 over the years from 1950 to 1970 (see Table 3). In 1970, a year in which there were 604,498 registered Republicans in the city, Governor Rockefeller garnered 1,057,964 votes, and he exceeded Goldberg's total on the Democratic line in all boroughs except Manhattan. Of the three remaining Democratic counties in the state, Rockefeller lost only in Erie.

Republican victories depended heavily on the ability to build and retain a suburban base. Over the 1950–1970 period, for example, the downstate Republican vote (New York City and the three suburban counties of Nassau, Suffolk, and Westchester) regularly constituted about two-thirds of that party's statewide total. The city component of this total declined, however, and the suburban component increased dramatically. New York City Republicans provided Thomas E. Dewey with 40 percent of his total in 1950, but delivered only 34 percent of Rockefeller's statewide tally in 1970 (a banner Republican

Table 2.   Vote for Governor as a Percentage of Party Enrollment in Respective Areas of Strength, New York, 1950–1970

Year	Republicans outside New York City			Democrats in New York City		
	Enrollment	Vote	Percent	Enrollment	Vote	Percent
1950	1,676,198	1,700,073	101	1,818,816	1,033,198	57
1954	1,586,285	1,784,149	112	1,606,275	1,260,426	78
1958	2,005,162	2,115,115	103	1,677,308	1,116,517	66
1962	2,283,238	2,003,294	88	2,202,162	1,118,215	51
1966	2,216,469	1,726,262	77	2,318,474	1,034,012	45
1970	2,353,410	2,047,256	87	2,068,116	920,875	44

Source: *New York State Legislative Manual,* 1951–1971.

Table 3. Vote for Governor as a Percentage of Party Enrollment in the Opposition Party's Area of Strength, New York, 1950–1970

	Republicans in New York City			Democrats outside New York City		
Year	Enrollment	Vote	Percent	Enrollment	Vote	Percent
1950	484,722	1,119,430	231	800,000	947,958	118
1954	506,931	764,464	151	701,297	1,036,219	148
1958	548,556	1,011,814	185	985,969	1,153,452	117
1962	767,526	1,078,293	141	1,259,749	1,191,528	95
1966	662,146	964,364	146	1,436,577	1,264,351	88
1970	604,498	1,057,964	175	1,498,136	1,237,480	83

Source: *New York State Legislative Manual,* 1951–1971.

year within the city). In contrast, the three suburban counties provided one-fourth of Dewey's total in 1950 and one-third of Rockefeller's in 1970.

The Democratic party was less successful in areas of Republican predominance than the Republicans were in Democratic areas. Though Democratic enrollment outside New York City almost doubled between 1950 and 1970, Democratic voting in gubernatorial elections increased by only about one-third during that period. In 1970, for example, the party outside New York City delivered only 83 percent of its enrolled strength to Arthur Goldberg.

In short, New York State Republican gubernatorial candidates were able to hold their base of strength outside the city and make considerable inroads in areas of Democratic strength, while the Democrats were unable either to hold their base in their areas of strength or to make inroads in Republican areas. Structural factors—the upstate–downstate split, off-year elections, and Republican dominance in the growing suburbs—go far toward explaining this situation. It is also significant that all the Republican victories during these years were won by two dominant political figures, Thomas E. Dewey and Nelson Rockefeller. Certainly their strength as candidates contributed to keeping the statehouse in Republican hands.[4]

Studies have shown that social class differences between adherents of the major parties are less strong in New York than in most other states,[5] perhaps because of the pervasiveness of cross-cutting ethnic appeals in the New York electorate. The major parties have acknowledged the importance of ethnicity by seeking to offer the electorate a "balanced ticket" in statewide elections, and in doing so have increased it. This balancing act was easier for the Republicans, who, because of their greater internal cohesion and the discipline imposed by incumbent governors, were able to avoid primary fights for places on the ticket. The Democrats often found their statewide ticket, carefully balanced by party leaders, unbalanced as the result of primary elections.

Generally, minority groups vote overwhelmingly Democratic in national elections.[6] Thus the Republican vote in presidential years in New York among blacks was only about 5 percent, among Jews only about 12 percent, and among Spanish-speaking voters only about 15 percent. Nevertheless, about 20 to 30 percent of those groups voted for Rockefeller in gubernatorial elections. Italians, the largest ethnic group, consistently supported Rockefeller.

An unusual feature of state politics in New York is the importance of the Liberal and Conservative parties. New York's election law permits a candidate for statewide office to run on more than one ticket and to have votes recorded on all lines on the ballot aggregated into a grand total for the purpose of determining the victor in the election. Thus third parties have come to play a pivotal role in state politics. Third-party roles are further enhanced by a psychological factor, the politician's belief that it is better to be safe than sorry. A third party's line on the ballot, with its habitual adherents, becomes an especially appealing form of insurance. In 1970, 109,311 voters were enrolled in the Liberal party and 107,372 in the Conservative party, but both parties attracted many more voters than formal adherents. In the 1970 election for governor, the Liberal line on the ballot delivered 263,070 votes to Arthur Goldberg. The Conservative candidate for governor, Paul L. Adams, attracted 422,514 votes, and the party's candidate for the United States Senate, James Buckley, was elected.

Enrolled Conservative strength was about evenly balanced between New York City and the rest of the state, though most Conservative voters reside outside the city. Conservatives in 1970 got three votes outside the city for every one they received in it. In contrast, Liberal party voting mirrored party registration. About seven of every ten Liberal party members in 1970 lived in New York City, and about two-thirds of those who voted Liberal resided there. It can thus be seen that the Conservative and Liberal parties duplicated in miniature the Republican–Democratic upstate–downstate split. Most Conservative votes came from outside New York City and were drawn from the geographic area of Republican predominance. Most Liberal votes came from within the city, the Democratic bastion.

During the last two decades the Liberal party sought to play a balance-of-power role in state politics by either granting or withholding endorsement from major-party candidates. For gubernatorial races, this tactic worked only once in the seven elections held from 1950 to 1974. Because of its occasional success the Liberal party retained statewide credibility. Any Republican gubernatorial candidate would breathe a bit easier knowing that the Liberals were naming their own man rather than backing his Democratic opponent. The hard fact was, however, that constant opposition by this party failed to undermine Republican control of the statehouse.

The Conservative party, conceived in 1962 to oppose "liberal Republicanism" in the state, as a consequence of its ideological origins worked only half of the Liberal party balance-of-power equation.[7] It functioned to deny votes to the major parties but did not try to add its strength to either of them in statewide races (in state legislative races, major-party candidates did receive Conservative endorsement). The Conservative party drew heavily from among voters in Republican geographic strongholds. After the Conservative party's entry into the political arena, the Republican upstate vote as a percentage of enrolled Republicans fell off considerably. Calculations show that it cut the Republican base by 300,000 votes and increased the statewide Republican reliance on the independent voter.

As in the rest of the nation, an important trend in New York in recent years has been the growth in the number and importance of voters not enrolled in a political party. During the past two decades, the number of independent voters in New York fluctuated between 1 and 1.5 million. In 1970 there were 1,262,359 unenrolled voters in the state, or 16 percent of the eligible voters. The high ratio of Republican votes to Republican registrants can be partly explained by support gained from independents. Although independent voters are the least likely to appear at the polls on election day, they hold the balance of power in the state. Even if their turnout was one-half that of enrolled party members, a low estimate, independents would have provided over half a million votes in 1970.

Rockefeller's Campaign Tactics

What formula did Nelson Rockefeller use that produced his extraordinary record of electoral success in seemingly Democratic New York State? The search for an answer reveals several major factors at work. Prominent among them were the governor's dynamic personal campaign style, his ability to tap vast financial resources, and his facility in attracting men who could put these resources to effective use. In three of his four gubernatorial campaigns, Rockefeller was behind the Democratic candidate in early poll results.

Governor Rockefeller's campaigns showed a high degree of organization and coordination. Organizational structure differed in detail from year to year but was clearly hierarchical, with primary directive power in the hands of a campaign manager responsible directly to the governor. In the Rockefeller system, campaign planning began early. For the 1970 campaign, for example, the first strategy session was held in April 1969, and a director of precampaign activities, R. Burdell Bixby, was appointed on May 5, 1969.[8]

Campaign strategy was formulated by a strategy board composed of the governor and his most trusted and experienced political aides. Among those who served in campaign after campaign were William Ronan, Malcolm Wilson, Hugh Morrow, George Hinman, R. Burdell Bixby, and William Pfeiffer. In 1966 there were five major functional subunits, the same number used by the governor in his first campaign in 1958. They were: political organization, research and planning, headquarters (which included speechwriting and scheduling), public and press relations, and special groups. In addition, separate units were established for the campaign in New York City and for fund raising.

One change in campaign organization took place in 1966, when Rockefeller, instead of coordinating his campaign entirely through Republican county leaders, as he had done in 1958 and 1962, instituted a system of regional coordinators. There were ten of these coordinators in 1966 and eleven in 1970, reporting directly to the campaign director.[9]

After Rockefeller became established as the incumbent governor, his campaign became further and further separated from the structure of the Republican party in New York State. Even in 1958, when the campaign was managed by Republican State Chairman L. Judson Morhouse, observers noted that Rockefeller waged a "personal and nonpartisan campaign."[10] In the 1962 and 1966 campaigns, managed by William Pfeiffer, treasurer of the state Republican party, and in the 1970 campaign, managed by R. Burdell Bixby, chairman of the State Thruway Authority, the governor's organization was separate and distinct from the state and local party organizations, though many state party leaders sat on the strategy board. The governor's studied independence and his campaign stress on the man rather than the party, so necessary for the candidate of a minority party, occasionally led to difficulty with local leaders. In the 1962 campaign, for example, trouble arose when county-level Republican fund raising clashed with that of Rockefeller citizens' committees.[11] But occasional problems with party loyalists were considered a necessary cost by the governor's aides, whose primary aim was to win the election for Rockefeller. If Rockefeller won, they reasoned, the party would necessarily benefit.

Whenever possible, of course, the governor did coordinate his campaign with those of other Republicans running in the state. In 1966 Assemblyman John H. Terry of Syracuse, the coordinator of the Republican Assembly campaign, maintained a full-time office in the governor's campaign headquarters. Coordination with candidates for the United States Senate, however, was often made difficult by arguments over the distribution of campaign resources. This was the case with Kenneth Keating's campaign in 1958 and Jacob Javits's in 1962. Problems arose in 1970 as well, when Charles Goodell's candidacy was a potential liability to the ticket.[12]

Another trend discernible in the Rockefeller campaign method over the years was an increased emphasis on the media and a decreased emphasis on personal campaigning. In 1958 and 1962 Rockefeller was the quintessence of the old-time barnstormer. He said of his technique:

> You've got to put yourself into this and reach out to people. It is not too easy at first, but it is very important, the ability to go up to the people on the street and talk in a friendly way. . . . People are tremendously aware of whether you are just going through this because you have to and it is extraordinary how, if you shake hands with them, look them right in the eye, you can establish in a split second a personal contact that really reaches them on a friendly basis, with a smile and a word.[13]

In 1966 he turned away from the personal approach and began to emphasize technology. Aides commented almost wistfully that the new techniques seemed to dull his spontaneity.[14] Increasingly the Rockefeller campaign effort was compared to a finely tuned machine, one that approached perfection in 1966 and 1970. Richard Rosenbaum, who was state chairman for four years, observed: "The machinery clicks like a giant computer. The planes and buses and helicopters arrive on time, the statements are available before deadline, the press is pampered, the luggage is always waiting in the hotel lobby, no meals are missed, reporters are supplied with local angles, film tapes are available for television, and crowds are not kept waiting."[15]

Opinion polls were a major factor in determining Rockefeller's strategic stance in each of his gubernatorial campaigns. Though polls were hailed as part of the paraphernalia of the "new media-oriented politics of the 1960s," they were widely used by Rockefeller in his first gubernatorial race in 1958, and he used them extensively in subsequent races. In fact, Judson Morhouse's judicious leaking of poll data that showed Rockefeller as the strongest of the potential Republican gubernatorial candidates before the state Republican convention in 1958 was an important factor in getting Rockefeller his first nomination.[16]

Polls were used by the governor's campaign team to determine the voters' mental picture of the governor, to measure the electorate's "trust and confidence" in him, to get a feeling for voter judgments on the kind of job the governor had done, to discover the voters' view of the governor's competence as compared to that of other candidates, and, of course, to run trial heats with possible opponents. Periodic polling allowed the campaign staff to identify trends and assess the impact of the campaign as it proceeded. The poll results shown in Table 4 document the success of the governor's 1970 campaign and the disintegration of Goldberg's. In addition to providing knowledge about the image of the governor and his probable success, polls were used to provide a profile of the potential electorate and to determine the issues and appeals that were most important for various segments of that electorate.

Polls also served a political purpose. During the 1970 campaign, announced poll results consistently overstated the governor's early disadvantage and then understated his later lead. In mid-September,

Table 4.   Percentage of Poll Respondents Favoring Gubernatorial Candidates Rockefeller and Goldberg, Early May–mid-October 1970

Time of poll	Rockefeller	Goldberg
Early May	34%	45%
Mid-September	43	45
Mid-October	49	37

Source: "Mandate for Leadership," unpublished history of the 1970 campaign of Nelson A. Rockefeller for governor of New York, 1971, Rockefeller Family Archives, Tarrytown, N.Y.

for example, Rockefeller's campaign headquarters announced polls that showed him fifteen points behind Goldberg but said that he "had started to move up." In fact, his latest polls showed him just 2 percent behind at that date (see Table 4). They were overstating Rockefeller's disadvantage so that he would appear to be the underdog. On October 6, Rockefeller's headquarters announced poll data showing that Rockefeller and Goldberg were "neck-and-neck," and on October 23 they revealed that he had pulled 7 to 8 percent ahead. In reality, the mid-October poll showed the governor 12 percentage points ahead of his opponent. They were understating his lead to avoid overconfidence that might keep his supporters from voting. If the private polls were not favorable, of course, they could simply be kept confidential.[17] While some would view this practice as questionable, others would regard it as legitimate campaign tactics.

From the analysis of poll data the Rockefeller strategy board devised a campaign theme. In 1958 the Rockefeller personality was stressed, his youth, his vigor, and his concern for state rather than national issues. In the area of issues, Rockefeller emphasized the alleged decline of the state's economy under Harriman, his opponent, and, especially outside New York City, raised the issue of bossism. In 1962, Rockefeller's least difficult campaign year, the theme was one of hard work, proven courage (the governor had raised taxes), and leadership. In 1966 the polls showed that the strategic problem was a low level of voter knowledge about state programs, and therefore the governor's record and his experience were stressed. Thus the motto was "Governor Rockefeller for Governor."

In 1970, research showed that the governor's assets were his likableness, vigor, articulateness, honesty, and courage. Voters viewed him as an advocate, specific and activist, while Arthur Goldberg, the Democratic candidate, was viewed as a mediator, judicial, and vague. The governor's liabilities were that many New Yorkers believed he had been too long in office, that he was not sincere, that he did not understand middle-class workers, and that he was an advocate of high taxes and excessive government spending. Knowing this, the governor and his aides decided to run on a personal image of decisive leadership, activism, and experience. The new motto was "Rockefeller—He's Done a Lot, He'll Do More."[18]

In the determination of the campaign strategy there was constant interaction between the governor's staff and media specialists. In 1958 and 1962 Governor Rockefeller used the Marschalk and Pratt Division of the giant McCann-Erickson advertising firm to bring his message to the voters of the state. In the more difficult 1966 and 1970 campaigns another division of that firm, Jack Tinker and Partners, was retained. The growing reliance upon media in campaigning was reflected in the growth of the advertising budgets of the four Rockefeller campaigns. Print media expenditures decreased over the years while those of radio and television skyrocketed. In 1958 Rockefeller emphasized the electronic media heavily but still spent about a quarter of his delegated funds for advertisements in daily newspapers. In 1970 only one major Rockefeller advertisement was run in the daily press across the state.

Over the 1958–1970 period, under the guidance of Tom Losee, Jerry Danzig, and other sophisticated television experts, Rockefeller's campaign style changed considerably. In the 1958 campaign the candidate appeared on fifteen- or thirty-minute television programs, either delivering a formal address or participating in a question-and-answer session. By 1966, and again in 1970, the emphasis was on twenty- to sixty-second spot announcements that dramatized a single issue and did not annoy voters by disturbing their viewing schedules. Often the governor's face or voice was not even used on these spot commercials.

The effectiveness of Rockefeller's media campaigning was enhanced by the knowledge that plans would not fail to be implemented because of lack of funds. The certain availability of funds for radio and television time, which must be planned and paid for long in advance, allowed confident outlining of a properly balanced, timed, and integrated media campaign. This was an advantage not enjoyed by Rockefeller's opponents. Both Frank O'Connor in 1966 and Arthur Goldberg in 1970 had to cancel reserved television time late in their campaigns for lack of financial resources.

The 1966 campaign provides a good case study of Governor Rockefeller's use of the media.[19] The campaign was targeted on the twenty-two largest counties in the state, which contained 86.7 percent of the registered voters and could be reached through advertising in six major television market areas. The television effort was divided into three phases. During the first phase, between July 15 and September 12, twenty sixty-second ads were run weekly in the New York City metropolitan area and ten in the five other major markets. These were low-key efforts emphasizing Rockefeller's achievements and personal qualities. They were presented after 11:00 P.M. on network stations and in prime time (between 7:00 and 11:00 P.M.) on independent stations in the New York City metropolitan area. In the second phase, from September 13 to October 10, the television schedule was doubled and accelerated in prime time and at the early dinner hour. The governor's voice and face were introduced, and anti-O'Connor commercials, twenty seconds long, made their appearance. In the final phase, October 11 to November 7, television advertising was tripled from the original concentration, even more prime time was used, and supplemental newspaper, transit, and outdoor advertising was scheduled. Commercials were shown during the daytime to reach homemakers, and spots were presented at station breaks.

The radio effort, divided into two phases, supplemented the television campaign and lasted eleven weeks. During the first nine weeks, six commercials a week were run on all the A-rated stations in major market areas in the state. During the last two weeks of the campaign the frequency of these commercials was doubled, and in addition, six a week were run on B-rated stations in these areas. Three-quarters of the Rockefeller radio commercials were run in prime listening time and one-quarter on weekends and during the day.

This massive use of the media was supplemented at various points during the campaign by four television specials: the governor's speech accepting the Republican nomination, a speech by Governor Dewey, a fifteen-minute program for upstate audiences by Malcolm Wilson, and a five-minute election eve broadcast. The cost of the Rockefeller media campaign alone in 1966 exceeded $2 million.

There is no doubt that the effort reached the New York voter. During the week of October 18, Rockefeller ran seventy-four television commercials in New York City, and market research estimated that they reached 91 percent of all the television homes in the city.[20] In 1970, in a campaign modeled after the 1966 effort, Rockefeller media advertisements reached 95 percent of the homes in the state, and the average New York City family saw 9.4 of these television commercials.[21] In fact, media saturation was so great in 1970 that the Rockefeller staff began to fear a backlash effect because of overexposure and the feeling on the part of the electorate that the governor was spending too much in his reelection effort. There was no firm evidence that such a backlash occurred, but there was some sentiment among the Rockefeller staff that they had gone too far with the media effort in 1970.[22]

Rockefeller supplemented his massive media blitz with a full complement of more traditional techniques. Though these techniques were more in evidence in 1958 and 1962, they were still used heavily in later campaigns. The governor, as a campaigner, showed himself to be indefatigable. His standard greeting, "Hiya, fella," came to be something of a legend in the state. In 1958 he traveled 8,300 miles, visited every county, shook almost 100,000 hands, and delivered 135 formal speeches and innumerable off-the-cuff talks.[23] In this aspect of campaigning the governor's excellent staffwork made itself felt. In 1958, under the direction of William Ronan, a county data book was prepared so that Rockefeller could speak with familiarity about local problems and issues. This effective technique was maintained through later campaigns, so that in each locality the governor could point to relevant state achievements and projects for which his administration was responsible.

One example of what thorough staffwork allowed Rockefeller to do in campaigning was a speech he made at Massena, New York, in 1962. In opening his local headquarters, Rockefeller emphasized the benefits that had come to the area during his first four years. State aid to local schools was up 37 percent from 1958. Seven and a half million dollars had been spent to upgrade the State University College at Potsdam and $1.4 million on the Agricultural and Technical Institute at Canton. More than $10 million had been spent on new state roads in St. Lawrence County, and $4.1 million on a new five-mile, four-lane highway. Sixty-two miles of roads had been resurfaced. The expansion of local industry, attributed by the governor to his efforts to improve the state economy, had brought hundreds of jobs.[24]

The county data book made this kind of speech possible in hundreds of locations throughout New York. To a listener in Massena, it seemed that the governor was concerned with the north country and was paying attention to its needs, progress, and problems. No Democratic challenger could hope to match Rockefeller's information resources. As the director of the state's governmental machinery, the incumbent governor had control of the sources of information; and in an election campaign, information, when well used, was power.

In the later campaigns, the governor's time was carefully allocated and his public schedule choreographed in detail. State ceremonies over which the governor presided were planned in advance to take place during the campaign and timed so that they could be easily covered on the evening television news. An intricate dual-communications network was established to keep the governor's motorcade in constant touch with campaign headquarters. Detailed advance work preceded the candidate at each of his stops with a degree of sophistication rarely seen outside of presidential campaigns.

In 1970, 28 million pieces of campaign literature were distributed, including eight special-interest and five regional brochures. Special staff was assigned in each campaign to research the record and follow the activities of the opposition. In 1966 these efforts resulted in a daily press release called "O'Connor's Errors," which got considerable press attention.[25] Here again the advantage of the incumbent was evident. Rockefeller had sufficient paid staff to pursue every possibly fruitful campaign tactic and the research resources to use this staff to best advantage.

Advertising in the ethnic and minority press supplemented regular advertising campaigns, as did telephone canvassing, direct mail, and massive last-minute get-out-the-Republican-vote mailings upstate. A major innovation in 1970 was the adoption of sophisticated, computer-based, personalized direct mail, a technique pioneered by the governor's brother Winthrop in Arkansas.[26]

Rockefeller's use of every available technique in campaigning sometimes led him into errors. In 1970 he asked his brother Laurance to help finance the publication of a biography of Arthur Goldberg written by Victor Lasky. Goldberg later called this book, which was critical of his political career, "obscene, pornographic, scandalous and libelous."[27] (Later he defined "pornographic" as meaning "dirty business.") At the Senate hearings on his confirmation as vice-president, Rockefeller admitted that this had been "a hasty, ill considered decision in the midst of a hectic campaign," though he also characterized the volume as "the most overrated, misrepresented, innocuous, political dud ever perpetrated in a partisan political campaign."[28]

Campaigning in New York City

In the last two Rockefeller campaigns a special organization was established for New York City, because a major part of the Republican victory equation was the minimization of the Democratic margin in that party's stronghold. In those years, the city was the source of between one-third and two-fifths of the Republican gubernatorial votes. In 1966 the New York City effort, directed by John Wells, was modeled after the successful 1965 mayoral campaign of John Lindsay.[29] The main vehicle for the campaign was a nonpartisan Citi-

On the campaign trail in "El Barrio"—Spanish Harlem (1958). Photo by Bob Wands. Wide World Photos.

Rockefeller invites Bella Abzug, who had heckled him, to share his public address system (1970). Photo by Bob Wands. Rockefeller Family Archives.

Rockefeller explains a point to his Democratic opponent, Arthur Goldberg, at the Columbus Day Parade (1970). Photo by Bob Wands. Rockefeller Family Archives.

zens for Rockefeller organization, though Republicans were approached through a citywide campaign committee composed of the county chairman of each of the five boroughs. The general plan was to build on the Lindsay base through the use of storefronts (seventy-five were opened by election day), walking tours by the governor, massive telephone and apartment house canvassing, and the use of mobile sound units.

Rockefeller's New York City effort reached its greatest sophistication under Fioravante Perrotta in 1970. In that year the governor attracted more votes on the Republican line than did Goldberg on the Democratic line in four of the five boroughs. Using computerized election data for the previous five years, Perrotta placed the city's assembly districts in three categories.[30] Priority I districts were conservative Democratic, mixed white, and contained 45 percent of the vote. Priority II districts were liberal Democratic and Republican, largely Jewish, and contained 43 percent of the vote. Priority III districts were very liberal and very Democratic, largely black and Puerto Rican, and contained 11 percent of the vote. The plan was to make heavy inroads into priority I areas with law-and-order appeals, to hold significant numbers of voters in priority II areas, and to keep some votes in priority III areas. In fact, after a telephone poll revealed the possibility of inroads in Puerto Rican areas, a special effort was mounted, under Manuel Gonzales, to attract the votes of this ethnic group.

Endorsement was sought and obtained from ethnic-group leaders, many of them prominent Democrats, to build up an appearance of wide support for the governor. Telephone surveys, canvassing, and follow-up letters were used extensively. The result was impressive: the governor attracted 40 percent of the enrolled Democrats who voted in the city and held on to 70 percent of the enrolled Republicans. In priority I areas Rockefeller obtained 55.8 percent of the vote, 17.8 percent more than he had in 1966, and losses in the other areas were not of major significance. The concentration of campaign resources in these key areas in the city was a master stroke of campaign planning and execution.

Campaign Financing

One of Governor Rockefeller's closest long-term personal aides has commented that campaigning for Rockefeller was like working in a milieu in which resources were virtually limitless. Indeed, the governor's war chest was vast. In a report issued in 1972, the Citizen's Research Foundation estimated that by the close of the 1970 campaign year Rockefeller had spent, all told, in excess of $27 million on his political career, more than half of which was either his personal funds or raised from his family.[31] Various estimates placed Rockefeller's campaign expenditures for 1970 at between $5.2 and $7.7 million, with between half and three-quarters coming from personal and family sources.[32]

In each of his campaigns Rockefeller enjoyed a financial advantage over his Democratic opponent. This advantage ranged from five Rockefeller dollars spent for every three Harriman dollars in 1958 to the disproportionate ratio of about 10 to 1 in the O'Connor race in 1966 (see Table 5). In all years but 1958, in which Harriman's wealth neutralized the question, Rockefeller's campaign spending was made an issue by his Democratic opponents. In 1966, Frank O'Connor called the extent of Rockefeller's expenditures "an evil thing" that was undermining the democratic process.[33] In the 1970 race, fought in the midst of a national debate on the limitation of campaign spending,

Table 5.   Campaign Spending in New York Gubernatorial Races, by Party, 1958–1970

Year	Republican expenditures	Democratic expenditures	Democratic expenditures as percentage of Republican
1958	$1,786,000	$1,138,000	63.7%
1962	2,184,000	420,000	19.7
1966	5,230,982	576,000	11.0
	4,900,000[a]		
	6,000,000[b]		
1970	6,900,000	1,330,000	19.3
	5,242,807[c]		
	7,700,000[d]		

Sources: Unless otherwise noted, figures are from the *New York Times,* November 26, 1958; November 29, 1962; November 30, 1966; November 28, 1970.

   [a] Rockefeller staff estimate reported in *New York Times,* November 30, 1966.

   [b] Estimate of James M. Perry in *The New Politics* (New York: Clarkson N. Potter, 1968), p. 135. Perry, a reporter for the *National Observer,* wrote a report on the 1966 campaign that was nominated for the Pulitzer prize.

   [c] Memorandum, Hugh Morrow to Nelson A. Rockefeller, May 5, 1972, Rockefeller Family Archives, Tarrytown, N.Y.

   [d] Estimate of the Citizen's Research Foundation reported in the *New York Times,* November 28, 1970.

Arthur Goldberg called on Rockefeller to limit his radio and television expenditures to seven cents per voter, the amount suggested in the proposed federal legislation.[34] The governor refused; such an agreement would have forced him to cut this area of his campaign budget by about 86 percent. Rockefeller's position was that the costs of campaigning were outrageous and that he would comply with any limiting legislation but that in the absence of such legislation he would use all the means at his disposal to win.

Even exclusive of the governor's personal and family resources, the Rockefeller campaign organization was able to collect funds far in excess of those available to Democratic gubernatorial candidates. One of the advantages of incumbency was the access it provided to campaign funds. In 1970 the Governor's Club raised $386,000 in $100 to $500 contributions, most of which went to the Rockefeller campaign.[35] The governor's name also opened up the coffers of New York City banks to his campaign committees. In 1958 the state Republican committee went $989,000 in debt in Rockefeller's behalf, $800,000 of which represented bank loans. In 1962 the Rockefeller campaign borrowed $600,000 from banks; in 1966, $350,000; and in 1970, $800,000.[36]

From an analysis of the Rockefeller gubernatorial campaigns, it is apparent that the control of most of the political money in the state was a major means by which the Republicans in New York were able to offset the Democratic enrollment advantage. But it would be simplistic to assume that Rockefeller buried his Democratic opponents under an avalanche of money. One interesting aspect of campaign spending is that no one knows how much is enough. The impulse of the candidate is therefore to spend all he can, for he cannot know at what point he ceases to receive a return on the marginal dollar spent. The governor was a good campaigner. He planned ahead and got started early. He put together a highly competent and well-organized staff that understood the underlying realities of state politics and could combine into a coherent whole the sophisticated techniques of media and polling with more traditional campaign methods. The fact that Rockefeller had almost unlimited financial resources made this kind of campaign organization possible.

The Governor and the State Party

Successful campaigning is only one measure, though the central one, of a politician's expertise. In New York, a state in which the chief executive can succeed himself indefinitely, a governor's survival at the polls allows him to build a reputation among his fellow politicians as a man with "sock" in the electorate, a man whom it is unwise to defy. This reputation is enhanced if the governor aggressively seeks his policy ends, visibly rewarding his friends and punishing his enemies. The governor's professional reputation grows out of his mandate but goes beyond it. Ultimately it depends on the way he uses his formal powers and informal resources and the way other political actors in the state regard his use of them.[37] Chief among these informal resources is the leadership of the state party.

After his election in November 1958, one of Governor Rockefeller's major tasks was to consolidate control over the state Republican party. This control was essential to the governor, both for the implementation of his program in the state and for the furtherance of his national ambitions. In seeking the presidential nomination Rockefeller had to retain control of the New York delegation to the Republican convention, a delegation that included some people whose philosophy of government and positions on public policy questions differed from his. He also had to illustrate, through a record of achievement in New York, that he was indeed presidential timber. Both of these imperatives required that he grasp firmly in his own hands the reins of the state party.

In the Republican party in New York there are three major potential centers of statewide power in addition to the governorship: the state committee (especially its chairmanship), the state legislative leadership,[38] and the state's incumbent United States senators of the party. Republican congressmen from the state have not been an active force in state party politics, perhaps because of the locus of their work in Washington, the nature of their constituencies, and the implicit sanction that the decennial redistricting holds for them. The story of Rockefeller and the Republican party in New York was thus the story of how the governor gained control over or neutralized these potential alternative power centers.

Before the incumbency of Governor Thomas Dewey, during the long period of Democratic domination of state politics under Al Smith, Franklin D. Roosevelt, Herbert Lehman, and Charles Poletti, the chairman of the Republican state committee was the key figure in opposition politics in Albany. During the early 1930s, Republican state legislators in the Assembly and Senate took their voting cues from W. Kingsland Macy, the Republican chairman.[39] After his victory in 1942, however, Dewey consolidated control of the party in his own hands and made the state chairman his agent. In 1958 Rockefeller inherited the Dewey system. Throughout the state, county chairmen and other leaders expected strong partisan leadership, in the Dewey mold, from the new governor.

Rockefeller moved early to consolidate control over the party and make it responsive to him. The executive committee of the New York State Republican party consisted of thirty-seven members, including the state chairman and vice-chairman, the secretary, the treasurer, the two national committeemen, the president of the state Young Republicans, two delegates from each of eleven judicial districts, and eight at-large delegates.[40] With the exception of L. Judson Morhouse, the state chairman and an early Rockefeller supporter, all other officers of the party were replaced by younger Rockefeller loyalists during the first few months of the administration. These changes were not anti-Dewey moves—many of the new appointees had been closely associated with the former governor—but were attempts to bring a new, younger, Rockefeller-oriented leadership to the party. Some of the displaced party officials were rewarded for their long service with high posts in the state administration to forestall the emergence of any early discontent with the new governor.[41] As the months passed, several members of the party executive board who had not been strong Rockefeller supporters lost their places, often as the result, direct or indirect, of the intervention of the governor or his agents. In September ten new executive committee members were appointed, and Rockefeller's control was firm.[42]

In addition to getting his loyalists on the executive board, in 1959 Rockefeller traveled throughout the state urging that the party be restructured and revitalized. On February 3, 1959, he met for three hours with 140 party leaders in the governor's mansion and stressed the need for a "close-knit organization" to overcome the Democrats' enrollment advantage.[43] The governor spoke then, as he had in January, of the need to attract young voters and women with vigorous leadership and attractive programs. In June, speaking at a $100-a-plate fund-raising dinner in New York City, Rockefeller, appearing with Dewey, asserted his desire to "spend as much time as possible with the state organization from here on in."[44] In July, the Rules Committee of the Party Executive Committee was convened for a "top-to-bottom study" of the GOP structure in New York State.[45]

Rockefeller's concern for party organization and his new overtly partisan stand can be traced to internal pressures within the party, to the difficulties the governor faced with his majority in the state senate during the 1959 term, and to his designs on the White House. It will be recalled that in the 1958 campaign Rockefeller deemphasized the GOP label and stressed his personal qualities. State leaders were concerned that the new governor would be "too much like Eisenhower" in his use of patronage, and these fears were fed by the early appointment of some Democrats to state posts.[46] Rockefeller, a patrician, was not comfortable at first with his patronage-dispensing and party-leadership roles, and consequently often delegated his job-filling prerogatives to Carl Spad and others. This "above politics" stance led to trouble in the state legislature, where Walter J. Mahoney, the Senate Republican majority leader and a rival in 1958 for the gubernatorial nomination, was able to delay the governor's taxing and spending programs.[47]

The emphasis on party building in 1959 was thus in large measure an attempt to reassert the party-leadership role vis-à-vis Republican legislative leaders. One means of access to Republican legislators that bypassed the leadership was the sixty-two county leaders, a group that was assiduously cultivated by the governor in 1959. Late in that year, in preparation for the 1960 legislative session, Rockefeller arranged four dinner meetings in Albany and New York with the county chairmen to discuss his program with them and enlist their aid in avoiding the difficulties he had had with Senator Mahoney in the previous session.[48] With all this the governor's presidential ambitions were intimately tied. If he could not control and direct his state party and implement his program within the legislature, how could he hope to capture the presidential nomination?

The test of Rockefeller's control of the state party came at the Republican national convention in 1960. Here he was able to hold the entire ninety-six-member state delegation uncommitted, with the exception of the Erie County contingent under Mahoney, despite strong pro-Nixon sentiments within the delegation and the centrifugal force of the Nixon bandwagon. Rockefeller hoped that if Nixon did not win the nomination on the first ballot, the convention would turn to him. Working personally and through Judson Morhouse, Rockefeller held meetings throughout the state before the convention to explain his strategy and hold the delegation in line.[49] Though reported to be for Nixon and afraid that the vice-president would get the nomination without New York, county leaders went along with the governor's strategy and, by staying uncommitted at the convention, supported his slim chance for the nomination.[50] Rockefeller had shown that he could perform his party-leadership role. Opposing him was impossible, even for a strong GOP county leader. The potential sanctions in the hands of a governor who would be in office at least two more years, in patronage and other intraparty matters, were too threatening.

After the convention, Rockefeller had to work hard for Nixon to avoid recriminations from those within party ranks whom he had prevented from endorsing the nominee at the convention. This he did, visiting 50 counties and making 237 speeches for Nixon.[51] Nevertheless, when the vice-president lost the state to Kennedy, charges that the governor had acted as a spoiler surfaced, though Rockefeller partisans worked hard to dispel them. Publicity was given to a statement by Nixon, made in Buffalo during the campaign, that "no one has worked as hard for the Nixon-Lodge ticket as Nelson Rockefeller."[52] In response to a survey by the Associated Press, thirty-one Republican county chairmen expressed the view that the governor had done all he could.[53] There was clearly a symbiotic relationship between the governor's state and national political roles; success in one area was necessary for success in the other, and difficulty in one meant difficulty in the other.

As he grew more comfortable in the administration of rewards and punishments in his party-leadership role, Rockefeller began to intercede directly in local party matters. In 1960, through Morhouse, he stepped into an intraparty fight in Suffolk County and implemented a complete overhaul of the candidate slate suggested by Arthur Cromarty, the county leader. Through his action, the governor averted a primary fight, placed three of the four state-legislature nominees from Suffolk in his debt, and put other county leaders on notice that he would use his power as party leader when necessary.[54] Similarly in 1963, when Rockefeller was confronted with an intraparty fight between Senate leader Walter Mahoney and Erie County leader Robert W. Grimm, he cut Grimm off as the patronage conduit in the county and began to take advice on appointments from Mahoney, whose support was essential for the governor's legislative program.[55] Rockefeller had come a long way from his posture "above politics" of early 1959. He had learned that the quid pro quo was a vital tool in seeking his policy ends. By the time of the 1970 campaign, Rockefeller could proclaim himself, in a speech before assembled party leaders, to be a firm believer in the patronage system.

Other examples of gubernatorial control and use of the state party for his ends are legion. In 1964 and 1968, delegations to the national convention were held solid for Rockefeller in a losing cause. In 1966 the governor dictated his own renomination even though his political fortunes were at a low ebb and his defeat seemed virtually certain. In 1969 Rockefeller imposed his choice for state chairman, Charles Lanigan, over opposing upstate and downstate factions. In 1970 he secured the unopposed senatorial nomination for Charles Goodell, an incumbent very unpopular with Republican leaders throughout the state. In 1972 the governor brought the party to a reluctant accommodation with the Conservative party and the endorsement of common electors for the Nixon-Agnew ticket, a course he had blocked in 1968. In 1973 he forced New York City leaders to accept the nomination of two-time Democratic mayor Robert Wagner on the Republican line, only to be embarrassed when Wagner declined to run.

Though Governor Rockefeller exercised control over the Republican party in New York State, he was careful to consult with local leaders and meet their needs whenever possible. As a consequence, these leaders expressed considerable satisfaction with their access to the governor and their patronage success with him. Of twenty-nine Republican county chairmen who responded to a survey conducted by political scientist Ronald Steinberg in 1970, 14 percent indicated that they were always successful, 62 percent felt they were sometimes successful, and 24 percent said they were occasionally successful in recommending names to the Rockefeller administration for appointive state positions. From the survey it appeared that "Republican leaders from the more rural portions of the state had been more successful than their urban counterparts in getting more recommendations and more valuable recommendations accepted by the Rockefeller administration."[56]

Other potential rivals to the governor for party leadership were the Republican United States senators from New York. Senators enjoyed the advantage of representing a statewide constituency without having to get involved daily in patronage and other decisions that might earn the governor intraparty enemies. They were thus the logical alternative choices for elements within the party that became disenchanted with the governor's leadership.

In 1966 and 1972 there was speculation that Senator Jacob Javits would challenge Governor Rockefeller for party leadership within the state. In 1965 Javits was urged by a conservative upstate state senator, John Hughes of Syracuse, to run against Rockefeller for the gubernatorial nomination. In a letter Hughes cited a poll that showed Javits to be the favored nominee of 30 percent of the Onondaga County Republican committee, while only 4 percent favored Rockefeller, and argued that Rockefeller could not win and would "take the party, the legislature, and many local officials down with him."[57] The short-lived Javits boom, reported to be supported by several upstate and suburban downstate leaders, lasted about a week and then was put to rest in a private meeting between the senator and the governor.

Similar rumors of a potential Javits gubernatorial bid emerged early in 1972.[58] On March 11 Senator Javits attended an exploratory meeting in New York City, this time convened by the downstate liberal wing of the party. Significantly, the state chairman, the governor's agent, was not invited to attend. The purpose of the meeting was to discuss the possibility of a Javits gubernatorial candidacy in 1974 to offset the impending efforts of Malcolm Wilson and Perry Duryea. As in 1965, the senator seemed the most viable alternative to the administration for the faction of the party that disapproved of the governor. In 1965 it was upstate conservative legislators, in 1972 downstate "progressive Republicans." When the governor seemed weak, as in 1965 because of his lack of popularity in the opinion polls, or in 1972 because of his seeming lame-duck status, the "anti" wing of the party turned to the senator as its champion. The 1966 experience illustrated, however, that if the governor wished to do so, he could crush any effort that challenged his domination of the state party. His control of patronage and the party machinery gave him overwhelming resources, resources that discouraged intraparty challenges.

Gubernatorial Patronage

It was often assumed that there was a central system for the dispensing of patronage in New York, organized around the governor's appointments secretary and the state party chairman. In a widely read book, for example, Martin and Susan Tolchin described New York as a major patronage state and estimated that Governor Rockefeller controlled about 40,000 state positions.[59] In fact, this number was far too high. Many of these posts were competitive but were filled without written examinations. What political influence there was in the appointive process was highly decentralized, functionally to departmental commissioners and their key subordinates and geographically to Republican county leaders. Thus politics might determine who got hired by the Finger Lakes State Parks Commission in Tompkins County, but it would be the politics of the relationship between the county leader and key local commission officials, not the preferences of the governor's office.

The nature of the patronage decision itself can be misunderstood.

As James Q. Wilson has pointed out, few patronage decisions are made purely to extend party strength and optimize partisan control.[60] A whole host of considerations—personal, political, and organizational—affect each appointment. The difficulty comes in attempting to reduce to a general description a process in which each decision is in some way unique.

The civil service system in New York was structured to hold to a minimum partisan political influence in the appointive process. In a fundamental sense, this system was a valuable resource for the governor and his staff, if only because its existence protected them from an overwhelming crush of job seekers, a crush that they were ill equipped to handle. It was doubtful that a government as large as New York's could function adequately without the orderly and continuing personnel management services provided by the civil service department acting under merit principles.

Pressures on the civil service system did arise from the partisan political arena, however, for a state job was one potential reward for party service, one incentive for involvement in the political arena. In his book on the dynamics of the American party system, Frank Sorauf noted: "Internally . . . [the political party] is a vast network of personal ties, authority relationships, and incentives to activity. Basic to these relationships are the rewards and sanctions, the political incentive system, which the political party commands and manages. If the party is to continue functioning as an organization it must make 'payments' in an acceptable 'political currency' adequate to motivate and allocate the labors of its workers."[61]

The appointments secretary in the governor's office and the Republican state chairman were the channel for patronage. Jobs, both paid and honorific, were only one kind of potential reward. Others included preferment (state contracts and special treatment by government departments), personal rewards (friendship with the governor and other high officials, social mobility, and psychic satisfaction), involvement in policy making, and pure ideological satisfaction. In distributing these rewards, the appointments secretary and the state chairman had subtly different commitments. Whereas the secretary's ultimate—and only—loyalty was to the governor, the state chairman, though of necessity the governor's man, had a fundamental commitment to building the party as an organization, and these two loyalties might at times clash.

In New York the handling of patronage went forward within broad parameters defined by the governor himself. Though he came to understand and value the use of patronage and partisanship in governing, Rockefeller insisted that his appointments secretary and state chairman understand that professional competence was the overriding consideration in the appointments process. Political aides, he said, had to meet party needs within the constraints of this criterion. The operation of this principle sometimes—as in the case of Joseph Swidler of the Power Commission and Ray Schuler of the Department of Transportation—resulted in the appointment of Democrats. Naturally, the state chairman preferred to see Republicans appointed, but he was consulted when the governor went outside the party. Democratic appointments were exceptions, not the rule, and the party leadership, convinced of the governor's overall commitment to building the party, learned to live with them. Richard Rosenbaum, who served as state chairman, noted that exceptions were most often made at the top. For middle-level posts, qualifications were more broadly defined, and consequently party loyalists who could fill them were more easily found.[62]

Generally the appointment process produced honest and competent officials during Rockefeller's early years, but there was one major exception. In 1965 L. Judson Morhouse, the Republican state chairman who had been instrumental in securing the Rockefeller gubernatorial nomination, and Martin C. Epstein, the governor's appointee as chairman of the State Liquor Authority, were indicted for seeking a bribe of $150,000 from the Playboy Club in New York City for the issuance of a liquor license. Epstein, appointed at the recommendation of John Crews, Republican county leader of Brooklyn, was fired by Rockefeller when he failed to waive immunity and testify in the case. Morhouse, who later was convicted, served a prison term.

Investigations by Anthony Scotti, New York County assistant district attorney, demonstrated that Morhouse had been involved in influence peddling well before he established his relationship with the governor. These earlier episodes should have alerted the governor to the seriousness of the situation. Morhouse had, however, passed routine state police Bureau of Criminal Investigation checks. He resigned his chairmanship and other state posts late in 1962, but the scandal jeopardized Rockefeller's reelection in 1966 and was a sobering experience for him. It led to a tightening of investigation procedures in the hiring process so that similar problems might be avoided.

In the first days of Rockefeller's governorship, appointments were screened through a committee chaired by Rockefeller and including

Roscoe Perkins (his counsel), William Ronan (his secretary), George Hinman, Malcolm Wilson, Louis Lefkowitz, and Carl Spad, appointments secretary. Each man suggested nominees from his own area of expertise, though most recommendations came from within the Republican party through county chairmen. Rockefeller was especially fortunate during this time to have the advice of Hinman and Wilson, both of whom were intimately familiar with the state party organization.[63]

The appointments secretary's concern was to merge professional and political qualifications. The particular qualifications differed with the job to be done. For example, in the case of the superintendent of banks, integrity, a lack of vested interests, and professional experience were most important. In the case of certain commissionerships— health, mental health, and welfare—the governor sought recommendations from professional societies, and party clearance was pro forma. In one way, Carl Spad recalled, this was good politics. If the governor accepted a recommendation from a profession group and the appointee turned out to be a poor administrator, he had someone to blame.[64]

After the rush of initial appointments, Spad attempted to establish a system in the governor's office to regularize the appointments process. A record was kept of every gubernatorial appointee, including his background, the person who recommended him, and his term of office. All potential appointees were investigated by the state police Bureau of Criminal Investigation as a matter of course before selection. When preparing to make an appointment, the secretary would seek nominees from selected county leaders. Without establishing a quota system, he attempted to achieve a geographic balance, especially between upstate and downstate. Though the governor instructed Spad not to consider racial and ethnic factors in selecting candidates for appointment, he felt it a political necessity to do so and did give some consideration to these factors. If the person selected for a position was originally suggested from outside party channels, he was cleared, at least formally, with the county leader before the process went forward.

If the law required that a Democrat be appointed to a post, the appointments secretary would seek the recommendation of the Democratic state chairman. Often, but not always, he would accept such recommendations. In later years the governor used these posts to reward Democrats who had given him needed legislative support. In 1969, for example, he appointed Charles F. Stockmeister of Rochester to the Civil Service Commission after Stockmeister had broken party lines to support the governor's proposed tax increase.[65]

After the Rockefeller administration became established, most vacancies arose through deaths or resignations. The pressure on the appointments secretary from county chairmen was intense and continuous. Carl Spad recalled that sometimes the chairmen would "hardly let a guy get cold and stop twitching" before they would nominate a successor. The appetite of the leaders for jobs was insatiable. There was never enough patronage to go around and it was in the nature of the process that some and often many were disappointed. When a county leader's recommendations failed, Spad viewed his role as "taking the heat" and "giving the local leaders a hearing."[66]

Several modifications of the system of the early and mid-1960s can be seen in the later operations of the office of the appointments secretary. Perhaps the major change was the political recommendations were sought solely through the state committee. The role of dispenser of rewards to the county leaders thus passed from the appointments secretary to the state chairman. The chairman served as a buffer for the secretary against pressure for appointments from the county level. The last appointments secretary, Phil Weinberg, did not commit himself to county leaders on appointments for fear of undermining the chairman and thus destroying this useful buffer function. "When they call," he said, "I tell them nothing. If I say we are considering their man, then they know what Rosenbaum [the state chairman] has done. If I say we are not, then they know he didn't give us the name—for reasons of his own which may be very good ones—and this puts the heat on him. So I just speak with them in generalities and make no commitments."[67]

From the perspective of the state chairman, it was critical that good candidates be recommended for state positions so that he could retain his "credibility" in the appointment process. Richard Rosenbaum, the chairman for the last four years of Rockefeller's governorship, had three staff people working solely on patronage matters. The governor demanded qualified candidates and Rosenbaum made the same demand of county leaders. "I will not," Rosenbaum told the leaders, "go to bat for a hack and won't come back to you for recommendations if you send me hacks."[68]

Rosenbaum worked closely with Rockefeller on all matters concerning the party. He attempted to establish the committee as a conduit for party demands on the governor and himself as the arbiter of these demands. Furthermore, he worked to convince heads of state departments that the party was a legitimate source of input in top-level personnel decisions. When making recommendations on jobs and other local party requests for gubernatorial aid (appearances and endorsements), Rosenbaum applied such criteria as party performance in past elections and support for statewide fund-raising efforts. Like Spad, he kept close records, worked for geographic balance, and sought to "spread the goodies around." Here, as elsewhere, criteria were flexible. There was a need to bolster the party in areas where it was weak as well as reinforce it where it was strong. There was some pressure for recognition from black, Puerto Rican, and Italian groups, but it was not, in Rosenbaum's view, a major problem. The questions of balance and recognition were perhaps most important in appointments to statewide boards and commissions.

Conflicting recommendations were rarely made to the governor by the state chairman, the appointments secretary, and the concerned department head. Usually they worked out differences among themselves. In this process, Weinberg saw himself as representing the governor's interest. What was good for the county leader or department head might not be good for the governor. The role of the state chairman was to protect the party's interest, but he also had to sell the governor's positions to party leaders and to absorb and quiet criticism.

In New York the civil service personnel system and the patronage system exist side by side in permanent tension. Each has significant sources of strength and significant weaknesses. The civil service system has a long tradition and a constitutional guarantee, and it has shown that it can function to staff the state bureaucracy effectively. In combination, these factors have made the state personnel system something of a political sacred cow. Few politicians could afford to challenge openly what has come to be called the merit system.

Yet the patronage system also has its strengths. These lie in the dynamics of the reward system of political life. As long as the people who work for political parties seek public jobs in the wake of victory, party leaders will challenge the civil service system in order to obtain those jobs for their workers.

In New York, the *potential* for gubernatorial control seemed enormous. Limiting factors, however, were at work. When an interviewer said to the state chairman, "Mr. Rosenbaum, I understand you have forty thousand state jobs that you fill with good and deserving Republicans," Rosenbaum laughed. He replied, "Heaven knows I try, but I don't succeed."[69] Among the 40,000 positions were faculty in the State University system, appointed by the university administration, and professional posts in the departments, to which appointment was made by the respective commissioners. A complicating factor was that department heads frequently did not notify the appointments secretary of existing vacancies. Often, too, service jobs were not filled. Party activists did not find them attractive because of their low status or their location.

In addition, the gubernatorial patronage mechanism was limited. The appointments secretary and state chairman were not equipped to handle a large volume of placements. They were organized to handle top appointments, honorific posts, and a limited number of lesser posts. Even here the system did not always work. During one interview the governor's appointments secretary pulled a file at random to illustrate how efficient the system was, but to his embarrassment he discovered a post on a community college board that had, through oversight, been left vacant for eighteen months.

In sum, patronage failed as an overwhelming tool of gubernatorial power in New York not because of the limited number of jobs but because the governor's office had neither the will nor the means to manage what was potentially a widespread patronage system. About 8,000 posts, paid and honorific, were controlled from the office of the appointments secretary, about 2,000 of them requiring decision annually. Though the governor had the power to influence a large number of other posts, the job of filling them was left to lower levels in the administrative and political processes.

Thwarted Presidential Ambitions

As powerful as Nelson Rockefeller was in the New York Republican party, he was unable to use this control as a springboard to the presidency. In fact, most of the explanation for the governor's failure to obtain his party's presidential nomination can be found within the imperatives of New York State politics.[70]

It has been said that Nelson Rockefeller could have been elected to the presidency if only he could have gotten the nomination of his party. A Harris poll in November 1967 offered ample justification for this contention. It showed the governor with 52 percent of the electorate in a projected race with Lyndon Johnson, but a survey of Republican county leaders across the country consulted on the same day revealed that they favored Richard Nixon for the nomination by a margin of 5 to 1. A later poll, completed on March 16, 1968, showed him still well ahead of Johnson with the electorate but behind Nixon among Republicans, 56 percent to 32 percent.

Four GOP national conventions were held while Rockefeller was governor. At three of them the nomination eluded the governor's grasp, and at the fourth the renomination of President Nixon blocked his path. Bowing to the inevitable in August 1972, Rockefeller himself nominated Nixon, his great rival over two decades and a man of whom he had said in 1960, "I hate the thought of Dick Nixon being president of the United States."[71]

What brought the governor to this pass? His failure to win the GOP presidential nomination was explainable by the interaction of three major factors. The most important were the dynamics of New York State politics and their contradictory implications for national Republican politics. Governors of New York had been automatically serious contenders for the presidential nomination of their party. Since 1900, five New York governors had obtained the nomination, and two of them had ultimately won the office. But, as has been demonstrated, Republican gubernatorial candidates in New York have to appeal to Democratic and independent voters. In 1970, for example, these two groups comprised about two-thirds of the enrolled voters in the state. New York is a polyglot state. Nearly half the electorate in 1970 was Catholic, one-third Protestant, and one-sixth Jewish. Three of every ten voters were union members. Large numbers of blacks and Latins were concentrated in New York City and other major cities. In order to win in New York, Rockefeller had to appeal to diverse groups, but it was precisely the kind of appeals that he framed for this end that alienated those who controlled his party nationally.

To be sure, Thomas Dewey, a Republican governor, was successful in capturing his party's presidential nomination twice. But the center of gravity in the Republican party when Dewey sought the nomination was in the Northeast rather than the Midwest and Far West. Moreover, the New York electorate in Rockefeller's day was different from that of Dewey's. Not only were there larger minority groups but they were more politically aggressive in their demands for government action. Thus in order to win state elections, Rockefeller had to be much more liberal than Dewey had been.

It was not only Rockefeller's liberal programs and rhetoric that made him persona non grata with large segments of his party, but also his approach to government. For Rockefeller was a problem solver, a man who through his administration in New York sought to prove that government at the state level could still be vital in the United States. But problem solving leads to activist government and expensive government. In 1958 New York State's budget was $1.79

billion; in 1973 it was $8.3 billion. To heartland Republicans, unfamiliar with the problems of urban states and convinced still that the government that governs best governs least, Rockefeller was a big spender, a Democrat in Republican clothing.

During the late 1950s and through the 1960s, the period in which Rockefeller actively sought the presidential nomination, the party was no longer controlled by the northeastern leaders who had dictated the nomination of Dewey and Eisenhower. Rather it was in the hands of mid- and far-western state and county GOP leaders, who had always been more conservative than the mass of the party's membership. To be sure, they had accepted liberal eastern presidential nominees (not without a struggle), but only because of the argument that such candidates could lead the party to victory. Thus in 1960, 1964, and 1968, Rockefeller's strategy was to demonstrate his strength in public opinion polls and in presidential primaries in selected states.

In 1960 the polls did not show him to have greater strength against likely Democratic opponents than Nixon, the incumbent vice-president. The publication of a Gallup poll a week before the 1968 convention that showed Nixon, with a 2–5 percent advantage over Rockefeller against Hubert Humphrey or Eugene McCarthy, undermined the governor's approach to the convention delegates. Later polls, by Harris and Crossley, in which Rockefeller was demonstrated to be doing better than Nixon in the country and the key industrial states, made poll data ambiguous, and in an ambiguous situation at a GOP convention, Rockefeller could not prevail.[72]

In 1964 the governor sought to prove his vote-getting ability through the primary route. The scattered results destroyed his hopes of showing himself the only possible Republican winner against Lyndon Johnson. In New Hampshire he lost to a write-in effort for Henry Cabot Lodge, and though he won in Oregon, Rockefeller's close defeat by Barry Goldwater in California laid to rest his hopes for the nomination.

Thus the kind of appeal that was necessary for Rockefeller to win in New York, and which made him potentially an attractive national candidate, also made him anathema to the Republican leaders who determined the presidential nomination. These men would turn to him only if he seemed a sure winner and only if no other possible winner was available. In each of his three efforts the governor fell short of proving clearly that these were the prevailing circumstances. One of the ironies of recent history was that as political necessity in

New York State moved Rockefeller to the right (or, as he would say, to the center) in the late 1960s and early 1970s, a development that made him more attractive to conservative Republicans, the route to the presidency was blocked by Nixon's incumbency. And so, in August 1972, Rockefeller abandoned his maverick role within the party and nominated Nixon, confirming his arrival at last in the mainstream of the GOP.

Other positions that Rockefeller took in political and personal matters also damaged his national career. In June 1960, after becoming convinced that some of the policies of the Eisenhower administration, both domestically and internationally, were contrary to the best interests of the nation, Rockefeller, who had publicly withdrawn as an aspirant for the nomination on Christmas Day of 1959, demanded that Vice-President Nixon make his views clear in nine policy areas. The subsequent threat of a floor fight over the party platform and the ultimate Fifth Avenue fourteen-point compromise gained Rockefeller his policy ends but labeled him a party wrecker among embittered conservatives.

Rockefeller's divorce and remarriage to Mrs. Robin "Happy" Murphy in 1963 was another factor in his failure to gain the 1964 presidential nomination. He had assembled a staff and had begun to work toward 1964 just a few weeks after the 1960 election. The prospects in 1963 were very bright. George Hinman and Emmet Hughes, however, warned the governor that his remarriage in the critical preconvention days would create a "morality issue" that would be used against him in the primaries, particularly in view of the fact that Mrs. Murphy had been recently divorced and was engaged in a custody fight for her five children. Yet Rockefeller remarried, at the worst possible moment for his political career. Before his remarriage a Gallup poll of Republicans showed Rockefeller with 43 percent of the vote and Goldwater with 26 percent. Immediately after the marriage Goldwater increased his total to 35 percent and Rockefeller declined to 30 percent. In the California primary fight the slogan used against Rockefeller by the Goldwater partisans was "We want a leader, not a lover." It became especially effective when Nelson and Happy Rockefeller's first child was born the Saturday before the primary. His advisers were right: his remarriage killed his candidacy.[73]

One of Nelson Rockefeller's main liabilities among his political detractors was what they viewed as his "selfish ambition." His June 1960 policy statements were presented as a desperate last-minute lunge at the nomination, without regard for its effect on the party's chances in the general election. His remarriage at such a politically sensitive moment was presented as evidence of arrogance. But in retrospect both of these actions entailed considerable political risks that did not have to be taken.

Some analysts assume that the holding of an important office is an advantage for a presidential candidate. In 1968, however, Rockefeller felt that it was a disadvantage. Unencumbered by the requirements of office between 1962 and 1968, Richard Nixon could travel throughout the nation, working for Republican candidates and placing them in his debt. Rockefeller, as governor of New York State throughout this period, had his campaign efforts constrained by the demands of his job at home.

Finally, Rockefeller was a victim of his own staff system. He believed in staffwork, in rational decision making. Early in 1959 he had an outstanding staff working on his presidential campaign. It included experienced politicians (George Hinman and Judson Morhouse), highly trained academics (William Ronan and Henry Kissinger), and lawyer-administrators well connected in the eastern Republican establishment (Richardson Dilworth and Roswell Perkins). Position papers were prepared on all issues. Data were collected on convention delegates. But when the results showed that a race would be futile, Rockefeller accepted the finding of this rational process of exploration. He withdrew. He later recalled that the "people who were running my campaign said it was hopeless."[74]

In 1968, too, staff analysis told Rockefeller that he could not be nominated. After a week of exploratory talks with advisers and Republican leaders and intensive examination of poll data, he decided on March 21 to announce that he would not be a candidate. Rockefeller's candidacy in 1964 had torn the party apart. He would stand aside this time, he thought, and play the role of kingmaker. Only when the business community asked him to run, a bit more than three months before the convention, did the governor reconsider and then launch a desperate last-minute bid. It almost succeeded. If Ronald Reagan had cut into Nixon's southern block, if Rockefeller had moved earlier and more surely, if he had avoided unnecessary alienation of such supporters as Spiro Agnew, then governor of Maryland, the convention might have been thrown open and the nomination might have been his. Nixon got 692 votes in Miami in 1968, only 25 more than the majority necessary to nominate.

A successful quest for a presidential nomination often requires almost an act of faith by the candidate. The candidacy of neither George

McGovern nor Jimmy Carter would have been launched had either man stopped overlong to assess his chances. Goldwater, confronted in 1964 by the Rockefeller juggernaut, never would have sought the nomination had he acted entirely rationally. Rockefeller's vast staff resources made him too cautious. The essential element of throwing caution to the winds, of starting early and going all out, was lacking in all but the 1964 presidential effort.

Governor Rockefeller's involvement in national politics, though unsuccessful, had a great impact on politics within the state. Other New York politicians were always aware that they were dealing with a potential presidential candidate, and this circumstance enhanced the governor's personal power within the state; as Joseph Schlesinger has noted, "a governor who has good prospects for advancement has a powerful instrument to affect other politicians—their own hope for advancement."[75] Further, Rockefeller's national involvement allowed him and his staff to develop relationships with other politicians within the party which no doubt helped him in seeking the resources to meet New York's needs in Washington.

On the other side of the ledger, the constant campaigning took the governor out of the state, sapped his energy, and directed his efforts away from state affairs. Activity in national Republican politics made Rockefeller enemies as well as friends around the country. His ambition helped ensure that he would work to make New York a leader among the states in many areas of policy but may also have led him to extend the state's efforts beyond its resources.

3

The Governor and
the Legislature

"Politics," Nelson Rockefeller said in looking back over his years as governor of New York, "is a kaleidoscope of constantly changing relationships." In no aspect of state government is this statement more true than in the evolution of gubernatorial relations with the legislature and its leadership over the years from 1959 to 1973.

When Rockefeller was first elected, the Republican speaker of the assembly, Oswald Heck, had held that post for twenty-two years. Walter Mahoney was a veteran of twenty-two years of legislative service and was entering his fifth year as Senate majority leader. The governor, new to state politics, had to deal with an entrenched GOP legislative leadership that had defined party positions without any constraints from the executive during the immediately preceding four years of the Democratic Harriman administration.[1] When Rockefeller left office, the Republican Senate leader, Warren Anderson, was entering his second year of service in that post, and the Assembly speaker, Perry Duryea, his fifth. The governor's fifteen years in office spanned all or part of the terms of four majority leaders and four speakers, one Democrat and three Republicans in each house. By the time he stepped down, Rockefeller had become the most experienced major participant in New York's legislative process—more experienced than even the staff aides on whom he relied for day-to-day legislative liaison.

As governor, Rockefeller was faced with every possible partisan circumstance in the legislature. Each situation required its own gubernatorial strategy in the marshaling of legislative majorities. Although both houses of the legislature were Republican-controlled during most of Rockefeller's tenure, in one year, 1965, the governor had to deal with a legislature in which both houses were controlled by the Democrats, and in 1966–1968 with one in which partisan control was divided between the two houses. In some periods the governor used partisan loyalties to hold together conservative GOP majorities in the Senate and Assembly that differed from his more liberal initiatives in public policy. In others, he dealt pragmatically with Democratic majorities in the Assembly but was constrained by the needs of his party's minority in that house and the priorities of its majority in the Senate. On some critical issues, the governor found it necessary to put together ad hoc coalitions centered on particular positions, adding Democratic votes to a core of Republican support. Rockefeller took his majorities where he found them and with increased tenure became skilled at the game of legislative politics. By the time he left office he had become a master of tactics, playing one house against the other, one party against the other, one leader against another, and even one faction against another within each major party, orchestrating all his formal and informal resources in order to gain his policy goals.

The partisan situation within the legislature, the balance of power within the Republican party, and the situation of individual legislators were all affected by legislative reapportionment during Rockefeller's administration.[2] When Rockefeller entered the governorship it was said that, because of state constitutional provisions on the apportionment of legislative seats, the legislature was "constitutionally Republican." The U.S. Supreme Court decisions in *Baker* v. *Carr* and subsequent reapportionment cases changed this situation. Between 1959 and 1973 the legislature was reapportioned four times. Though Republican control of the Senate remained secure, reapportionment made the Democratic threat in the Assembly very real. With narrowed majorities and a tenuous hold on power, the Republican Assembly leadership after 1968 was not so free to negotiate with the governor as the leadership during Rockefeller's first years in office. Within the Republican party, the balance of power in the legislature shifted from rural areas to the suburbs of New York City. In 1962, 36.1 percent of Republican senators and 45.9 percent of Republican assemblymen were from rural areas; in 1968 the percentages were 24.2 and 26.9. In contrast, the percentages of Republican senators from the New York City suburbs rose from 21.2 to 30.3 during this period. In the Assembly a similar trend, from 18.8 to 26.9 percent, was discernible. This situation also presented problems to the governor. Suburban legislative districts were more competitive than rural ones, and it was in the suburbs that the state's Conservative party grew fastest. Suburban legislators, more cross-pressured than their rural counterparts, were less likely to support gubernatorial programs out of party loyalty.

Reapportionment also resulted in increased turnover in the membership of the legislature, a development that further attenuated leadership control. Rockefeller himself recognized this trend as contributing to the difficulty of the governor's job vis-à-vis the legislature. In an interview in 1971 he noted that when he came into office

> there was little turnover in the membership of the legislature. The leaders had good disciplinary control over the members. Many of the most prominent members of the legislature had interim committee assignments for which appropriations for staff were made. This gave them a certain amount of patronage and helped in maintaining discipline. Consequently I worked closely with the two majority leaders, and once they agreed to a program, there was usually little difficulty in getting it through the legislature. . . .
>
> [However] . . . since the one-man–one-vote ruling there has been much more rapid turnover in the membership of the legislature, with the result that you do not have as many experienced legislators with loyalty to the leaders. Consequently, negotiation involves a much larger group of people and it is more difficult to get legislation through.[3]

Despite this trend, New York had long been known as one of the states with a strong legislative party system. In 1948 Warren Moscow wrote of "tight control" by the leadership as "an important key to the relative success of the state legislature."[4] Since the administration of Alfred E. Smith in the mid-1920s, it has also been a state with a strong governor. Thus the study of legislative politics in New York has often been considered to be primarily the story of personal negotiations between the governor and the legislative leadership. The expectation of strong executive leadership has also led to the assumption that the executive controls the legislature in New York, and, in fact, to charges that Rockefeller functioned as a "one-man legislature" in Albany.[5]

It is ironic that many of the same legislators who criticized Rockefeller for being too dominant in his legislative relations complained of lack of leadership when his successor, Malcolm Wilson, followed a conscious policy of constraint in this area. As Rockefeller noted in June 1974: "I think Malcolm accomplished exactly what he set out to do, which was to . . . allow the legislature, which had been critical of my form of leadership, to have the opportunity to express themselves. And then, of course, as is the case with life, they then said, 'Where's the leadership?'"[6]

In the context of the vast social and political changes in New York during the 1960s and 1970s, changes that fundamentally affected the nature of legislative majorities, the assumption of absolute gubernatorial control, even under Rockefeller, was incorrect. Legislative leaders could no longer deliver the votes of their colleagues to the governor. Deep differences in ideology and in geographic perspective split both parties. The Democratic threat to capture control of the Assembly was a real one in Rockefeller's later terms as governor, and indeed the Democrats did obtain control of that house in 1974. During the late 1960s and early 1970s, the legislature began to develop independent staff and information resources to reduce their reliance on the executive, and leaders of the governor's party took an increasingly independent public stance. The governor could still have his way on key issues if he was willing to pay the price in effort and resources, but few issues were worth the legacy of resentment, especially within his party, that such dealing caused. As Rockefeller said in replying to a journalist's question on how far he would go to support a bill on no-fault automobile insurance, "I have a pretty good sense of what is do-able and what isn't do-able and when it's do-able. This is political."

Most often the chief executive, knowing that he would have to deal with the legislature again another day and realizing the political realities that constrain legislators and their leaders, compromised in order to secure the most important parts of his program and budget. The governor's power was predominant, but it was not absolute.

The Governor's Resources

The governor brought to his relationship with the legislature a variety of resources, both formal and informal. Experts have ranked the formal lawmaking powers of New York's governor among the strongest in the nation. He defined legislative debates and priorities through his annual and special messages. The executive budget was shaped by him and offered to the legislature with his approval. He possessed a veto on legislation which was exercised freely, and though it could be overridden by a vote of two-thirds of both legislative houses, it never was during Rockefeller's tenure. He also had the sole power to call the legislature into special session and to define its agenda when it was called.

One gubernatorial power challenged in 1971 was the constitutionally given prerogative to issue "messages of special necessity." The New York Constitution required that a bill be on each legislator's desk for three days before it could be passed into law. The waiting period could be circumvented, however, if the governor issued a "message of special necessity," which he could do by simple declaration. One legislator described the consequences of this constitutional exception:

> Using this device, the governor can call upon the legislature to vote on legislation at any time. By eliminating the three-day waiting period, votes can be called on bills which have not been studied, publicized, or in some instances even read. In New York, the governor's program bills are often held until the closing hours of the session. They are then submitted to and reported out of the Rules Committee through prior arrangement with the Speaker. Called immediately to the floor upon the utilization of the "message of special necessity," the bills are passed and few members of the legislature have had a chance to analyze or even read them.[7]

In 1971 the American Civil Liberties Union, in cooperation with the United Federation of Teachers, the National Welfare Rights Organization, and a group of liberal Democratic legislators, brought a suit charging that the governor had issued messages of special necessity on seventy-nine occasions in the 1971 legislative session when no emergency existed. This practice, it was charged, was an abuse of gubernatorial power, violated the intent of the state constitution, and short-circuited the legislative process. Nine months later State Supreme Court Justice Irving Saypol dismissed the suit. Judge Saypol found the challenged messages "constitutionally sufficient" and allowed the legislation in question to stand because, he said, the state constitution established no standard of "facts" upon which a message of special necessity had to be based. Judge Saypol's decision was affirmed on July 2, 1973, by the State Court of Appeals, New York's court of last resort.[8]

Another formal power that attracted considerable criticism was the governor's sole authority to call the legislature into special session. Under the New York Constitution, the governor established the date for a special session and set the agenda. No matter could be taken up without his authorization, and he could withhold details of legislation until the session began. This power to call special sessions was used by the governor to meet intraparty needs (for example, selection of new Assembly leaders in 1959), to meet fiscal crises, to help secure GOP control in legislative reapportionment, and to reassert personal power after a defeat in the regular session.

The Citizens Conference on State Legislatures recommended that a constitutional amendment be passed allowing the legislature to call itself into special session.[9] The first passage of such an amendment by bipartisan supporters during the 1974 legislative session indicated the increasing desire of state legislators to buttress their role in the policy process.[10] The governor's sole power to call a special session, however, served to give the opposition party an issue. New York City Democrats often demanded special sessions to meet particular problems of the city. When the governor failed to call such a session or to include on the agenda measures desired by city Democrats, he could be blamed for inaction and its consequences.

The fact that New York's governor served a four-year term and might succeed himself indefinitely never allowed legislators to assume that he would pass from the political scene and did permit the governor to trade on the presumption of his future candidacy. Research by Sarah P. McCally has shown that indefinite eligibility is an aspect of the governor's formal powers that is strongly linked to his legislative success. A governor's success in having his vetoes upheld was shown to be strongly correlated with his success in primaries held following the legislative session. Thus, as McCally noted, gubernatorial influence "builds on a future reward, rather than a past success."[11] It was Rockefeller's indefinite eligibility that made such rewards possible.

The less formal sources of persuasive power that the governor of New York may marshal were also formidable. He was the most visible public official in the state, and, because the national media were headquartered in New York, he was perhaps the most visible state official in the nation. His visibility and access to television, radio, and the press gave him power to shape the public debate on issues before the legislature and marshal public sentiment in support of his views. As leader of his party, the governor could use the partisan appeal for legislative support. He controlled a good deal of patronage—most important, the power of appointments to judgeships, posts coveted by many legislative leaders.[12] Because the bureaucracy reported to and through him, the governor controlled much of the information that legislators needed in order to act intelligently on substantive legislation and budgetary matters, and, if information was lacking, it was he and not the legislature that had the necessary staff support to develop source material. Finally, the governor possessed the great advantage that inheres in the expectation that he would lead. The initiative in public affairs was always with the governor, the debate his to define.

To the informal resources of any governor of New York must be added those peculiar to Nelson Rockefeller. A leader of the legislative staff who worked closely with Rockefeller once commented that the remarkable thing about his governorship, especially in the later years, was that running the state was only one of several enterprises in which he was involved. Rockefeller was at home in several worlds— business, finance, society, culture, the arts. Each of the worlds to which his wealth and interests gave him access was a potential resource that could be used in the political realm. Usually he kept these worlds separate, but occasionally he would invite legislative leaders to a party at his Pocantico Hills mansion, where they might mix with the greats of American business and commerce. Used carefully, this technique of subtle flattery occasionally helped ease the way for some gubernatorial priorities in the legislature. In a more direct way, Rockefeller's wealth provided him with a larger and better staff than that available to a governor who had to rely solely on public pay schedules and job availabilities, and it gave him tremendous flexibility. Few governors have commanded such resources.

The Legislative Leaders

Wide as the governor's powers were, it would be a mistake to assume that the legislature was powerless. Indeed, a study published in 1971 by the Citizens Conference on State Legislatures, which examined the fifty state legislatures in five broad categories (functional, accountable, informed, independent, and representative), ranked the New York legislature second only to California's as the strongest in the nation. According to this study the New York Senate and Assembly enjoyed a "high volume and wide range of resources" that offered them at least the opportunity for action independent of the governor. [13] Another survey in the 1970s showed that the New York legislature was tightly organized under the control of the Senate majority leader and Assembly speaker:

> The leaders' powers are similar and quite extensive. Each appoints the members of standing committees and interim joint legislative committees in his house (minority members on the recommendation of the minority leader) and selects committee chairmen (often on the convenient basis of seniority). Each has final control over the appointment and salaries of the hundreds of legislative employees. . . . Each supervises the auxiliary offices and controls the space of his house. As chairman of the Rules

Committee, a leadership committee lopsided with loyal majority party members, the leader controls whatever bills he chooses to refer to the committee throughout the session, has the power to expedite the consideration of bills on the floor, controls the flow of bills coming from the other house, and regulates the flow of bills to the floor during the important closing weeks of the session. Leadership control of the Rules Committee is especially important in the Assembly when the other committees have stopped functioning in the waning days of the legislative session.[14]

The role of the leadership is central. One expert in gubernatorial–legislative relationships commented: "No factor is more important in determining a governor's legislative success than his relationship with the legislative leaders of his party. . . . These are the governor's spokesmen and representatives in the legislature. If they are ineffective or uncooperative, the governor is seriously handicapped. If he tries to bypass or undermine his leaders on one bill, he damages the effectiveness of their leadership on other legislation."[15] Even within his own party, however, the governor has relatively little to say about leadership selection. One long-term Senate staff aide who has been in a position to observe several leadership changes in that body went so far as to comment: "A gubernatorial endorsement in a fight for the majority leadership in the Senate would be a positive disadvantage in the Republican party caucus."[16] Rockefeller knew this. In an interview in 1970 he commented that there were "serious political risks in attempting to influence the outcome of contests of this nature . . . the members of the legislature are rightfully jealous of their prerogatives." As a consequence, he said, his policy was one of "respecting the sensibilities of lawmakers and avoiding interference with their leadership preferences."[17]

Rockefeller did admit, however, that he might have tried to influence legislative leadership selection "if someone really objectionable had [had] a serious chance of success."[18] Such a situation, the governor commented, had never arisen, despite the abortive move in 1965 to capture the Senate leadership by John Hughes of Syracuse, a Rockefeller foe on tax and fiscal policy. Legislators were aware that, though the governor was not directly involved, whoever was selected would have to deal with him. It did the legislative party little good to select men with whom the governor could not bargain.

Over his fifteen years as governor, Rockefeller had to deal with men of various political strengths and styles in legislative leadership posts. Walter Mahoney, the Senate majority leader and his chief rival for the gubernatorial nomination in 1958, had such great strength that he often felt free to commit the Senate to a position without consulting the Republican senators. Mahoney came to prominence in 1949 by leading a successful revolt against Governor Dewey's budget and came within two votes of seizing the majority leadership from Arthur Wicks in 1950. When Dewey forced Wicks's resignation in 1953 because of the senator's association with labor racketeers, Mahoney won the leadership. Mahoney's style was much like that of Lyndon Johnson in the United States Senate. He attached men to him through personal favors. He sought to build loyalty to the Senate as an institution, for he knew that success in this endeavor would add to his power as a leader of that institution. When issues arose about which he felt strongly, the power that he built through personal relationships served him well. In 1964, for example, a bill whose impact would be felt almost entirely in New York City was defeated in the Senate by a vote of 30–27. Mahoney had pledged his word to the governor that it would pass, and Rockefeller in turn had given his word to Democratic boss Charles Buckley of the Bronx. Coming to the floor, Mahoney made this appeal: "Do this for me. I have never asked that before. . . . Don't vote on the merits. Vote for the institution we love."[19] A second vote was taken and the bill was passed unanimously.

Mahoney was a political force before Rockefeller entered state politics and remained independent of him. He was able to force concessions in Rockefeller's 1959 tax package and to block a bill barring racial discrimination in the sale and rental of private housing which was part of the governor's 1960 legislative package. Because he was not consulted, he refused to allow Wagner-Rockefeller compromises on judgeships in 1960 and in the Fifth Avenue Coach strike in 1962 to pass the Senate. After Mahoney's record eleven-year tenure as Senate majority leader was ended by the 1964 Democratic landslide, no comparable force emerged in the state legislative leadership. In the Assembly, long-term speaker Oswald Heck died soon after Rockefeller's tenure began, and Joseph Carlino, who succeeded to the job from the majority leadership, was most often a reliable partner for the governor. Carlino never viewed himself as Mahoney's peer in legislative power. In an interview he noted: "Mahoney could count on his majority through thick and thin. I couldn't match his control, since the Assembly was so much bigger and the members were not as mature and sophisticated."[20]

In later years, many of Rockefeller's difficulties with the legislative leadership of his own party focused on his relationship with one man, Assembly Speaker Perry Duryea. Duryea seized the minority leadership from George Ingalls in 1965 and became speaker when the Republicans recaptured the majority in the Assembly in 1968. He sought to establish a posture independent of the governor, partly because his gubernatorial ambitions demanded it but also because of the imperatives of his position in the Assembly. Whereas Mahoney opposed the governor from a position of strength—a large majority in the Senate was personally loyal to him—Duryea bargained from a tenuous base. His majority in the Assembly was narrow and composed of shifting coalitions of intraparty blocs strongly influenced by the emergent Conservative party. Duryea, like Mahoney, stressed institutional loyalty, but unlike Mahoney, he could not make an effective personal appeal that would transcend members' feelings about issues.

Duryea's own gubernatorial ambitions suffered a severe setback in 1972, when, in the midst of his jockeying for position for the nomination with Lieutenant Governor Malcolm Wilson, he was indicted for election irregularities on the basis of evidence gathered by Republican Attorney General Louis Lefkowitz. The case against the speaker was later thrown out on the ground that the law he had allegedly violated was unconstitutional, but the litigation effectively blocked his race for the governorship. Duryea held Rockefeller responsible for his difficulties, and his wife publicly opposed the ex-governor for the vice-presidential nomination on the ground that his conduct in this case made him unfit for office.

After a Democratic interlude in 1965, the Senate Republican leadership was held by Earl Brydges of Niagara Falls. Brydges was much more supportive of the governor than Mahoney had been, especially during the period 1965–1968, when Democrats controlled the Assembly. He was also less likely to use personal indebtedness to cement his coalition, and was more consultative in style. Under Brydges and his successor, Warren Anderson, individual members had greater impact on policy, which more and more frequently was being decided in the Republican caucus. Though centers of power outside the majority leader's office grew in the Senate during his tenure, Brydges, unlike Duryea in the Assembly, enjoyed a large and cohesive majority. His house, more Republican, remained the more disciplined one.

During periods of Democratic legislative control, 1965 in the Senate and 1965–1968 in the Assembly, Rockefeller had to deal with Senator Joseph Zaretzki and Speaker Anthony Travia. Both men reached their positions by virtue of Republican votes, after the Democratic caucuses of both houses were prevented from organizing the legislature for over a month by a conflict between the forces of Robert Wagner and Robert Kennedy. Though losers in the leadership fight alleged that Republican support was given in exchange for a pledge by the Wagner group to provide the votes for the governor's proposed 2 percent sales tax, Rockefeller denied it and claimed that he simply supported the established leadership, with whom he knew he could work.

Zaretzki was a long-term minority leader who was accustomed to working with the Republican majority. Travia was an extraordinarily hard-working and hard-bargaining leader who found it difficult to delegate any aspect of his job to subordinates. Rockefeller established strong personal ties to both men and even had direct telephone lines established to their offices during the legislative session, something he had not done with their Republican predecessors. In retrospect, Rockefeller recalled that he enjoyed as much success with the Democratic leadership in the legislature as with the Republican, perhaps more.[21] Indeed, after 1965 Democratic control of the Assembly and Republican control of the Senate gave the governor added flexibility. Rockefeller bargained separately with Brydges and Travia, sometimes striking a deal with the Democrat and then telling the Republican that a "liberal solution" had been forced upon him, sometimes settling first with the Republican and presenting the speaker with a *fait accompli*. Rockefeller was often more able to direct policy in his role as "honest broker, bringing together different points of view in the legislature in the interests of the people of the state as a whole," than in his role as a partisan leader.[22]

Whatever the partisan stripe of the legislative leadership, the leaders were faced with a continuing dilemma. Clearly, under the state constitution the governor had the initiative in policy design. Therefore, legislative leaders had to work with him to enact a program. This imperative to work with the governor was most compelling for Republican leaders, who were members of Rockefeller's party, but it was felt by Democrats as well. Nevertheless, the leaders were legislative men, and their power base remained in the party caucuses of their respective houses. Consequently they could not be too closely identified with the governor; their posture had to be one of cooperative independence as representatives of a coequal branch of government if they were not to undermine the very source of their leadership and power. This became especially true in the period after the mid-1960s, when reapportionment and social change produced narrower, less secure legislative majorities and legislators who consequently wanted a larger hand in policy making and left the leadership less freedom. In the Republican party, change was evidenced by the resurgence in both houses of a fiscally conservative central New York bloc with its geographic center in the Syracuse area, by the appearance of a cohesive Nassau County group in the Assembly, and by pressure on some issues of voting blocs of New York City and Hudson Valley Republican assemblymen. The Democratic leadership task was made more difficult not only by ideological differences between reformers and regular Democrats but by splits along geographic, racial, and ethnic lines that made it difficult to take partisan advantage of Republican troubles when they did emerge. As time passed, while negotiating with the governor in weekly meetings during the legislative session, leaders of both parties had to ask themselves more often, "What will the members accept?" And more often, too, they faced the need to win concessions from the governor to make policies and programs salable in their respective houses.

Partly as a consequence of changing internal politics, but also as a result of growing sensitivity on the part of legislative leaders to the need to find means of balancing the governor's formal and informal resources in the policy-making process, the professional staffs of the Senate and Assembly grew and became more specialized during the late 1960s and early 1970s. In this development, New York's experience reflected a national trend toward legislative revitalization.[23] In the Assembly, the development of a professional staff in the fiscal area stemmed from recruitment in the early 1960s of such Budget Office veterans as Al Roberts and June Martin, and continued as a result of the need perceived by Democratic Speaker Travia in 1964 to provide a focal point for intelligent opposition to executive fiscal initiatives. Under Travia's Republican successor, Perry Duryea, the size of the fiscal staff reached about twenty professionals for the majority party and seven for the minority. By constitutional provision, the legislative finance committees receive departmental estimates and participate in executive budget hearings in addition to holding their own. The development of fiscal staff capacity transformed this formal power into the ability to develop alternatives to the executive expenditure plans and to make independent projections of anticipated revenues and tax needs. In other areas, the Assembly established a central staff for ongoing research, established a scientific staff, streamlined its committee structure, and became committed to the concept of a five-year fiscal plan.

In the Senate, professional staff increased over 300 percent between 1964 and 1974. Recent years saw the development of two separate groups of aides, attorneys, and social scientists. The Senate also drew on outside consultants on policy and employed highly skilled ad hoc task forces to investigate particular problems. In addition, staffs of legislative committees were increased, and more employees worked on an annual basis rather than for the duration of the legislative session.[24] All these steps contributed to the legislative capacity to respond intelligently to gubernatorial initiatives and allowed legislative leaders to begin to seize the initiative in the design of public policy in New York.

To help the legislature determine whether state agencies were "faithfully, efficiently and effectively" carrying out authorized programs in accord with legislative intent, a Legislative Commission on Expenditure Review was established in 1969. The commission was composed of twelve members, ten of them leaders of the majority and minority in both houses of the legislature. Its professional staff made "program audits" of various state agencies which could be used by the legislature in the evaluation of agency budgets. In commenting on the commission's "notable success," one analyst of legislative performance noted: "In some instances departments and agencies have taken corrective action as a result of commission criticisms; in other instances, the legislature has altered the scope, thrust, or funding levels of programs as a result of commission assessment."[25]

While legislative staff and Rockefeller's budget office were occasionally at odds, for the most part working relationships were cooperative. Although both groups were composed of professionals, the Budget Office was much larger and had easier access to information in the executive agencies. Furthermore, legislative efforts were often fragmented between the two houses and duplicated by leaders who insisted on maintaining separate staffs personally responsible to themselves. There was no way of ensuring that professional analysis would be considered in policy making. Nevertheless, developments in the legislature, especially the desire of its leadership for an independent legislative role, strengthened the legislature in its long-term relationship with the governor.

Enacting the Legislative Program

The best way to illustrate the workings of the balance between the governor's powers and those of the legislature is to describe the enactment of the legislative program. During the Rockefeller years, only after priorities were largely decided and announced in the governor's annual message were legislative leaders advised of his program and their comments sought. The advice the governor sought from the leaders was tactical. They were not asked what the state government should do but how to get through the legislature what the governor had already decided should be done. Legislative leaders were at times able to alter the program by insisting that it could not be passed in one or both houses. This tactic was especially successful with regard to fiscal policy. Once the essential features of the program were settled, the nuances of legislative tactics—deciding who would sponsor administration bills, what committees they were to go to, and how the bills were to be shepherded through the legislature—were left to the leadership. This was one of the lessons of the 1960 experience, when bypassing the leadership to find sponsors for program bills caused the governor considerable difficulty with Republican leaders in both houses.[26]

Governor Rockefeller's long tenure allowed him to plan his program strategically as well as tactically. The growth of the State University, for example, was achieved incrementally over several program years. The fact that a bill was introduced as part of Rockefeller's program did not mean that it would be passed. Some of his proposals met with strong opposition and failed to obtain legislative approval. Such setbacks did not discourage him from making the same proposals in succeeding legislative sessions. This was the case, for example, with open housing legislation in 1959, 1960, and 1961. Another example was the repeal of the full-crew law for railroads, which the governor included in his program in every year between 1959 and 1966. Annual reintroduction, however, did not guarantee eventual passage. A later pet idea of the governor's, compulsory health insurance for workers in the state, financed out of a payroll tax, was introduced in several legislative sessions beginning in 1967 but was successfully opposed by employers and employees alike every time it was offered.

During the legislative session, Rockefeller personally remained in close touch with Republican leaders in both houses and with Democratic leaders when they held the majority. The tradition of weekly leaders' meetings is of long standing in New York. Under Governor Dewey the meetings were attended by the president of the Senate, the Assembly speaker, the majority leader, the Finance Committee chairmen in both houses, key gubernatorial aides, and other Republican state officials. Dewey stressed the formalization and synchronization of these meetings, a practice that, his counsel Charles Breitel wrote, "provided the binding quality of precedents and fashioned a new instrument of government." No bill, according to Breitel, became "a party or administration measure unless it [had] been canvassed and resolved upon at a leaders' meeting." Dewey required unanimity at leaders' meetings before he would have a bill taken to the floor, a process that transformed the meetings, in Breitel's words, into "a legislative cabinet responsible to the members of the legislature and speaking for them." It also made the leaders "the liaison, but not the controlled voice of the administration in the support of its programs in the legislature." It was, the counsel concluded, "the equivalent for the close responsibility of the parliamentary cabinet without the instability of the parliamentary system."[27]

During the Harriman governorship, the leaders' meetings were never really successful because the Republicans controlled both houses. Harriman tried unsuccessfully to alter the Dewey institution by bringing leaders of the Democratic legislative minority into the weekly conferences. Under Rockefeller, meetings were held weekly on Sunday nights and then daily toward the end of the session as legislative business reached its apex. The agenda was prepared by the counsel to the governor, though in Mahoney's later years and during the tenures of Brydges in the Senate and Duryea in the Assembly the leaders began to assert the right to add items to the agenda. Gubernatorial control of these sessions was also attenuated by the insistence of the legislative leaders on including their key staff members and committee chairmen. The governor had always exercised the prerogative of inviting his top aides and commissioners when necessary.

Leaders' meetings during the Rockefeller governorship were less formal than under Dewey and bound by no rule of unanimity. They provided a forum for the frank exchange of views between the governor and the leaders. One top Republican legislative staff aide commented: "There are tough fights in every session, though few of them reach the public eye." After compromises were hammered out there, Rockefeller usually left the gathering of Republican votes to the leader in each house. But there were occasions when he took a very active part in corralling votes himself. The governor recalled that while legislators rarely hesitated to ask for patronage as the price for their votes on measures in which he was interested, they did not always stay bought. Sometimes, on reflection, they would withdraw their commitment, but of course without losing the patronage.

With respect to Democratic votes, however, Rockefeller did not face the constraint of having to be solicitous of leadership prerogatives. On occasion, as in the 1969 budget fight, he made patronage trade-offs to capture individual Democratic votes. The votes in support of the governor's budget by Assemblymen Charles F. Stockmeister, who was later appointed a civil service commissioner, and Albert J. Hausbeck, who later switched to the Republican party, enraged the minority Democratic leaders, but their attempt to discipline these party members was blocked by Speaker Duryea.

Other gubernatorial efforts were more complex and involved Democratic leaders outside the legislature. In 1973, for example, Rockefeller desired Democratic votes in support of his transportation bond issue in order to present it to the voters as a bipartisan measure. Through an intermediary the governor advised Abraham Beame, the New York City comptroller and the prime contender for the mayoralty in that year, that unless he could get city Democratic votes for this measure in the legislature he would push through a bill requiring a runoff election in the city if no candidate for mayor received 40 percent of the vote. This proposal was anathema to Beame, who had already had to face a runoff primary. He told Rockefeller that he would need the backing of the incumbent mayor, John Lindsay, to produce the votes in the legislature, and that Lindsay's price was an annual preaudit of the Metropolitan Transportation Authority. Rockefeller had Lieutenant Governor Wilson work out wording in the legislation that "seemed to give Lindsay what he wanted" and the bill passed with bipartisan support.[28]

In situations of divided or Democratic legislative control, the governor's tactical situation was altered significantly, and as a consequence the pattern of gubernatorial–legislative relationships was altered. In this regard, Rockefeller's behavior followed a pattern similar to that of other governors in like situations. One authority summarized it this way:

> A governor whose party normally has a minority in the legislature faces certain fundamental problems from the outset. He must temper overtly partisan appeals, rely more heavily on public opinion, distribute patronage to both parties, and constantly base his tactics on the necessity of ultimate compromise with the opposition party. All of the tools of party leadership are dulled because they cannot be used with maximum effectiveness, but these tools still have utility. Particularly if the governor's party controls one house or has a large minority in the legislature, he is able to bargain with the opposition from a position of considerable

strength *if* he can depend on unified support from his own party in the legislature. Very often, then, the successful governor must be effective both as a partisan leader and a bipartisan leader.[29]

During periods when dealing with Democrats was essential, Rockefeller met with leaders of each party separately, stressing partisan ties with the Republicans and policy similarities with the Democrats. The governor developed close personal ties with leaders of both parties. Not the least of his tools was a subtle understanding of the egos of the leaders. Democratic Speaker Travia, whose outspoken ambition was to be governor someday, was often invited to sit in the ornate governor's chair during conferences at the statehouse.

Wide as were the governor's powers in legislative matters, it is important to note that they had limits, some imposed by the substance of policies, others dictated by political factors. Rockefeller avoided commenting on bills not in his program. As he once said, "I have tried increasingly to refrain from promising to sign or veto a bill when it is before the legislature. I learned from experience that when I took a position in advance, legislators sometimes would vote for unwise measures knowing that I would veto them. Thus they would get the benefit of the vote without having to take any responsibility."[30]

Limits of Gubernatorial Power

Every session of the New York State legislature has a dominant theme, an issue or a group of issues that preoccupies public and legislative attention. Not all of these issues emanate from the governor's office. Some, such as leadership selection, are uniquely legislative issues and involve considerable risk for the governor, with few gains likely from participation. Two such issues during Rockefeller's tenure were reapportionment and legislative ethics. The governor's office became involved in reapportionment in 1964 and 1965 because of his staff's expertise and the close deadlines imposed by the courts. By calling a special session of the lame-duck legislature elected in 1962, Rockefeller had a major impact on the partisan shape of the legislature (both houses of the 1964 legislature-elect were Democratic), but district lines were still largely determined by legislative leadership and staff. Later reapportionments, after legislative expertise had been assembled, had minimal gubernatorial involvement.[31] The ethics issue surfaced as the result of a series of articles in the *New York Herald Tribune* attacking the behavior of legislators in several areas, especially their practice of representing clients before state agencies and in suits against the state in the Court of Claims. The governor first endorsed a strong reform law recommended by the La Porte commission, but later signed a weaker law passed by the legislature.[32] He saw little political gain in trying to force further reform on a legislature that already resented the emphasis that the press had given to this issue. Gubernatorial intervention not only would be unsuccessful but might arouse opposition to other measures to which the governor was committed.

Rockefeller also had little involvement in the legislative politics that occasionally arose out of the clash of deeply held moral positions. When such matters as divorce law reform and abortion reform legislation forced their way to the floor of the legislature, normal political controls were suspended and partisan alignments were smashed. In 1970, Earl Brydges, the powerful majority leader and a Catholic, wept openly on the floor of the Senate as the abortion reform bill he had allowed to come to a vote passed in his house. In the Assembly, the decisive vote for passage was cast by an upstate Democrat, George M. Michaels of Auburn, who remarked as he voted that he realized that the act would terminate his political career but "I have to keep peace in my family."[33]

Rockefeller found that the usual compromise solutions that could produce a legislative majority did not work in regard to abortion reform. Later he recalled: "As an observer of this scene, one who has been pretty intimately connected with politics, probably there is no more divisive issue before America today than abortion."[34] The governor took positions on such issues—he signed the abortion reform legislation and vetoed a later attempt to repeal it—but he minimized his involvement in the ongoing debates. Active participation on either side only served to alienate a good portion of the governor's legislative party.

Thus the governor did not define every major political debate in the legislature, and indeed he found it both prudent and politic to keep out of some matters. Nevertheless, he did define many of the major issues, and when he took a position it was imperative that he win to sustain his strength in future battles.[35] This was especially true for a governor of a major state who harbored presidential ambitions. Once committed to legislation, Rockefeller had to get it passed or leave himself open to the charge that he was ineffective in managing state affairs and thus ineligible to move on to the national scene.

In late March of 1964, a series of liquor law reforms proposed by

Governor Rockefeller failed to pass the legislature. Key aspects of the proposed changes, vigorously opposed by retail liquor store owners throughout the state, included an end to "fair trade" (fixed) prices in liquor retailing and a resumption of the granting of new liquor licenses. The governor's reforms, motivated by scandals in the State Liquor Authority and recommended by a subsequent investigatory commission, were a threat to many "ma and pa" liquor store owners. The governor's proposal, by allowing new licenses, would drastically force down the value of the old ones, and by permitting price competition would change the very nature of the business. Rockefeller, who was then seeking the presidential nomination, reacted to the legislature's failure to enact his program with a speech in which he pictured the situation as "the people against the liquor lobby," and called his effort an attempt to clean up a "breeding ground of corruption." He would not, he said, accept the legislature's action; a special session would be called specifically to reverse it.[36]

Legislators of both parties were angered by the tone and substance of the governor's remarks. William C. Brennan, Democrat of Queens, called them "despicable," and Thomas La Verne, Republican of Rochester, said, "This is a vicious attempt to intimidate us into voting according to what he thinks is in the public interest. In trying to create an image and to cover up executive scandal he is trying to throw the onus on the legislature. The chances for a compromise on the liquor bill in my view are completely gone."[37] Nevertheless, by the time the smoke of the special session had cleared, three weeks later, Rockefeller had his reform bill passed essentially in the form he desired. Intense lobbying by the governor and aides in leaders' meetings and party caucuses on the eve of the session produced twenty-nine Republican votes in the Senate and seventy-three in the Assembly. The margins of victory in the Assembly and comfort in the Senate were provided by votes of Democrats, mostly from the Bronx, as the result of an accommodation on other matters reached between Rockefeller and Charles Buckley, the Bronx Democratic leader.[38]

In a similar situation in 1968, Rockefeller publicly committed himself to a multibillion-dollar Urban Development Corporation. With the governor out of the state attending the funeral of Martin Luther King, a coalition of Democrats and suburban Republicans who feared the corporation's power to override local zoning ordinances blocked the measure in the Assembly. Enraged, Rockefeller threatened to "stop doing personal favors for legislators, signing pet bills, and appointing their friends to jobs." Legislative leaders of both parties brought UDC opponents to the governor's office for conferences with top staff aides, and pressure was applied to Republicans through Charles Schoeneck, the state chairman. "These guys have never seen this side of me before," Rockefeller told the press. The UDC result was reversed in a midnight vote on April 9, 1968.[39]

The governor did not often have to bring such overt pressure on individual legislators. Few issues required it, and legislative business could normally be managed without it. Such action, if repeated often, could also leave a residue of resentment that would be counter-productive in the long run. When his public prestige was at stake, however, and he saw an issue as encompassing his power to govern not only now but in the future, Rockefeller did show his other side.

The Veto

The governor's legislative concerns did not end with the close of the legislative session. The legislature transacted much of its business in the last few frantic days that it met, leaving the great bulk of gubernatorial legislative decisions for the "bill-signing period" after the lawmakers had gone home. The state constitution provided that the governor would have ten days in which to decide upon bills enacted before the last ten days of the session and thirty days in which to consider measures enacted during this final period.

The end-of-session rush was partly the result of the rhythm of legislative business and partly the result of design. When the date of adjournment was fixed, legislative action in a host of policy areas was forced. Furthermore, the resulting legislative logjam fed upon itself. Legislators contributed to the problem by attempting to shepherd low-visibility legislation through during this period. Nevertheless, it was true that the extent of the logjam was overstated by newspaper editors. In 1974, 17 percent of the bills passed by the Senate were voted in the last eight days of the legislative session, including a twenty-one-hour-marathon last day. These days constituted 12 percent of the days during the session on which votes were taken.[40]

There was an informal agreement between the legislative leaders and the governor that they would not send much legislation in final form to the governor's office during the session while intricate negotiations on legislation were going forward, bills were being drafted and redrafted, and compromises were being drawn. The additional work load during the session would have simply over-whelmed the governor's office. As a consequence, no more than sixty bills were sent down each Thursday by both houses for gubernatorial action, and only about 20 percent of all legislation was signed before the session ended.[41]

Indeed, a somewhat lighter work load during the session allowed the governor to have sponsors recall for amendment bills that would otherwise be vetoed for technical reasons. In 1973, for example, seventy-five bills were recalled by the Senate and Assembly, and 56 percent of them later became law (see Table 6). This figure is somewhat higher than the average for the Rockefeller years but reflects the general trend. During years of Democratic or divided legislative control the governor was somewhat less likely to sign into law bills returned to the legislature for further action than he was during years of Republican control. During 1964, the only year in which the Democrats controlled both houses, recalls by the legislature seemed to be a device through which Rockefeller avoided formal action.

After the close of the legislative session, the full strength of the governor's office was focused on the consideration of legislation that

Table 6. Acts Recalled by the New York Legislature from the Governor's Desk, 1957–1973

Year	Total recalled	Recalled and vetoed	Recalled and returned to law	Percent returned to law
1957	71	16	29	40.8%
1960	82	13	41	50.0
1961	64	4	41	64.0
1962	107	18	47	43.9
1963	66	7	36	54.5
1964	39	6	7	17.9
1965	144	16	51	35.4
1966	288	54	158	54.8
1967	90	14	35	38.8
1968	152	23	66	43.4
1969	77	6	35	45.4
1970	109	18	57	52.3
1971	90	28	47	52.2
1972	37	3	28	75.6
1973	75	19	42	56.0
Annual average	99.4	16.3	48	48.3%

Source: Eugene J. Gleason, Jr., and Joseph F. Zimmerman, "Executive Dominance in New York State," paper delivered at the annual meeting of the Northeastern Political Science Association, Albany, November 9, 1974, p. 33.

had passed both houses. The work was highly organized. Comments were sought from a mimeographed list of potentially interested state agencies, interest groups, and individual advisers to the governor. Those asked to comment were given five days to respond, and a record was compiled in a "bill jacket." A memorandum based on the replies was prepared, summarizing the bill and its effects and recommending action.

During the early part of the bill-signing period, Governor Rockefeller often took a short vacation, since he could do little before the staffwork in the counsel's office was complete. Upon his return, he reviewed the memorandums prepared by his staff, often spreading them and supporting materials out on a twenty-foot table in the conference room in his West Fifty-fifth Street office in Manhattan. Given the procedures that were followed, the degree of agreement between the governor and his top advisers in these sessions was not surprising. In the later years, however, a seemingly minor detail was sometimes subjected to probing gubernatorial questions. Having served so long, Rockefeller could often recall facts that his staff had overlooked in drafting recommendations on new legislation.[42]

Unlike the president, the governor of New York could veto individual items in appropriation bills. This power, while not unique among the states, was an important one. New York has traditionally been among those states in which the governor's veto has been most freely used.[43] Between 1927 and 1951, a period spanning both Democratic and Republican administrations, about 26 percent of the bills that passed the legislature were vetoed by the governor.[44] During the Rockefeller years the proportion of bills vetoed varied between 35 percent in 1965 and 20 percent in 1971. Rockefeller seemed to use the veto most frequently in his first year and then in periods of Democratic or divided control of the legislature (see Table 7). During his last six years, he consistently vetoed between 20 and 24 percent of the bills that passed the legislature.

Whenever possible, the governor sought to base his veto on technical grounds rather than on the substance of the legislation. This practice allowed him to buy time, reserving action on the merits of a bill to a later year. It also allowed him to explain his actions more easily to interested groups upset by his use of the veto. In fact, technical vetoes often masked substantive gubernatorial objections to measures passed by the legislature.[45]

Since no veto of a piece of legislation by a New York governor had

Table 7. Rockefeller's Use of the Veto, 1959–1973

Year	Total bills passed	Signed by governor	Vetoed by governor	Percent vetoed
1959	1,202	880	322	27%
1960	1,389	1,089	300	22
1961	1,293	970	323	25
1962	1,278	1,013	265	21
1963	1,288	1,004	284	22
1964	1,326	974	352	27
1965	1,642	1,075	567	35
1966	1,328	1,025	303	23
1967	1,127	817	310	28
1968	1,412	1,096	316	22
1969	1,523	1,155	368	24
1970	1,340	1,048	292	22
1971	1,519	1,214	305	20
1972	1,298	1,016	282	22
1973	1,333	1,045	288	22

Sources: *New York Times* and *Legislative Record.*

been overridden since 1870, the threat of veto carried considerable weight.[46] Earlier governors, particularly Governor Dewey, had used the threat of veto—or "preveto," as it was called—effectively in legislative bargaining. Governor Rockefeller had a great stake in ensuring that the legislative leaders never perceived the overriding of his veto as a viable option.

Confident that as a practical matter the gubernatorial veto could not be overridden, legislative leaders sometimes let legislation pass so that the onus for blocking it would fall on the governor—sometimes even with the governor's acquiescence, especially when his veto could be traded for some other legislative action he desired. On occasion, however, the governor refused to use the veto to get legislative leaders off the hook, and as a consequence signed bills into law that neither he nor the legislative leaders favored.

Each house of the legislature was sensitive to being one-upped by the other on popular legislation, especially when partisan control was divided. On one occasion Republican Earl Brydges got a bill through the Senate requiring nominations by direct primary, assuming that Democratic Speaker Travia would block it in the Assembly. Travia, not to be upstaged, had it passed. Both Brydges and Travia then visited the governor and asked for a veto. Rockefeller refused, and a bill that no major politician on the state scene favored thus became law.[47]

The Governor, the Legislature, and Fiscal Policy

For several reasons, fiscal policy is one of the best areas in which to examine gubernatorial–legislative relations. First, it is axiomatic that the getting and spending of state resources is an issue of primary and continuing importance to the state's people, politicians, and political system. As two experts in state politics noted: "The executive budget occupies the central position on the agenda of all legislatures. As a rule, sessions of the state legislature are unable to achieve any momentum until the governor's budget has been received; by the same token, when the critical budget decisions have been made, the legislators ordinarily are ready to return home."[48] In another study legislators were asked to identify the key issues in their respective states. Taxation was the issue mentioned most often, and finance, a separate category, ranked fourth. When these classifications are combined, well over one-quarter of the issues mentioned by the legislators surveyed may be said to concern fiscal policy.[49] Certainly this issue is salient to participants in the legislative process at the state level.

Most issues on which the governor asks the legislature to act are not recurrent; once legislative action has been taken, the matter may not arise again for decades. The budget, however, requires legislative action every year. As a consequence, an examination of this policy area provides a favorable milieu for an analysis of the changing relationships between the governor and the legislature in varying partisan contexts and fiscal circumstances.

The power of fiscal issues is reflected in the fact that they affect the tone of entire legislative sessions. The legislative process is not compartmentalized. Difficulties between the executive and the legislature in such an important policy area can spill over into other matters, as they did in New York as a result of the bitter fight over tax increases in 1968. During that legislative session, one Rockefeller aide remarked, "This unusual strain over the budget and the taxes required to balance it is coloring everything else we're trying to do. If communications with the legislature have diminished, and they have, it's because of the enormous worry over taxes."[50]

The executive budget document submitted by the governor to the legislature is a summary of policy choices. As such, it subsumes almost all the tensions of the state's political system. Because the state can do almost nothing without raising and spending money, all participants in the political process are interested in the way it is raised and spent. And because it is a document of major political concern, the politics of budgeting often force to the surface divisions that are less apparent in other policy areas.

While governor, Nelson Rockefeller submitted fifteen budgets to the New York State legislature. Four were not reduced by the legislature at all, and in three years reductions were held below 1 percent of the budget total (see Table 8). There remained eight years in which legislative cuts in the governor's budget exceeded 1 percent. In six of these years, including the only two that occurred before 1965, reductions were made in response to gubernatorial requests for tax increases. Lower expenditures were an alternative to higher taxes. After 1965, when an independent legislative fiscal staff began to be developed, no year passed without some reduction in the budget submitted by the governor. In fact, it is not too much to say that legislative budget cutting became institutionalized in New York during the later years of the Rockefeller period. Thus, rather than subordinating

Table 8. Legislative Budget Cuts, New York, 1959–1973

Year	Submitted (billions of dollars)	Approved (billions of dollars)	Percent reduction
1959	$2.041	$2.0005	1.9%
1960	2.035	2.035	—
1961	2.388	2.394	0.2
1962	2.591	2.591	—
1963	2.889	2.822	2.3
1964	2.920	2.920	—
1965	3.480	3.480	—
1966	3.980	3.806	4.4
1967	4.700	4.650	1.1
1968	5.500	5.400	1.8
1969	6.700	6.400	4.5
1970	7.300	7.140	2.2
1971	8.450	7.700	8.9
1972	7.900	7.870	0.4
1973	8.800	8.770	0.3

Source: *New York Times*, 1959–1973.

the legislature, Rockefeller, through his taxing and spending powers, provided the stimulus for that institution to take an increasingly independent policy-making role during his governorship.

Further evidence for this point is the fact that budget reductions were greatest in 1966, 1969, and 1971, all years in which an increasingly conservative Republican majority controlled one or both houses of the legislature. The most severe cuts, totaling over $750 million, or almost 9 percent of Governor Rockefeller's budget request, came in 1971, a year when the Republicans controlled both houses. Thus it was clear that any difficulties the governor had in getting his budget passed were due more usually to clashes with the legislature as an institution than to partisan opposition. Indeed, the governor often exploited divisions in the Democratic party or the availability of Democratic votes in support of social programs to bring legislators of his own party into line or to bypass intransigent intraparty opposition.

Several clear trends are evident from a review of tax and budgetary politics in the legislature during the Rockefeller governorship. First, no tax increase was ever suggested in a gubernatorial election year, and only two were sought in years in which legislatures had to face the electorate without the governor on the ballot. In fact, the electoral cycle caused Rockefeller to restore in 1970, a year in which he was seeking reelection, cuts that he had made the year before. This decision led directly to an even greater fiscal problem in 1971.

The governor and his budgetary advisers were not averse to using fiscal gimmicks—nonrecurring revenues, deferring local aid payments to the next fiscal year, accelerating collection schedules, and the like—to balance the budget in years in which it served their political purposes to do so. When he decided that tax increases were necessary, however, Rockefeller most often sought them in major revenue sources such as the personal income tax or the state sales tax. Thus in 1959, 1968, and 1971 income tax increases were sought. In 1965, the establishment of a state sales tax was successfully advocated, and this levy was increased in 1969. (A major exception to this tendency occurred in 1963, when a "no tax" campaign pledge in 1962 forced Rockefeller to seek an increase in a variety of "fees.")

For the governor, it seemed a more appropriate strategy to fight for major tax increases that would meet current needs and provide a growing base for the future than to have to fight the same battle over again in each legislative session. Legislators, however, were wary of increases in such broad-based taxes and fees as the automobile registration fee, which would generate hostility throughout the electorate.

When confronted with tax increase proposals, legislators sought budget cuts, increased use of borrowing (which deferred expenditures and shifted them out of the expense budget), and the use of more narrowly based consumption taxes, such as those on cigarettes and liquor, which could be justified on moral as well as fiscal grounds. That is not to say that the governor was hostile to these more limited revenue sources; they simply did not make sense to him as keystones of a fiscal program.

An example illustrates the point. In 1968, a legislative election year, the governor sought $494 million in new taxes to help balance a budget that reflected $856 million in new expenditures. Rockefeller's tax package, offered to a legislature in which the Republicans controlled the Senate and the Democrats the Assembly, included a 20 percent income tax surcharge, an increase in business taxes, an increase of 1 cent a gallon in the gasoline tax, a rise of 10 cents a fifth in the liquor tax, and an increase in the parimutuel tax. Fearful of tax increases in an election year, legislators sought budget cuts and other alternatives to the Rockefeller plan. Eligibility levels for Medicaid in the state were raised, an action that in effect cut the budget by $300 million and removed the necessity to raise this much revenue.

Fiscal committees of the Assembly and the Senate recommended further budget cuts of $141 million, and a bloc of twelve fiscal conservatives in the Republican Senate pressed for further cuts that would remove the necessity of the 20 percent surcharge (expected to yield $270 million) and the gasoline and liquor tax increases (expected to yield $21 million and $15 million respectively). Late in March, both Earl Brydges (R) in the Republican Senate and Anthony Travia (D) in the Democratic Assembly offered alternative tax plans. Brydges advocated a cut in the surtax to 10 percent, a five-cent cigarette tax increase, and the elimination of the gasoline and liquor taxes. Travia suggested elimination of the surtax entirely with the difference made up by an increase in the income tax in the higher brackets and the postponement of certain state aid payments to balance the budget. This soak-the-rich plan, focused on a limited number of top-bracket, mostly Republican voters, earned Travia the nickname of Robin Hood in the legislature. The presentation of these alternative tax plans by both leaders was unprecedented, and was made possible by the availability of expert fiscal staff hired by the legislature as one result of an earlier budgetary battle in 1965.

Since the governor was a Republican, the Democratic Assembly insisted that the Republican Senate act first. Again under the pressure of the oncoming fiscal year and desperate to avoid all three of the governor's major tax proposals (the surcharge, the gasoline tax, and the liquor tax), the Senate in the early hours of the morning of March 30 passed a package that included a five-cent cigarette tax increase, the delay of $149 million in school aid, and the calling in of $93 million in state loans. Republicans who voted for this legislation conceded that it was "a lousy package," but insisted that it was simply a negotiating position from which to approach the Assembly and the governor.

As the senators had anticipated, this plan, especially the cigarette tax increase, was opposed by both the governor and the Assembly leadership. After an attempt by the Democrats to pass expenditure bills before the tax package was blocked in the Assembly, the two houses reached a compromise. The income tax surcharge, gasoline tax, and liquor tax were all scrapped, and the Senate abandoned the cigarette tax in return for the Assembly's abandonment of an increased income tax in the top brackets. The compromise was essentially based on deferment of $200 million in state aid payments and repayment of $95 million to the state for funds advanced in anticipation of passage of a transportation bond issue. The business tax package and other minor taxes from the governor's package were retained. Democratic Senate Minority Leader Joseph Zaretzki noted that it was a "paper budget put together with spit."[51]

When confronted with the action, Governor Rockefeller denounced it as "fiscally irresponsible" and insisted that the "kiss of gimmickry" had to be removed from the budget package. The legislative plan, he said, would simply delay major tax increases for one more year.[52] Under the pressure of a threatened veto, the Senate and Assembly recessed without final passage of the budget. Abandoning the surtax, which legislative leaders viewed as politically suicidal in an election year, the governor continued to press for increased levies on gasoline and liquor. In late April, after the legislature returned from recess, he also explored the possibility of the Democratic idea of an increased cigarette tax and income tax increases in the top brackets and expressed a willingness to accept at least some of the budget-balancing devices employed in the April 3 compromise between the Senate and the Assembly. More and more the governor took a mediating role, insisting on the need for some new taxes beyond those already passed but remaining flexible on particular measures. During the intense negotiations of early May, he personally shuttled back and forth between Brydges and Travia, trying to negotiate a compromise.

Finally, in the early-morning hours of May 8, under increasing pressure from the governor and with the cooperation of both parties in each house, a package was passed that created new brackets with higher rates at the top of the state income tax schedule and included increases of one cent a gallon in the gasoline tax, two cents a pack in the cigarette tax, and ten cents a fifth in the liquor tax, and a reduction of depreciation credits for business. The passage of the budget required open horse trading on the floor of the legislature until almost the moment of the vote, and in the end the governor was reduced to saying, "At this point, I'll take anything that the bastards will give me."[53] The budget battle kept Rockefeller from the presidential primary trail for several weeks, and he recalled the 1968 session as "the worst legislature I've ever had to work with."[54]

The 1968 budget battle, so illustrative of the different fiscal priorities of the governor and the legislature, ushered in a period of recurring budgetary crises in New York State. Though each situation was of course unique, a few general tendencies may be discerned in the budgetary politics of the next five years. Within the Republican party, a conservative bloc led by Senator John Hughes of Syracuse opposed new taxes and pressed for budget cuts in the state purposes and local assistance budgets, especially in social services areas. These outlays, after all, were felt more keenly in Democratic than in Republican districts. Another Republican bloc, centered on the powerful thirteen-member Nassau County delegation, opposed any cuts in education assistance that would lead to increased property taxes in suburban school districts. The result was compromises that put even greater pressure on the health and welfare areas.

After 1968 both the Senate and the Assembly were Republican, but the Republican margin was more precarious in the Assembly. It was thus in the lower house that most of the crucial budgetary politics of the late 1960s and early 1970s were played out. Organized Republican groups in the Assembly could wring concessions from the governor by denying passage to his entire budget. The control on such conduct was that, if pressed too hard, the governor could seek votes from the minority party.

The threat of seeking Democratic votes gave the governor a weapon against conservative Republican demands. Indeed, when Democrats dominated both houses of the legislature, the governor had a good deal more flexibility, since he could call upon the Republican minority for partisan backing while dealing, legitimately and necessarily, with the majority. Rockefeller did this sort of thing well, establishing personal relationships with the Democratic leadership. Dealing with the Democrats was fundamentally different from dealing with his own party, as they demonstrated in the 1971 special legislative session; they were more interested in maintaining social service levels and in aid to New York City than in tax minimization and budget cuts.

The most difficult circumstance for Rockefeller was one of divided control in the legislature or reliance on Democratic votes for tax increases. Concessions that produced Democratic votes lost those of Republicans. The coalitions were fragile, and legislators sought to avoid the responsibility of voting for taxes whenever possible. The governor had to deal with the Democrats while remaining loyal to his own party and maintaining the allegiance of Republicans in the legislature, a difficult pair of tasks.

By 1971 the governor's fortunes in budgeting had reached their nadir. Rockefeller proposed a budget in which all major taxes were to be increased and expenditures were to rise $1.5 billion. After resistance developed, the governor offered to make $300 million in cuts, but ultimately had to accept reductions of more than $700 million. During this time the process of budget cutting took on a dynamic of its own, and conservative members—especially from the Syracuse area, where media pressure was intense—found it difficult to back off from extreme positions taken earlier. Some reporters felt that the leaders of the budget-cutting group had attracted more followers than they had anticipated, and now they could not accept a lesser gain without compromising their new adherents. Attempts by Governor Rockefeller to meet with publishers of the Syracuse-area newspapers and have them ease the pressure on central New York legislators and thus give more flexibility to the bargaining situation proved to be, at best, minimally successful.

The 1971 budget cuts were widely viewed as a defeat for the governor. Rockefeller himself conceded that the conservative Republicans in the legislature "got their pound of flesh," and one legislator described the result as a "coup d'état that has swung the power to the Assembly."[55] Republican Speaker Duryea, who harbored ambitions to be Rockefeller's successor in the governorship, hailed the result as evidence of a restoration of balance between the executive and legislative branches in the budgetary process. In a retrospective interview he commented: "I think philosophically we have made the turn, with the legislature showing it in improved staffwork and greater involvement in the budget than ever before."[56]

Throughout the Rockefeller years budget battles were not fought on the merits alone. At first the governor was somewhat hesitant about using direct pressure on legislators. In 1959 one Republican legislator found his blandishments exceedingly mild, especially when compared to those of former governor Dewey. On leaving Rockefeller's office he remarked: "The governor made no demands. He was a perfect gentleman."[57] During this time, the state chairman, Judson Morhouse, working through county leaders, did the heavier persuasion, threatening primary fights, the loss of patronage, and the death of pet bills. By the early 1970s Rockefeller was directly involved in the wheeling and dealing, operating out of the Senate majority leader's office and striking man-to-man bargains with recalcitrant legislators. During the regular session in 1971, after agreement was reached with legislative leaders, chairmanships and special expense allowances were used as bargaining counters to attract Republican votes. During the budgetary special session in December of that year, the governor held a legislative reapportionment plan on his desk unsigned so that he could use it for political leverage in support of his fiscal plan.

April first was the beginning of the state's fiscal year. In the early Rockefeller period this deadline strengthened the governor's hand. His budget was submitted to the legislature early in January. If the legislature had not passed the budget by April 1, it was viewed as a legislative failure. If the legislative leaders reached agreement with the governor but members were recalcitrant, as in 1965, the approaching beginning of a new fiscal year and the concomitant specter of missed paychecks for state workers and missed aid payments for local governments could be used to bring the rank and file into line. Time was thus a resource for the governor. Its passage brought pressure on those legislators who blocked action, because the state simply could not act without a budget.

Once the legislature developed an independent capacity for revenue and expenditure projections, the situation was changed. Its leadership no longer had simply to react to gubernatorial initiatives, but could offer its own alternatives. The governor's budget was no longer the single base for discussion, and thus the political costs for any delay past the beginning of the fiscal year had to be more equally shared between the executive and the legislative branches. With alternatives on the table, the process of compromise demanded that the governor give more ground.

Thus, in budgeting as in other areas of legislative action, Governor Rockefeller was not the overwhelmingly dominant force in New York that he was often considered to be. In fact, throughout Rockefeller's tenure the trend was toward greater independence of the legislature. Though on some matters Rockefeller won substantial victories—the 1959 tax increase and the liquor law reform are prominent examples—he also suffered some major defeats. One was the 1971 budget battle. And there were important areas, such as legislative leadership selection, reapportionment, and abortion reform, where the governor felt it politic to avoid major involvement in the legislative process.

In general, an analysis of the legislative process in New York during the Rockefeller years reveals a pattern of bargaining rather than one of dominance. In the bargaining process the governor possessed major resources. When he gave an objective priority and thought that a defeat would affect his power and influence on other matters, he employed these resources ruthlessly. Yet during Rockefeller's term as governor the legislature strengthened itself, perhaps as a defense against his strong leadership style. It developed the capacity to deal critically with gubernatorial initiatives and occasionally to seize the initiative in policy making. Overall, the process was one of accommodation. In the final analysis, Rockefeller's success was rooted in his ability to master this process.

4

The Executive Staff

No chief executive can govern alone. It is through his immediate staff that a state's governor seeks to advocate, pursue, and implement major policy choices. By the use of key aides, too, the governor may monitor the infinitely changing political and administrative environment within the state government and in the larger polity. Most of the time, those who seek some action by the governor deal with his staff and not with him directly. Ultimately, the evaluation of the governor by others in the political system—legislators, lobbyists, federal and local officials, newsmen—may hinge more on their views of his staff than on their opinion of the man himself. Are his aides loyal? Are they competent? Are they effective? Positive answers to such questions enhance the power and prestige of the governor who has assembled the team.

In New York, staff support for the governor was located in the Executive Department, an agency created during the reorganizations of the 1920s. At the time this department was established, it was intended to unite the governor's principal staff officers. Since constitutional amendment forbade the creation of more than twenty departments, however, and as the state government expanded into new areas of concern, a number of operating agencies in search of a home were also placed in the Executive Department. By the time Rockefeller became governor in 1959 there were some seventeen agencies in the Executive Department. Except for the Budget Division, those most closely involved with the governor were grouped in a unit called the Executive Chamber within the Executive Department, and these terms sometimes led to confusion.

The Budget Division, whose director was always one of the governor's principal staff assistants, was part of the Executive Department but not of the Executive Chamber. All of its personnel except for the director and his deputies were tenured civil service employees. Personnel in the Executive Chamber except for those involved in routine housekeeping were exempt from the tenured civil service. Thus when a new governor assumed office, even if he were of the opposite political party, one could expect little immediate change in the Budget Division except for the three or four top officials, though the Executive Chamber would reflect the political affiliation of the individual holding the governorship.

For the development and administration of policy in New York State, Governor Rockefeller relied on a few key aides: the secretary to the governor, the counsel, the budget director, the director of communications, the director of the Office of Planning Services, and the press secretary. Over the fifteen years of Rockefeller's tenure, turnover in these posts was minimal; only fifteen persons served in them during the entire period, several in more than one capacity at various times. Long tenure gave the governor's staff a considerable advantage in dealing with high-ranking civil servants. For example, Mike Whiteman had longer service in various posts on the governor's staff than most of the department heads with whom he dealt. Norman Hurd not only served as principal fiscal adviser to Rockefeller but also had had similar experience under Dewey. Thus, as time passed, Rockefeller's staff could rely more on their own experience than on the advice of the permanent governmental establishment in Albany.

Though the size of this inner group remained relatively stable, the Executive Chamber staff just below the top levels grew considerably during the Rockefeller years in both size and scope. An appointments office, an office of the press secretary, and a number of special assistants in specific policy areas were added, the number of professional employees increased from fourteen to sixty-three, and the total staff, including clerical, doubled (see Table 9). The staffs of governors in all the states increased during the period 1959–1972, as one might expect with the increase of state activities. California, which was closest to New York in population in 1972, had approximately the same number of professional posts in the governor's office.

Fortunately, a study was made in 1969 of the characteristics of gubernatorial staffs generally in the United States, so it is possible to compare Rockefeller's staff with those of other governors. The study reported that governors' staff members tended to be younger than persons in higher administrative positions in the civil service or on

Table 9. New York Executive Chamber Professional Positions, 1958/59–1971/72

Position	1958/59	1959/60	1960/61	1961/62	1962/63	1963/64	1964/65	1965/66	1966/67	1967/68	1968/69	1969/70	1970/71	1971/72
Secretary's office		9	10	12	12	12	13	13	18	17	17	17	17	13
Counsel's office		9	9	9	9	9	9	9	9	9	9	9	9	9
Press secretary		4	4	4	5	5	5	5	6	6	5	5	5	6
Appointments office		2	2	2	2	3	3	3	3	3	4	4	4	5
Special assistants		3	4	3	5	6	5	6	7	9	14	20[a]	20	12
Executive assistant		—	—	—	—	—	4[b]	5	1	—[c]	—	—	—	—
Communications (established 1969/70)												—	4	7
Director of State Operations (established 1971)														11
All positions	14[d]	27	29[e]	30	33	35	39	41	44	44	49	55	59	63[e]

Source: Prepared by the governor's office, Albany.

[a] Washington office transferred in 1969 from Commerce budget to Executive Chamber. Did not represent real increase.

[b] New designation.

[c] Merged with special assistants.

[d] Only the total figure is available for 1958/59, the final year of the Harriman administration.

[e] Total staff, including clerical: April 1960, 126; April 1972, 229.

staffs of mayors and legislators. They were well educated, with 71 percent possessing at least a college degree and 34 percent graduate or professional degrees. Although staff members customarily held their offices at the governor's pleasure, 84 percent expected to serve during the governor's full term. About one-third of the staff members covered by the study had been recruited directly from business, one-fourth had previously worked in government, one-fifth had already been on the governor's staff when he took office, and one-seventh had served the previous governor.[1]

From the first, Rockefeller's top staff was older and more experienced than the staffs of most governors. The average age of the top four was forty-six years. All of them were college graduates; indeed, two held doctorates and two law degrees. Three had extensive previous experience in government service and one was a member of one of New York City's largest law firms. Below the top level, Rockefeller's staff tended to conform to the pattern of governors' staffs generally. They were young, well educated, and new to the government service.

Governors generally tended to regard staff appointments as personal matters rather than partisan rewards. Party regulars had to cope with the problem of dual loyalty—to their political sponsors as well as to the administration. Civil servants might be loyal to the governorship but not necessarily to the incumbent governor. As one scholar observed, "No governor wants his staff disagreeing *too* sharply with him on content of policy and the manner in which he wants to perform his role."[2] Rockefeller's staff were his personal choices rather than nominees of the party organization. Some he had known before taking office, but others were recruited through friends, primarily on the basis of ability. Junior staff were recruited on the basis of academic records and general competence. The question of political affiliation was secondary.

Outside observers—newspapermen, lobbyists, and heads of state agencies—have been generally quite critical of gubernatorial staffs. One study of a representative group of fourteen states showed that in only five did outsiders believe that the governor's staff was competent or respected.[3] In contrast, similar observers viewed Rockefeller's staff as highly able and dedicated. While commissioners sometimes differed with them on policy, they did not question their ability.

Throughout his later years as governor, rumors persisted that at least part of the reason for his personal staff's loyalty to him was that Governor Rockefeller supplemented salaries. Then, during the confirmation hearings on his nomination for the vice-presidency in 1974, leaks to the press from income tax returns filed with the Senate committee caused Rockefeller to reveal publicly that he had given gifts and loans to individuals totaling $2,777,501.50 between 1958 and 1974. About 80 percent of this total comprised gifts to twelve of his closest associates in state government. Almost half had been loans made while the Rockefeller aides worked for the state and forgiven after they left public service. Three individuals who received the largest gifts were: William J. Ronan, secretary to the governor (1959–1966) and later chairman of the Metropolitan Transit Authority, $625,000; Alton G. Marshall, secretary to the governor (1966–1970), $306,867; and Edward Logue, chairman of the Urban Development Corporation, $145,000. Gifts to each of six other persons totaled $100,000 or more. Another gift, not to a state official, that attracted considerable attention in the press was $50,000 to Henry Kissinger, who, before he entered the Nixon administration in Washington, was a long-time adviser to Rockefeller on foreign policy.[4]

Several concerns emerged in the House and Senate hearings and in the public debate that ensued as a result of the revelation of Rockefeller's gifts and loans. The first was the question of whether the governor's actions violated the state's antitipping statute and public officer's law, both of which barred payments to state employees for the performance of their official duties or as a reward for action while in office. Rockefeller's detractors argued that loans made at little or no interest and then forgiven at the termination of public service or during a brief interlude between periods of public service constituted a violation of the spirit, if not the letter, of these statutes. Rockefeller claimed that the gifts and loans were not made to supplement salaries, but were acts of generosity to close associates to enable them to deal with individual cases of personal and family need. Not all close aides received gifts, and none of the gifts was made regularly or periodically. In some cases, Rockefeller said, outlays were made to attract to the service of New York people who were uniquely capable in their fields. Other gifts were intended to cover extraordinary family medical or educational expenses. In no case did the governor have to make payments to influence official conduct, he said, since he had the power to appoint or remove these officials and thus they already were subject to his direction.[5] Louis Lefkowitz, the state attorney general, later concluded that no violation of state law was involved.

The Senate Rules Committee gave considerable attention to the matter of Rockefeller's gifts and loans to his staff, friends, and associates. The committee found no evidence of "any ulterior motive, personal or economic gain, or wrong-doing for any purpose."[6] The

House Judiciary Committee took a somewhat more critical view. Though it voted 26 to 12 to confirm the governor as vice-president, ten dissenting members wrote: "Mr. Rockefeller should have known that his practice of giving loans and gifts would raise serious questions . . . concerning the ability of such officials to render independent judgment."[7]

For those who believed that the massive commercial and industrial holdings of the Rockefeller family meant that any public service by one of its members necessarily involved a conflict of interest, the gifts and loans were supporting evidence.[8] For the governor's partisans, on the contrary, they were indicative of his interest in the personal problems of the people who worked most closely with him; Rockefeller's record in the executive mansion for fifteen years, they believed, was evidence enough that he could and did avoid any such conflicts.

Access to the governor's inner circle resulted from political, institutional, and personal relationships. Malcolm Wilson, the lieutenant governor and a major original backer of Rockefeller for governor, had his elected post as a base and, because of his long experience in the state legislature and statewide party contacts, came to be a key political adviser. (The exclusion of Mary Anne Krupsak, Wilson's successor as lieutenant governor, from the highest circles of the Carey administration in New York indicates that the post alone did not ensure such access.) T. Norman Hurd, budget director and head of the Budget Division, had formerly served in this capacity in the Dewey administration. The counsel, a post held first by Roswell Perkins and then successively by Robert MacCrate, Sol Corbin, Robert Douglass, and Michael Whiteman, handled the governor's legislative liaison and thus was of key importance to him. The secretary and the executive assistant were historically close personal aides to New York's governor, and Rockefeller continued this tradition by appointing William Ronan as secretary to the governor. Ann Whitman, who had served in the White House as Dwight Eisenhower's executive secretary, was the governor's executive assistant. In effect, she was keeper of the gate, scheduling his engagements and handling confidential correspondence. The first press secretary, Frank Jamieson, had a personal relationship with Rockefeller that dated back to the 1930s. His successor, Hugh Morrow, later director of communications, came to enjoy a similar status. Indeed, the communications director and press secretary were continually required to speak for the governor and therefore needed almost constant access to him. These were uniquely personal staff posts during the Rockefeller years.

Rockefeller with his perennial running mate and gubernatorial successor, Malcolm Wilson (1970). Photo by Bob Wands. Rockefeller Family Archives.

Rockefeller with his principal staff in the garden of the Executive Mansion, October 3, 1972. Clockwise: Governor Nelson A. Rockefeller; Mrs. Ann C. Whitman, executive assistant to the governor; Michael Whiteman, counsel; Richard Wiebe, director of planning services; Ronald Maiorana, press secretary; Charles Lanigan, former Republican state chairman; Hugh Morrow, director of communications; Mary McAniff, assistant secretary to the governor for intergovernmental relations; Richard Dunham, director of the budget; T. Norman Hurd, secretary to the governor. Photo by Donald Doremus. Rockefeller Family Archives.

Not all close Rockefeller advisers had government posts. George Hinman, a Binghamton lawyer and political leader from central New York, became a national party committeeman and a key aide in the governor's presidential bids. Emmet Hughes, a political journalist, served as a speechwriter and adviser and was a major influence during Rockefeller's early years as gvernor. L. Judson Morhouse, the state Republican party chairman, was a major political aide, until his involvement in a scandal in 1962 forced his resignation.

Within this core group of advisers, William Ronan, the secretary to the governor, emerged as first among equals early in Rockefeller's first term. This development probably came about because the institutional role of this office was augmented by Rockefeller's great confidence in Ronan, whom he later called "one of the most brilliant men I have ever known."[9] Ronan was born in Buffalo on November 8, 1912. After graduating from Syracuse University in 1934 with a B.A. degree, he continued graduate studies at New York University, receiving a Ph.D. in 1940. Later he joined the faculty of New York University, rising through the academic ranks to become professor and dean of the graduate school of public administration in 1953. In the intervening years he was frequently consultant to various government agencies at city, state, and federal levels. While deputy city administrator of New York in 1957 he was recommended to Nelson Rockefeller by Frank Moore, Tom Dewey's lieutenant governor, as an academic unusually knowledgeable in government administration. Thus began a close association that lasted over many years. A big, imposing man, Ronan was highly articulate and the intellectual spark plug in the group of advisers that surrounded Rockefeller.

Ronan's own view was that the secretary served the governor as *chef du cabinet*. In describing his job further, he said:

> By tradition and long usage, the secretary to the Governor acts on behalf of the Governor and, in his name, deals with the departments and agencies of State government in liaison, also with the legislature in many matters, and ... with various individuals and public groups who have business with the chief executive of the State. ... Under Governor Rockefeller, the office of secretary to the Governor became the Governor's arm for assuring that his programs were being carried out and, in addition, the office was given a responsibility for program development.[10]

Contrary to Ronan's view, however, the secretary had not historically been the dominant figure on gubernatorial staffs in New York. Both John Burton, the budget director who served Dewey, and Paul

Appleby, who held a similar position in the Harriman administration, were, in effect, first ministers to the governor on both fiscal and program matters.[11] The shift during the early 1960s was due not only to Ronan's relationship with Rockefeller but also to the role perception of T. Norman Hurd, the governor's long-term budget director, a thorough, talented, knowledgeable, experienced public official. Hurd was called "a major institutional force in state government" because of the eighteen years he served in that key post. But Hurd's forte was data gathering and administrative oversight rather than policy development. One former associate remarked: "Hurd is a detail and desk man more than a wide-ranging adviser. He does the bookkeeping and turns the results over to Rocky for diagnosis."[12] Ronan was the idea man, the policy innovator. Hurd was the administrator, older, more experienced in state government, with a remarkable memory for detail.

In 1965 Ronan was succeeded as secretary to the governor by Alton Marshall, who served until December 1971. While Ronan had been an imaginative developer of new policies and innovations, Marshall was primarily a public relations man, of solid, substantial character, but also with a flair for the flamboyant. His suggestions were not so numerous as Ronan's. Personally, he was somewhat more exuberant. He loved a crisis. On his first day as secretary, in December 1965, the state experienced a power failure. Office gossips quipped, "Maybe Al planned it that way." Marshall took complete control of the situation, moving in portable generators, and was really in his element. It was said, "Al goes around with a pocketful of decisions in search of a place to use them."[13]

Marshall was sensitive to the public image of the governor and approached problems with a sense of the probable public reaction. He had come from Syracuse University's Maxwell School to the Budget Division in 1948. Later he became deputy director of the budget and then executive assistant to the governor before becoming secretary. Relations between the secretary's office and the Budget Division were much closer under Marshall than they had been under Ronan. As secretary, Marshall insisted that his staff discuss all program proposals with the Budget Division before putting them before the governor. In comparing Marshall's influence with that of Norman Hurd, the budget director, one long-term aide to the governor remarked, "Both men came up with an equal number of good ideas, although Marshall came up with more ideas."[14]

But the differences between the secretary's office and the Budget

Division went beyond personal relationships to institutional factors. One study noted: "The Division of the Budget had become highly bureaucratized and already overburdened by existing responsibilities. It was reported . . . that Budget had lost its capacity for program innovation."[15] Furthermore, the Budget Division staff, composed, in New York as elsewhere, of civil servants, took a more institutional view of the governorship than did the secretary's staff.

The major reason for the division of the program development staff role from the budget role and the growth in importance of the secretary in policy making was the style of the governor. Rockefeller viewed himself as an activist, a pragmatic problem solver. In one interview he described his decision process in this way: "You sit down and study what the problem is, what the factors are, and then you study out what the steps are that need to be taken to deal with it, and you take those steps. You don't say, 'Am I going to take a liberal or conservative position on this?' If you did, you would be like the man who says, 'Don't confuse me with the facts; my mind is already made up.'"[16]

As a consequence, the Rockefeller staff viewed its job as "telling the governor how to do what he wanted to do rather than telling him he couldn't do it."[17] Yet, institutionally, the Budget Division tended to emphasize constraints, to stress the limiting effect of finite resources. The secretary's office generated broad-scale, dramatic programs, and, because of Rockefeller's predispositions, therefore gained an advantage. As one former budget official recalled: "[Rockefeller] is very receptive to new ideas—too much so, in my opinion—and his enthusiasm needs to be curbed. Some of his staff feel a way to get mileage with Rockefeller is to feed him ideas. . . . The Budget Division tried to discipline Rockefeller by channeling facts and data to him largely through the Director of the Budget, in the belief that yesterday's decisions are today's budget problems. But Rockefeller is very program-oriented and less oriented toward fiscal controls."[18]

Once during the Rockefeller years, the Budget Division made a major effort to increase its program role with the partial implementation of a planning-programming-budgeting system (PPBS). Richard Dunham, who succeeded T. Norman Hurd as budget director, recalled that PPBS was originally embraced because the budget director was "anxious to have greater input in the governor's annual messages and his programs." The changed budget system, however, generated massive volumes of additional paperwork and, in Dunham's words, "did not produce the data in usable form to give the desired input." Agencies soon learned that what they said in a PPBS submission did not make any difference in regard to what happened. The regular budget procedures went forward, without regard to PPBS. Indeed, the Budget Division, in efforts antedating PPBS, attempted to increase program and policy sensitivity, but the confusion surrounding PPBS interfered with this more orderly development. Ultimately, PPBS was abandoned.[19]

The influence that the Budget Division did have in policy making came from its role in the ongoing budgetary process. It reviewed agency requests for funds, held hearings, produced the executive budget, and was involved in budget negotiations with the legislature. Division projections of revenue estimates were crucial to the governor as he prepared his tax program. Its administrative management unit was often called on by the secretary's office for help in planning reorganization or meeting administrative problems. In addition, the Budget Division was essential to the governor as an aid in day-to-day administration, as it monitored and controlled department expenditures of funds already appropriated.

Staff Role in Legislative Programs

Rockefeller made much more extensive use of staff in preparing his legislative program than previous governors had done. Ronan's office had the primary responsibility for collecting data each year. To accomplish this task, Ronan created within his office a new section, headed by an assistant secretary and staffed by five or six individuals called "program associates," each of whom was assigned one or more policy areas.[20]

Each program associate throughout the entire year, but especially during the summer months, collected information from state agencies in his area about emerging problems as he perceived them. He also watched the daily press and the governor's mail for other ideas. As this research went forward, the program associate queried other states, particularly California, and federal agencies concerning their perceptions. They were also asked what if anything they were doing to solve the problem if they were conscious of one. On most subjects he was free to seek the advice of politically knowledgeable people in the state. Finally, in the fall he would reduce all of this information to a brief memorandum, which would be submitted, along with some two hundred similar documents, to the scrutiny of the secretary, budget director, and counsel.

As reactions accumulated, a loose-leaf notebook of the developing range of attitudes on each issue was kept in the secretary's office, and copies were circulated to gubernatorial policy and fiscal staff and to departmental staff for comment. Thus, when the closed policy meetings between the governor and his chief aides were held in December to make final choices on the program, a developed record was available for comment. It was in this final stage that Rockefeller's imprint was placed on the program. His many contacts outside the government enabled him to add further data to what already was available. The broad outlines of the program went into the annual message; details followed much later in special messages.

Rockefeller's procedures in developing his legislative program were in some ways similar to those used by his immediate predecessors. Under Dewey, the process was coordinated by his counsel. A master list of problems was prepared in November by the counsel, commented upon and amended by Dewey, and then submitted to major staff aides and legislative leaders for further comment before final gubernatorial programmatic decision.[21] During Harriman's governorship the program was developed under the direction of the secretary to the governor, Jonathan Bingham. After tentative approval by Harriman, initial drafts were prepared during October and cleared with the budget office and Democratic legislative leaders before they reached final form.[22] Thus the preparation of the program under Rockefeller seems to have been the further institutionalization of a process that was beginning to develop under his predecessors, though background research was much more extensive.

The counsel to the governor was the third member of Rockefeller's "troika." His primary concern, as well as that of his assistants, was to see that the governor's program got translated into law. In addition he had the responsibility of seeing that bills were correctly drafted and of preventing legislation contrary to the governor's program. Five counsels served Rockefeller, and the relationship between the governor and each of the five was partly a function of personality and role perception. Roswell Perkins, the first counsel, who had been active in the 1958 gubernatorial campaign, served only through the first legislative session. He was succeeded by thirty-seven-year-old Robert MacCrate, from the prestigious law firm of Sullivan and Cromwell. MacCrate was primarily concerned with legal craftsmanship and only secondarily with political advice. MacCrate was followed in succession by Sol Corbin, a *cum laude* graduate of Harvard Law School, Robert Douglass, and Michael Whiteman.

Douglass, who later served as secretary to the governor, was a protégé of George Hinman and only thirty-three years old when appointed counsel, and he was very close personally to Rockefeller. He combined political with legal advice. One associate said of Douglass, "When Bob asked you to do something, you did it because you wanted to do it for him, not because you had to." Like the Budget Division, the counsel's office was restive with the program dominance of the secretary and periodically tried to assume a larger role. It was most successful in areas, such as criminal law reform, that were clearly within the professional expertise of attorneys.[23]

Bills in the governor's annual legislative program were drafted in the counsel's office to ensure that they reflected Rockefeller's views. Drafting work was divided among the six or seven assistant counsels, roughly according to subject matter. Unlike some governors, who were attorneys and often became mired in the detail of legislative drafting, Rockefeller, who was not an attorney, relied on his counsel for this work and concentrated on broad principles.

Bill drafting went on through January, February, and March, with changes continually being made as a result of negotiations with legislative leaders. Rarely were bills available at the beginning of the session. During the drafting period, major bills were also discussed with the lieutenant governor, attorney general, and appropriate department heads. Interest groups in the state were often consulted for reactions, but one counsel to the governor, Michael Whiteman, said he tended to "talk concepts" with legislators and lobbyists to avoid getting mired in detail. Only infrequently did he circulate draft legislation for outside comment.[24]

At its peak, in one year in the late 1960s, the counsel's office drafted 121 program bills. In addition, from 400 to 600 bills that originated in state agencies were reviewed by the counsel and his assistants annually. Though these bills usually concerned technical matters—minor changes in state laws suggested by experiences in the day-to-day work of those who administered them—some were of major significance and, if they interested the governor, became part of his program.[25]

During the legislative session, the counsel's office maintained an ongoing monitoring system on the status of bills. Weekly, then later in the session, daily status reports were compiled by each assistant counsel on the program bills under his purview. Assistant counsels often attended legislative committee meetings and made presentations on program bills to caucuses of both parties in both houses.

The bill-signing period in Albany. Flanking the governor are, left, Robert R. Douglass, counsel to the governor, and Attorney General Louis J. Lefkowitz (1970). Photo by Bob Wands. Rockefeller Family Archives.

They negotiated with legislators and the legislative staff on the content of the key bills, often serving as the governor's agent. As a general courtesy, program bills were not amended by legislators without consultation with the governor's counsel on detail or with the governor on substance.

The development of the budget was a necessary complement to preparation of the legislative program. Prepared under the direction of the budget director for submission to the legislature between mid-January and February, the annual budget was the result of a process that had begun the previous April within state departments and agencies. Key gubernatorial inputs into the budget under Rockefeller came in December, after he received the recommendations of the budget director. Gubernatorial decisions resulted in a financial plan later summarized in the budget message. This document represented the governor's priorities reduced to dollars and cents and, especially when unpleasant new taxes were recommended, often defined the key issues for the legislative session.

Thus the secretary, the counsel, and the budget director were Rockefeller's "big three" staff resources for programs and administration. One man who served as counsel suggested that the difference between the three offices of secretary, budget director, and counsel was one of time perspective. The secretary, he said, planned over several years, the budget director worked in one-year increments, and the counsel thought in terms of legislative sessions.[26]

In addition, a separate planning establishment was created because of the governor's conviction that the planning function would have to be separated from program development and implementation if it were to be viable. The Office of Regional Development was established in the Executive Chamber in 1961 and replaced in 1966 by the Office of Planning Coordination (OPC). When this agency fell victim to legislative budget cutting in 1971 (legislatures are notoriously hostile to planning agencies), it was replaced by the Office of Planning Services (OPS). The influence of this office, much smaller than its predecessor, was guaranteed by the appointment of Richard Weibe, an assistant secretary for whom Rockefeller had very high regard, as the agency's first director.

Rockefeller's close circle of advisers took on special importance because the governor valued collective advice on policy making. Unlike Governor Dewey, who used a single aide to carry out an assignment, Rockefeller was likely to assign one staff agency to develop alternatives and then to turn policy making into a group effort. Top-level staff were expected to be generalists, to be open to any and all possible assignments, but the governor was most comfortable with an institutionalized rather than an ad hoc decision process. In staff meetings, disagreement was encouraged until a decision was reached; at that point Rockefeller expected all aides publicly to support the decision.

Rockefeller's techniques in employing his staff can be compared to the various approaches employed by presidents on the national level. One analyst of the presidency has termed these approaches competitive, formalistic, and collegial.[27] Franklin D. Rossevelt as president used a competitive pattern of management. He sought controversy and thrived on it. He pitted advisers against one another, delegating responsibility and authority in overlapping segments. Jurisdictional boundaries of assignments were left deliberately vague so that the president could be the final arbiter. Thus he hoped to provide creativity and at the same time provide himself with a constant flow of information on government operations.

In contrast, Eisenhower's management style was formalistic. He set up a strict chain of command under a chief of staff, using specialists with fixed responsibilities. It resembled the staff organization with which Eisenhower had been familiar during his military life. Information to the president was channeled through a single chief of staff, Sherman Adams. Eisenhower delegated responsibility and did not wish to be bothered with details of administration. He tended to vacillate on tough decisions and strove for cooperation among his staff members.

Outwardly, Kennedy's staff organization was like that of Roosevelt. The president himself was chief of staff. His staff was composed of generalists, but the resemblance to Roosevelt's staff operation stopped there. One aide spoke of "equal status, equal salaries and equal access to the President."[28] Kennedy emphasized collegial working relations among his staff members and did everything in his power to dampen the competitive spirit.

In Rockefeller's staff there was some personal competition, though the governor did not foster it; indeed, he tried to discourage it. But he also sought to avoid the Eisenhower practice of having a single chief of staff. He had had a negative experience with this approach in Washington during World War II, though William Ronan and later Robert Douglass approached the status of being Rockefeller's primary aide. On balance, his use of staff in New York came closest to that of President Kennedy.

When the governor's secretary, his counsel, and the budget director work together in harmony, they are a powerful force for the effective management of the state's business. To be effective, each must recognize the others' institutional roles. Such cooperation was notable under Rockefeller but succeeding governors had difficulty in this area.

Governor Rockefeller directed his staff operations from two locations—the Executive Chamber offices on the second floor of the state capitol in Albany and his two privately owned town houses, 20 and 22 West Fifty-fifth Street in New York City. Under the multigabled roof of the cavernous state capitol building, which houses the legislature, the governor was provided with office space for himself and his staff and a public hearing room called the Red Room, which contained a stately executive desk, a massive fireplace, and staid wood-paneled walls. In general, the New York City and Albany offices contained duplicate staff services, although the top aides usually followed the governor to each location. The administration of the state bureaucracy and the implementation and monitoring of programs were handled by the Albany-based staff. Unlike Governors Dewey and Harriman, however, Rockefeller did not make the Executive Mansion his permanent residence, nor did he work full time at the capitol. He lived and worked in New York City, remaining in Albany for long periods primarily during the legislative session.

The governor's New York offices, owned by the Rockefeller family, were similar in appearance to hundreds of other town houses just off Fifth Avenue and were marked only with a brass number 22 on the front door. The forty-two rooms of these buildings, converted by the governor to office use, were the nerve center of state government during the Rockefeller administration. As one aide remarked: "Nelson likes it because it's in the center of town—and who can blame him? Albany isn't the kind of place he was brought up in, you know."[29] "Fifty-fifth Street," as it came to be called, contained offices for the governor, lieutenant governor, and about a half-dozen top staff aides and their assistants. It housed facilities for staff conferences and press relations, but contained no living quarters. A converted town house, it had certain disadvantages for office use. A top official might find himself assigned to what was originally a maid's room and a stenographer might have her desk in what was formerly a kitchen.

The expanding state involvement in urban problems had a direct impact on the location the governor chose as the center of his activities. There were certain advantages in governing from Albany, midway between the state's northern and southern boundaries. But the money, the talent, and the resources for dealing with problems were in New York City. Consequently, governors were drawn there to an increasing degree. Dewey maintained an office in his old law firm, and Harriman had one in the family suite. Rockefeller, however, was the first to establish a permanent office in New York City. Through much of his incumbency, he personally paid for the entire cost of this operation, an expense that exceeded $200,000 a year. Feeling the same need, his successors Malcolm Wilson and Hugh Carey maintained city offices, paid for by the state.

One of the hallmarks of Rockefeller's approach to decision making was his emphasis on study prior to decision. In one interview, when asked about the sources of new program ideas, the governor commented: "Ideas come to me from all over and it is difficult to know why one has intuitive feelings about the essence of a problem. Once I determine that there is a problem, I usually try to get a group together to study it."[30]

Rockefeller relied on three types of study groups: task forces, temporary state commissions, and governor's conferences. One study in 1972 pointed out that Rockefeller had publicly announced the establishment of eighty-one such groups during his first three terms (see Table 10). This total did not include the study groups that generated more than eighty research papers for the 1958 campaign or the forty task forces formed by William Ronan to generate new ideas for state policy initiatives in Rockefeller's first two years.[31]

Political scientists have pointed out that commissions and other study groups have both manifest and latent functions.[32] Manifest functions are those publicly announced by the chief executive when the group is appointed; they include the gathering of information, the development of policy alternatives, education of the public, and generation of input from outside the government. Latent but equally important functions include the provision of recognition for constituency groups, the delaying of decisions, the building of support, and the insulation of the executive from the decision process. Like the study groups of the nation's presidents, Rockefeller's served each of these purposes at one time or another. In each case, the mix of goals was different. In-house task forces consisting solely of state personnel, such as the one that designed the Pure Waters Program in 1965, were primarily low-visibility policy-development tools that were useful to the governor for transcending parochial departmental perspectives. External task forces (temporary state commissions) helped redi-

Table 10. Publicly Announced Study Groups Appointed during the Rockefeller Administration, 1959–1970

Year	Task forces			Temporary state commissions[a]	Governor's conferences	All study groups
	In-house	Mixed	External			
1959	8	1	4	2	1	16
1960	2	—	—	—	—	2
1961	—	—	4	—	1	5
1962	1	—	1	1	2	5
1963	—	1	2	—	—	3
1964	—	1	4	—	—	5
1965	2	4	2	—	—	8
1966	1	—	4	—	4	9
1967	—	1	6	—	2	9
1968	1	3	4	1	4	13
1969	1	1	—	1	1	4
1970	1	—	—	—	1	2
All years	17	12	31	5	16	81

Source: William J. Daniels and James Underwood, "Program Innovation and Program Output: The Role of Governor Rockefeller," paper delivered at the annual meeting of the American Political Science Association, Washington, D.C., 1972. Data compiled from *Public Papers of Nelson A. Rockefeller* (Albany, N.Y., 1959–1971).

[a] Only those temporary state commissions all of whose members or chairmen were appointed by the governor are included.

rect policy but also served to build a constituency for the changes they suggested. Larger groups called governor's conferences—for example, on public employee relations, aging, and youth—helped Rockefeller attract attention to issues in which he was interested.

One former Executive Chamber aide commented that Rockefeller also used a study group on occasion as "a buffer between himself and the decision." Such a group "insulated the governor from the problem and allowed him to make an independent judgment."[33] It thus allowed Rockefeller to delay his final decision on a controversial matter and still give the appearance of taking action. Having a widely representative panel of experts formulate and then propose a plan helped the governor to build support for it. And if the recommendations turned out to be politically troublesome, Rockefeller could call them an interim report and say that final proposals would emerge later.

Public Relations

Though the role of public relations in politics is most visible during election campaigns, the process of learning and shaping public opinion is continuous, and is the daily preoccupation of a significant portion of the governor's executive staff. By meeting with opinion leaders, monitoring the press, television, radio, and incoming mail, and occasional opinion polling, Governor Rockefeller sought to keep in touch, through his staff, with the changing currents of opinion in New York State. Through public meetings, speeches to selected audiences, media appearances, and a vigorous daily public relations effort, he sought to shape public opinion toward specific support of particular programs and general support for the efforts of his administration.

It is axiomatic among students of public affairs that policy initiatives win neither passage nor public approbation on their intrinsic merits alone. The success of a program within the state is often as dependent on the way it is perceived as on its measurable social, economic, or political impact. From Frank Jamieson and later from Hugh Morrow, Rockefeller learned that the leader who could define the arena, the one who could shape the way in which issues were seen by others, could often win his objectives. The governor's public relations effort was thus inextricably bound up with the policy process, and an examination of it gives considerable insight into the daily workings of the executive staff.

Some governors emphasized learning what the public wanted and followed what they learned. Others stressed leading public opinion to support policies to which the electorate of the state might not otherwise be receptive. Rockefeller generally sought to lead opinion, often making critical remarks to staff members about politicians who "seek a hundred percent support before they act." "They are," he told one aide, "like the man chasing down the streets of Paris after a mob. 'Why are you running so hard?' he was asked. 'I must, I am their leader,' he replied."[34]

Rockefeller had tremendous energy and an overwhelming personality, resources he used to good advantage when in public view. Like Lyndon Johnson, he liked to get physically close to people when talking with them. Frequently when shaking hands, he also grasped one's forearm. Among politicians in Albany, this was known as the "half Nelson." On other occasions he might throw his arm around one's shoulders while shaking hands. This was the "full Nelson." In conversation with others he customarily responded enthusiastically. Some of his favorite expressions were "Wonderful idea!" "I'm thrilled!" "I'm interested in that!" "Good for you!" "You're a brave man!" "That's fabulous!" "You're a great guy!"[35]

Rockefeller's personality was also effective in larger public meetings, even with hostile audiences. On the campaign trail and in town meetings he would sometimes receive rough criticism from members of the audience. Far from resenting such criticism, he welcomed it, because it gave him the opportunity to turn it to his advantage by saying: "What a wonderful democratic system we have here in America, where people of courage can stand up and openly criticize the governor! I wish to compliment the gentleman for his frankness."[36]

Rockefeller's attitude toward opinion leadership often entailed risks that members of his staff would have preferred him not to take. One of them described his feelings about the governor's tendency to ignore polls and advice and follow instinct in four lines of doggerel:

> It matters not how steep the freight,
> How charged with negatives the poll,
> I am the captain of my state,
> I have the comfort of my role.[37]

This attitude brought Rockefeller both successes and failures. He failed in his campaign for public support of the 1970 transportation bond issue, but succeeded in standing fast in the face of adverse opinion on the abortion reform question.

One of Rockefeller's tenets was that "you can't kid the people very long." This was a lesson that had been emphasized by his first mentor in public relations, Frank Jamieson, and reinforced by later experience as governor. In his campaign for reelection in 1962, in accordance with projections available to him at the time, Rockefeller pledged not to raise taxes for four years. When, after the election, it was found that a change in the economic climate made earlier projections inaccurate, the governor decided to seek more revenues within the constraints of his earlier pledge by raising automobile registration fees. Though technically based on a valid distinction used in public finance, this action made the governor's pledge look like an attempt to deceive the public during the election and cost him considerable credibility. He later listed the pledge to impose no new taxes as one of the major errors of his administration, and it was a seminal learning experience for him in public relations.[38] From that time on, he avoided pledges unless he was absolutely certain he could deliver.

The governor likened public goodwill to "a bank account, which can be built up during certain periods, and then drawn upon to get unpopular things done." The best way to handle a difficult problem, he felt, was to go where it was and "meet the issue." To illustrate this point, Rockefeller gave the example of his stand on the operation of the Long Island Rail Road during the early days of the Metropolitan Transportation Authority. Local Republicans were urging that he come out against the authority and its chairman, William Ronan. Instead, he went to a meeting on Long Island and took full responsibility for what Ronan was doing. This, he recalled, saved the local politicos and "bought time until the thing could be turned around." In the short run, Rockefeller took a public beating, especially when he enthusiastically said that the Long Island would be the best railroad in the country, but, as he noted, "I wasn't running that year."[39] Over time the governor found financing for the road, ironed out labor problems, increased productivity, and slowly rebuilt his credibility with Long Island voters.

Similarly, in July 1972, he spoke in support of highly unpopular Urban Development Corporation (UDC) low-income housing plans for Westchester despite strong local opposition. Such risks, however, had their limits. Rockefeller bowed to the local will in the matter of the Rye–Oyster Bay Bridge. Here the impact of the four-year election cycle on the governor's willingness to take locally unpopular stands was apparent. The imminence of an election advised prudence in opinion leadership.

Some of Rockefeller's public relations successes can be laid to the timely seizing of opportunities. The question of a shield law to protect newsmen against the forced divulgence of their sources, for example, was largely a national issue in 1973. Fortuitously, New York had passed such a law in 1970, and when the governor spoke out strongly in favor of a similar national measure he received more than eighty favorable editorial comments on this stand in newspapers around the country.[40]

Rockefeller's political instinct was sometimes spectacularly successful in helping him seize the leadership of public opinion and use it as a resource. An excellent example was his 1973 narcotics program, which aroused enormous opposition in the media. In his initial proposal the governor called for mandatory life sentences for hard-drug pushers and certain drug-related crimes, no plea bargaining in drug cases, and a major expansion of the court system to deal with the additional burden this program would place on it. In order publicly to reinforce his commitment to this program, Rockefeller made an unprecedented two-and-one-half-hour appearance in behalf of it before a joint legislative committee. This appearance was broadcast on the statewide educational television network and made available to commercial stations.

During the controversy over the hard-line 1973 drug law, the skill of the governor's staff in employing the techniques of public relations came into play. When they heard the governor's drug program characterized as antiblack, a group of black ministers from Harlem who disagreed with this assessment approached Rockefeller's office and offered their aid. At first it was proposed that they issue a statement or hold a press conference, but the governor's press staff argued that such action would have little impact on the media. They suggested instead a gubernatorial press conference in Albany at which the group would appear with Rockefeller. This alternative was adopted, and the conference received major coverage by newspapers and television stations over the state. Later it was edited into a half-hour tape and distributed for use at public meetings by the women's division of the Republican party.[41]

The effect of this public relations effort was a deluge of mail to the governor that ran 5 to 1 in favor of his drug program. His stand on the issue stimulated debate, provided a safety valve for public frustration over the drug epidemic, and offered the impetus for a possible major strengthening of state drug laws. On this issue, Rockefeller took a position and worked hard to create favorable public opinion on it. The supportive opinion he precipitated was then used as a resource to make his position credible in the public policy debate that his stand had created.

Rockefeller did not take positions solely for public relations purposes, though the policy directions he adopted were affected by his judgment of the state of public opinion.[42] Public relations considerations followed his decisions. He started out with ideas, made an independent analysis, and then used polls to determine the level of public awareness and expectation about a problem. Often his feelings about the essence of an issue were intuitive.

Elections, a time of stocktaking, served to reveal many problems. Other problems, such as prison reform, arose out of crises. Rockefeller's reliance on intuition was paradoxical, because in dealing with problems he was enamoured of data. He often made his case with charts and graphs, facts and figures. This, he said, "is the way I work. The impact is slower but it builds more solidly. Emotions may sway feelings for the moment, but in the long run they do not convince."[43] One observer noted that Rockefeller represented the new breed of politician who used visual communications effectively in an age when visual communications were part of the experience of all Americans.[44]

Here, as in other areas of action for New York's governor, success bred success and failure bred failure. Effective decisions on substantive matters could make the governor appear strong and help him on issues that might arise later. Ineffectual decisions contributed to the appearance of gubernatorial weakness and thus had high costs. Perhaps the best public relations technique that the governor could employ was to avoid highly visible errors. In the state political arena, at least, Rockefeller for the most part was able to do so.

The visibility of the governor of New York, always high, is enhanced by the fact that the state is the home of the television industry and of some of the nation's most widely read newspapers and magazines. But the attention that the governor gets may be a liability as well as an asset. He may use the public interest in himself and his office as a potent informal resource to enhance his power and ability to get things done within the state, but, as the most identifiable symbol of state government, he must also suffer the blame for publicly perceived governmental failings, some in areas over which he may have little control.

It is probably true that politicians, concerned about their public image, read the press with much more care than do average citizens. After his election as president, John Kennedy remarked that he was "reading a lot more and enjoying it less."[45] Studies have shown that the average newspaper reader, unlike the politician, reads very selectively and filters out much of the political content of the paper as he goes through it.[46] The news media's immediate effect on state politics, therefore, may stem less from their impact on the electorate than from their impact on the politician.

In disseminating information and trying to shape opinion in the state, Rockefeller, like any other governor, was constrained by the manner in which people form and hold opinions. One study of gubernatorial influence offers some hope for a governor as a shaper of opinion. It reported that a governor generally enjoys the advantage of public trust as he pursues his opinion-shaping objectives. In 1969, Louis Harris Associates conducted an opinion survey in a group of southeastern states to determine the percentage of their respondents

Governor Rockefeller in a typical chart presentation (1960). Photo by Bob Wands. Rockefeller Family Archives.

that agreed with the proposition that "the governor can be trusted to do what is good for the people." The results showed that 67 percent of those queried agreed. This level of trust in a governmental institution in that year was exceeded only by that in the presidency. A governor's ability to shape opinion, however, is limited by the nature of the issue and the low level of public knowledge and participation in most public-policy matters: "On the average . . . a state governor faces the prospect of having an inherent source of negative feeling toward his administration resulting from taxing and spending matters, and unless he has an issue such as law and order to create some positive response to his administration, it would seem unlikely that he could sustain, or even achieve, a favorable level of popular support for his administration."[47]

Low participation and knowledge, rather than blocking gubernatorial opinion leadership efforts, may at times offer governors unique opportunities to take the initiative. In general, research shows that governors are more successful at shaping the broad parameters of opinion—at making the public more receptive to them in general—than at precipitating strong support for particular policies. Appeals to public opinion are more likely to mobilize potential support from the governor's partisans than to convert opponents or attract new supporters.[48]

Within the constraints of the process of mass-opinion formation, Governor Rockefeller employed many tools. A small but highly skilled and organized communications staff maintained liaison with both the electronic and the print media and served a dual advocate role. With the press they sought the best possible coverage of the governor. Within the administration, they strove for gubernatorial sensitivity to media needs. The governor enjoyed a reciprocal relationship with the media; they needed him because he was news, he needed them because they controlled the channels of communication to the broader public.

The Communications Staff

Because the communications task for the governor was complex and essential, Rockefeller developed an entire subunit, one of four in the Executive Chamber, to perform this function. The governor's director of communications was Hugh Morrow. At the time of his appointment, Morrow had over two decades of experience in political public relations and had seen the politician–reporter relationship from a variety of perspectives. He had been a *Saturday Evening Post* writer and associate editor, a speechwriter and press secretary for United States Senators Irving Ives and Kenneth B. Keating, and, between 1960 and 1969, a special public relations assistant in Rockefeller's private employ. His appointment as director of communications, a post created for him in 1969, was, according to Morrow, a matter of "logic and convenience"; it formally established his theretofore informal position as director of the entire communications effort of the governor's office.

The governor's press secretary, Ron Maiorana, worked closely with Morrow. Though he would appear subordinate to the director of communications on an organization chart of the governor's office, in fact Maiorana's relationship with Morrow was collegial, and he was almost totally autonomous in the area of day-to-day gubernatorial press relations.

The communications staff varied in size from fourteen to eighteen persons and had a budget of about $500,000 a year. When circumstances required, its efforts were supplemented with people from other state agencies, or with private firms that supplied advertising and polling services. Besides Morrow and Maiorana, other key people included the deputy press secretary, two assistant press secretaries, and two special assistants, one for television and the other for speechwriting. In addition to his other duties, the deputy press secretary handled gubernatorial proclamations and the informal coordination of the thirty information officers in the state's departments and agencies. One assistant press secretary was stationed full time in New York, and the deputy press secretary and the other assistant were based in Albany. The director of communications and the press secretary traveled between the two cities with the governor.

When Franklin D. Roosevelt was governor of New York, he could meet with all the interested press in his office in Albany. Under Rockefeller, press conferences filled the huge Red Room of the capitol. The high level of development of the press relations staff during the Rockefeller administration reflected a trend evident in both national and state government.[49] In New York prior to the Dewey administration, there was no differentiation of the press function in the gubernatorial staff; press relations were handled by the secretary to the governor or his assistant. Under Dewey, an office of press relations was established and its chief given the rank of executive assistant to the governor. The first holder of this post was James C. Hagerty, who later became President Eisenhower's press secretary.

The efforts of the gubernatorial press staff were supplemented by those of public relations officers throughout state government. Though these press officers worked primarily for heads of state departments and agencies, they were expected to bring major policy questions to the attention of the governor's office. In 1946 Governor Dewey established a Public Information Council to draw together the public relations work of the administration. Governor Harriman's press secretary held periodic meetings with departmental press officers. During the early Rockefeller years there was a mechanism for clearing administrative agency press releases through the assistant secretary for reports and an executive assistant to the governor. With the establishment of the position of director of communications, responsibility was consolidated in his office. In general, however, coordination of press relations efforts in the Rockefeller administration was informal.

One factor that provided informal coordination, or at least great awareness of the governor's stake in the release of information, was that all chief public information specialists in state agencies were political appointees and in a sense were all members of the team. Some of them—Harry O'Donnell, the assistant commissioner of commerce, for example—had been key men in press relations in Rockefeller's gubernatorial campaigns. On the other hand, the governor and his staff were sensitive to the charge of "managing the news." Both Morrow and Maiorana held that it was better to have the governor's side of the story told than to attempt to close off news sources and be vulnerable to charges of news management.[50]

Morrow was on the strategy board of the governor's last three gubernatorial campaigns, and both he and Maiorana regularly participated in policy discussions at the high staff level.[51] As the official spokesmen for the governor, they had to know what he thought and how and why he took a particular position. Both Morrow and Maiorana had ready access to Rockefeller and neither hesitated to interrupt his schedule on occasion, when they considered the matter at hand of sufficient importance to warrant Rockefeller's immediate personal attention.

The Governor and the Reporters

The relationship between the modern politician and the journalist is a curious one, made up in almost equal parts of conflicting interests and mutual dependence. The reporter's job, as defined by the canons of the profession and the pressures of daily work, is to get the story and to publish it regardless of the political consequences. Awards and recognition come if the journalist breaks a spectacular exclusive or perhaps exposes chicanery or corruption in high places. The governor, however, must govern. The premature public disclosure of information about delicate political negotiations or programs in the formative stages could disrupt the political bargaining process or forearm the enemies of the program. Even when a governor has nothing to fear so far as the integrity of his administration is concerned, leaks to the press can make his political and administrative life much more difficult.

Reporters need the governor's cooperation; without it, reporting about state government and politics becomes difficult and with his active opposition may be virtually impossible. As the American Institute for Political Communication noted in its 1966 study of press relations in Washington: "Government officials and newsmen are mutually dependent to an extent which makes it virtually impossible for each to function in the long run without the cooperation of the other."[52]

The press is not only a potential aid for the governor in policy formation and implementation and a watchdog over gubernatorial behavior but also a multidimensional internal communications network for the state political system. When the governor speaks publicly, he, like the president, speaks to many publics, and the news media enable him to reach these multiple publics. The press also provided the governor with an image of his administration that was not filtered through his staff. Rockefeller was not always pleased with what he read. In June 1972 he told Charles Dumas of the *New York Daily News* that "his works have not been accurately portrayed and that he is not fully understood." For this, Dumas reported, Rockefeller was "inclined to blame the writers."[53]

In releasing news stories, the governor's press staff was aware of the substantive and timing needs of both the print and the electronic media. When dispensing the news, the press office attempted to avoid playing favorites in the press corps. Morrow and Maiorana shared the belief that exclusive interviews with Rockefeller, for example, were counterproductive in the long run. Such techniques necessarily disappointed more reporters than they satisfied. This did not mean that reporters did not occasionally get exclusive stories from the governor in off-the-cuff interviews.

During the Rockefeller administration, stories were most commonly leaked in connection with the governor's annual message, which, because of its complexity, would not otherwise have received widespread attention. By releasing parts of the message over a one- or two-week period and making sure that the major outlets received the information—the metropolitan dailies, the Gannett chain of newspapers, and the television networks—the governor's office could ensure maximum exposure for his policy positions.[54]

Geographic considerations were taken into account in releasing stories; some were issued in Albany and some in New York City, especially after 1973, when Albany finally received color television transmission capability. Sometimes, and often with the consent of the reporters who covered state politics, available stories were released over the weekend. This timing gave newsmen something to write about on Sunday, when "nothing ever happens except natural disasters," and assured more complete coverage of lesser stories originating in the governor's office. Judgment and experience were also important in knowing when to release news items. Items for which the administration wanted high visibility were timed to meet the deadlines of the morning dailies and the six-o'clock news. Those for which it desired less visibility might be held beyond those deadlines.

Despite the personal accessibility of the press staff, reporters complained of their limited access to Governor Rockefeller. Members of the press corps based in Albany felt especially disadvantaged because Rockefeller did not live in that city except during the legislative session and then did not hold frequent press conferences. According to Dick Zander, state political editor of a Long Island daily, *Newsday*, Rockefeller was "not very available . . . except in election years."[55] Similarly, Charles Dumas of the *New York Daily News* said Rockefeller as governor had "been less accessible than any in the memory of veteran hands in and around state government."[56]

Most of the criticism came during legislative sessions when the press would have welcomed the governor's views on controversial issues. Rockefeller readily admitted that he was not so available to the press as some other governors. During the legislative session that was particularly true. But he said, "If I am to do a good job, I've got to get the legislature to pass the bills that I think are important for the state. The press may criticize me for not being available sufficiently, but I would rather be successful in my dealings with the legislature."[57]

One universal complaint of reporters who covered the governor was similar to that of the Washington press corps about President Nixon—he held formal press conferences infrequently. In 1971 Governor Rockefeller held twenty formal press conferences—fewer, for example, than Governor Milton J. Shapp of Pennsylvania, who held thirty-one formal conferences in Harrisburg in that year and numerous less formal ones throughout the state, or Governor Thomas J. Meskill of Connecticut, whose press secretary stated that he had frequent conferences in 1971.[58]

Governor Rockefeller on occasion used a press conference to rally public opinion on a controversial action, and to gain support from the public at large for a program that was in difficulty in the legislature. In 1959 and 1965, for example, he used televised press conferences to help sell tax increases that were being opposed by legislative majorities.[59] Clearly the press conference evolved into a device for gubernatorial opinion leadership. It was held at the governor's initiative and on his home ground. He controlled its length and, by his responses, its tenor. Governor Rockefeller, like President Kennedy, was comfortable with the press conference; he excelled at the give-and-take of the question-and-answer session. Though reporters complained, in fact he was relatively accessible. A combination of ease with journalists and good staffwork made the governor reasonably successful in using the press for his political and administrative ends.

Speechwriting and Special Media Projects

Though the press secretary was relatively autonomous in his area of responsibility, the director of communication, Hugh Morrow, played a more active role in the drafting of speeches and the administration of special projects. Speechwriting was the special assignment of Joseph Persico. The problems inherent in preparing a speech for the governor were a little different from those of any similar operation. A speech had to state the governor's position and at the same time had to appeal to the particular audience before whom it was given. Each speech was carefully planned. First, Morrow and Persico determined the physical surroundings of the place where the speech was to be given and carefully analyzed the potential audience. Persico then prepared a first draft, based on known positions of the governor, which was circulated to the executive staff and frequently to other state officials and political advisers. Suggestions, additions, deletions would produce other drafts to be further discussed and debated. When a consensus had been reached and a draft satisfied Morrow, it would be ready for the governor.

A day or two before the speech was to be delivered, Persico and Morrow would go over the text with the governor line by line, phrase by phrase, nuance by nuance. At this point Rockefeller began rewriting and revising the speech to make it his own. The governor had an "almost obsessive concern with every possible interpretation of a phrase." He was "terribly sensitive about possible interpretations that can be put on something he says."[60] Rockefeller was much more attuned to what a speech said than the way it sounded, a fact that sometimes distressed his staff. In one instance the governor included in a speech to be delivered before a Jewish group in New York two very long sentences on American military aid to Israel. This was a classic example of a case where the governor wanted his thoughts expressed "just right," which meant including every qualifying phrase necessary for a complete, literal expression of his thought. The result was two long sentences of sixty-five words each. A staff assistant reworked these two sentences into ten or twelve short ones to make them read better. The governor was clearly annoyed at this tampering with the sentences that he believed conveyed his exact meaning. The original language was restored.[61]

One obvious aim of a good speech is a good headline in the press. Good headlines, in turn, require ample lead time for the reporter to file his story. Hence the value of a text prepared in advance. The governor's penchant for vigorously editing speeches meant that on occasion texts were being revised up to delivery and well past reporters' deadlines.

Rockefeller was a good speaker when he remembered to read slowly and stay with his text. Because of a mixed dominance, the tendency to reverse the order of words when reading, he had some trouble scanning prepared texts, especially when he was tired. Consequently, whenever possible, he liked to speak extemporaneously, and it was impossible to predict how he would treat a text when he finally approached the lectern. What he said would depend on the nature of the occasion and the way he felt. If he was familiar with the subject, he was likely to depart at some point from the text. That too posed a problem for the press secretary; the evening papers got the text of the speech, and the morning papers got what the governor actually said.

As with any other incumbent executive, Rockefeller after a time faced the problem of proposing new ideas without opening himself to an opponent's charge of past neglect. The governor, with understandable pride in his record, was unusually sensitive to the charge that he had been inattentive to a problem. Thus, for example, he could not announce a proposal for state aid to local police forces by saying, "We are going to fight crime by putting more policemen on the street," because opponents could charge, "If you knew the need, why didn't you do it before?" He had to say rather, "We have been and we are now fighting crime vigorously. We will continue to fight crime with a new state aid program to put more police on your streets." Weaving these kinds of convoluted qualifiers came to be known among the staff as writing in the "future past perfect" tense.[62]

The number of speaking engagements the governor accepted was a function of his particular political goals and policy objectives at the time. Some speeches, such as the State of the State address and annual budget message to the legislature, were mandated by the state constitution. Others—the September 1973 speech to the American Political Science Association, for example—were chosen to maximize his visibility on the national scene. Sometimes the state party chairman arranged for Rockefeller to speak to a local Republican organization as a reward for a job well done. The choice of forum, the choice of subject, and the emphasis of the speech, when combined with media coverage, were potent tools for opinion leadership.

An examination of the public addresses delivered by the governor during his first three terms reveals, as one might expect, that he was most likely to take to the podium in gubernatorial election years and was much more active in upstate areas during these times (see Table 11). The three peak years for speechmaking by the governor were 1962, 1966, and 1970.

Rockefeller's speeches could be divided into two major categories. In the politically ritualistic appearance, the governor's mere presence at a particular occasion, such as a county Republican picnic, was more important than what he said. On other occasions the governor appeared to be heard; he might launch a new initiative, argue a point of view, or press for new legislation. The communications staff advised the media of forthcoming speeches not only to ensure coverage but also to protect the credibility of the administration by distinguishing between speeches of substance and addresses of lesser importance.

One trend evident from an analysis of the governor's speeches was a move away from full-length television and radio addresses to explain his positions and programs. Nevertheless, Rockefeller was aware that the most radical development in political communication in recent years was the displacement of newspapers by television as the prime source of news for a majority of the people. He recognized

Table 11. Geographic Location of Public Addresses Given by Governor Rockefeller, 1959–1970

	New York City		Albany		Rest of state		Out of state		All
Year	Number	Percent	Number	Percent	Number	Percent	Number	Percent	addresses
1959	47	43	15	14	35	32	13	12	110
1960	45	35	12	9	47	37	23	19	127
1961	15	24	13	21	30	48	4	6	62
1962	49	30	5	3	94	57	16	9	164
1963	29	43	10	15	15	22	13	19	67
1964	15	21	3	4	6	8	47	66	71
1965	37	35	15	14	43	40	11	10	106
1966	84	35	13	6	139	59	1	—	237
1967	65	55	17	14	36	30	4	3	122
1968	31	42	5	7	11	15	26	36	73
1969	39	46	5	6	33	39	7	8	84
1970	104	47	26	12	88	40	2	1	220

Source: Compiled by the authors from *Public Papers of Nelson A. Rockefeller* (Albany, N.Y., 1959–1970).

the importance of coverage of his speeches by television news programs. Thus a speech could not be viewed simply in terms of the audience that would hear it on the scene or of newspaper coverage. It had to be weighed heavily in its potential to win a minute of television news time. As one campaign aide noted: "In the current communications context, a political event is largely judged in these hard terms: If it didn't happen on television, it didn't happen."[63]

During the Rockefeller administration, television and radio were used in several ways. The governor appeared on network news programs such as "Meet the Press," gave special interviews, and held televised press conferences. Parts of these appearances were often taped by his staff for later use. In addition, special in-house quarter-hour programs, film clips, and feature films, often based on Rockefeller's public appearances, were prepared and distributed to all the state's radio and television stations. An hour-long feature based on Rockefeller's town meetings, for example, was taped and later distributed through the Republican state committee.

Perhaps the most ambitious undertaking to explain state programs on television was a series of eight half-hour shows entitled "Executive Chamber," presented in 1964 and 1965. These programs were fi-

Rockefeller appears on Dave Garroway's television show to publicize his fallout shelter program (1960). Photo by Bob Wands. Rockefeller Family Archives.

nanced with more than $200,000 of the governor's personal funds and were carried by eighteen television stations throughout the state. In the first program, the governor laid out the essentials of his legislative program. Each of the later presentations attempted to dramatize one major issue facing the state, such as mental health, transportation, or water pollution. Though the governor of course derived political benefits from this effort, it was a major attempt to increase public awareness of the operations of state government.[64]

Learning Public Opinion

The governor's staff was as much concerned about listening for him as speaking for him. The staff believed that Rockefeller's greatest political asset was his reputation for personal honesty.[65] If any rumors of official misconduct in the governor's administration arose, the allegations were checked by any means necessary, from a few discreet telephone calls to a full-scale state police investigation. In these matters, it was felt that it was best to err on the side of discretion. Rockefeller had to be kept from even the appearance of impropriety. "The best way to deal with sin," Morrow said, "is to banish the sinner and cry loudly about how he has betrayed you."[66] Indeed, the Rockefeller administration, judged on the basis of what happens generally in political life, suffered from relatively few scandals.

In addition to guarding the governor's image, an exceptional function, the process of information gathering served to guide and inform public policy. The governor and his staff used a variety of sources—the news media, contacts in the political, professional, and business communities in New York, direct communication with the electorate through mail and town meetings, and opinion polling.

Polling, because of its expense, was used much less frequently in connection with policy questions than in political campaigns. When polls were used on policy questions, they were designed to determine the degree of support in the state for gubernatorial positions. In June 1969, for example, the governor's office commissioned a survey on three questions: school decentralization, narcotics addiction, and campus disorders.[67] On school decentralization, the poll showed that about two-thirds of the electorate in New York had heard of the issue, about three-fourths of them in New York City and its suburbs. Of these, opinion was divided about 50–50 on the issue. On narcotics addiction, about 85 percent of those polled agreed with the governor's position requiring compulsory treatment of addicts. On campus disorders, though seven of ten polled believed in the abstract right to protest, eight of ten favored tighter enforcement of college rules, and 75 percent would expel students who broke laws in demonstrations or would cut off government aid. Certainly such information was helpful to the governor as he planned his public positions, especially with an election in the offing.

The media also provided the governor with some of the feedback he needed. A vast clipping file was maintained by the governor's office, covering major daily newspapers not only in the state but all over the country.

One innovative technique that Governor Rockefeller developed to measure opinion on public issues in New York was what came to be called the "town meeting." They were of two types—gatherings of some four hundred people open to the public, and smaller, intimate "leader groups" of twenty-five or thirty influential citizens. Started in 1961, these meetings were means to promote regional development and defend Rockefeller's controversial fiscal policies. The number of town meetings in a series generally was between ten and eighteen, and sites were well scattered throughout the state. In 1972, for example, town meetings were held in Syracuse, Elmira, Utica, Olean, Lake Placid, Buffalo, Cheektowaga, Poughkeepsie, Colonie Hill, and Binghamton—all upstate; in other years meetings were also held in downstate suburban communities. Over the ten years that they were in use, the governor's town meetings evolved from a consultation with local business and community leaders into a more general and open forum that allowed Rockefeller and his staff to test statewide opinion during the months just before the annual legislative session.

Town meetings entailed considerable advance work by the governor's staff. Press releases were prepared for the various news media in the local area in which Rockefeller would speak and individual invitations were sent to local public officials. Accompanying these invitations was a list of suggested "issues for discussion." For example, in 1972 this list covered eight areas: criminal justice, education, environment, health, housing, community development, no-fault insurance, and public transportation. Follow-up work was also extensive, as the governor urged people with further questions to write him or promised to look further into problems raised at the meetings. At some meetings in 1969 envelopes addressed to the governor were distributed, but this technique was too expensive and was soon abandoned.

Rockefeller was generally accompanied by several aides and ranking state officials at each meeting, depending on the questions he thought might be discussed. At one meeting it might be the commissioner of environmental conservation, at another the commissioner of education. On other occasions he was accompanied by the other elected Republican state officials, Lieutenant Governor Malcolm Wilson and Attorney General Louis Lefkowitz. The format for the meetings was simple. The governor generally opened the session with a prepared statement and then took questions from the audience. The first questioners were generally selected from among invited local officials. Queries that the governor could not answer himself were referred to aides or noted for later research.

Several techniques were used to control the nature and direction of questioning. The distribution of the "issues for discussion" both before and at the meetings served this purpose, though aides to the governor claimed that their objective in using this device was to open up discussion during the reluctant moments at the beginning of each session rather than to limit it to the topics listed. Subjects the governor wished to avoid, such as abortion, were not listed. Control over the meetings was also facilitated by judicious preparation. The size of the hall limited the audience to three hundred to four hundred people, half of whom were invited public officials.

Despite all these built-in precautions, on occasion a town meeting was a difficult two hours for the governor. At a meeting on Long Island he tried to shut off debate on the abortion issue by selecting a questioner who was wearing a volunteer fireman's badge. Once the fireman got control of the microphone he denounced the 1972 veto of the repeal of New York's liberal abortion law and shouted that the law was "a ridicule on what we as firemen do."[68]

When speaking extemporaneously, Rockefeller risked committing himself precipitously on questions of public policy. In Buffalo during the 1972 series of town meetings, he caused something of a sensation by commenting that he thought the Niagara frontier jetport was "for the birds." Later, his assistant press secretary, Gerry McLaughlin, had to explain that the governor was referring only to the Batavia site, which he opposed, and not to the Wheatfield-Pendleton site, which was still under consideration.[69]

Though such problems recurred, Rockefeller seemed to enjoy the confrontations and was able to draw valuable information from them. The governor stated repeatedly that the town meeting provided him with a major information input, an opportunity to "get the public point of view—first hand, and forcefully put across." His enthusiasm even led him to recommend this technique to other governors. In 1966 he wrote Governor Pat Brown of California: "I am delighted that the town meeting technique has worked well for you. Recently I set up another series of such meetings—actually I find they probably are more beneficial to me than the audience."[70] Later, when Rockefeller became vice-president, he induced President Ford to try the town meeting technique. Still later, it was used by President Carter.

The meetings provided other advantages for the administration as well. Usually the governor got a good press by showing that he was willing to travel widely to talk directly with people. Editorial opinion throughout the state generally favored town meetings as examples of responsive government.[71] The attitude of Emmet O'Brien, expressed in a 1969 column that appeared in the Albany *Times-Union*, was typical of that of the press: "I think the governor has shown a great deal of courage in arranging these meetings and offering himself as a target for anyone who cares to wander in from the street. He didn't have to. He could have fought for his program from behind the shield of high office, allowing others to go into the highways and byways."[72]

Town meetings also provided the governor with the opportunity to build relations with local politicians—in effect, to give them a chance to show the folks at home that they were carrying local concerns to the governor's doorstep. Aside from a few consistent themes pressed by statewide lobbying groups, local issues predominated at the meetings. In 1972, for example, the Elmira meeting was largely concerned with flood relief, the one at Olean with the Route 17 expressway, and the meeting at Utica with the declining local economy. Just as congressional hearings gave lobbyists in Washington the opportunity to show their constituents that they were looking after their interests, so town meetings gave local officials the same opportunity.

Though their primary function was communications and public relations, town meetings also provided the governor with a resource to use in later political negotiations. In fact, Rockefeller could use the meetings to justify any set of priorities he wished to bring to state politics. Having gone out to "talk with the people," the governor could claim to know what public opinion was and then use this claim as a political tool. In 1972, for example, in a growing debate over the way the projected state budget surplus was to be used, the governor asserted that "testimony that he had heard at his recent town hall meetings around the state . . . [had convinced him] that welfare improvements were necessary."[73] Similarly, Rockefeller based his controversial proposal for life sentences for hard-drug pushers, presented in his 1973 legislative message, partly on what he said he had learned of the public's mood in the town meetings.[74] Curiously, neither of these issues was prominently discussed in press coverage of any of the meetings in the 1972 series.

Gubernatorial Mail

Mail to the governor was another, though minor, source of opinion input to the executive office. In 1972, 313,903 pieces of mail addressed to Governor Rockefeller were received at his office in Albany. This was about half as much as had been received the year before but two and a half times as much as in 1960, the first year of the Rockefeller administration for which there are complete tabulations (see Table 12). Aid to parochial schools was a highly controversial subject in 1971, and accounted for a large amount of the governor's mail in that year. About 71 percent of his mail in 1972 arrived during the five months of the legislative session. In one peak week at the end of the session, 52,318 pieces were received, an enormous number, exceeded only by that of the president's mail at the White House.

Rockefeller had a regular weekly statistical summary of his mail

Table 12. Number of Letters Received by Governor Rockefeller, 1960–1972

Year	Letters
1960	136,509
1961	188,772
1962	194,895
1963	233,728
1964	192,052
1965	178,694
1966	158,806
1967	184,264
1968	274,743
1969	227,334
1970	436,522
1971	802,522
1972	313,903

Sources 1960–1966: Last weekly mail report each year, Executive Chamber, Albany, New York (figures may be understated, as they are cumulations of figures to the last full week that ended in any calendar year, not to the last day of the year); 1967–1972, memo, Joeanna Brown to Charles Palmer, "Annual Mail Report, 1972," January 9, 1973.

prepared for his information, a practice generally used in the White House.[75] Letters were recorded according to subject, issue, and direction of preference. Items were included in the report if twenty-five or more letters were received on the subject during the week.

There was little consistency in the subject matter of letters to the governor over the period of his tenure. Subject matter was largely defined by the visibility of public issues and the choice of tactics by pressure groups. In 1972, the subject most frequently brought to the governor's attention through the mail was pornography, closely followed by state aid to nonpublic schools and abortion. Among them, these three subjects accounted for well over half the gubernatorial mail for the year (see Table 13).

Mail was handled by the governor's staff in various ways. Complaints about failures of state departments to provide services were referred to departmental heads for remedial action. Five correspondents worked full time answering individual letters and queries. Mail that the staff considered motivated by pressure groups was recorded but not answered. The staff also determined which mail should receive the personal attention of the governor. Mail forwarded to Rockefeller, unlike that shown to Kennedy during his administration in Washington, was not randomly selected but was chosen for its perceived importance to the governor.[76]

Generally, Governor Rockefeller, like most politicians, placed little credence in the volume of mail as an accurate measure of public opinion. Though he might use positive mail as evidence of public support for a position he advocated, Rockefeller knew that, generally, mail campaigns could be easily contrived and manipulated by pressure groups. Self-motivated letter writers, furthermore, as shown by studies of opinions expressed in newspaper letters to the editor, tend to be intensely interested in and committed to the issues they write about and therefore hardly reflect the general public views on these issues.[77]

Letters on public issues received by the governor rarely reflect the range of opinion on these issues. Of the twenty-four issues listed in Table 13, only four elicited significant numbers of comments on both sides. In over half the cases, no opposing views were recorded. It is not surprising that the governor's office tended to be most responsive to individual letters expressing personal concern and exhibiting a personal stake in the outcome of a decision. But letters to the governor played a minor role in public policy making in New York.

Whether in analyzing the governor's mail, preparing speeches, or

Table 13. Subjects of Gubernatorial Mail, New York, 1972

Topic	Total	Pro	Con
		Letters received	
State aid to nonpublic schools	57,043	56,452	591
Abortion			
Bill S26	48,258	25,797	22,461
Veto	6,403	4,815	1,588
Budget cuts: mental hygiene	3,533	0	3,533
Animal shelters (A109 et al.)	1,627	1,627	0
Unemployment benefits to strikers	290	206	84
Public school aid	12,197	12,197	0
Office of Mental Retardation	2,799	2,096	703
Return to capital punishment	1,234	1,163	71
Housing bonds	636	636	0
Knorr-Gallagher bill	1,657	1,564	93
Cuts to drug abuse programs	2,311	0	2,311
No-fault insurance	266	180	86
"Fair" dismissal bill	905	615	290
Banning pornography	62,331	62,325	6
Jeff Smith	248	248	0
Preller Field	1,521	1,521	0
Willowbrook investigation	4,156	4,156	0
Pollution	1,209	1,209	0
Pension abuse	1,578	0	1,578
Day care centers	873	873	0
Senior citizens	443	443	0
Canarsie Junior High School	753	0	753
Adirondack Park	684	684	0
Reapportionment	616	86	530
	213,571	178,893	34,678
Other	45,671		
All topics	259,242		

Source: Memo, Joeanna Brown to Charles Palmer, "Annual Mail Report, 1972," January 9, 1973.

dealing with the news media, Rockefeller's public relations effort was extraordinarily successful. This success could not be explained solely by the size of the professional staff. It was adequate, but other politicians had staffs as large or larger and were not so successful. The reason lay elsewhere.

Three additional factors account for the success of the Rockefeller effort. The top staff were sophisticated professionals experienced in the political world. Hugh Morrow, who was chief of this group, had the confidence of the news media and was unusually sensitive to public reaction to Rockefeller's programs. His frank advice both on the substance of policies and on their presentation to the public was invaluable.

Rockefeller was eminently "salable." He was used to public relations advisers. He believed that public opinion was a potent political resource, and that facts and figures could be used to influence citizen attitudes. Moreover, he had a warm personality to which people responded easily.

The final factor in Rockefeller's success was the ability to augment the state budget with personal funds. Outside consultants and pollsters could be retained, television time obtained, special projects developed and financed by the governor's private resources. The availability of these funds did not guarantee their intelligent use, but when combined with the quality of people Rockefeller was able to attract and retain, they provided the governor with a public relations resource few other executives in American politics were able to develop or employ.

5

Administration, Reorganization, and Crisis Management

Like all bureaucratic organizations, state agencies in New York tend to be creatures of habit, inflexible, and enmeshed in the process of administering ongoing programs. Around them emerge a complex of interest groups and legislative supporters, all committed to the survival and growth of extant bureaus and their programs. One of the fundamental contrasts between agencies and the executives elected to control and direct their programs lies in differing time perspectives. As one writer on the presidency noted:

> Bureaucracies move like glaciers, marking progress, it would seem, to the pace of geologic time. In contrast, most Presidents, as creatures of politics, have reflexes attuned to daily changes in the public pulse.... The cyclical demands of electoral politics impose an unavoidable constraint upon Presidential management: how does the President reconcile the short-term demands of electoral politics with the long-term requirements for bureaucratic change?[1]

The president's situation is similar to that of all political chief executives faced with large organizations, and the governor of New York was no exception. Indeed, New York's governor had much more formal authority over the various departments and administrative agencies of the state than did most other governors, as a result of the constitutional revisions designed by Robert Moses and pushed through during the governorship of Alfred E. Smith in the 1920s. At that time, Walter Lippmann called New York's administrative reorganization "one of the greatest achievements in modern American politics."[2]

153

The governor's great formal authority helped him with one of his two primary administrative problems, gaining firm control of the major functions operated directly by the state. There were, however, few such functions in New York. The second problem, a more difficult one, was to direct, commensurate with the state's financial contribution, policy in areas where the state did not deliver services directly. In addition, as the visible and responsible political executive in the state, the governor may at any time be thrust to center stage by a crisis in state or local government. The ability to manage crises thus becomes one of the key tests of the governor's administrative will and ability.

Growth of the State Bureaucracy

During the 1960s, state and local government was one of the nation's biggest growth industries, and New York reflected this trend. The new York State Civil Service Commission reported an increase of 60,000 state employees during the period 1960–1971.[3] This increase, steady until the state fiscal crisis of 1970, roughly paralleled the general trend of a 5 percent rise per annum for all American state and local governments during this period.

New York ranked first among the states in number of employees in 1958, but by 1970 it was second to California. Despite the growth in absolute numbers of state employees, New York expanded its payrolls at a slower rate than most other large industrial states and was able to maintain a highly favorable ratio of employees to population. In 1958, with a ratio of 71.1 to 10,000, it ranked fourteenth among the states by this measure of efficiency. By 1970, with a ratio of 101.7 to 10,000 it was seventh. Further, New York was one of the first of the large industrial states to establish a low employee–population ratio and thus to reflect the advantages of economy of scale in the provision of state services.[4] State payrolls were expanded in all personnel categories, but the growth was greatest in the unclassified services, which increased over 400 percent. These were mostly professional positions in the State University system, and their creation reflected the major commitment to this area during the Rockefeller years. With respect to jobs under civil service jurisdiction, laborer positions more than doubled during this eleven-year period, exempt posts increased 61 percent, competitive posts 53 percent, and noncompetitive posts 42 percent. Under civil service law, competitive posts were those filled by written examination; noncompetitive posts were considered not appropriate for written examination, but were filled by the Civil Service Commission after it examined and ranked the credentials of applicants. Exempt posts, small in number, were filled through political appointment.

The state also became an increasingly generous employer during the Rockefeller governorship. In 1958 the average salary for a state employee in New York was $404 a month, $52 below the highest paying state (California) but $39 more than the average for state employees in the United States. In this category, New York ranked eighth highest among the states. By 1970 it had advanced to fourth highest, paying an average of $809 a month, double the 1958 figure. This was $211 below the average for Alaska, $74 below California, and $12 below Michigan, but $112 above the national average. By 1972 the average monthly pay for a state worker had advanced to $936, and the state ranked third highest. Over this period, New York also improved its position in regard to fringe benefits. Its hospitalization and medical plans for state employees were among the most generous in the nation.[5]

Increases in pay and benefits were the results of several factors. Early in his administration, Rockefeller, who had commissioned consultant reports on the subject, became convinced that remuneration had to be increased if New York was to compete with private industry and with other states for top administrative and professional talent. Consequently, he committed himself to this goal in several budget messages. In 1967 a modern labor-relations system was established for the state under the Taylor law. Public employees, guaranteed the right to organize and bargain under the law, made financial gains under this system, though they remained critical of several aspects of it, including its no-strike clause.[6]

Comparison of the distribution of New York's employees over the functional areas of state responsibility with the distribution of employees of other states is difficult because of the great variety of ways in which states divide administrative responsibilities between the state and local levels. In New York the emphasis was on the local provision of services; about two-thirds of the state budget consisted of transfer payments to localities in support of local efforts in substantive areas. In 1972 only 18.1 percent of total state and local salary payments in New York went directly to state employees, the lowest percentage for any state in the nation. Geographically, most state personnel were located in the Big Six cities (Albany, Buffalo, Rochester, Syracuse, Yonkers, and New York). During the period between

1962 and 1971, state employment in these cities grew 63.5 percent, compared to statewide growth of 41 percent. Despite the concentration of these jobs in cities, rural areas remained heavily dependent on the state for employment and income. In some rural counties, more than half of all earned income was from government payrolls.[7]

The two areas of greatest direct state administrative effort were mental hygiene and higher education. Between them these two departments commanded the services of almost half the employees of the state in 1970. In that year the New York State Department of Mental Hygiene, which operated the mental hospitals, employed more than twice as many people as did its sister agency in Pennsylvania, the state with the second greatest commitment in this service area. In contrast, New York in 1970 ranked fifteenth among the states in the number of state employees in the welfare area. While social welfare employees composed about 3.6 percent of all persons on state payrolls in the United States in 1970, workers in this area in New York made up only 2.2 percent of the state labor force. Most social welfare workers in New York State were on local payrolls.[8]

The Process of Administration

One of the least heralded tasks of a governor is day-to-day administration. As a matter of policy, Rockefeller tried not to become involved in the internal management of the departments. He preferred to rely on his commissioners for this work and to oversee them through the use of personal staff. One former high-level aide recalled: "The Governor depended heavily upon this staff to manage state government and had relatively few dealings with the commissioners directly. He was not very much interested in administration. He was more concerned with solving problems, putting together big programs, and he depended upon his staff to watch the administration, confident that if they ran into a mess it would be brought to his attention."[9] Rockefeller himself summarized his views on administration at the hearings on the Attica prison uprisings: "After the policies were determined, I have always tried to pick the ablest people to carry out those policies and to administer the programs. Having done so, I've given them my fullest support and backing, followed the operations through top flight staff but I'm always available to the administrators to discuss their programs and problems and to give them the necessary counsel and support."[10]

Subordinates often confirmed that Rockefeller backed them fully in difficult political circumstances. Edward Logue, head of the Urban Development Corporation, commented, for example: "I served at his pleasure and often chartered [*sic*] . . . a difficult or politically unpopular course for UDC. If anything, he bent over backwards to support my decisions when many in his own party, and outside, expressed their doubts."[11] In another case, when the Department of Mental Hygiene adopted what were generally regarded as progressive policies and refused to accept senile patients for custodial care in state hospitals, family physicians and local politicians protested vigorously to the governor. Rockefeller, however, refused to intervene. Much of the correspondence of the governor's office on this subject in the last three years of his administration concerned this problem. But, once convinced that the department's policy of more intensive treatment of the mentally ill rather than massive custodial care was correct, he did not waver in support of Dr. Alan Miller, commissioner of mental hygiene.

Generally the head of a department in the state government would deal first with gubernatorial aides, either at their request or on his own initiative; if he was not satisfied with their decisions, he could appeal directly to the governor. Commissioners had varying access to the governor. Some of them might see him several times a week when developing a new program or when the agency faced some crisis and then not see him again for several months. Commissioners who fancied themselves privileged because of their frequent conferences sometimes felt hurt when Rockefeller seemed to lose interest in the internal problems of their departments, as his attention turned to other matters.

Rockefeller's habit of concentrating on policy decisions and relying on the departments, supervised by personal staff, to implement these decisions did at times lead to major errors. The controversial decision of the state Department of Mental Health regarding senile patients and the implementation of the federal Medicare program led to the massive growth of the nursing home industry in New York in the late 1960s. Responsibility for nursing homes was diffused among several state departments and local welfare agencies. Though this growth should have been closely supervised by the state, it was not. Later investigations unveiled a pervasive pattern of fraud and abuse of patients in these institutions.

One top Rockefeller aide commented: "We were aware of the fact that the nursing home problem was increasingly important but we had no inkling of the extent of the fiscal problems."[12] Moreover, the

Health Department did not aggressively advocate state action in this area. Later, in testifying before one commission investigating the matter, Rockefeller acknowledged that he knew of problems with nursing homes, but budgetary constraints prevented him from acting upon this knowledge. Evidence showed, however, that much of the cost for additional Health Department auditors would have been borne by the federal government.[13]

As on the national level, cabinet meetings were not an important forum for decision making in New York during the Rockefeller years. The cabinet, which included the heads of all state departments and major units of the Executive Department, had about forty members and was too unwieldy to be an effective policy-making body. Continuing a practice instituted by Al Smith, Rockefeller called cabinet meetings once or twice a year. He used them for ceremonial purposes, to announce new policy initiatives, and sometimes to test ideas being developed by his staff. Not only were cabinet meetings unwieldy, but commissioners, jealous of their jurisdictions and prerogatives, preferred to talk privately with the governor rather than bring up sensitive matters in the presence of their colleagues.[14]

One way in which problems could be brought regularly to Rockefeller's attention was through the Friday Report, compiled by the secretary's office. Begun in June 1962 under William Ronan, it was continued on a weekly basis until September 1963, then begun again under T. Norman Hurd in February 1971 and continued through the remainder of Rockefeller's term as well as through Governor Wilson's. The reports written under Ronan differed somewhat from those prepared under the system used by Hurd. Ronan requested each department of the state to submit items that it thought ought to be brought to the governor's attention. These reports were condensed, the items paraphrased in a paragraph or two, and some ten typed pages given to the governor on Friday afternoon to be read over the weekend.

Ronan's report was more informal than Hurd's and included items from the press, telephone conversations, and letters written to the governor.[15] Most of the items were marked simply "for information," but a few bore the notation "for action." Among the latter might be those calling attention to vacancies that must be filled on the governor's nomination or perhaps appointment papers that were before the governor awaiting his signature. Sometimes the Friday Report included suggestions—for example, that the state's Washington, D.C., office submit a statement in behalf of the governor regarding certain legislation pending before Congress. Others were relatively minor concerns on which the governor might be questioned by the press corps: the loss of a child who had wandered away from a summer camp, the removal of a state police captain, the eviction of a book dealer from a store to make way for a highway, an accident involving a runaway truck in which thirteen people were injured and a church and eleven houses destroyed. But the report also included information on new social welfare facilities, new industrial developments in the state, changes in the number of state employees in various categories, progress on the construction of the Albany Mall, improvements in higher education, and federal legislation, either past or under consideration, that might affect New York State.

When Hurd began issuing the reports again in February 1971, he used a different system. He asked for a monthly report from each of forty state agencies but rotated the due date so that ten reported each week. He suggested "brief written reports concerning the activities of your department which you have not previously brought to the Governor's attention and important developing problems which may lead to future action by the Governor and concerning which it would be desirable for him to have advance warning."

The reports were supposed to be limited to three or four typewritten pages, but some commissioners could not resist the temptation to write at considerably greater length. In submitting these reports to the governor, Hurd attached a covering letter, which he called "High Lights," summarizing in a sentence or two the most important item in each commissioner's statement. Heads of agencies probably liked Hurd's approach better than Ronan's because at least the department report went unedited to the governor, although Hurd might note in his "High Lights" that a department had no important problems. The governor, who was a voracious reader of memorandums, had an opportunity to read the commissioner's full report if he desired to do so. On the other hand, Ronan's report might be of more use to the governor because it was shorter and contained less irrelevant material.

Despite this mechanism for regular oversight, the governor most often became deeply engaged in an agency's ongoing operations either because of the emergence of a major problem of administration or because of a desire to redirect agency policy and reorder priorities. Both of these circumstances often required reorganization. During the Rockefeller administration, agency reorganization occurred for several reasons.[16] In the early years, an attempt was made to restructure the entire state government "according to purpose rather than process." This attempt, only partially successful, reflected the views on organization of Rockefeller's first secretary, William Ronan, who had been a professor of public administration. In later years, reorganization relied less on theory than on pragmatic efforts to emphasize new thrusts in policy. This was the case in the creation of the Departments of Environmental Conservation and Transportation and in the lowering in status of such constituent subunits as the Department of Public Works. Even when new agencies were not created, an organizational shakeup could be used to impose new policies on old departments and to centralize highly decentralized state agencies. Finally, reorganization could be used to meet and ward off external critics of state operations. For example, the State Liquor Authority was reorganized in 1962 and the Human Rights Commission in 1967. Politically, agency restructuring gave the governor visible evidence to offer to his constituency that he had "done something" about a problem and was an especially attractive option because it could serve as a substitute for an actual expenditure of funds. But structural change was not merely symbolic, as one leading student of administration on the national level has noted: "Organizational arrangements are not neutral. We do not organize in a vacuum. Organization is one way of expressing national commitment, influencing program direction and ordering priorities. Organizational arrangements tend to give some interests, some perspectives, more effective access to those with decision-making authority."[17]

The Ronan Report

In his first annual message to the legislature on the state of the state, in January 1959, Rockefeller said: "With respect to the Executive Branch, I have initiated a study of its entire structure, with a view toward reorganization to achieve greater efficiency, economy, and improved services. There has been no such review for three decades."[18] The reorganization of the administrative structure of the executive branch was one of the primary early goals of the Rockefeller administration. It should be remembered that Rockefeller had long been interested in problems of administrative organization. At the federal level, he had chaired President Eisenhower's Committee on Government Organization. Later, the chairmanship of the Temporary State Commission to Prepare for the Constitutional Convention was his springboard to the governorship. With regard to the commission's work, Rockefeller once said that it had given him "a wonderful insight" into the needs of the state.[19]

William Ronan, newly appointed secretary to the governor, who had been staff director of the preparatory commission for the constitutional convention, was assigned the task of drafting reorganization plans. Working closely with management specialists from the Budget Division, Ronan organized a series of task forces to study various segments of the state government. He found that the number of agencies reporting to the governor had increased dramatically since the close of Smith's administration, from 65 in 1928 to 136 in 1959. Over the years a number of governing and advisory agencies also had been established, as well as temporary agencies that were continued from year to year.

The Ronan report was delivered to Governor Rockefeller in December 1959. In general, it reflected orthodox theories of public administration and was aimed at strengthening the governor's control over the administration. "Sound management principles" were guidelines for the report. Related programs, it said, should be integrated within major departments according to purpose rather than process. The number of departments should be kept small, and each department should have a single head. Department heads should be appointed by the governor, who should have an adequate management and planning staff. The governor should also be responsible for fiscal management. Specifically, the report viewed with alarm the use of the Executive Department as a catchall for new agencies. It recommended that the Executive Department be abolished and that it be replaced by six staff agencies in the governor's office, among which would be a new Office of General Services and an Office of Civil Service. The report also proposed the transfer of a number of agencies from one department to another, the creation of a Department of Municipal Affairs built around the existing Office of Local Government, and the elimination of the constitutional specification of departments by name.[20]

Some of these suggestions caused major controversy. Ronan's recommendation that the Department of Audit and Control be replaced by a "little comptroller general's office" responsible to the legislature angered Arthur Levitt, the comptroller, who headed the existing agency and was the sole Democratic official elected statewide in New York. Since abolition of the department required a constitutional amendment, Ronan advocated as an interim measure stripping Audit and Control of all but its postaudit function. This recommendation, too, enraged Levitt, and led him to denounce the entire reorganization as an unseemly power grab by the governor.[21]

The Republican attorney general, Louis Lefkowitz, was also unhappy with the report's suggestion that the Law Department, which he headed, be replaced by a Department of Justice headed by an attorney general appointed by the governor. Undoubtedly the opposition of the attorney general and the comptroller had a good deal to do with the fact that the governor did not propose the changes that were recommended in the report. He later handled the problem in a less formal way by making Lefkowitz a member of the Rockefeller team. As for Levitt, the Democratic comptroller, the governor established good working relations with his office through Hurd, the director of the budget. While Rockefeller did not succeed in muting criticism from the comptroller, especially in regard to debt management, he was able to avoid having these questions become major political issues during his tenure.[22]

When in January 1960 Rockefeller presented to the legislature proposals based on the Ronan report, they were much more limited in scope. The number of state agencies reporting directly to the governor's office was left at ninety-one, whereas the report suggested forty-one. One constitutional change that was suggested and later approved by the legislature and the voters deleted the names of the departments from the basic document but left the number of state departments at twenty. This gave the governor greater flexibility in later reorganizations. Most of the other changes were minor, and even then the legislature refused to accept some of them. Legislative leaders were angered by the fact that they had been confronted with a *fait accompli* in the Ronan report. They had not participated in the various task forces and they charged that the governor was attempting to reduce them to rubber stamps. Ronan, as director of the task forces, was a particular target for the lawmakers, who referred to him sarcastically as "the professor."

Thus Rockefeller learned that, however sound the principles of administration might be, massive reorganization was not possible. Every proposed change involved reshuffling political power and patronage. Sweeping reorganization broadened the base of opposition to any change. The problem had to be tackled piecemeal. And indeed, there were already means at hand that would strengthen the governor's power if they were properly used.

Reorganization to Symbolize Change and Redirect Policy

In 1961 the constitutional amendment deleting the names of the departments permitted the governor to recommend to the legislature the creation of new departments through reorganization. In 1967, as part of an overall transportation package, Rockefeller sought the creation of a Department of Transportation. In 1970 he suggested the establishment of a Department of Environmental Conservation. The new Department of Transportation, constructed largely from the existing Department of Public Works, was to symbolize the state's movement from a highway-oriented policy to one stressing integrated transportation planning with a major role for mass transit. The new Department of Environmental Conservation, created from major parts of four state departments and minor segments of several other agencies, was to symbolize, in an election year, New York's involvement in the environmental movement. The creation of each of these agencies was a major political move by the governor and one through which he sought to shake up organization to redirect policy. He met with mixed success.

The Department of Public Works had been primarily concerned with highway construction and maintenance. Early in the Rockefeller period it had lost its role in the design, operation, and maintenance of public buildings to the Office of General Services. It still was responsible for the maintenance of the state's canal system, but this program was dwarfed by its highway functions. The department was a classic example of the closed bureaucracy.[23] Most of the top positions were filled by promotion from within, and, aside from clerical employees, civil engineers filled all but a few of the professional posts. The governor's office had long felt that engineering problems were the main concern of the department and that little attention was being given to the social and economic effects of new highway construction or to how highways related to other modes of transportation. Indeed, in 1960 a transportation office was established in the Executive Department to deal with problems of mass transit not addressed elsewhere in state government.

The reorganization and renaming of the department entailed considerable reshuffling and the addition of airport-related responsibilities from the Commerce Department, but the retention by the governor of the long-time commissioner of public works, J. Burch McMorran, as the top man in the new agency worked against major change. McMorran kept his old staff, many of whom had opposed the

reorganization, in top positions. The statewide master plan for transportation, submitted by this leadership in 1969, was heavily highway
oriented. It was damned with faint praise by the state Office for
Planning Services and "released" but not "approved" by the governor, who requested a revision by December 1972.[24]

In 1970, in conjunction with a reorganization of the Public Service
Commission, the Department of Transportation was given responsibility for the regulation of railroads, trucks, buses, and other private
carriers, but the major responsibility for operating mass transit remained with the Metropolitan Transportation Authority and other
emerging regional transportation authorities that the state agency did
not regulate. The overwhelming preponderance of Department of
Transportation resources and personnel were still devoted to highway work. A new master plan was released in 1973. It included a
twenty-year projection. Prepared under General T. W. Parker, new
commissioner of transportation, and his successor, Raymond
Schuler, it heavily emphasized urban mass transit needs and
suggested no new major roads. This plan was accepted by the governor, though its implementation was severely limited by the defeat of
the $3.5 billion transportation bond issue in November 1973.[25]

In transportation, Rockefeller's reorganization did not immediately
result in policy changes. Its redirection came only with time, as the
leadership and political circumstances changed. Rockefeller's experience here was in accord with the general findings of students of
public administration. As one scholar concluded, after a review of
twelve cases of reorganization at three levels of government: "Reorganizations which tend to involve substantial changes in behavior
and human relationships are slow and time-taking.... In most...
that had any significant effect the process ... of change went on over
a number of years."[26] Thus the governor learned that reorganization could not bring about the quick and dramatic changes he desired,
at least without the infusion of new leadership. This was a lesson
he applied in the area of environmental conservation.

Though serious consideration was first given to the creation of a
Department of Environmental Conservation in 1968, it was not until
late in November 1969 that Governor Rockefeller approved, with
some changes, a proposal for a "department of ecology."[27] With a
gubernatorial election year approaching, the governor saw in this
proposal an opportunity to have New York take the lead among the
states in identifying with a popular issue of increasing importance. As
indicated in the proposal finally sent to the legislature, the respon-

sibilities of the proposed department included all the functions of the old Conservation Department except parks and recreation (which were to be located in a new Executive Department office), all the functions of the Water Resources Commission, the environmental-health functions of the Health Department, the pest-control activities of Agriculture and Markets, and minor activities from several other departments. The Department of Environmental Conservation was to be responsible for development of a state plan for the development, use, and conservation of natural resources and would be charged with formulation and enforcement of antipollution and noise-control policy and with maintenance of a "natural and historical preserve."[28]

The quickness with which the proposal for a Department of Environmental Conservation (DEC) emerged from the governor's office caught prospective opponents by surprise. Health Commissioner Hollis Ingraham did not even know he was going to lose part of his agency until December 1969, and by that time the decision in the governor's office to go ahead was final. Nevertheless, the core of opposition that did emerge was located in Ingraham's department and in the Conservation Department, headed by R. Stewart Kilborne. County health officials, who were receiving state aid from the Health Department for certain antipollution activities, were concerned that they might suffer financially if control of these funds were transferred from Health—"their" agency in Albany—to a new department. Opposition from this source was eliminated fairly effectively, however, by assurances that no county's funds would be reduced as a result of the restructuring. Sportsmen feared that "their" commissioner would in effect be demoted a step and that hunting, fishing, and camping interests would take second place behind urban-oriented pollution-control activities in the new department.[29] In joint legislative hearings on the reorganization bill, Kilborne and representatives of the New York Conservation Council urged that no hasty action be taken and that full consideration be given to all problems involved and all possible consequences.[30]

But in the governor's office there was concern that delay would give the bill's opponents time to organize further and block action during the 1970 legislative session. Moreover, there was, at various places within the administration, an impressive supporting coalition for the governor's plan. The Office of Planning Coordination had long favored something like this; it was consistent with the idea of functionally integrated planning. Alton G. Marshall, secretary to the governor, was a strong supporter. Laurance Rockefeller reportedly wanted parks and recreation in a separate office directly under the governor, rather than subordinate to the conservation commissioner. There was increasing support for such a change from the urban-oriented and rapidly growing "recreation profession." Even in the Health Department, environmental health personnel, mostly sanitary engineers who had long felt subordinated by agency medical chiefs, supported the plan.[31]

Swept along by the national tide of environmental concern, the legislature passed the bill with little debate in February 1970. But for two reasons, there was a very short lead time left for implementation of this mandate. First, Rockefeller wanted to get something concrete going by the time his campaign for reelection got under way in the fall of 1970. Second, he wanted to get major organizational decisions made before the groups that had opposed the reorganization at the legislative stage had a chance to exert pressure at the implementation stage. It was reported, for example, that certain industrial interests in the state were pressing for strong representation of a sportsman-oriented point of view in the agency, so as to keep the pollution-control people in second place, as they had been in Health.[32]

Rockefeller, applying the experience gained in the Transportation reorganization, appointed a new commissioner, Henry Diamond, to get the new agency moving. Diamond, a long-time associate of Laurance Rockefeller in conservation work, was given unusually broad discretion in organizing the Department of Environmental Conservation (DEC) by the enabling legislation, but also faced unusually serious organizational problems. The agency took over some of the field operations of eleven other agencies, all of which had different interests, different geographic structures, different procedures, and different lines of communication.

In July 1971, after a six-month study done under the direction of his deputy, E. Stanley Legg, a former budget official recruited from the Office of General Services, Diamond implemented a reorganization that divided the state into ten conservation regions. The reorganization blueprint, intentionally called an "interim plan," set out an ultimate goal of parallel organization for each of the regions, but recognized that movement toward this goal would be gradual. Regional directors were recruited internally, with the prime criterion for appointment being the individual's ability to command the respect of his peers in the area. Thus no single activity or profession within the department came to dominate the field structure, and many of the "natural leaders" of the environmental movement in the field were co-opted for the reorganization. Nevertheless, progress toward an integrated agency with a new ethos was slow, with internal rivalries remaining, especially in the central offices in Albany, between departmental subunits and their supporting constituencies. Again the lesson was that, to be effective, reorganization required a major commitment and constant reinforcement over time by the commissioner and his chief aides.

Reorganization to Enhance Internal Control: The Feudal Baronies

Less dramatic than the creation of new departments, internal reorganization of state agencies during the Rockefeller years was often undertaken to centralize power in the hands of commissioners responsible to the governor. Though the organization chart of the New York State government presented a more symmetrical pyramid leading up to the governor's office than those for most other states, the actual day-to-day management of some agencies was in the hands of district officers who ran their fiefs like feudal baronies. Superintendents of state mental institutions, district public works officers, and park superintendents, among others, awarded contracts, hired personnel, and determined policies with little control from departmental headquarters in Albany.

State regional offices and institutions were often at the center of a complex web of local political and administrative relationships that made them highly resistant to central direction. Local autonomy, dating from a time when problems of communication and distance made central direction impracticable, was reinforced by the patronage opportunities it offered to county political leaders and state legislators. In some rural counties, heavily dependent on state employment, this patronage was the keystone of Republican power.

Organized as a loosely knit collection of formerly independent institutions in 1927, the Department of Mental Hygiene in 1959 operated nineteen hospitals for the mentally ill, nine schools for the retarded, and the Craig Colony for Epileptics. New York's rate of hospitalization for mental illness in the mid-1950s was more than double that for the rest of the country, and its hospitalized population (93,000 in 1955) was twice the size of that in any other state. Further, perhaps because they had been established very early, New York's hospitals were much larger than those in any other state, each housing up to 14,000 patients at a time when excessive size was regarded by mental health professionals as a major evil.[33]

New York State law charges the commissioner of mental hygiene with the care and treatment of "the mentally ill, the mentally retarded, and the epileptic." For generations state authorities had chosen to give this mandate a minimal, residual interpretation, limiting state efforts on behalf of the disturbed and the retarded to those persons who were not attended to by other agencies and who received little from the state aside from what was necessary to keep them out of harm's way. As a consequence, the Department of Mental Hygiene found itself providing custodial care for a large, semipermanent, and growing population of institutional inmates. In the state hospitals and schools for the retarded were not only the hopelessly insane and uneducable but also the senile, the addicted, the impoverished neurotic, the brain-damaged, and the alcoholic. This vast array of persons had little in common except their inability to survive elsewhere and their fate of long-term isolation and neglect.

Paralleling national trends, substantial efforts had been made to change this situation during Governor Harriman's administration. Under the Community Mental Health Services Act, passed in 1954, the state sought to encourage the development of effective community-run treatment facilities by reimbursing local governments for 50 percent of their costs. Under the leadership of Dr. Paul Hoch, commissioner of mental hygiene in the late 1950s, an effort was made to convert the state hospitals into "therapeutic communities," providing an environment that was more pleasant and conducive to treatment. The introduction of tranquilizing drugs allowed the department to take the bars off the windows and the locks off the doors, so that the patients might move freely about the hospital grounds. A further attempt to reduce the coercive nature of confinement appeared in Dr. Hoch's proposal to base admission on a medically determined need for hospitalization.[34]

The first seven years of the Rockefeller administration produced only limited gains in the effectiveness of the mental health services offered by the state. Through 1965, the number of residents in the state's institutions had been only marginally reduced, the local-services program had produced no effect on the admissions rate, and the plans to modernize the hospitals themselves had languished. While the use of tranquilizers had allowed other states to reduce patient population by up to 30 percent between 1955 and 1965, New York managed only a 9.4 percent decrease in the same period. The fact that even heavily urban states had done substantially better suggests that New York's Department of Mental Hygiene lacked the ability to manage its own operations efficiently enough to take full advantage of therapeutic innovations.

In fact, there was very little power exercised in departmental offices in Albany. Each mental hospital in the state system was headed by a director, invariably a psychiatrist, who appointed employees. With resident patient populations ranging from 1,900 to 14,000, each institution was operated as an independent community. Hospital employees baked bread, made and laundered staff and patient uniforms, and generally supplied the services needed to maintain the institution. Because the hospitals were major employers and major purchasers in their respective communities, directors were often able to establish close ties with local officials and with state legislators from the area.[35]

By contrast, the central departmental offices were meagerly staffed; only 715 of the agency's approximately 41,000 employees worked there. For example, the central office of the Mental Retardation unit, responsible for supervising nine schools employing more than 8,000 persons, had only two staff members. Other divisions with broad supervisory responsibilities were similarly understaffed. With the possible exception of the commissioner and his immediate aides, no unit was responsible for supervising all activities or for developing an overall program of treatment. In addition, the top posts in the department traditionally had been filled from the ranks of hospital directors.[36]

In light of these circumstances, it is hardly surprising that the central office was largely limited to the more technical aspects of administration. Departmental budgets, for example, were for the most part simply a consolidation of the budgets submitted by the directors of the various hospitals and their financial officers.

There were some exceptions to this generalization in the area of treatment practices. In 1955, drug therapy was established as an official departmental policy for all hospitals. Several new programs also resulted from central office initiative. Intensive treatment, at first limited to new admissions, was later extended to geriatric patients and to chronic schizophrenics. An open-door policy modeled on the British system of the therapeutic community was begun in 1958, with each hospital allowed to set its own pace of involvement.[37] To the extent that these programs represented systemwide initiatives from the central office, they were significant departures from decentralized policy making. None of these programs, however, challenged the directors' authority within their own hospitals, particularly with regard to such matters as budget making and personnel. Consequently, the actual operation of most of these programs depended to a considerable extent on the degree to which they were supported by the directors.

An attempted reorganization in 1963 failed to redress the balance of power in the department. The Department of Mental Hygiene's organizational inadequacies became glaringly obvious when it was asked to implement a massive program of capital construction conceived in the governor's office. In the latter part of 1963 the legislature, after some debate and modification, approved the governor's proposal to establish a Mental Health Facilities Improvement Fund in order to finance this capital construction. The fund was authorized to issue bonds, secured by patients' fees. This independent authority would bypass such state bureaucracies as the Budget Division and the Department of Public Works, which were thought to be obstacles to the quick construction of badly needed facilities.[38] Thus the problem of financing, long a roadblock, was solved.

The department, however, lacking a comprehensive program for treatment, could not provide specifics on what facilities should be built and where they should be located. Dr. Hoch's death in the fall of 1964 and vacancies in other top positions in the department made the situation even more difficult. Ad hoc arrangements were made to fill the gaps, but the experience convinced the governor's office of the need to strengthen the central office.[39]

After a nationwide search, a new commissioner, Dr. Alan Miller, was appointed in 1966. The selection of Miller, who had worked in the National Institute of Mental Health and then had served as the New York department's director of local services, was a break with the tradition of selecting a hospital director to head the department. The new commissioner, a relatively young man identified with the community mental health movement, soon gathered around him associates with similar commitments from outside New York.

With the cooperation of the state Budget Division and the support of the governor's office, Miller wrote a reorganization plan designed to strengthen the central office.[40] The functional organization of such staff services as nursing, physical medicine, and social services was abolished and operations were divided among three divisions: Mental Health, Mental Retardation, and Local Services. The creation of a separate Division of Mental Retardation was a compromise response to pressures being brought by the New York State Association for Retarded Children, which felt that its interests were being ignored in the Department of Mental Hygiene. In 1965 and 1966, the association found support in Senator Robert Kennedy and State Senator Harry Kraf, chairman of the Joint Legislative Committee on Mental Retardation. The staff at the deputy, associate, and assistant commissioner levels was almost doubled.

The plan was written quickly and in relative secrecy, and Miller presented it as a *fait accompli* at a quarterly meeting of the hospital directors. Consequently, the directors were unable to mobilize their considerable political resources against this move to reduce their autonomy. Nevertheless, they were able to block legislation that would have shifted the power to appoint personnel from the individual directors to the commissioner.[41]

With his reorganized structure in place, Miller sought to implement programs to reduce the patient population and reform the custodial approach to treatment at the large state hospitals. Under the "unitization" program, a system of multidisciplinary teams was organized for each therapeutic unit within each hospital. Unitization, implemented gradually and over the objections of most old-line hospital directors, helped meet the shortage of psychiatrists by giving other specialists clinical authority. Regional program analysts, new officials through whom hospital budgets now had to be submitted, provided a link between these institutions and the central office and oversaw the introduction of this new program.[42]

Unitization and the introduction of geriatric screening in 1968, despite much political pressure against it, dramatically improved the DMH discharge rate. In 1969, as the new programs were implemented across the state hospital system, the admissions rate, which had risen steadily for over sixty years, began to decline. Between 1968 and 1974 the patient population in state institutions dropped from 78,000 to 36,000.[43]

Though defeated on several organizational matters in the late 1960s, the directors of individual institutions remained a strong force in the Department of Mental Hygiene. In 1970 the central office attempted to recodify the mental health law and strengthen the administrative and regulatory powers of the commissioner of mental hygiene. The directors of the state hospitals and schools, who had joined together in 1968 to create the New York State Branch of the Association of Medical Superintendents of Mental Hospitals, vigorously opposed this effort and in the end retained the power to hire personnel locally. The recodification effort suffered generally from concessions made to special interests in various parts of the agency's constituency. The commissioner lacked a broad political base, for though there was organized support for programs designed for subgroups served by the Department of Mental Hygiene— alcoholics and the mentally retarded, for example—there was little support for the agency as a whole.[44]

Nevertheless, the attempt to reorganize the department had some successes. Some control of hospital spending was obtained through a central budget system. Centralization of purchasing and nutrition meant better and more nutritious food for patients. New hospitals were better designed—less like fortresses and more like hospitals— and more quickly constructed. These were remarkable achievements. Even if feudal baronies continued to exist, they were not so independent as they had been and were better managed.

The major change, however, was in the treatment programs and the shift from long-time custodial care to intensive treatment and early release. Another aspect of the new policy was the refusal to accept elderly senile patients on the ground that incarceration in a mental hospital would only make their condition worse. Both of these policy changes were regarded as highly progressive by professionals but they soon led to new problems.

Under the early-release program patients usually were expected to receive continued treatment in outpatient clinics. Senile oldsters unable to care for themselves would be placed in nursing homes. Unfortunately, local governments and private groups were slow to develop clinics under the Community Mental Health and Retardation Act of 1963. The Department of Mental Hygiene's attention was more concentrated on hospital treatment than on local mental health centers. Nor was there an adequate number of nonprofit nursing homes for senile patients. To meet the demand, hundreds of proprietary nursing homes were opened, all too frequently by persons more concerned with making a fast buck than with providing adequate services. The state Department of Health had the responsibility for inspecting and regulating nursing homes but it was slow to perceive the extent of the problem. While it did request funds for additional inspectors from the Budget Division, it did not make the case in strong terms. In fact, it had a reputation among budget officers for not requesting increased funds.

Moreover, when the Health Department found conditions in a proprietary nursing home poor, it was reluctant to close the home because alternative facilities were not available. To be sure, there should have been better coordination between the Department of Mental Hygiene and the Health Department, and program coordination certainly was a responsibility of the governor's office, particularly of the secretary to the governor, but unfortunately the problems did not receive sufficient attention. The helter-skelter growth of nursing homes inadequately monitored by the state was accompanied by massive fraud and shocking patient neglect.

Of the 31,000 patients discharged from state mental hospitals in 1973, 14,000 were living in New York City in proprietary nursing homes or single-room occupancy hotels. Critics charged that though the Department of Mental Hygiene based its program on community treatment, it had devoted insufficient resources to building small community facilities and thus had endangered the whole concept.[45]

Commissioner Miller resigned amid a storm of protest in late 1974, and the new Democratic governor, Hugh Carey, promised a "sweeping overhaul" of his department. Pressure groups interested in mental retardation renewed their efforts for the creation of a separate department. Complaints of the Coalition of Voluntary Mental Health and Mental Retardation Agencies about the veto power of the directors of state mental institutions over local programs and their monopolization of available resources, as well as a demand for meaningful power in the planning stages, indicated that the power of the directors in the department, though diminished, was not broken. Institutional reform aimed at solving old problems had led to new and equally intractable ones.[46]

The centralization of authority over the state parks, though at first as difficult as in mental health, was ultimately more successful. Parks in New York State were administered for almost half a century through a structure designed to place them outside of gubernatorial control.[47] In 1924, Robert Moses, in drawing up the bill formally creating a State Council of Parks to coordinate diverse small, independent park agencies, made the council theoretically responsible to the commissioner of conservation. Actually, however, all budgetary and policy-making power for parks was placed in the state council and eight regional commissions. The council was made up largely of regional commission chairmen, who served for terms longer than that of the governor and were removable only for cause. Moses used his power as chairman of the state council and president of the Long Island State Park Commission to dominate parks policy in New York State from 1924 to 1966, a period that spanned the terms of seven governors.

When Rockefeller came to power, Robert Moses, entrenched in a variety of state and city posts, resisted any reorganization of the parks that would threaten his hold on them. In 1960 the Ronan report suggested that authority over parks be taken from the council and given "in fact as well as theory to the Department of Conservation." Moses's open opposition was enough to scuttle the plan. Rockefeller abandoned it in his final reorganization request to the legislature, and in a personal letter assured Moses of his continued support.

In 1966 Moses was finally deposed. Rockefeller appointed his brother Laurance, who had been vice chairman, to the chairmanship of the State Council of Parks.[48] Laurance Rockefeller, like Moses, had long been a dominant figure in parks policy, his power enhanced by his personal relationship to the governor. With the transition, the commissioner of parks and recreation remained relatively powerless. Unlike Moses, however, Laurance Rockefeller was unable to affect the local power bases of the eleven regional commissions. Park policy in New York State thus became the product of negotiations and compromises between Rockefeller and the regional commissions. When agreement was reached among them, success in establishing a policy was reasonably assured. The governor followed the lead of his brother, and the legislature, faced with the endorsement of the governor and locally powerful regional commissions, usually complied.

The reorganization of 1970, which created the Department of Environmental Conservation, transferred the Division of Parks and Recreation, formerly in the Conservation Department, to the Executive Department (where it became the Office of Parks and Recreation). This change, however, did little to alter the power relationships among the commissioner, the council, and the council chairman. The commissioner of parks, Sal J. Prezioso, attempted—and usually failed—to establish central control over finances, budgeting, personnel, and standards. One of his techniques was the use of budgets based on programs rather than regions. Regional commissions, however, jealous of their independence, resisted Prezioso's attempt to reallocate resources among regions.

With his brother Laurance rather than the recalcitrant Robert Moses as chairman of the Council of Parks, the governor was finally able to make sweeping changes in the organization of the state parks agency in 1972.[49] In a series of four laws, all operating authority was taken from the state council and the regional commissions and given to the commissioner of parks. In each region, the commission retained the right to issue rules and regulations concerning the parks, but day-to-day control of the operation of all state parks (with the exception of the Adirondack preserve, which was to be administered by the Department of Environmental Protection) was centralized in the hands of the commissioner and his staff in Albany. Two leadership changes symbolized this change in power relationships. In 1972 Alexander Aldrich, the governor's cousin, became parks commissioner, and early in 1973 Laurance Rockefeller stepped down as council chairman.

Reorganization to Defuse Political Criticism

For the governor, reorganization was also useful as a tool of partisan politics. By changing an agency's structure he could take potential issues away from the opposition before they became major liabilities. Through the same means, he could demonstrate responsiveness to public criticism and could deal with less visible concerns that were potentially explosive. The manner in which Rockefeller dealt with problems in three multiheaded agencies—the Division of Alcoholic Beverage Control, the Human Rights Commission, and the Public Service Commission—demonstrated his use of reorganization to avoid or minimize political liabilities. Integral to his approach in two of these three cases was the use of study commissions to buy time and develop policy options.

In 1962 the New York State political scene was jolted by revelations of corruption in the Division of Alcoholic Beverage Control (DABC). Graft had been a chronic problem in DABC, but this case was more serious than any that had preceded it. The chairman of the State Liquor Authority, Martin Epstein, was indicted, as was Judge Melvin Osterman of the Court of Claims. Governor Rockefeller forced the resignation of one of his closest political associates, State Republican Chairman L. Judson Morhouse, when Morhouse refused to testify in the case without being granted immunity from prosecution.[50] He was later convicted and imprisoned.

The governor's initial response to the scandal was to appoint two groups to study the problems that gave rise to it. In September 1962 he appointed a Moreland Commission to study the adequacy of the state's Alcoholic Beverage Control Law (ABC Law) and DABC's enforcement procedures. (The Moreland Act, passed in 1906, empowered the governor to appoint a commission with broad investigative powers to look into the operations of a state agency.) He chose Lawrence E. Walsh, a retired federal judge, as chairman, along with William C. Warren, dean of the Columbia University School of Law, and Manly Fleischmann, a Buffalo attorney. Then, in January 1963, he ordered a study by the Budget Division of the organization and management of the DABC. The two studies were completed in December 1963.

The state's liquor-control system at the time consisted of the State Liquor Authority (SLA), a five-man commission appointed by the governor, not more than three of whose members could be members of one political party; the DABC central offices, which were largely a paper organization, virtually indistinguishable from the New York City zone office; three zone offices (New York City, Albany, and Buffalo), each headed by a deputy commissioner and largely autonomous; and fifty-eight local alcoholic beverage control boards, one in New York City and one in each of the fifty-seven other counties, theoretically responsible for the investigation and evaluation of license applicants but in reality doing very little outside New York City and Erie County.[51]

The Budget study, initiated by Rockefeller in January 1963, focused on administrative operation. It concluded:

> Development of a responsible, responsive, and effective liquor control organization requires radical changes in the administrative framework established by the ABC Law, overhauling of an antiquated and ineffective field organization, and creation of an adequately compensated, well-trained and professional career service. Any steps short of this approach will invite a repetition of the situation which has needlessly sacrificed a large measure of the public's confidence in liquor control administration.[52]

One of the study's findings was that inefficiency in processing applications led to long delays, which in turn brought on corruption. Since applicants for licenses had frequently invested substantial sums in their prospective operations, delay could prove costly. Applicants were thus open to temptation from influence peddlers who promised to use their connections to get prompt and favorable action. In addition, the Budget Division report recommended major organizational changes.[53]

In contrast to the Budget Division group, the Moreland Commission focused on needed legislation. Summarizing its findings, Governor Rockefeller said that "most of the controls and regulations [on the sale of liquor] piled up under the law through the years have in practice defied objectivity, encouraged corruption, added nothing to promote temperance, and have served to [encourage] public disrespect for law. . . . The liquor industry has acquired a dominant hold in a field properly regarded as one requiring public regulation. . . . It is contrary to the public interest to have the regulated industry in such a dominant role."[54]

The commission recommended that tavern licenses be established as a separate category from restaurant licenses, and that the food requirement for the former be drastically reduced. It called for repeal of the distance requirement and an end to the moratorium in granting new licenses, so that anyone who met the requirements of the law concerning character, absence of a criminal record, and financial resources could be granted a license. It was further suggested that licenses be granted to retail establishments engaged in the sale of nonalcoholic items (for example, supermarkets and department stores), provided that the alcoholic beverages be sold in physically separate areas of those stores and that package stores be allowed to sell soda and other mixers as well as wines and liquor. Finally, the commission recommended complete repeal of the ABC Law's price-fixing provisions, allowing free competition among retailers.[55] The recommendations were strongly endorsed by the governor and became the heart of a liquor reform package that he sought to push through the legislature. In taking this course, Rockefeller failed to focus on structural changes in the SLA recommended by the Budget Division, and these were left by the wayside.

In a major legislative battle, Rockefeller was at first defeated in the regular session after a massive lobbying effort by the liquor industry. Returning to the fray, he called a special session and gained partial acceptance of his liquor-reform program.[56] In light of the intense opposition that Moreland Commission proposals engendered within his own party, it is not surprising that the Budget Division ideas for reorganization were not pressed by the governor. They would have added the county leaders to the coalition opposing him. The local board system, which the Budget Division would have abolished, provided considerable patronage. Board members were salaried but did very little work. Just as political considerations dictated that administrative reform be undertaken, after the issue cooled political considerations contributed to limiting this reform.

The basic defects in the Division of Alcoholic Beverage Control's organization that led to the 1962 scandal were never really corrected. An internal inspection and audit system never got off the ground. Long delays and seemingly arbitrary decisions still plagued the agency. The clarification of the chairman's executive responsibility at first overloaded him with administrative duties, although this situation was later corrected through shifting some of the work to the executive officer. A series of articles in the *New York Daily News* in 1970 indicated that cooperation between the division and local police was still lacking. A member of the SLA agreed that the delay in granting new licenses had not been solved and that it still provided opportunities for influence peddlers.[57]

The Human Rights Commission, charged with protecting minority rights in employment and housing, was another agency that was reorganized to defuse political criticism. It had long been known that the agency was having organizational difficulties. In the words of then Budget Director T. Norman Hurd, "changes would be desirable." One of Hurd's subordinates stated it more plainly when he said: "Everybody from the governor on down knew the thing was screwed up."[58] The agency was seriously crippled by personal conflicts among the commissioners. In 1965 its chairman, George H. Fowler, and a rump group of commissioners submitted two totally different budget requests, and in one closed session Fowler and one of his colleagues reportedly traded punches. The civil service classification system was neglected and chaotic. Hiring practices were haphazard. A consultant, paid by the commission to plan implementation of the legislature's 1965 authorization of a unit that could initiate antidiscrimination action without waiting for individual complaints, had produced nothing by 1967.[59] The governor's office initiated no change, however, until the commission's difficulties began to be discussed prominently in the daily press.

On February 4, 1967, the directors of the New York State Conference of the NAACP voted to support a bill sponsored by Senator William Thompson of Brooklyn, aimed at restructuring the commission in order to eliminate lengthy delays in the processing of complaints. Explaining the directors' position to the press, Conference President Eugene T. Reed charged that the racial situation in the state was "more critical and more serious than at any time since the Civil War."[60] A few weeks later the NAACP effort gained support from the Long Island Council for Integrated Housing. Jesse Hentzow, council chairman, urged Rockefeller to dismiss and replace all nine commissioners, and said: "We've got the best housing laws on the books and the worse commission. . . . [It] completely fails to function as a law enforcement agency."[61] About two weeks later, Senators Thompson and Basil A. Paterson, in a symbolic action showing black disaffection, sought to have $1.2 million budgeted for the commission transferred to a fund for assistance to poverty-area students at the City University. Their amendment was defeated on a voice vote.[62]

The protest against the commission that led to action by the governor's office was the threat by Roderick Stephens, Jr., and others to resign en masse from the commission's New York City Advisory Council. The council members charged that Chairman Fowler had ignored them completely. Rockefeller thereupon ordered the Budget Division to undertake a thorough study of the commission and its operations.[63]

Working with civil rights groups, local human rights agencies, and state officials, the budget team substantiated the major charges made against the commission.[64] Personal differences among its members had seriously disrupted administration; delays were serious and discouraged recourse to the commission; there was no machinery to ensure compliance with its rulings; the arrangement under which each commissioner was in charge of a regional office prevented coordination and policy consistency; there were no consistent standards for staffing; and the chairman had ignored the advisory councils.

The report of the budget group recommended a series of changes in the commission's organization and operations: establishing the post of executive director to relieve the chairman of administrative responsibilities; placing regional directors, rather than commissioners, in charge of regional offices; restricting the commissioners' role to hearing appeals and reviewing policies; establishing procedural controls to assure quick receipt and disposition of cases; and improving relations with local agencies and advisory groups.

In the case of the State Liquor Authority, the Budget Division management study, and the more public Moreland Commission study of legislative change went forward simultaneously. In the case of the Human Rights Commission, Budget Division recommendations led the governor to appoint a prestigious public commission to study a revision of the law and prepare informed public opinion for such a revision. The twenty-three-member commission, appointed in August 1967, was chaired by Eli Whitney Debevoise. It was broadly representative of the civil rights establishment in the state and was asked by the governor to report by December, in time for the 1968 legislative session. Earlier, in June, Rockefeller had cleared the ground for the commission's work by implementing many of the Budget Division's proposals that did not require legislation, and by replacing Commissioner Fowler with Robert Mangum, a Democrat.

The Debevoise committee did, indeed, draw up proposals for sweeping changes in the antidiscrimination laws. They were so sweeping, in fact, that the governor's staff was convinced that few of them stood much chance of passage by the legislature. In early 1968, the governor's counsel and members of the committee, after some negotiation, agreed on a set of eleven separate bills. At a news conference in March 1968, Rockefeller unveiled the proposals and endorsed them "very enthusiastically." He pointed out as "most significant" the proposed abolition of the commission and its replacement by a single executive.[65]

The seven incumbent commissioners who would lose their positions (there was one vacancy) were unanimously opposed to abolishing the commission, but the change was supported by a coalition of sixty-one rights groups from around the state. As it turned out, this was the only bill of the eleven that was passed by the legislature,[66] much to the dismay of some agency staff, who believed that, without more legislative change, organizational change was meaningless. In the case of the State Liquor Authority, political factors had allowed some legislative change but had blocked reorganization. In the case of the Human Rights Commission (later called the State Commission against Discrimination), the same factors had allowed reorganization but not an increase in agency powers. In both cases, the governor's hierarchy of priorities in pressing for some ends and compromising on others was decisive.

While reorganization was a means by which Rockefeller could respond to public criticism, it was also one by which he could anticipate such criticism and turn it to his own advantage. Through much of the Rockefeller period, the Public Service Commission (PSC) was a little-known state utilities regulatory agency and its five commissionerships were safe havens for fortunate and faithful Republicans. Then, in the late 1960s, increasing concern for the environment, service failures by the New York Telephone Company and Consolidated Edison, and rapidly rising electrical rates brought the agency to center stage. In February 1969, Assemblyman Albert Blumenthal, a Democrat and chairman of the Joint Legislative Committee on Consumer Protection, called the PSC "a fiasco" and suggested a series of reforms. The attack from the legislature became bipartisan later that year when Thomas F. McGowan, Republican chairman of the Senate Committee on Public Utilities, called for a "reorganization and beefing up" of the agency.[67]

Anticipating that the Public Service Commission might become a difficult issue for him in his 1970 reelection bid, the governor put his staff to work on the problem. The result was a series of bills that became part of his 1970 legislative program.[68] The PSC was turned into a bipartisan agency, and consumer groups were given a voice in rate hearings. Terms of the commissioners were reduced from ten to six years, and executive power was centralized in the hands of the chairman, who was to serve in that capacity at the pleasure of the governor. While these bills were still before the legislature, the governor recruited Joseph Swidler, a Democrat and former head of the Federal Power Commission, to be the agency's first chairman under its new structure.[69]

By his rapid action, Rockefeller took the PSC issue away from the Democrats. Instead of having to defend himself in the 1970 campaign against charges concerning the agency's shortcomings, he could now point to its revitalization as an achievement of his administration. At the same time, the reorganization had the added advantage, from the governor's point of view, of bringing the chairman, who had formerly served for a fixed term, more firmly under the control of the chief executive.

Crisis Management: Attica and Prison Reform

In the early-morning hours of September 9, 1971, inmates at New York State's prison at Attica took control of cell block A and seized thirty-nine guards as hostages.[70] After five days of negotiation between Russell Oswald, commissioner of corrections for the state, and a prisoner negotiating committee failed to effect release of the hostages, Governor Rockefeller ordered an assault on the prison by the state police. In the assault nine hostages and thirty-one prisoners died. Other deaths brought the total number of casualties to forty-three.

The decision to regain control of Attica prison by force was the most controversial one in Rockefeller's career as governor. Defended by him as a step to block "the start of anarchy" and the attendant "loss of all the values we cherish as a nation" and attacked as demonstrating his insensitivity to the value of human life and the underlying racism in American society, Rockefeller's actions during the Attica crisis became central to the popular perception of his term as governor.[71] Unlike any other major decisions made by the governor, those taken with regard to Attica were crisis decisions. Unfolding events forced the governor's hand. There was little time for staffwork, little opportunity to shape the decision context, no time to prepare. Thus, more than most of Rockefeller's decisions, those made during the five days of the Attica disturbances revealed his personal style and the underlying values that developed as he served as governor.

As the inmate population in New York State prisons became increasingly black and Puerto Rican over the two decades before 1971, the already tense relationship between prisoners and correction officers—primarily white—became complicated by racial differences. Although the Corrections Department had endeavored to recruit guards from minority groups, it had not been very successful because few blacks and Puerto Ricans were willing to live in an all-white rural community such as Attica.[72] These racial problems, compounded by differences in generations and cultures, led to a breakdown of communications between prisoners and staff and some apparent discrimination in prison jobs and treatment. Matters were further complicated by the emergence of militant black inmates, who believed themselves to be political prisoners and were not disposed to abide by strict rules. Prisons work only with the tacit cooperation of the prisoners; Attica officials were ill prepared to handle prisoners who refused this cooperation.

It was ironic that the Attica uprising occurred in a state penal system that was already moving toward reform. In an effort to change the state prison system's emphasis from custodial to rehabilitative care, a special commission on criminal offenders appointed by Governor Rockefeller in 1966 recommended reorganization. On January 1, 1971, the Department of Correction and the Division of Parole were consolidated into the Department of Correctional Services. The purpose of this consolidation was to achieve continuity from arrest to release. It was hoped that many persons convicted of crimes would be admitted to a work-release program after a short time in an institution.

As part of the redirection of the prison system, a nationwide search was made for a progressive new commissioner to head the department. Russell Oswald, who was highly regarded as one of the nation's leading penal administrators, was selected for the post. Upon taking office as the state's new commissioner of correctional services in January 1971, Oswald vowed to institute reform programs that would restructure the state correctional system. His first reforms included granting the news media greater access to state prisons, revising censorship rules to liberalize mail and visiting privileges for inmates, directing that more nutritional food be purchased even if a fiscal deficit resulted, providing an alternative to pork for Muslims, and generally relaxing the rules of tight discipline.

Soon after his appointment, Oswald found that, like other state services and programs, the institution of massive rehabilitative programs for the prisons was governed by the iron grip of economics. The state in 1971 was going through a major fiscal crisis. In Oswald's words, the prison system was "fiscally starved." Without money to pay additional officers, Oswald argued, prisoners could not be released from their cells for long periods, and innovative rehabilitative programs could not be expanded. Although state appropriations for correctional services increased between 1967 and 1971, most of the increase was spent on administrative overhead. In fact, the proportion of the state budget appropriated for correctional services decreased from 4.8 to 3.0 percent.[73]

Within five hours after the beginning of the Attica uprising, Commissioner Oswald was on the scene and had taken charge of the situation. The state police, using ordinary riot equipment, had succeeded in retaking half of the portion of the prison that had been closed by the rioters. It was a long-established principle among corrections officials not to negotiate during an uprising with prisoners holding hostages. But Oswald urged the governor to stop further police action and permit him to negotiate with the prisoners. Rockefeller reluctantly agreed. Later he characterized that decision as "the most serious mistake I made." He said that he should have continued steady police pressure while the situation was still fluid.

Indeed, there was ample precedent for refusing to negotiate with prisoners in revolt, even within New York State. Governor Franklin D. Roosevelt and Lieutenant Governor Herbert Lehman faced similar situations in 1929. In July of that year some 1,300 inmates at Clinton prison in Dannemora rioted and rushed the walls in an attempt to escape. Three prisoners were killed and a score wounded when the guards stormed the prison to restore order. Six days later, a similar riot at Auburn led to two deaths. In December there was another uprising at Auburn in which the chief warden was murdered, eight guards were seized as hostages, and several others were wounded. Roosevelt was out of the state at the time of the second outbreak, and Lehman was acting governor. The leaders of the revolt demanded release from prison with the promise of safe conduct and transportation elsewhere. Lehman's answer was "Impossible. As long as I am here there will be no compromise, no matter what the circumstances or what the result may be."[74] He ordered the National Guard to retake the prison, which they succeeded in doing.

During the first two days of negotiations at Attica, little progress was made. Then, at the request of the prisoners, a citizen observer committee was formed to serve as an ad hoc mediating body. The committee included, among others, U.S. Representative Herman Badillo, state Senator John Dunne, *Amsterdam News* publisher Clarence Jones, attorney William Kunstler, Black Panther leader Bobby Seale, and *New York Times* columnist Tom Wicker. With the committee's assistance the prisoners drew up a list of thirty demands for reform of the prison. After lengthy discussion Oswald agreed to twenty-eight of the thirty demands if the hostages were released and order in the prison restored. He refused, however, to promise complete amnesty from criminal prosecution, passage to a "nonimperialist country," and removal of Vincent P. Mancusi, superintendent of Attica. The prisoners' insistence on complete amnesty came one day after the death of prison guard William Quinn, who was injured by the prisoners during the takeover and died two days later at a Rochester hospital. Unconditional amnesty, therefore, was seen by the McKay commission, which later investigated the uprising, as a way in which the prisoners could avoid prosecution for the death of Quinn as well as the deaths of three prisoners placed on house arrest by inmate leaders and found murdered when the prison was retaken.

In an endeavor to break this deadlock, Commissioner Oswald and the observers' committee urged Rockefeller to come to Attica and take charge personally. Rockefeller's refusal has been a central point in the controversy concerning his handling of the situation. From Rockefeller's perspective there was little to be gained from going to Attica. His closest associates—Robert Douglass, the governor's secretary, and T. Norman Hurd, director of state administration—as well as an assistant counsel, were already at Attica. The critical point in the dispute with the prisoners was amnesty, which in Rockefeller's view was outside his constitutional authority. Also, the governor said he would not personally enter into direct negotiations with inmates holding hostages.

Tom Wicker, a member of the Attica observers' committee during the uprising, later recalled that he had urged the governor to come to the prison "so that he could see and sense *for himself* the building mood of hatred, the eagerness to shoot. . . . The governor had to come to Attica to understand the threat of bloodshed in its full dimension."[75] It has also been argued that Rockefeller's presence would at least have demonstrated concern for the lives at stake.[76] Though unsure that the governor's presence would have produced a negotiated settlement, the McKay commission later concluded that he "should not have committed the state's armed forces against the rebels without first appearing on the scene," since the "prison system was in need of major reform," a circumstance that was "a major contributing factor to the uprising."

After Rockefeller declined to go to the prison, he instructed Oswald to make a final effort at negotiating a settlement. At the second meeting between Oswald and the prisoners, eight hostages were lined up, blindfolded, and tied. An executioner held a knife at each one's throat. The prisoners refused to change their demands, nor would they release the hostages. Oswald, with the governor's concurrence, then ordered the assault. Five days had passed since the prison erupted.

Plans for dealing with prison fires and riots, however modest, had been developed by Commissioner Oswald after he took office in April 1971. In an interview with Walter Cronkite, the television newsman, Oswald said, "The plan . . . was that in any emergency of this kind, the State Police would lead the way because it is always assumed that correction officers, being embroiled in a situation such as this, might be vindictive in going in and the State Police, who are a tremendously well-disciplined group, would go in coolly." He added that "correction officers would follow behind for mop-up operations and the National Guard and local officials would be on the outside." Rockefeller did order that correction officers be excluded from the assault force because of the doubts about their ability to control their personal feelings, but this order was not implemented by the State Police or correctional supervisors.

From the description of the circumstances surrounding the assault on the prison, it appears that the tactical plan produced much crossfire that ultimately caused death and injury. Though officials at first claimed that some hostages had been killed by the prisoners, autopsies later revealed that all those who died in the assault, prisoners and hostages, had been shot by the State Police and correction officers. With regard to the hostages, the commission found that "no official, including the police commanders, believed that the hostages could be saved if the inmates were intent upon killing them." Indeed, Governor Rockefeller, who was in touch by telephone with officials at Attica during the assault, expressed amazement that so many persons emerged unharmed. The McKay commission did note, however, that "had the majority of the assault force not acted with restraint, the toll of dead and wounded would undoubtedly have been greater." The commission recommended further police training, the development of new prison riot procedures, and the development of adequate nonlethal weapons.

There were lessons to be learned from the Attica experience, and politicians in other states were quick to learn them. The rule of "no negotiations with prisoners holding hostages" was sound and should be followed. Early police action as soon as possible after a riot began, while the situation was still fluid, was important. Outside civilian negotiating committees, newsmen, and television cameras should be kept out of the prison during the rioting since they encouraged violence. Finally, the public expected the chief executive of a state or a city to be personally on the scene and take command during a crisis.

In the wake of Attica, more than two score prisoners who were charged with participating in the riot were indicted. But allegations that little attention was paid to illegal actions by police officers in the retaking of the prison caused considerable controversy and led to several state investigations. Years later the issues that arose from Attica were still being debated in New York, with considerable bitterness on both sides. Finally, in 1976, Governor Carey took action to close the book on Attica. He pardoned or commuted the sentences of inmates for actions taken during the uprising, and dropped all plans to prosecute police officers for their behavior during the retaking of the prison.[77]

Events at Attica in September 1971 made prison reform a major issue in the 1972 session of the New York State Legislature. In proposing his budget for 1973, Rockefeller exempted the Department of Correctional Services from expenditure restrictions placed on all other state agencies and, in anticipation of the report of the Select Committee on Correctional Institutions and Programs (the Jones committee), called for significant reforms in the prison system. Later, in April, Rockefeller proposed an additional $12 million for the Department of Correctional Services, $1.3 million to be spent for a "maximum program, maximum security" facility requested by the department and the rest for additional personnel and the upgrading of prison services.

As a result of this recognition of the need for change, more than 150 prison-reform bills were introduced in the legislature during the 1972 session, but only eight were passed. The most important included the governor's $12 million package of new funds, a bill authorizing short furloughs for carefully screened inmates within a year of their release date, and a measure equalizing parole eligibility for men convicted before and after penal law reform in 1967. Also the legislature passed for the first time a constitutional amendment removing the commissioner of correctional services as head of the commission of correction that was charged with overseeing the operations of the department.

The final report of the Jones committee, released in May 1973, noted that "the Department's efforts since January, 1972, . . . achieved mixed results. . . . Change which has a fundamental impact on the day-to-day existence of the inmate population remains elusive."[78] In April 1973 the Department of Correctional Services offered a $276.8 million master plan designed to diversify facilities. One prime objective of the plan was to reduce the number of prisoners held in maximum-security facilities from 80 percent to 20 percent and to establish smaller community-based facilities. Yet in that year the legislature reduced authorizations for new minimum-security, community-based facilities by $15 million, effectively killing four of six proposed centers. In addition, the legislature in the 1973 session killed a major package of prison reform measures proposed by a bipartisan group of legislators. As Attica passed into history, political commitment to prison reform began to wane. Outside of the immediate context of violence and crisis, Rockefeller found, as Franklin D. Roosevelt did in 1931, that in the scramble for state funds the legislature placed budgetary requests of the Correction Department far below state aid to local school districts, which had a much greater impact on their chances for reelection.

Conclusions

Like most other politicians, Nelson Rockefeller was clearly more interested in policy development than in ongoing administration. Political payoffs emerged from rapid and visible results that could be cited as achievements during election campaigns. Unlike many governors, however, Rockefeller delegated responsibility well. A regular information system was developed and used to keep him apprised of state operations, and an informal appeals procedure ensured that his staff would not shield him too well from commissioners who believed that they had a pressing need to see him.

Often this process, and good staff work, helped Rockefeller fend off crises before they became visible. Sometimes, however, as in the case of the nursing home problem, the underlying social consequences of decisions were not recognized and adequately dealt with. Even when timely action was taken, as in the case of prison reform and reorganization, the potential for crisis was not necessarily defused. And, as the handling of the situation at Attica demonstrated, the need to act under crisis conditions increased enormously the stakes involved in decision making and the potential for error.

In the area of reorganization, Rockefeller's early experience demonstrated that, despite public administration theory, comprehensive change through reorganization could not be achieved. The basic interests of too many actors in the administrative process—bureaucrats and their network of supporting state legislators, local leaders, and interest groups—were simultaneously challenged by such an approach. Coalitions for mutual benefit among disparate groups emerged in order to face the common threat to the status quo brought by such a comprehensive plan offered by the governor.

Even when problems were taken up one by one, because of an intra-agency difficulty or awakened gubernatorial interest, the prospects for change were uncertain. Surely, one lesson was that rapid change through reorganization was not possible. The redirection of state efforts in transportation and environmental conservation, for example, began to take hold only after Rockefeller had left office. Often, as in the case of the state Human Rights Commission, the governor was unwilling to put on the line sufficient political resources to push a total reform package through the legislature. The result was change that was sometimes more symbolic than substantive. In other cases—the State Liquor Authority, for example—agencies were able to ride through a storm of public controversy by making visible concessions that had little impact on actual day-to-day operations.

Clearly, the difficulty of change ensured that most of the time any governor's impact on the bureaucracy he headed could be only incremental. In Mental Hygiene, one of the largest state departments, attempts at reorganization did lead to some erosion of the power of the feudal baronies and, as a result, to improved treatment and more professional service delivery. But this was a struggle never completely won. In the end, the hold of local bureaucrats and politicians over the department was not broken. Nevertheless, Rockefeller's long service and constantly shifting attention did allow him to have incremental impact across almost the entire gamut of state operations. In some areas, as in Parks, where gubernatorial authority was finally established in 1972, major change was, in the end, accomplished.

6

Fiscal Policies and Financial Programs

"Tax, tax, tax, spend, spend, spend, elect, elect, elect." This is how Harry Hopkins was said to have described the strategy followed by Franklin D. Roosevelt in the first years of the New Deal.[1] If this strategy was the formula for Roosevelt's success, it provided a major lesson in politics for Nelson Rockefeller, who first entered public life as an aide to FDR. Between 1959 and 1973, the New York State legislature took eighteen separate tax actions. No other governor in this century came to his legislature with so many requests for tax increases as did Rockefeller. No other New York governor spent so freely to meet societal needs and public demands for increased services. And no other governor served so long.

The fiscal history of New York State during the Rockefeller years is, in large measure, the story of pressures that led to changes in Rockefeller's most basic assumptions about public finance. In 1959 the governor was convinced that the state could meet the needs of its people from its own resources, if only its leaders showed political courage in seeking those resources. The people of the state, Rockefeller thought, would not take political retribution on legislators who enacted tax increases if it were clearly explained to them that the money was needed to provide the public services they demanded. By the late 1960s, however, the governor became convinced that the fiscal capacity of the state had been strained to its limits and that help from the national government was needed if the federal system was to survive. From 1967 until the enactment of Federal Revenue Sharing in 1972, one of Rockefeller's highest priorities was the pursuit of large-scale federal fiscal assistance for state and local governments.

In the area of borrowing, Rockefeller began his tenure with a strong commitment to a hoary Republican principle in New York State, pay-as-you-go financing of capital improvements. This principle, inherited from the Dewey administration, became the linchpin of Rockefeller's approach to state finance, and, in part, the justification for early tax increases. Partly as a consequence of his highly visible commitment to this principle, which foreclosed politically the option of full-faith-and-credit borrowing in the manner prescribed by the state constitution, the governor sought to exploit other methods of financing capital improvements. The result was a major expansion of such devices as Public Benefit Corporation borrowing, financing through lease-purchase agreements, and the encouragement of capital improvement by local governments through state-aid guarantees. Ultimately, Rockefeller chose to abandon pay-as-you-go and, with mixed success, sought voter approval for massive bond issues in the policy areas of environmental protection, transportation, and community development.

These trends, in both taxation and borrowing, engendered major controversy in the state political system. Additional controversy arose from executive budgetary practices. The Democratic comptroller, Arthur Levitt, was highly critical of the state's cash-basis budgeting system, and the attendant flexibility that this system offered the governor to meet the constitutional requirement of a balanced budget by manipulating reserve funds, using one-time payments, accelerating expenditures, rolling over expenditures, and employing other devices at the end of the fiscal year. Levitt advocated long-range fiscal planning and putting the state's accounts on a modified accrual basis. The comptroller also found fault with the fact that the state's budget was not comprehensive. The financial operations of public benefit corporations were not reflected in it, nor, since it did not require legislative action, was most federal aid. The governor and the budget director defended their actions by asserting that Levitt's criticism was largely partisan in nature and that he did not use the powers that were legally his to block the practices that he chose to criticize. Rockefeller's reply to Levitt was, in effect: "If you believe I am acting unconstitutionally, sue me."

The Land of Taxes

The first budget prepared by Nelson Rockefeller for New York State, in 1959, totaled just over $2 billion. Rockefeller's last budget, for the 1973 fiscal year, was more than four times as large; it totaled

$8.7 billion. This vast increase in the magnitude of state spending in New York was not unique, but was indicative of a national trend. During the period from 1962 to 1972, expenditures by the national government grew 170 percent. In comparison, expenditures by all the states from their own sources during the same period increased 197 percent. This trend was especially evident in such states as California, Illinois, and Massachusetts, with growing urban problems. Nevertheless, New York's rate of increase exceeded that of even these states. Between 1962 and 1972 its expenditures grew 250 percent.[2]

Great expenditure growth could be achieved only with increased taxation. Again, the trend was general, but New York exceeded the average for all states. Between 1950 and 1972, the number of states using both a full-fledged personal income tax and a broad-based sales tax climbed from seventeen to thirty-six, and the Empire State was numbered among them. New York had adopted an income tax in 1919, and it was the state's greatest revenue producer during the Rockefeller period. By the early 1970s, though rates at low-income levels were moderate, in the higher income brackets they were the steepest in the nation. When state revenues were segregated from those of localities, New York's heavy dependence on the individual income tax became clear. This levy produced 40.5 percent of New York's revenues in 1971, more than twice the average for all of the states.

New York adopted a 2 percent state sales tax in 1965, and later increased the rate to 3 percent. Nevertheless, it was among the least dependent of the states on this revenue source in 1971 (see Table 14). Most states with high state taxes had low local taxes. New York, however, demonstrated high tax effort at both the state and local levels. In 1973 it ranked first in per capita local tax effort and third in per capita state effort.[3] In fiscal 1972 New York per capita state and local taxes combined were one and a half times the national average for states, and per capita state taxes alone were almost seven times as large as they were in 1957 and more than two and one-half times as large as those for the median state.

In another measure of tax effort, taxes as a percentage of personal income, New York was also the leading state. In 1971, state and local taxes combined in New York amounted to 16.14 percent of adjusted personal income. This was more than 1 percent higher than Vermont (14.88 percent), the next highest state in effort, and over 3 percent higher than California (12.95 percent). Over the decade of the 1960s, New York moved increasingly farther from the national mean. In 1961

Table 14. 1973 Tax Revenues for the Six Most Populous States and United States Average (percent)

Revenue source	United States	New York	California	Illinois	Ohio	Pennsylvania	Texas
General sales and gross receipts tax	30.5%	21.9%	33.5%	33.9%	31.5%	25.8%	34.4%
Individual income tax	23.0	40.3	22.6	25.6	15.0	24.2	—
Corporate net income tax	8.1	10.3	13.1	6.5	6.8	11.7	—
Selected sales and gross receipts tax	24.2	18.5	18.1	23.3	30.8	22.7	34.0
License taxes	8.2	4.7	5.7	8.5	11.7	10.7	12.6

Source: Advisory Commission on Intergovernmental Relations, *Federal-State-Local Finances: Significant Features of Fiscal Federalism* (Washington, D.C.: Government Printing Office, March 1977), pp. 23–24.

Note: The columns do not total 100 percent because some minor revenue sources were excluded.

it was 1.1 percent above the mean; in 1971 the figure was 4.24 percent.[4] By 1973, New York was collecting about twelve cents of every tax dollar collected by all the states in that year. If, as Justice Oliver Wendell Holmes noted, "taxes are the price we pay for a civilized society," the Empire State during the period 1959–1973 made great strides toward civilizing itself.

High taxes in New York were not without consequences for the state's economic system. Governor Rockefeller, the scion of an enormously wealthy business family, was well aware of this fact. From the first days of his administration one of his stated goals was to improve the business climate of New York State. In a speech at the annual meeting of the Associated Industries of New York State in September 1959, for example, Rockefeller said: "A primary objective of my administration has been the development of a climate for an accelerated growth of our economy to provide the necessary job and income opportunities for all of our people."[5] Later, in an interview in 1961, the governor described "promotion selling" of New York. With regard to economic development, he commented, "I think that New York has been complacent about its own future, and I don't think that labor and business are on opposite sides, nor is the government. I think that all three are completely in this problem, inseparably together."[6]

In Rockefeller's view, his early program for "fiscal integrity," balanced budgets and pay-as-you-go, had a strong, positive psychological impact on the industrial leaders he sought to lure to New York. More concretely, he offered tax and borrowing advantages. By 1962 he had pushed through the legislature a reduction in the corporate franchise tax for businesses shipping to other states, a revision of the unincorporated business tax which excluded 44 percent of covered businesses from it entirely and gave relief to an additional 22 percent, and revisions in tax administration to make New York conform more closely to the federal system and thus ease the paperwork burden on business people.[7] In his 1962 budget message Rockefeller claimed that during his administration New York had passed more than sixty pieces of legislation helpful to business development.[8]

Over the years, the Rockefeller administration sought systematically to minimize increases in business taxes in order to improve the state's competitive position and thus retain indigenous industries and attract new ones. The result was an increased reliance on taxes on individuals (personal income and sales taxes). In 1955 individuals paid sixty cents of each tax dollar. By 1973 individuals were providing through taxes seventy-four cents of every dollar of state income. In 1959, business tax accounted for 19.9 percent of the total collected. By 1973 the figure had declined to 15.0 percent. "This decline," noted a special study commission preparing for the 1967 state constitutional convention, was the "direct result of the state's efforts to develop a more favorable business climate in New York. In contrast to consumer taxes, no new taxes have been imposed on business [between 1959 and 1967] . . . and tax rates have remained fairly constant."[9] In 1965, a year of major tax increases, Rockefeller rejected "significant increases in business taxes . . . [because] such tax sources would serve as deterrents to expanded business and increased job opportunities and because the potential yield would be small in terms of our total needs."[10]

A glimpse of the governor's priorities emerged again during the 1971 budget battle. When it was evident that his tax package would not pass the legislature, Rockefeller wished to give first priority to the avoidance of business and income tax increases that might affect New York's ability to attract and retain industry. At a press conference on March 15, 1971, he expressed a desire to avoid taxes "that affect the present economic structure of the state."[11] Legislative leaders, on the other hand, gave first priority to the elimination of new automobile registration fees, the burden of which would fall on individual car owners in their districts. For Rockefeller, the major limiting factor in raising new state taxes was the potential erosion of New York's economic base. As he said in a meeting with eleven county executives during the 1971 fiscal crisis, "New York State is very close to the limit of what we can raise through additional taxes without very seriously affecting the growth and vitality of our economy and future job opportunities."[12]

In fact, development efforts did not avert severe economic difficulties in New York, especially during Governor Rockefeller's last two terms. Between 1966 and 1974 the state lost 314,000 manufacturing jobs. However, there were employment increases in other sectors of the economy, clerical, service, and governmental (federal, state, and local). Thus, at first glance, it did not seem that New York's economy was in trouble. Manufacturing contributed more to the state economy, however, since it generated wealth, had a high multiplier effect, and thus ultimately produced more taxes. In addition, by 1974 New York faced a decline in total employment, including former areas of growth. The headquarters of twenty-one corporations listed among the five hundred largest in the nation left New York State during the period 1966–1974.[13]

Whether Rockefeller's relatively successful efforts to hold down corporate taxes had much effect on New York's business climate remained an open question. Taxes were not the primary determinant in business location. Closeness to markets and supplies of raw materials and the availability of trained labor were the decisive factors. As the center of population in the nation shifted to the south and west, New York lost some of its earlier locational advantages. Unionization made labor more expensive. Street crime and generally higher living costs, particularly in New York City, also influenced business decisions. Intangible factors, which do not appear in textbooks, such as the tax department's reputation for rigorous enforcement, weighed heavily against New York. Business people were upset, too, about New York's practice of offering unemployment benefits to striking workers. An additional fact, and an ironic one in light of the thrust of Rockefeller's tax program, was that corporate executives who might make the actual decision to move into the state were discouraged by the high state personal income taxes.[14] Those dollars, after all, would have to come out of their own pockets. On balance, it must be concluded that Rockefeller preferred to raise taxes in order to provide higher levels of service to New Yorkers.

Tax increases in the early years of the Rockefeller governorship reflected the governor's conviction that states had to seize the initiative and generate their own resources for new programs if they were to remain viable participants in the federal system. In his 1962 Godkin lectures on the future of federalism Rockefeller said: "If a state government lacks the political courage to meet the needs of its people by using its own taxing power—if it prefers to escape by letting the national government do the taxing and then return the money to the state—the leadership of this state puts itself in an exceedingly poor position to weep over the growth of federal power. The preservation of states' *rights*—in short—depends upon the exercise of states' *responsibilities.*"[15]

While Rockefeller recognized early in his administration that federal grant-in-aid programs worked to the disadvantage of New York, he was prepared to accept that fact. As he said in an interview with newspaper reporters of the Gannett chain in 1961: "Well, I could go screaming to Washington all the time saying 'we are being shortchanged by Washington,' but I think we have to have some maturity and recognize that the areas which are highly developed and have high incomes have a responsibility, either in a federation or within a state, to help those areas which are less fortunate."[16] Acting on the views he later expressed at Harvard, in 1959 Governor Rockefeller sought and obtained major increases in the gasoline tax (two cents a gallon) and the income tax (the addition of three new brackets at the top of the scale), and the institution of tax reforms such as a uniform $600 exemption for each taxpayer and dependent and the withholding of state personal income taxes at their source.

The institution of withholding, a "good government" provision that caused little controversy at the time, was the major hidden asset of this tax package. It was well known that many people evaded paying income tax in New York State, but there was no way of accurately telling the extent of this phenomenon. As Rockefeller wryly noted in his 1961 budget message, one result of withholding was to bring about half a million people "who formerly overlooked their obligations" into the taxpaying fold.[17] During the first two years of Rockefeller's 1959 tax revisions, the state income tax produced over $100 million more than the budget office projected. This administrative change thus provided the state government with a major income bonus that was not anticipated and helped the Rockefeller administration more easily to achieve its early fiscal goals. In fact, revenue production of the new income tax provisions in New York in 1960–1961 allowed a one-time 10 percent refund to taxpayers in fiscal year 1961–1962 at an expense to the state of $90 million.

Increasingly in his second term, Rockefeller's publicly stated positions on fiscal matters limited his options. Pay-as-you-go eliminated the possibility of full-faith-and-credit borrowing. His views on states' rights and responsibilities foreclosed the possibility of adding his voice to the chorus calling for increased federal aid. Finally, his campaign pledge in 1962 precluded the introduction of new tax legislation. As a consequence, Rockfeller increasingly relied on fiscal gimmicks, administrative changes that produced increased revenues for one year, to meet the constitutional requirement that the budget be balanced. In fiscal 1963, for example, a change from quarterly to monthly payments by businesses of state personal income tax withheld produced $115 million in increased revenues. In fiscal 1964, acceleration of the payment schedules of corporation, bank, and unincorporated business taxes produced $175 million. But this was robbing Peter to pay Paul, for these funds collected in fiscal 1964 would normally have been fiscal 1965 revenues.[18]

In 1965 Rockefeller had to abandon both his no-new-tax pledge and pay-as-you-go to submit a balanced budget to the legislature. By 1967 he began to move away from his cherished concept that the state could meet its problems from its own resources. In his third-term inaugural address Rockefeller pointed out that the federal government collected two-thirds of all tax revenues in the United States, but that it was "too distant from local conditions" efficiently to use its funds. "To an increasing degree in recent years and months," Rockefeller pointed out, "a multiplication of inadequately financed domestic federal programs have raised aspirations and aroused hopes of many citizens, only to produce grave disappointments." New York, the governor continued, sought a "full fair share" of federal funds. These funds, he said, could best be administered through the state, "unencumbered by needless restrictions or bureaucratic regulation." This speech, calling for "bloc grants" as "a partial refunding of federal income tax revenue," was the first shot in the battle Rockefeller led that successfully culminated in federal revenue sharing.[19]

After 1967, every effort to increase state taxes was accompanied by a claim that New York was shortchanged by the federal government through formulas that worked to the disadvantage of populous states. In his 1968 annual message, Rockefeller also attacked the federal government for underfunding domestic programs. The consequence of this action, he said, was to create expectations in the citizenry that could not be met and to force the states into increasingly heavier taxes from their own, relatively narrow tax bases. No longer optimistic about the ability of state and local governments to meet domestic problems from their own resources, Rockefeller said: "We may well be reaching a point where the level of expectation of the American people is rising at a rate which is outrunning our capacity to raise the revenue on a sound basis—on a basis that will not seriously affect economic growth and increased job opportunities."[20]

With the national Republican victory in 1968, and facing a budget gap of $620 million, Rockefeller in 1969 proposed a sales tax increase, a 5 percent across-the-board reduction in state expenditures, and a developed program for federal assistance "to share a greater proportion of Federal revenue with state and local governments and share it in a way that recognizes the particular needs of heavily urbanized states."[21] This national program included the institution of bloc grants; the limited continuation of categorical grants; authorization, subject to congressional veto, for the president to consolidate grant programs; the establishment of federal welfare standards, preparatory to federal assumption of total costs in this area; the institution of universal health insurance; and a national study of the cost and quality of elementary and secondary education. Since the national effort was not immediately forthcoming, new state taxes were necessary, but the governor no longer spoke of using revenues for new state services, urging rather "the need to reorder and reschedule our priorities so that pressing needs [were] met while a healthy climate for economic growth [was] preserved."[22]

In 1970, a gubernatorial election year, Governor Rockefeller offered a budget in which he asked for no new taxes, but continued to emphasize the need of states and localities for aid from the national government. Citing New York's difficulties in attracting and retaining industry because of its high level of state and local taxes, Rockefeller condemned the federal tax cut in December 1969 and called on local government officials to join with him in urging the adoption of a major federal revenue-sharing program. He said:

> I urged the President and Congress to set aside 35 percent to 40 percent of the growth of federal revenues annually [projected at $15 billion a year to 1976] for the cities and the states to help them to meet the needs of our people at home. This growth sharing would have produced from $5 billion to $6 billion this year, and between $35 billion and $45 billion additional aid for cities and states by 1976. Only increased financial aid on this scale can meet our need on the home front and the federal government is the only level of government that has the tax resources to provide it. . . .
> A single state government cannot, by itself, raise the revenues neces-

sary to meet the demands made on it. States such as New York, which have led the way in meeting their responsibilities to their people and their local governments, now find themselves in a critical position where they will jeopardize their economies, drive out business and drive away jobs if they raise taxes.[23]

With the national economic slowdown causing a revenue shortfall of $237 million in fiscal 1970 and inflation driving up costs, New York confronted a major crisis as it entered the new decade. The 1971 budget showed a deficit of $23 million, the first such deficit since fiscal 1950, and it was kept from being greater only by the deferment of $195 million in state payments to the following year. In his 1971 budget Rockefeller requested increases in every major state tax, totaling $1.114 billion. Even with these funds, to balance his budget the governor had to include in it $300 million of revenue from borrowing not yet authorized by the voters. Although he continued to push hard for revenue sharing, he did not include federal funds from this source in his budget, Rockefeller told reporters at a news conference in March 1971, to "dramatize the problem."[24] Earlier he had said that, if federal revenue sharing passed Congress in time, he would cancel his request for a 10 percent income tax surcharge and a 1 percent sales tax increase, and if Congress funded revenue sharing at the $10 billion level, no new taxes would be necessary.[25]

Instead of giving the governor his new taxes, the legislature made major cuts in his budget. Further, Congress failed to act, the proposed bond issue was rejected by the voters, the economy remained sluggish, and litigation blocked reductions in welfare and Medicaid costs. The result was a projected deficit, in December 1971, of $780 million for the last quarter of fiscal 1971 and $720 million for fiscal 1972. To meet the crisis Rockefeller called a special legislative session and proposed $250 million in new taxes (many of them rejected that past spring), postponed $400 million state aid payments to the next fiscal year, froze hiring and other state expenditures when possible, and relied on the passage of the federal revenue-sharing program.

Revenue sharing finally passed in 1972, the national economy improved, and the crisis in New York State finance abated. In 1973 the state was able to return aid payments to a current basis, and it had the uncharacteristic if short-lived luxury of a dollar surplus. Normal spending patterns were resumed in 1974 as Malcolm Wilson, Rockefeller's long-time lieutenant governor and successor as governor, sought to please a variety of constituencies and retain his post. He failed, and by late 1974 it was apparent to the newly elected Democratic governor, Hugh Carey, that New York State was in a deep financial crisis, caused in part by the failure of its economy to recover as well as others from the severe national recession and in part by the cumulative impact of fiscal decisions made during the Rockefeller governorship. For a time, the bond market was closed to New York State and its agencies. Still another round of tax increases and a severe austerity program were thus necessary, and were undertaken in order to restore New York to financial health.

Analysis shows that over his years as governor, Rockefeller moved from the confident use of state taxing power to provide additional services and meet citizen demands to the reluctant use of this power to meet rapidly rising mandated costs without the expansion of services. He left New Yorkers the highest taxed people in the nation at the end of his term in office. Though he often expressed a concern for economic growth and sought to act on this concern, when forced to choose, the governor nearly always gave priority to tax increases in order to maintain or improve service levels. He pushed the state to the limits of its capacity, and perhaps beyond those limits. At first convinced that it could act vigorously and effectively from its own resources, Governor Rockefeller was compelled to the view that unrestricted federal aid to state and local governments was necessary if the federal system was to survive.

Trends in State Expenditures from State Sources

The large increase in New York State expenditures during the Rockefeller years can be best understood through an examination of the major categories of state appropriations. As is the case with most other states, New York made its expenditures from a variety of funds, not all of which were reflected in the executive budget. The budget that the governor submitted to the legislature primarily covered resources that required annual appropriation and was called the General Fund. This fund had four basic parts: the local assistance fund, the state purposes budget, the capital construction budget, and debt service requirements. Over the period of the Rockefeller governorship, the General Fund diminished relative to total state expenditures. In 1958 this fund included 79 percent of state expenditures; in 1973 it encompassed 62 percent of these expenditures.

This change was not due to any absolute decline in the General Fund but rather to its slow rate of growth compared to the rate of growth of income not included in it. Because they did not require legislative appropriation, federal aid payments to the state, with the exception of general revenue sharing, were not included in the General Fund. In addition, New York, like most states, had a wide variety of special funds that did not appear in the General Fund budget. Some (the Conservation Fund, the State University Income Fund, the Outdoor Recreation Development Account) contained money collected from charges for the provision of state services, the sale of land and property, federal grants, and the sale of lottery tickets. They were used to finance the acquisition of land or other capital investment, or for other specific purposes authorized by law.

Tax stabilization reserve funds were another category of special funds. Built up during periods of state surpluses, these funds were used to meet unanticipated deficits in the local assistance or state purposes budgets. Tax stabilization reserves were drawn on in 1971 and 1972 for a total of $66 million; this entire amount was replaced in the reserve in 1973. There were also a number of trust funds (the Unemployment Insurance Benefit Fund, the State Employees Retirement System Fund) and a $4.5 million governmental emergency fund, which could be drawn on only by the governor when the legislature was not in session and then only with the approval of six of seven designated legislative leaders of both major parties.

Local Assistance

New York has traditionally been among the states most generous to its localities, and during the years of the Rockefeller governorship the emphasis on state aid to localities through the Local Assistance Fund for the delivery of basic services was continued and reinforced. In 1958, 52.7 percent of the state budget was earmarked for local assistance. In 1973, 61.6 percent of the budget was allocated in this category. Between 1958 and 1973, the Local Assistance Fund, consisting of money that the state returned to localities to subsidize locally delivered services, increased 465 percent, from $940 million to $5.34 billion. Even after the effects of inflation were removed, the growth of this segment of the state budget, 365 percent, is impressive. The era of greatest increase in the Local Assistance Fund came between 1965 and 1970. In the seven years between 1958 and 1965 this fund rose by 76 percent. Then in the next five years it grew by 125 percent, before resuming an average annual rate of growth of just over 9 percent for the 1970–1973 period.

The trend in New York State's support for its localities is evident both in the percentage of local budgets that is made up of state aid and in comparison with efforts made by other states (see Table 15). In 1961 New York provided 28 percent of local revenues, slightly below the national mean (28.4 percent). By 1971 New York State was paying 43.1 percent of local bills, while the national average for state governments in this category was 33.8 percent. By 1973 the state was providing $2.5 billion in aid to New York City alone, a fivefold increase in ten years and about one-fourth of the city's budget. Overall, by 1967, the first year of Governor Rockefeller's third term, New York was clearly leading the states in per capita aid to local government. And by 1971, the first year of the governor's final term, the Empire

Table 15. Expenditures from Local Assistance Fund, by Function, New York, 1958/59 and 1973/74

Function	Fiscal year 1958/59 (in thousands of dollars)	Percent-age of total	Fiscal year 1973/74 (in thousands of dollars)	Percent-age of total	Percent increase 1958–1973
Elementary and secondary education	$564,646	59.70%	$2,497,000	49.70%	370%
Environmental conservation	59	a	23,256	0.44	39,317
Health	33,435	3.5	91,477	1.70	174
Housing and community renewal	15,855	1.70	76,739	1.40	384
Mental health	10,845	1.10	64,000	1.20	490
Narcotics addiction control	—	—	72,900	1.40	
Probation	450	0.05	19,900	0.40	4,322
Social services	140,968	14.90	1,337,635	25.00	849
Community college operating aid	2,750	0.30	112,400	2.10	3,987
Per capita local aid (revenue sharing)	140,385	14.90	662,680	12.40	583
Veterans' affairs	450	0.05	653	0.01	50
CUNY	8,250	0.90	132,300	2.50	504
Youth	3,200	0.30	25,500	0.50	
Total	945,393	—	5,345,134	—	465

Source: State of New York, Division of the Budget, Annual Budget Messages, 1959–1974.
Note: Columns do not add to totals because of the exclusion of some minor categories of aid and of some categories in 1973 that did not have antecedents in 1959.
a Less than 0.01 percent.

State was providing its localities with 25 percent more than was California, the state that ranked second in the nation in local government assistance.[26]

During the years of the Rockefeller governorship, the major components of the Local Assistance Fund (LAF) remained the same. In 1958, aid for elementary and secondary education, social services, and unrestricted local use accounted for 89.5 percent of the fund; by 1973 this figure was 87.0 percent (see Table 15). This essential similarity, however, masked considerable differences, since within these three categories the Rockefeller administration rearranged priorities and altered formulas for the raising and distributing of resources.

Aid to elementary and secondary education accounted for about six of every ten local assistance dollars in 1958, and of this total, 97 percent was distributed under the general aid formula. By 1973, educational aid included slightly under fifty cents of every local assistance dollar, and the general formula distributed 94.5 percent of this fifty cents. In addition to programs of aid for school lunches, libraries, and physically handicapped children—all inherited from the Harriman administration and augmented under Rockefeller—there was instituted in 1968 a program for educationally disadvantaged inner-city areas, and in 1970 a system of support for certain functions of nonpublic schools. In 1973 these two programs, outside the general aid formula, cost the state $108 million.

Early in 1959, Governor Rockefeller commissioned a task force to make the "first thoroughgoing study of state aid that has been undertaken in recent years."[27] Subgroups of this task force ultimately produced twenty-two reports on state aid programs, which were consolidated into one final report in 1960. The basic finding of the task force was that there were no "gross inequities or basic unfairness in state aid programs," but that much consolidation was needed. Federal involvement blocked consolidation in the social welfare area, but more could be done in education, which was almost totally financed by the state and localities.

Between 1960 and 1962 the issue was studied by the Joint Legislative Committee on School Finance (the Diefendorf committee). In the interim, $5 million a year in "special assistance for cities of over a million population" was appropriated in 1960 and 1961 in implicit recognition that the extant formula was shortchanging New York City. Under the Diefendorf law, adopted in 1962, school aid statewide was increased $150.2 million, but the basic criteria for the distribution of aid remained unchanged:

The distribution continued to depend largely on two key factors: a count of pupils derived from average daily attendance and the yield of a specified tax rate applied to the full value of taxable real property per pupil. . . . As in previous laws, there was a minimum guarantee of state money per pupil as well as a maximum allowable expenditure per pupil for purposes of computing the state money payable.[28]

Later years brought alteration of aid ceilings and other technical changes, but no change in the basic Diefendorf formula, despite claims by cities (especially New York City) that the use of weighted average daily attendance (WADA) rather than total population or a count of pupils enrolled and the emphasis on taxable property per pupil left them short-changed in this aid category. The city, with a large truancy problem that reduced its average daily attendance, naturally preferred to have aid based on the number of pupils enrolled.

Per capita aid to local governments, a form of general assistance, constituted 14.9 percent of the local assistance fund in 1958. When Rockefeller came to office, localities were being aided through a per capita aid plan devised in 1946 to replace a variety of formulas based on different revenue sources that resulted in "wide and unpredictable revenue fluctuations and disparities among localities." The purpose was "to institute a system of general state assistance, without program limitations or other requirements which could be applied as a supplement to local taxes or as a source of local tax relief."[29] In addition to aid provided to cities, towns, and villages under this formula, counties were assisted through the return of a share of motor fuel taxes and motor vehicle fees.

After Rockefeller took office, pressures for alteration in the state aid formula grew. The result of the 1960 census, which showed a population decline in many municipalities in New York, would have caused a decline in per capita aid in these areas if the legislature had not enacted "hold harmless" provisions for the 1961 and 1962 fiscal years. In 1962 a Temporary State Commission on Per Capita Aid (later the Commission on State–Local Fiscal Relations) was created. In 1965 its recommendations were enacted into law. The result was an aid formula that provided new assistance to towns and counties, substantially increased basic per capita rates to cities and villages, and introduced an "ability to pay" factor. Overall, these changes increased the level of local assistance by about $100 million between the 1964 and 1965 fiscal years, and its adoption was tied to state tax increases in 1965.[30]

Despite these efforts, fiscal pressures on cities continued, owing to rapid population change (and the increased demand of low-income families for public services) and to constitutional local tax limits. As a consequence, in 1968 the governor recommended and the legislature passed a program of special per capita aid for cities. This three-year program provided $40 million for cities in 1968, $100 million in 1969, and $150 million in 1970. This aid was not enough to meet urban needs, however, and pressure from the cities, especially New York City, continued.

In 1970, in anticipation of a difficult race for reelection in which urban votes were crucial, and also to add to his bargaining power as he lobbied in Washington for federal revenue sharing, Rockefeller took a new initiative. Moving away from grant formulas based on fixed per capita amounts, he adopted the concept of revenue sharing for state aid. Aid to localities was tied to the income tax, the most productive source of state revenue. An amount equal to 10.5 percent of income tax collections was to be shared with all counties, towns, and villages, and 10.5 percent was to be used to replace the special per capita aid programs instituted in 1968, a total of 21 percent. Later, the severe fiscal pressures experienced in 1971 caused the governor and the legislature to cut back the total percentage of income tax revenue shared with localities to 18 percent. It has been a major goal of cities ever since to restore the original 21 percent level.

Despite the changes made during the Rockefeller years, little was done in response to the underlying criticism leveled at the local assistance formula by all the groups that had studied the problem since 1946. Though included in the 1965 formula changes, counties, which were assuming increasing responsibility for local services, continued to be shortchanged. Since jurisdictional classification remained a major factor in the revenue-sharing formula, cities automatically received more aid per capita than did towns, villages, or counties, regardless of need, capacity, or effort. The pressure for reform continued into the mid-1970s.[31]

Social services were the fastest growing segment of the Local Assistance Fund. In 1958, aid in this category totaled $141 million. By 1973 it had reached $1.337 billion, a tenfold growth in a decade and a half. In 1958, social service constituted about one-seventh of all local assistance; in 1973 it constituted about one-quarter of all assistance. Some of this growth can be traced to the establishment of a broad-based Medicaid program under gubernatorial initiative. In 1967, the first full year of this program, federal and state costs for it in New York were $606.7 million. By 1968, total costs exceeded $1 billion, and by 1973 they were approaching $2 billion, despite executive and legislative efforts to hold them down.[32]

Beyond the increases in Medicaid, a new initiative, increases in social service costs were inherent in the very nature of the programs themselves. As one authority noted: "The growth seems to be the result of the basic character of social service aid: everyone who qualifies for assistance and applies for it, receives it. Sufficient funds are appropriated to meet the costs that the program has authorized. In this sense, appropriations are automatic."[33] Throughout the 1960s, the number of eligible applicants grew. In New York City alone, welfare rolls increased from just over 500,000 in 1965 to 1,250,000 in 1972. In 1973, after major efforts at cost reduction, the state had 1,694,229 recipients, about 70 percent of them in New York City. By that year, New York's relative generosity in payment levels and the continuation of traditional migration patterns had resulted in the location of 12 percent of the national population of public assistance recipients in New York.[34]

In addition to these three major aid categories, localities were provided with aid through the Local Assistance Fund (LAF) in a host of substantive areas. Aid for local programs in aging, the arts, and narcotic addiction control and methadone maintenance were innovations during the Rockefeller administration. In higher education, New York under Rockefeller came to fund half of the City University (CUNY) operating budget, to support the development of doctoral programs at the university, to establish a program for disadvantaged students at City University (SEEK), and to pay one-third the operating costs and half the capital costs of the state's community colleges. In 1973 the cost of CUNY to the state was $132.3 million, and an additional $12.3 million was provided for the SEEK program. Community college operating aid cost the state $2.75 million in 1958; in 1973 the figure was $112.4 million.

In the areas of physical and mental health, LAF payments supported local health departments and medical clinics and community facilities for mental health, mental retardation, and alcoholism. In environmental protection, operation and maintenance costs of sewage-treatment plants were shared with localities. In housing, local agencies were provided with subsidies and capital grants. In probation services, funding for local agencies was increased from $450,000 in 1958 to $19.9 million in 1973. In all major areas of local assistance during the 1958–1973 period, support by the state outstripped the level of inflation as programs were enriched and expanded (see Table 15).

State Purposes

During the Rockefeller governorship, the state purposes portion of the general fund grew from $608.2 million to $2.42 billion, an increase of 298 percent.[35] Since the state purposes budget contained only funds that New York collected from its own revenue sources, and since the state constitution gave the governor predominance in budget making, an analysis of changes in this portion of the budget between 1958/59 and 1973/74 is useful for uncovering the priorities of the Rockefeller administration in those areas where the state government delivered services directly. The first striking fact that emerges from such an analysis is that few resources were devoted to operations that were entirely new. In the 1973 budget, seventeen agencies had no antecedents in the budget of 1958/59, and in aggregate these agencies accounted for $95.2 million, or 3.9 percent of expenditures for state purposes. Of this amount, close to 70 percent was spent on one agency, the Drug Abuse Control Commission; seven of these new organizations were funded at levels below $1 million. Even if two other agencies, the Office of General Services and the Division of Youth, were included in this "new" group because the changes in their functions over the Rockefeller years made them qualitatively different from their antecedent organizations (the Division of Standards and Purchase and the Youth Commission), the percentage of the state purposes budget devoted to new agencies reached only 7 percent. Clearly the major changes made during the Rockefeller administration in the direct provision of state services resulted from reorganization and redirection of resources in established policy areas rather than from entry into entirely new areas.

Corresponding with the popular perception that governors tend to husband resources and release them during election years, growth spurts in the state purposes budget seem to correspond with quadrennial gubernatorial election years. Of thirty-three state departments and agencies with antecedent organizations in the 1958/59 budget, fourteen had budgets that increased at a rate faster than that for the state purposes as a whole (see Table 16). Nine of these fourteen were commissions, divisions, or offices of the Executive Department (Executive Chamber, Budget, Equalization and Assessment, General Services, Housing and Community Renewal, Human Rights, Parks and Recreation, State Police, and Youth). Of these, two—the Executive Chamber and the Division of the Budget—were direct arms of the governor in controlling the rapidly growing state government. The 232.5 percent real dollar increase in the Executive Chamber budget reflects a growth of the governor's immediate staff during the Rockefeller years. The real increase in the Division of the Budget was 343.5 percent, a degree of growth substantially greater than that for the state purposes budget but less than the growth of the budget as a whole.[36]

Outside the Executive Chamber, departments whose budgets increased at a faster rate than the entire state purposes budget included Education, Environmental Conservation, Law, State University, and Transportation. Two of these departments underwent major reorganization, Transportation in 1967 and Environmental Conservation in 1970. Evidence indicates, however, that growth was steady during the Rockefeller administration and was not the result of the concentration of resources during and after reorganization. In fact, reorganization may have been a highly visible substitute for a major new commitment of state dollars from general tax resources.

The Department of Law, administered by Republican Attorney General Louis Lefkowitz, was one of two state departments headed by a statewide elected official not directly responsible to the governor. This department's budget grew at almost twice the rate of the overall state purposes budget. On the other hand, the Department of Audit and Control, under Arthur Levitt, a Democrat, grew slightly less rapidly than the overall state purposes budget and at less than half the rate of the Department of Law. Nevertheless, Levitt's budget was 293 percent larger in 1973/74 than in 1958/59.

Growth in the Department of Education and the State University reflect the Rockefeller administration's emphasis on higher education. The State University budget went from 7.3 percent of the state purposes total in 1958/59 to 19.2 percent of that total in 1973/74; it grew four times as fast as the entire state purposes budget during this period. The high rate of growth of state purposes expenditures for the Department of Education was largely attributable to increases in Regents scholarships and scholar incentive programs and in grants to nonpublic colleges and medical and dental schools.

Agencies that did poorly during the Rockefeller years include Veterans' Affairs, State, Military and Naval Affairs, Health, and Banking.

Table 16. Agency State Purposes Budgets, New York, 1958/59 and 1973/74

Agency	1958/59	Percentage of 1958/59 state purposes budget	1973/74	Percentage of 1973/74 state purposes budget	Percentage of increase, 1958–1973	Percentage of increase with effect of inflation removed[a]
Executive Chamber	$ 1,227,399	0.20%	$ 5,238,900	0.22%	327%	232.5%
Agriculture and Markets	5,629,310	0.93	13,071,716	0.54	121	26.5
Alcoholic Beverage Control	3,260,932	0.54	7,221,711	0.30	132	37.5
Audit and Control	5,454,137	0.90	21,435,100	0.89	293	198.5
Banking	234,420	0.04	463,395	0.02	98	3.5
Budget	1,219,875	0.20	6,567,992[b]	—	438	343.5
Civil Service	3,096,834	0.51	11,372,600	0.47	267	172.5
Commerce	3,071,929	0.51	9,032,366	0.37	196	121.5
Corrections (Commission and Department)	42,937,825	7.06	128,347,458	5.30	199	104.5
Education	27,461,848	4.51	259,366,940	10.71	844	749.5
Environmental Conservation	4,653,570	0.77	37,286,917	1.54	1,111	1,016.5
Equalization and Assessment	1,255,440	0.21	6,048,278	0.25	380	285.5
General Services	2,107,051	0.35	47,465,845	1.96	2,153	2,058.5
Health	23,587,714	3.88	47,698,071	1.97	102	7.5
Housing and Community Renewal	993,584	0.16	4,824,556	0.20	386	291.5
Human Rights (Division and Appeals Board)	743,024	0.12	4,282,190	0.18	476	381.5
Insurance	380,939	0.06	878,227	0.04	131	36.5
Labor	8,431,641	1.39	19,658,843	0.81	133	38.5
Law	3,646,777	0.60	23,864,800	0.99	554	459.5
Mental Hygiene	194,113,785	31.91	539,093,495	22.26	178	83.5
Military and Naval Affairs	6,077,480	0.10	12,021,329	0.50	98	3.5
Motor Vehicles	8,563,388	1.41	28,613,212	1.18	234	139.5

	1958/59		1973/74		Index	
Parks and Recreation	10,537,112	1.73	42,206,474	1.74	301	206.5
Probation	328,348	0.05	956,220	0.04	191	96.5
Public Service	3,979,583	0.65	11,063,000	0.46	177	82.5
Social Services (Board and Department)	9,886,998	1.63	24,018,761	0.99	143	48.5
State	3,590,926	0.59	57,420,529	2.37	432	337.5
State University	44,505,083	7.32	464,359,000	19.18	943	848.5
Taxation and Finance	28,218,978	4.64	66,841,499	2.76	240	145.5
Transportation	53,638,865	8.82	221,511,832	9.15	313	248.5
Veterans' Affairs	2,208,802	0.36	3,364,179	0.14	52	42.5
Youth	331,988	1.05	30,979,429	1.28	9,231	9,136.5
State Purposes total[c]	$608,240,422		$2,421,557,877		298	203.5

Source: State of New York Executive Budgets, 1959–1974.

Note: In order to make the data comparable across years, the following adjustments were made: Alcoholic Beverage Control Commission and Local Beverage Control were considered together. The budget of the Division of Parole (1958/59) was added to the budget of the Department of Corrections (1958/59) and the budget of the Probation Division of the Department of Corrections (1958/59) was considered separately. The budget of the Department of Conservation (1958/59) was compared with Environmental Conservation (1973/74). The budget of the Division of Standards and Purchase (1958/59) was compared with that of the Office of General Services (1973/74). The budget of the Division of Housing (1958/59) was compared with that of the Division of Housing and Community Renewal (1973/74). The budget of the Commission against Discrimination (1958/59) was compared with the combined budgets of the Human Rights Division and the Human Rights Appeals Board (1973/74). The budget of the Bureau of Motor Vehicles, which was part of the Department of Taxation and Finance in 1958/59, was considered separately from that of the department. The budget of the Division of Parks of the Conservation Department (1958/59) was compared with that of the Office of Parks and Recreation (1973/74). The budget of the Department of Social Welfare (1958/59) was compared with that of the Department of Social Services (1973/74). Budgetary totals for the Department of Public Works, the Civil Defense Commission, and the Division of Safety (all 1958/59) were considered together and all were compared with the budget of the Transportation Department (1973/74), which assumed the functions of these agencies. The budget of the Youth Commission (1958/59) was compared with that of the Division for Youth (1973/74). The budget of the Department of Public Service (1973/74) was borne by regulated companies and thus was not included in the General Fund.

ᵃ Adjustments in this column were made by use of the State and Local Goods and Services index, in Council of Economic Advisers, *Economic Message of the President* (Washington, D.C.: Government Printing Office, 1974), p. 253.

ᵇ The actual total for 1973/74 for this division was $11,417,992, but this figure included a nonrecurring expense of $4.85 million, which was deleted for the purposes of this analysis.

ᶜ Detail does not add to totals because of exclusion of certain agency budgets and budgets for the legislative and judicial branches.

When the effect of inflation is taken into account, the budget of the Division of Veterans' Affairs declined 42.5 percent and the functions of the four other departments showed virtually no growth. Several of these departments did receive funds outside the state purposes budget. Other departments of low growth (less than 25 percent of the rate for the state purposes budget) included Agriculture and Markets, Alcoholic Beverage Control, Insurance, Labor, and Social Services. It must be remembered, however, that all of these agencies except Alcoholic Beverage Control had significant funding outside the state purposes budget.

Federal Assistance

In 1958, fifteen state departments and agencies shared in federal aid to New York, which, after the inclusion of refunds of state first-instance advances, totaled slightly over $400 million. In that year, state departments receiving and administering the bulk of federal funds were Social Welfare and Labor (for New Deal–instituted public assistance and unemployment insurance programs) and Public Works (for highway construction under the Public Defense Highway Act). In the last year of the Harriman administration these three departments spent among them about seven out of every ten federal dollars provided to New York state government. By 1973, the number of state agencies receiving federal funds had increased to twenty-five, and many of them received aid under several programs.[37] During this fifteen-year period, the amount of nonappropriated federal assistance increased almost nine times, to $3.54 billion.[38] (In New York, unlike some states, most federal aid funds were not subject to legislative appropriation.) There were few areas of state government that were not in some way the beneficiaries of federal aid.

The greatest growth in federal assistance during the Rockefeller years occurred in the social welfare area, which alone accounted for more than seven of every ten dollars of such aid given to New York in 1973. In addition, education assistance increased from 5 percent of total federal aid to New York in 1958 to 12 percent in 1973 (or 14 percent if support for higher education is included in the total). In contrast, aid provided to the state Department of Labor diminished from 9 to 4 percent of the total federal funds received, and highway assistance dropped from 26 percent to 3 percent.

The pattern of growth of federal aid to New York paralleled the passage of federal social legislation during the 1960s. Growth in the social welfare and education areas, for example, began in 1965 and 1966 with the passage of Medicare and Medicaid legislation, the Elementary and Secondary Education Act, and the Higher Education Act. Education aid grew again in 1969 and 1970 with the renewal and augmentation of the 1965 federal legislation. Similarly, assistance in the areas of law enforcement, corrections, probation, and parole came to the state after the passage in Washington of the Safe Streets Act in 1968.

Often it seems that state agencies were established largely to receive and expend federal aid. This was the case, for example, for the state Office of Equal Opportunity, established in 1965 after passage of the Federal Equal Opportunities Act, and for the state Office for the Aging, established in 1966 after passage in 1965 of the Older Americans Act.

Though New York thus experienced formidable increases in federal assistance during the 1958–1973 period, it remained less dependent than most states on aid from the national government. Thus, though the Advisory Commission on Intergovernmental Relations reported that New York's percentage of state and local general revenue from federal sources increased from 5.5 percent to 13.9 percent between 1957 and 1971, New York remained well below the mean figure for federal aid to all the states during this period. Indeed, the Empire State consistently ranked among the lowest of the large industrialized states in percentage of state and local revenues provided by the national government and, though over the 1960s it moved toward the national mean in this area, progress was reversed as the 1970s began (see Table 17).

When particular functional areas are examined, the same picture emerges. In 1973 the national government paid an average of 7.7 percent of school costs in the fifty states; in New York it paid 6.0 percent. In 1971 an average of 26.8 percent of state highway costs, 52.0 percent of public welfare outlays, and 4.8 percent of health and hospital expenditures were provided by the federal government. In New York, the comparable figures were 17.9 percent, 44.0 percent, and 1.8 percent, respectively. Despite the levels that federal aid had reached in the state by 1973, New York was still largely paying its own way in the major areas of state and local responsibility.

It is notable that Rockefeller's predecessor as governor, Averell Harriman, had first raised questions about the small amount of federal money coming back to New York. Testifying before a congressional committee in 1957, he observed that New York State received

Table 17.   Percentage of State and Local Revenue from Federal Aid, United States and Ten Largest States, 1957–1975

	1975	1971	1970	1967	1962	1957
United States	20.6%	18.0%	16.7%	16.9%	13.5%	10.1%
California	18.6	19.3	19.2	19.0	14.0	10.7
Florida	18.1	14.1	13.0	14.9	11.0	10.0
Illinois	18.2	16.4	14.2	13.5	11.2	6.9
Indiana	15.2	13.2	12.5	12.3	10.8	6.6
Massachusetts	19.0	16.8	15.8	14.0	11.6	7.2
Michigan	20.5	15.4	13.8	14.6	11.2	7.9
New Jersey	17.7	15.0	12.3	11.2	8.7	4.6
Ohio	18.8	14.4	14.0	14.4	12.7	8.0
Texas	20.7	19.2	17.9	18.0	13.8	12.8
New York	17.9	13.9	13.6	12.1	7.1	5.5
Percentage by which New York falls below United States average	2.7	4.1	3.1	4.8	6.4	4.6

Source: Advisory Commission on Intergovernmental Relations, *Federal-State-Local Finances: Significant Features of Fiscal Federalism*, 5th ed., 1977. (Washington, D.C.: Government Printing Office, 1974), p. 32.

only 7.3 percent of all federal grants to states and localities in fiscal 1956, whereas it had nearly 12 percent of the nation's population and contributed more than 13 percent of total federal tax revenues. Harriman characterized these disparities as being "excessive" and criticized federal policies that failed to account for the cost, complexity, and magnitude of problems in huge urban industrial states such as New York, which, for the most part, were of a "completely different order" from those of smaller, more agricultural states.[39]

The disparities between the state's share of the federal tax burden and federal grants returned to it remained largely intact during the 1960s. In 1968, New York residents paid an estimated $22 billion in tax revenues to the federal government and received back $1.4 billion for state and local aid, some 6 cents on the dollar. In 1971, this figure was 11 cents on the dollar, and by 1973, with the passage of revenue sharing, it reached 18 cents returned to New York for every dollar of federal taxes raised there.[40] This later figure was still far below the 1971 figures for Arkansas (27 cents on the dollar) and Oklahoma (25 cents on the dollar). If in 1971 New York had received proportionately the same amount as had either of these two states in federal grants, it would have received between $6 and $7 billion in federal aid rather than $2.5 billion. Some claims have been made, however, that New York's argument that it is shortchanged by the federal government has been overstated. When all federal payments were counted, and not just payments to the state government, New York received 11.6 percent of all federal outlays, while providing 13.9 percent of federal taxes. It led the nation in both categories.[41]

Governor Rockefeller was critical not only of the amount of aid flowing into New York but also of the fact that the form, manner, and management of the grant allocation system worked to the disadvantage of his state. His critique had three major foci. First, many categorical grants to the states were skewed in the direction of rural rather than urban poverty. Second, states were limited by statutory ceilings in the total amount of federal funds any single state could receive. Third, states with high levels of services, such as New York, which already had program standards above the national average, were prevented by "maintenance of effort" requirements written into federal legislation from substituting federal funds for previous levels of state expenditures. They were forced to raise standards further and to spend more of their own money merely to obtain increased federal funding.[42]

During the late 1960s and early 1970s, New York State's circumstances in relation to other states changed dramatically. Fiscal disparities among some states lessened. The economies of other states became more mature, and several became more industrialized. Hence the amount of federal tax dollars flowing to New York increased gradually. New federal grant programs slowly moved away from a rural orientation, becoming more urban and suburban in their thrust and directed more at human resource areas than at bricks-and-mortar types of programs. Nonetheless, a certain time lag existed between changing economic conditions and federal responsiveness to these new circumstances, particularly in view of the fact that allocation formulas depended on outdated census data. Rockefeller recognized this. Many of his "fair share" and "magnitude of need" arguments were directed at bridging the gap between obvious social changes and federal responsiveness, and between trends that would bring greater federal aid to New York and the more immediate transfer of these new funds. "These grants," Rockefeller observed, "are heavily weighted in favor of the so-called poor, rural states, a definition established during the Depression which is no longer applicable in light of the tremendous poverty in the nation's industrial and urban centers."[43]

The Hill-Burton Hospital and Medical Facilities Construction Program, which dated from 1946, had an allocation formula that weighted the population of each state with the inverse ratio of per capita income squared. The net effect was a distortion of the per capita income standard, so that New York, with more than five times the population of Alabama, received annually roughly the same amount of federal funds for hospital construction and modernization as Alabama. New York State alone had nearly as many "medically indigent" people as the entire population of Alabama. In virtually dozens of programs—such as mental health, vocational rehabilitation, airport development, water pollution, library services, elementary and secondary education, and maternal and child health services—similar formulas were at work, and as a consequence New York obtained substantially less money from the federal government than its population warranted.[44]

In program after program, Congress provided that grants to any one state could not exceed some fixed upper limit, usually 12.5 or 15 percent. This upper-limit provision, necessary to get broad-based congressional approval of many programs, severely hurt New York State. In mass transit, for example, New York had over 40 percent of the nation's riders but could receive only 12.5 percent of the available federal funds. In urban renewal and public housing the limit was 15 percent of available federal funds. In public housing, additional upper limits for allowable construction costs per unit further inhibited New York because costs in New York City far exceeded those for other areas of the country.

A classic example used by Rockefeller to illustrate the impact of these federal upper-limit and maintenance-of-effort provisions in New York concerned the Medicaid program. Title XIX of the 1966 social security amendments provided for a 50–50 matching program to support medical assistance for the poor. Since federal funds would be provided to the states only if they improved and enriched existing programs, New York—which had the oldest and most generous program for the medically indigent—raised its annual net income standard for eligibility from $5,200 to $6,200 for a family of four. Had the New York program been approved, as it was unofficially, New York State would have been eligible for $217 million of federal assistance, the entire amount of funds planned for the nation's Medicaid program in its first year. Summoned by the New York delegation to Washington to explain how this occurred, Rockefeller argued that he and his staff had merely complied with the law in order to get the maximum funds. As Rockefeller recalled the situation, one upstate congressman at the meeting spoke up. "If I had known what was in this legislation," he said, "I never would have voted for it." Rockefeller responded, "Great, Congressman. Go back to your constituents and tell them just that. They will have tremendous confidence in your representation."[45]

As a result of New York's aggressiveness in seeking Medicaid funds, Congress placed a ceiling on the amount of funds any one state could receive. Caught in a fiscal bind, New York State consequently had to change its legislation. The result was the removal from the eligibility list of 1.2 million people who for the first time had been promised government assistance for medical care. Rockefeller repeatedly drew on this incident to stress the dilemmas of state and local government in responding to federal programs. As he said of the war on poverty: "The federal government aroused the expectations, then did not adequately fund the program, and it falls back on the state."[46]

Often the administration of federal programs penalized New York for being innovative and anticipating national trends. In the early 1950s, for example, New York completed a considerable stretch of its portion of the national interstate highway system prior to enactment of federal legislation that established the multibillion-dollar program. New Yorkers paid for most of the Thomas E. Dewey Thruway out of bond funds. The state was ineligible for a 90 percent reimbursement that was given to other states that began their interstate programs later.

With regard to its Pure Waters Program, instituted in 1965, New York State not merely financed its share but advanced the federal portion (up to 55 percent of total costs in some cases) for many projects. Congress and federal officials encouraged the state to proceed with promises of reimbursement, only to have the Treasury Department balk at prefinancing as a back-door raid on the federal treasury. Not only did the state go out on a limb for $1.3 billion but so did local communities, which sold bonds to finance sewage-treatment plant construction. By the end of the Rockefeller administration New York was compensated roughly $400 million for the $900 million prepaid federal grants promised for the Pure Waters Program. The remaining amount was at least three years overdue and still in dispute.

Rockefeller placed his criticism of federal aid to New York in the wider context of a general critique of the federal grant-in-aid program. The virtual explosion of new federal programs produced myriad problems for the state and local governments. Between 1960 and 1970 the number of federal grant programs increased from 45 to 430. The Eighty-ninth Congress (1965/66) alone enacted twenty-one new programs for health, seventeen for education, fifteen for economic development, twelve for aid to cities, and four for job training. As Rockefeller noted before a subcommittee of the House Government Operations Committee in 1969, the sheer number of federal grants was evidence of their narrow, specialized thrust. The Department of Health, Education, and Welfare, for example, had 209 separate programs. This proliferation of programs caused red tape to abound. In his testimony the governor, denouncing the requirement to file "plans" that were never read or followed, said: "The splintering of grants produces a maze of plans, regulations, and rulings. The seventeen grants in welfare alone have led to five thousand pages of federal program operating requirements. In the case of education grants, a state is required to submit twenty separate plans."[47]

Further, most of the grants of the 1960s were of the project rather than the formula variety. By 1970, 380 federal grant programs, about five of every six, allowed federal officials considerable discretion in establishing grant conditions and selecting recipients. The establishment of such programs fostered competition among state and local governments (since there were not enough resources to go around), and, because of matching fund requirements, tended to alter their priorities. Earlier federal assistance provided funds largely for established state and local functions; money was given for building schools, highways, and hospitals. In the newer approach, grants were extended to aid the federal government in achieving its purposes. To be sure, these new programs were also accompanied by increased federal support in more conventional categories—highway and hospital construction, sewage disposal, mental health, and mass transit—which were largely oriented toward capital rather than operating aid. But in both cases, matching requirements necessitated expenditure of more of the localities' own funds to get additional federal funds. As Rockefeller noted before a congressional committee, categorical grants ultimately limited the flexibility of the states and localities: "Present narrowly defined federal programs keep states and counties from concentrating or focusing fiscal and manpower resources on the most critical problems. States cannot transfer funds from one federally aided project to another. Without flexibility, priorities set by states become almost meaningless."[48]

Federal grant programs also entailed political risks for state officials. If governors failed to seek federal funds, they were open to attack by opponents for not being aggressive enough in seeking "free money from Washington." If they did obtain funds, they confronted the problem of the termination or underfinancing of the federal programs. The Congress frequently failed to appropriate funds in the amounts it had previously authorized. In 1966 the national government appropriated 81.2 percent of authorized federal aid. In 1970, only 65.8 percent of the funds authorized were appropriated, and some appropriated funds were impounded.[49] Too often in the 1960s the federal government used categorical aid authorizations to lure the unwary states out onto a limb while using actual appropriations to saw the limb off the tree.

Finally, Governor Rockefeller complained of trends in federalism that diminished the role of elected officials and of state government in the ongoing process. Too often categorical programs resulted in what Terry Sanford, governor of North Carolina, called "picket fence federalism," with thousands of vertical programs constituting the pickets but without any horizontal cross slabs to enable the fence to stand up.[50] James Sundquist, in one of the more insightful studies documenting the consequences of federalism transformed in the 1960s, found that each federal agency actively involved in domestic grants had developed autonomous policies, doctrines, strategies, and field structures in implementing intergovernmental programs.[51] Governors, mayors, and elected federal officials alike protested against proliferating federal programs and confusion and lack of coordination in their administration.

Often the federal government took action to bypass the states by dealing directly with cities because the states were unresponsive to urban needs. Rockefeller felt that a flexible system was needed, one that would put these funds through those states that would take responsible action. "The urbanism of today's society with its areawide problems," the governor argued, "made local planning inadequate." In light of the states' greater resources, powers, and jurisdiction, he thought, "they should serve as the leaders in planning, and the catalysts in development of cooperative action at the local-state-federal levels."[52] Over the strong objections of several mayors, Rockefeller persuaded the Advisory Commission on Intergovernmental Relations to adopt a recommendation that federal grants-in-aid for urban development be channeled through state government when a state provided appropriate administrative machinery to carry out its responsibilities.

As the gap in resources narrowed between the rich and poor states over this period and as federal programs changed, often under intense lobbying, New York's share of the federal pie did increase. Ranked forty-second among the states in per capita direct federal aid in 1960, the Empire State moved into the top ten in this category in 1974. But federal help was predicated in part on the demonstrated willingness of the states to take up the burden from their own resources, both in delivery services and in aiding local governments. Here, too, New York was at the forefront.

Capital Construction

In fiscal 1958, the first year of his governorship, Nelson Rockefeller asked the state legislature for a capital budget of $255 million; by 1973, his last year as governor, the capital budget had reached just over $760 million.[53] Unlike the budgets for state purposes and local assistance, however, the capital budget did not follow a trend of constant increase over the Rockefeller years. A peak was reached in fiscal 1969, when $1.289 billion was appropriated for capital projects. The lowest capital appropriation during the Rockefeller years was $213 million, during the fiscal crunch of 1963. In fiscal 1972 another low, $296 million, was reached during a period of intense financial difficulty in the state.

Of the major categories of the state budget, capital construction was most complex. It had two major components, regular or hard-dollar appropriations and first-instance appropriations. Regular appropriations were made from state taxes or full-faith-and-credit bond revenues. First-instance appropriations were start-up money, and were made in anticipation of reimbursement from sources outside the General Fund. They were, in effect, interest-free short-term loans to departments and agencies.

One of the major changes in capital financing during the Rockefeller years was the enormous growth in the use of first-instance financing. This growth was a concomitant of the development of public benefit corporations by Rockefeller as primary vehicles for capital programs. In 1957, 95 percent of a total of $782 million of first-instance appropriations in force in New York was reimbursable from federal sources. By 1973, the total of these appropriations in force had reached $3.466 billion, of which only 48 percent was reimbursable by the federal government. The rest, a total of $1.795 billion in first-instance capital appropriations, was reimbursable from state sources, largely public authorities.

A major concern during the later years of the Rockefeller administration was the use of first-instance appropriations as a method of back-door financing for public authorities. Of all such appropriations made by the state between 1964 and 1972, only about 15 percent, $63.1 million, had been repaid by June 1972. In contrast, well over one-third, $154.1 million, was written off. That is, the legislature made hard-cash appropriations to cover these loans, in effect relieving the authorities of the obligation to repay. About 40 percent of the first-instance appropriations forgiven ($87.2 million) were made to the Metropolitan Transit Authority (MTA).

Of the $203.6 million in such appropriations remaining outstanding in mid-1972, the comptroller commented, "much . . . now appears to be of doubtful collectability." First-instance appropriations, he concluded, were often a means of providing a subvention to public authorities unable to meet their obligations from their own funds.[54]

Another complexity of the capital budget was that, unlike the state purposes and local assistance budgets, not all of the funds appropriated in it were expended in the fiscal year in which the appropriation was made. Thus for fiscal 1974 the governor recommended $524.7 million of capital appropriations, of which the budget office estimated $148.2 million (28.2 percent) would be spent in that fiscal year. In addition, expenditures of $311.7 million of capital construction funds appropriated in previous years were estimated for expenditure in fiscal 1974.

It was the general practice under Rockefeller to appropriate the entire cost of a project in the year that it was budgeted and then to make reappropriations as necessary until the project was completed. This practice allowed the legislature to consider total project costs at the time of the initial appropriation. It also, however, caused a major backlog of funds appropriated but not spent to grow during the Rockefeller years. Between 1958 and 1973 regular capital appropriations in force increased almost threefold, from $924 million to $2.615 billion, and first-instance appropriations in force went from $783 million to $3.467 billion, an increase of over five times.

Increasingly the priorities in actual capital expenditures of the state reflected past choices and were less responsive to choices made in the current fiscal year. The difficulty of controlling cash flow through capital budgeting was especially evident to the governor in years in which he faced fiscal problems. Capital budget cuts made in 1963, 1971, and 1972 were not reflected in expenditures until one or two years later. In those years, actual cash expenditures far exceeded regular capital appropriations. Even in very tight situations, experience indicated that once a project was 25 percent along the way to completion, it would cost the state more to cancel it than to fund it.[55]

Another reason for the backlog of appropriations in force was the state's tendency under Rockefeller to appropriate in one or two years all the funds authorized under major bond issues, though these funds would not be borrowed or expended for some time. Thus in 1969, for example, $600 million of the transportation bond issue of 1967 was appropriated for the New York City subway system. As one expert on capital budgeting in the budget division noted, successful bond issues became targets for a variety of interest groups and localities throughout the state. A capital appropriation was an assurance to a local government that it could enter into commitments that were contingent on the state's commitment.[56]

In general, the regular capital budget was used for construction for which full-faith-and-credit borrowing was authorized by the voters: transportation (primarily highways, but increasingly mass transit in the late 1960s), parks, and environment. In the early Rockefeller years, before the creation of the State University Construction Fund and the Mental Health Facilities Development Fund, the capital budget was used for State University and mental hygiene construction. After 1962, regular capital appropriations for SUNY were largely for community colleges. In 1961, $101 million was appropriated for civil defense projects. In the mid-1960s, over $100 million was appropriated for facilities for the Narcotics Addiction Control Program. A major trend during the Rockefeller period was the increasing capital budget of the Office of General Services. This budget reached $61.6 million in 1973; its major component was lease-purchase payments for the Empire State Plaza in Albany and similar projects throughout the state.

The Burden of Debt

Among the most controversial of Nelson Rockefeller's legacies to the Empire State was the debt incurred during his tenure. By 1973, New York's long- and short-term debt aggregated over $11.8 billion, 20 percent of the amount owed by all the states combined. In addition, the state had lease-purchase obligations with public authorities, municipalities, and retirement systems totaling $2.7 billion. New Yorkers in 1973 carried a per capita debt burden that was more than twice the national average (see Table 18).

The rate of growth of indirect state debt incurred through lease-purchase agreements (excluding other forms of indirect debt) was greatest during the 1962–1965 period, when direct debt was being avoided, but still averaged over 20 percent in the last Rockefeller term. In contrast, the highest rate of growth for full-faith-and-credit debt occurred during the later years of the 1968–1971 fiscal crisis and slowed appreciably in 1972 and 1973 (see Table 19). In 1973, New York ranked fourteenth among the states in per capita long-term full-faith-and-credit debt, fourth in long-term per capita moral obligation debt, and first in short-term debt. Among the ten most populous states, New York was the leader in combined per capita debt (see Table 18).

The extent of debt in New York was the result of two major groups

Table 18. Per Capita Debt of the United States and the Ten Most Populous States, 1973 (in hundreds of dollars)

| | | Long-term debt | | | |
	Total	Guaranteed	Nonguaranteed	Short-term debt	Percent of U.S. total
United States	$281.50	$134.10	$129.89	$ 17.51	100.0%
California	292.43	258.05	34.38	—	10.2
Florida	162.72	—	162.59	0.12	2.1
Illinois	174.14	61.31	111.30	1.53	3.4
Indiana	115.35	—	106.25	9.10	1.0
Massachusetts	535.44	278.11	168.74	88.59	5.3
Michigan	156.54	38.85	96.25	21.45	2.4
New Jersey	376.13	184.62	168.30	23.21	4.7
New York	647.88	193.84	333.95	120.09	20.0
Ohio	209.30	95.95	112.43	0.91	3.8
Texas	137.06	62.42	74.64	—	2.7
New York's percentage above U.S. mean	130.1 %	44.5 %	157.1 %	585.8 %	

Source: Calculated from U.S. Department of Commerce, Bureau of the Census, Social Statistics Division, *State Government Finances in 1973*, GF 73, no. 3 (Washington, D.C.: Government Printing Office, 1974), p. 40; and *Statistical Abstract of the United States, 1976* (Washington, D.C.: Government Printing Office, 1977), p. 11.

Table 19.   Debt Service Costs, Aggregate Debt, and Per Capita Full-Faith-and-Credit Debt, New York, 1959–1973

| Year | Debt service costs | | Aggregate debt (in millions of dollars) | Per capita full-faith-and-credit debt |
	Millions of dollars	Percentage of General Fund expenditures		
1959	$ 53	6%	$ 897	$ 54
1960	49	5	988	59
1961	49	4	1,035	62
1962	39	3	1,050	61
1963	38	3	1,072	61
1964	38	2	1,082	62
1965	40	2	1,089	62
1966	39	2	1,236	70
1967	55	2	1,323	74
1968	64	2	1,769	90
1969	100	3	2,258	124
1970	139	4	2,523	138
1971	176	5	3,130	171
1972	223	4	3,362	183
1973	264	6	3,451	187

Source: Annual Financial Report of the Comptroller, State of New York, 1968 and 1973.

of fiscal policy decisions made during the 1960s. The first, and less discussed, was the decision to abandon pay-as-you-go capital financing for a massive full-faith-and-credit borrowing program in several policy areas. The second was the decision to use public authorities, lease-purchase agreements, and other devices to circumvent state constitutional restrictions on borrowing in order to provide a whole range of public services, many of them related to pressing urban needs. Though each of these decisions made a good deal of sense when examined in its own discrete context, their cumulative impact severely threatened New York's fiscal health by the mid 1970s.

A central aspect of the Rockefeller platform of fiscal integrity in the 1958 gubernatorial campaign was the avoidance of borrowing for capital projects. Early in his first term, in a speech before the Empire State Chamber of Commerce, the governor reaffirmed his commitment to this idea: "Personally, I feel that to the maximum degree possible, we should finance out of current income in government, because we make the taxpayers pay up to and over fifty percent more for their roads, their hospitals, and their mental institutions, by financing out of bond sales."[57] Rockefeller noted that businesses borrowed to build new revenue-generating facilities; the state's borrowing did not produce such facilities. Furthermore, he justified pay-as-you-go as a technique for holding state borrowing capacity in reserve, so that it might be used during difficult economic periods to stimulate the economy.[58]

Unanticipated revenues from the withholding of state income taxes combined with a strict review of state expenditures and the encouragement of business expansion to broaden the state tax base allowed the Rockefeller administration to reach its goal of a pay-as-you-go budget earlier than had been anticipated. The 1959 budget included $84 million in bond funds, but of this amount only $33 million was actually borrowed.[59] In his 1960/61 budget message Rockefeller announced that he expected to achieve pay-as-you-go capital financing without tax increases in the coming fiscal year. "I am happy to report," the governor told the assembled legislators, "that we have restored fiscal integrity to the Empire State."[60] In the next year, when asked by a reporter how long he thought the state could stay on pay-as-you-go, Rockefeller replied, "I see no end as far as my administration is concerned," and in 1963 he commented, "I am opposed to deficit financing except in a major depression."[61]

But there was more to pay-as-you-go than met the eye. Although the extent of borrowing by New York diminished in every year between 1959 and 1965, in no year did the state cease entirely to issue general obligation bonds.[62] Some such bonds, totaling $4.6 million between 1959 and 1964, were used to acquire parkland. When asked about these bonds by a reporter, Rockefeller claimed that no violation of his pay-as-you-go policy was involved. The borrowed money, the governor explained, was being spent on "a basic commodity, which is land, which is going up in value very rapidly," and furthermore, this was "a one-shot . . . program to match local communities, to permit them to buy land that was disappearing for availability for the future, and it will be amortized out of fees paid for by the parks."[63] Other borrowing was done in a halting attempt to combine public and private resources in a Limited Profit Housing Mortgage Corporation in order to make available funds to stimulate the construction of low- and middle-income housing under the lagging Mitchell-Lama program. Though technically not state debt—the bonds involved were issued by local governments, local public housing authorities, and limited profit corporations—the state was pledged to pay interest charges on these securities through local assistance housing subsidies. Between 1959 and 1964, debt in this category increased by $184.5 million. The governor and the comptroller differed on whether park and recreation and housing debt should be included under the category of "state borrowing" in the presentation of the General Fund budget. The governor excluded this borrowing and thus was able to show a regular decline in both debt service and net debt between 1959 and 1965 and to claim that he had placed the state on a pay-as-you-go basis. The comptroller included them and thus presented a picture of a lesser decline in debt service costs and a small increase in net debt during this period.

By 1965, the same pressures that caused Rockefeller to seek a statewide sales tax caused him to include extensive use of bond funds in his budget proposal to the legislature. Citing the "urgent need for accelerated highway and mental hygiene construction programs" (community mental health centers), Rockefeller in his budget message provided for the use of $223 million in highway bonds and $9 million in mental health bonds, both already authorized by the voters.[64] He justified the use of bonds by saying that they allowed him to avoid seeking even higher taxes and that, by abandoning pay-as-you-go, he was acceding to Democratic criticism made in previous years. On February 7, 1965, on the WCBS radio program "Let's Find Out," Rockefeller made this argument:

> I've used for the first time, reluctantly, bonds in this budget. . . . This will reduce the amount [of new taxes] . . . that's needed this year. The majority party [Democratic] in the legislature has been urging the use of bonds, instead of current expenditures, for this purpose. I'm sure that if I don't recommend them that they would insist on that. But it has made it possible to hold down the increased revenue source for this year.[65]

In 1965, as well, Rockefeller sought and obtained voter approval for a massive $1 billion Pure Waters bond issue. In his 1965 annual message the governor justified this, his first recommendation of "a state bond issue drawing upon general revenues for debt service," on the basis of "the urgency and magnitude of the problem of water pollution, the long-range benefits to be secured, and the staggering costs and crises which would result from further delay."[66]

Nevertheless, pay-as-you-go died hard. Even after balancing his budget in 1965 with almost $250 million in borrowed funds, Rockefeller declared: "I still believe in the principle of pay-as-you-go, and consider this as an exception."[67] In the 1966 budget message he cited "a sound fiscal policy that has generally been on a pay-as-you-go basis" as one of the major achievements of his first eight years.[68] In that year, nevertheless, the budget was balanced by the use of $210 million more in funds borrowed for highway and mental hygiene projects. In the next year, 1967, the governor sought and obtained legislative and voter approval of a $2.5 billion bond issue for transportation. During the massive publicity campaign he waged in favor of the authorization of the bond issue, Rockefeller often found himself advocating positions he had dismissed out of hand eight years earlier. On January 30, 1967, for example, in response to a question put to him by Charles Dumas of the *New York Daily News* on the radio program "Dateline Albany," the governor said:

> Now my feeling is that to meet this major need in transportation statewide, we can only do it by a large bond issue for transportation. I personally feel that this is justified in the interest of convenience to the citizen, plus the fact that the costs of construction are going up. In the pure waters field it is about five per cent a year now. On the basis of compound interest, that would be a doubling of costs in ten years. Therefore it is more economical, as the businessmen point out, to borrow the money and pay the current charges on the money . . . than it is to postpone the building, delay the economic benefit to the state and pay higher costs anyhow.[69]

From 1966 onward, all budgets offered by Governor Rockefeller to the legislature relied largely on full-faith-and-credit borrowing to achieve the balance required by the state constitution. This borrowing reached a peak in 1971, when it provided about one in every ten dollars of state income (the figures of the executive branch and the comptroller differ; see Table 20), but was reduced in importance with the increase of taxes and upturn in the national economy in 1972 and 1973. Dropping to less than 2 percent of state General Fund expenditures in 1966, debt service requirements for full-faith-and-credit borrowing climbed to 6 percent of these expenditures in 1973, the last year of the Rockefeller administration. Per capita full-faith-and-credit debt, $54 in 1959, had more than tripled by 1973, reaching a level of $187 in that year (see Table 19).

Toward the end of the 1960s and into the 1970s, New York voters, made sensitive to fiscal issues by ever increasing taxes, became less receptive to the governor's penchant for massive bond issues. Two

Table 20.   Governor's Budget Office and Comptroller's Figures on New York State
Full-Faith-and-Credit Borrowing, 1959–1973 (in millions of dollars)

Year	Governor's Budget Office figure	Percentage of General Fund income	Comptroller's figure	Percentage of General Fund income
1959	$118	6.6%	$186	11.3%
1960	33	1.6	136	6.6
1961	—	—	95	4.4
1962	—	—	66	2.8
1963	—	—	67	2.6
1964	—	—	56	2.0
1965	—	—	54	1.9
1966	119	3.5	196	5.6
1967	122	3.3	142	3.6
1968	390	8.4	501	9.1
1969	436	7.9	560	10.1
1970	304	4.9	350	5.7
1971	608	9.9	700	10.5
1972	204 (est.)	2.9	342	4.9
1973	143 (est.)	1.8	219	2.8

Sources: New York State, Executive Department, Division of Budget, June 1972;
Annual Financial Report of the Comptroller, 1968 and 1973.

transportation bond issues, for $2.5 billion and $3.5 billion, were defeated in 1970 and 1973, respectively, and in 1972 a $1.15 billion En-
vironmental Protection borrowing proposal was rejected by the voters.

The Growth of Public Authorities

The use of public benefit corporations to finance capital improvements was not new to New York, nor, for that matter, to other states.
Local public authorities authorized by the legislature had proliferated
in New York during the Depression, as they did in other states, as a
device through which to finance major capital projects. In the case of
Robertson v. *Zimmermann* the New York Court of Appeals held these
authorities to be constitutional.[70] Between 1921 and 1958, more than
sixty authorities (including housing authorities) had been established
in New York State. In the New York City metropolitan region, under
the hand of Robert Moses, public authorities became a major factor in
the political and governmental processes.[71]

Rockefeller's innovation was in the purposes to which he put these corporations and in the scale on which he used them. Authorities created during the 1930s and 1940s were usually limited to one project or a group of projects in a single function area. Bonds were issued for each project and were secured by the revenues of that project. In the later years of the Rockefeller administration, authorities were created in areas traditionally served by established state agencies (the most prominent examples were housing and transportation). Bonds were issued not on a project-by-project basis, but rather on the basis of all the operations of the agency. The primary concern was not the security of the bond issues but the creation of a quasi-governmental device with the capacity to infuse massive amounts of private capital into areas that had proven intractable to more conventional approaches by state and local governments. Unlike traditional authorities, which were wholly financed out of user fees and other nontax revenues, some later authorities, such as the Metropolitan Transportation Authority, received appropriations in the state capital budget.

The increasing difficulty the governor faced in getting voter approval of proposed borrowing provided part of the motivation for his search for ways to circumvent the constitutional requirement that "no debt shall be hereafter contracted by or in behalf of the state, unless such debt shall be authorized by law, for some single work or purpose, to be distinctly specified therein. No such law shall take effect until it shall, at a general election, have been submitted to the people, and have received a majority of all votes cast for and against it...."[72] At least at the outset of the Rockefeller administration, however, another reason for seeking methods to borrow outside the debt limit was to maintain pay-as-you-go financing while entering into major capital programs.

Thus, in 1961, the governor sought and obtained voter approval for constitutional amendments allowing the state to guarantee the borrowing the Port of New York Authority (for commuter railroad cars) and the newly created Job Development Authority (JDA).[73] These amendments were needed since under New York's constitution the state could not be made liable for the debt of public corporations and could not extend its credit to a private corporation. Unlike later public authorities, the Job Development Authority was established by accepted constitutional methods. Its attractiveness to the governor lay in the fact that it allowed him to use public-sector borrowing, which, because of its tax-free status, could be done at very low interest rates, to attempt to attract industry to New York while still keeping the costs of that borrowing out of the General Fund budget. Later, however, as the JDA program developed, there was some question about the actual effectiveness of this approach.[74]

In 1961, at the same election in which the voters approved state guarantees for Port Authority and JDA borrowing, they defeated a proposed constitutional amendment that would have allowed direct state debt up to a limit of $500 million for university construction. Expanding the State University was a top priority of the governor's. Another attempt at constitutional amendment would mean a two-year delay, for under the amending clause of the state constitution such action required legislative approval in two consecutive sessions. A more expeditious alternative had to be found, and an earlier initiative in another policy area offered a possible answer.

In 1959 the governor had appointed a task force under Otto L. Nelson, Jr., a vice-president of the New York Life Insurance Company, to study means of stimulating private investment in middle-income housing. The high cost to private builders of borrowing money had brought construction of middle-income housing, especially in New York City, to a virtual halt. By use of the state's credit, the money could be borrowed at a much lower rate than could be obtained by private builders. On the basis of the report of this task force, Rockefeller in 1960 sought legislation that would create the New York State Housing Finance Agency. This agency would raise its own funds from private sources by issuing tax-free bonds and would then relend these funds to developers to build housing. Rockefeller envisioned initial borrowing of about $500 million with a potential for the level to rise to $1.5 billion if the program proved viable. The obligations of the agency were not to be obligations of the state, and thus the constitutional referendum requirement was bypassed. Nevertheless, the Internal Revenue Service, in granting these securities an exemption from federal taxation, ruled that they were "issued in behalf of the state," and in the bond market they were viewed as moral, if not legal, obligations of New York.[75]

The structure of HFA financing, a prototype for many later Rockefeller public benefit corporation initiatives, was not an issue when the bill creating the agency was passed. Democrats, eager for housing in New York City, feared only that the bill would not work to provide apartments that middle-income people could afford. In the state senate, the bill passed 49 to 5, with all opposition coming from upstate Republicans.[76]

In 1962, after the original functions of the Housing Finance Agency became established, the governor obtained legislation to allow the agency to enter into the financing of construction for higher education, which had been blocked the previous year by the voters' rejection of the 1961 constitutional amendment. Under the 1962 law the State University Construction Fund (SUCF) was established as "a public benefit corporation to receive and administer monies available for State University construction and improvement." The construction fund, with income from student tuition and fees, was authorized to lease facilities built for it by the Housing Finance Agency. The legislature placed no limit on borrowing by the HFA for the construction of university facilities, and by mid-1972, $1.55 billion in debt had been incurred in this manner.[77]

Legislation later authorized the financing of construction of mental health facilities by the HFA, reconstruction and repair of state highways by the Thruway Authority, and construction of state health and correctional facilities by the State Dormitory Authority. The latter two agencies were established well before the beginning of the Rockefeller administration but their functions, like those of the HFA, were expanded to accommodate the broader role that the governor envisioned for them.

In addition, to finance the construction of state office buildings, the state made lease-purchase agreements directly with retirement systems and municipalities. One of the most controversial projects undertaken was the construction of the Empire State Plaza in Albany.

The Empire State Plaza

Few would question that the natural setting of Albany is beautiful. The city rises abruptly from the Hudson and spreads out over the plain. The state capitol, an architectural wedding cake dating from the middle of the nineteenth century, crowns the hill half a mile from the river's edge. But in 1958 block after block of grim, late-nineteenth-century homes and commercial buildings surrounded the capitol. For the most part, these buildings were neither beautiful nor livable. As in so many other urban areas, Albany's well-to-do had moved out of the downtown areas, and business establishments followed them to outlying shopping centers.

The capitol building provided inadequate space for legislators, who were crowded, two or three together, in small offices created by temporary partitions erected in a building poorly designed for a rapidly expanding state government. The legislators used their offices most frequently during sessions of the Assembly and Senate, but it was almost impossible to conduct business there. As regular sessions grew longer and special ones more frequent, the inadequacies of the capitol became more evident.

Office space built or rented to meet the needs of burgeoning bureaucracies was scattered over the area within a radius of ten miles from the capitol building. Earlier administrations attempted to cope with this problem in various ways. In Al Smith's day, the multistory office building that bore his name was erected across the street from the capitol. Lehman and Dewey added office buildings in various places across the city. When these offices proved inadequate, rental space was obtained and the state offices were fragmented further.

Harriman explored the idea of building one or more skyscrapers in the capitol area, but when it was reported that the subsoil would not bear the weight of such buildings, he abandoned the idea. Instead, the state campus complex was erected some ten miles from the capitol building. This construction did nothing to slow the decay of the downtown area. Moreover, further scattering of state offices made the conduct of day-to-day business even more inconvenient.

On his arrival in Albany as governor, Nelson Rockefeller was aghast at the bleakness of the state's capital city. When Queen Juliana of the Netherlands was invited in 1960 to attend the anniversary of the founding of the capital (Fort Orange), her route from the airport to the capitol had to be changed repeatedly in order to avoid some of the city's worst slum areas. This episode convinced Rockefeller that something would have to be done, not only to centralize and improve government facilities but also to make Albany worthy of its position as capital of the Empire State.

In March 1961 the governor established the eighteen-member State Commission on the Capital, charged with developing a master plan.[78] In January of the following year, the commission unanimously recommended that a new government complex be located in downtown Albany—a recommendation that the mayor and other city officials enthusiastically endorsed. Alternate sites on the outskirts of the city, said the commission, were not nearly so attractive. Moreover, engineering developments made construction of high-rise buildings downtown possible, although more expensive than they would be if located in the suburbs. It was thought that the downtown location would not only improve the attractiveness of the city by removing slum areas but bring together scattered state agencies and legislative offices near the capitol. Rockefeller enthusiastically hoped that the new center would be aesthetically and architecturally worthy of the most populous state in the nation.

The ultimate result of the commission's work was the South Mall project (now known as the Empire State Plaza), a complex of government buildings covering eighteen acres between the capitol and the executive mansion. In days past the area had been called "the Gut," and was known primarily for its bordellos. Upon completion, the mall was to have eleven buildings, including five twenty-three-story agency buildings, a forty-four-floor office tower, a legislative office building, a justice building, a quarter-mile-long center for the state Department of Motor Vehicles, and several special purpose buildings, including a meeting center and a cultural center. The most expensive and ambitious feature was called the Main Platform, a colossal construction 1,440 feet long and 600 feet wide, which had five levels and was surmounted by the five high-rise office buildings and the Meeting Center. The platform's three lower levels contained mechanical and storage areas, garage space for 3,300 cars, and a tunnel for a four-lane highway; the fourth level contained a concourse with offices, cafeterias, shops, meeting halls, exhibition areas, and a bus terminal; the top level had landscaped plazas with fountains, pools, and walkways; the platform also housed a health laboratory and a 13,000-square-foot fallout shelter.[79]

When the South Mall project was announced, the director of the Office of General Services gave a horseback cost estimate of $250 million, but the actual construction contracts specified $450 million. When a member of the Budget Division's construction staff estimated the cost to be over $1 billion, according to one account, his chief was told not to send "so negative a man" to future meetings. Later, difficulty arose in financing the new construction, for the governor knew that there was little chance that the citizens of the state would approve a major bond issue to rebuild the capitol. Thus when Albany Mayor Erastus Corning III suggested that the city's credit be used for this purpose by way of a lease-purchase agreement, it is said that Rockefeller went for the idea "like a trout for a fly."[80]

Legislation passed in 1963 permitted cities with populations greater than 75,000 to contract with the state to build state office buildings within their boundaries. In 1964 the law was expanded to allow similar action by counties with cities of 75,000 or more people. During the next eight years such agreements were completed with three counties, Albany, Suffolk, and Jefferson, and two cities, Utica and Binghamton. The most famous of these arrangements was the one with Albany County to provide the financing for the massive South Mall project.

At first the lease-purchase agreement to finance the mall was to be made with the city of Albany, but a switch was made to the county after Mayor Corning claimed that its broader tax base and lower indebtedness would provide more favorable interest rates in the bond market.[81] After several delays, the final agreement was signed in 1965. It conveyed to the county title to all affected land between the capitol and the executive mansion and provided that the county would lease it back to the state for a term ending December 31, 2004 (or earlier, if the bonds were retired). County bonds were to be sold for the mall construction and related costs, up to a total of $480 million. Construction was to be undertaken by the state superintendent of public works in accordance with plans of the commissioner of general services. The state agreed to pay rent to the county to cover bond costs starting on March 26, 1967. In addition, it agreed to pay the county an amount equal to the real property tax levy in 1961 on all mall land (except external highway land) for the years 1965 through 1967. This money was to be divided between the city and the county of Albany in the same proportion as reflected in the 1961 tax base. The state agreed to make certain additional payments, linked to the amount of bonds sold.

This final provision proved to be profitable to the city and the county, since by early 1975 the total amount borrowed for the mall project reached $985 million, and thus these localities were entitled to an additional $22 million in payments from the state. The comptroller estimated that the Albany mall would cost about $1.5 billion by the time all principal and interest payments were made.[82]

The lease-purchase agreement that provided the financial basis for Albany County's borrowing for the mall was typical of state "moral obligations" of this character. In retaining a rating of "A" for Albany County bonds after a review in 1973, *Moody's Bond Survey* commented:

> The lease rental contract provides that the state's obligation is absolute and unconditional, but it is subject to an "executory clause." This clause means that one session of the New York State legislature cannot legally bind a succeeding session, and that each Legislature must vote the rental payment for the succeeding year. Should the state fail, for one reason or another, to make a rental payment, a debt of such magnitude could no longer be serviced by the County on its own.[83]

These circumstances made the bonds riskier for the investor than direct obligations of New York, which have first claim on the general revenues of the state.

The controversy over the mall extended beyond the method by which it was financed. The project became a symbol of excessive capital spending, a lightning rod for all Rockefeller's critics in New York State. The nineteenth-century housing displaced by the mall was viewed by some as interesting landmark architecture, despite its decrepit appearance. The planned public housing for families that had to move was later canceled. Costs were increased by labor troubles, inflation, and poor planning. The project was called "Rocky's Folly," and the governor was charged with building a monument to himself as useful as the pyramids. Although the mall was justified on the ground that it would centralize in one place state operations scattered around Albany, even after its completion the state still required 800,000 square feet of leased office space in the capital.[84]

Rockefeller defended the high cost of the design and materials for the mall (the Vermont and Georgia marble used alone cost $20 million) on the ground that a capital should "fulfill us esthetically as well as serve us practically." "Mean structures," he said, "breed small vision."[85] He defended the method of financing by arguing that it had helped avoid the long delays that the full-faith-and-credit borrowing process would have engendered and thus the heavy impact of inflation. Nevertheless, the full cost of the project was more than twice the governor's first estimate, and some argued that "the interaction of grandeur, tight scheduling, and the workings of the state construction system proved to be synergistic. . . . *Haste* itself greatly delayed the project, and also exacted a heavy penalty in waste."[86]

Like the financing, the mall's grand design has not met with universal acclaim: Jane Jacobs, advocate urban planner, called the project "planning insanity," and *New York Times* architecture critic Paul Goldberger described its buildings as "foolish," "silly," and "impractical."[87] Nevertheless, by late 1976 the positive effects of the mall were beginning to be felt in downtown Albany. The nearby Center Square neighborhood was being renewed by middle-class homesteaders who were buying row houses near their offices and renovating them. Government officers fought for space in downtown buildings, and citizens returned after dark and on weekends to ice skate, visit the museum, and view the acclaimed state collection of contemporary art. For the first time, residents commented, there was something to do in the heart of the city. Even Democratic politicians who

The Empire State Plaza in Albany, under construction as Rockefeller left the governorship (1973). State of New York, Office of General Services.

had been highly critical of the project, such as Lieutenant Governor Mary Ann Krupsak and Assemblyman Mark Siegel, were commenting positively on its attractiveness and value as a focal point for the activities of state government.[88]

Other Moral Obligation Financing

The principle of the lease-purchase agreement was used by the state not only to finance state projects but also in projects of local government for which the state provided capital aid. For example, a law passed in 1972 permitted local governments to contract with the state Dormitory Authority for construction of community college facilities, with costs to be repaid later from tuition. The effect of this program was to allow the state to avoid lump-sum capital costs in one fiscal year by spreading them over a number of years, and to remove the need to support financing from general revenue receipts. Since interest charges were involved, the ultimate cost to the state was higher under the 1972 plan. The state was further involved in debt service under this plan in that the law provided for the appropriation of money to a reserve fund should the balance in that fund be insufficient to cover payments required in any fiscal year. Similar arrangements existed for the financing of City University construction by the Dormitory Authority and for the construction of municipal health facilities by the Housing Finance Agency (HFA). Aggregate debt under these three programs in mid-1972 was $481.3 million.[89]

A somewhat different arrangement prevailed for the financing of senior citizen centers, community mental health and mental retardation facilities, and youth facilities, all through the HFA. Here legislation authorized authority borrowing for mortgage loans to local nonprofit corporations. The corporations then leased the facilities to municipalities that received state aid to provide the service. Part of the state aid was then used to meet rental payments to the HFA for borrowing costs. In addition to the state commitment to keep the reserve fund at the necessary level to meet annual debt service requirements, bonds issued to provide loans for youth facilities and certain senior citizen centers were guaranteed by the Community Facilities Guarantee Fund. This fund represented an actual appropriation and direct encumbrance of state money in the amount of at least 10 percent of the loans outstanding. In 1972, $3 million was appropriated to this fund; outstanding loans totaled $11.5 million.[90]

A final area of state debt commitment beyond the full-faith-and-credit bonds involved the guarantee of public authority debt. Generally, the law required that authorities establish a reserve fund sufficient to meet debt service requirements anticipated for the next year. As the comptroller noted, "these reserve funds . . . constitute a margin of safety to an agency's bondholders in that they provide funds to meet the succeeding year's debt service requirements."[91] The reserve fund requirement also provided a check on authority borrowing. New obligations could be incurred by an agency only if total debt service payments could be met by available reserve funds (borrowed money from a new bond issue, however, could be used to augment the reserve to meet this requirement).

State involvement came with statutory language that indicated that it would appropriate each year enough money to bring authority reserves up to a level sufficient to meet debt service requirements if authorities, from their own resources, fell short of this level. This language was considered by the financial community to make authority securities a moral obligation of the state, though disclaimers in the law pointed out that such funds had to be appropriated by the legislature and that future legislatures would not be bound by law to make the required appropriations.

The enabling legislation of only four of the agencies for whose debt the state assumed a moral obligation provided for repayment of state reserve fund payments made out of general revenue. In mid-1972 the comptroller found that the moral obligation of New York State amounted to $2.278 billion; since seven authorities had no limit in law on the debt they could incur, the potential debt of New York in this category could not be calculated.[92]

Moral obligation financing began to cause difficulties after Rockefeller left office. In 1975 the Urban Development Corporation (UDC) defaulted. Governor Carey was forced to ask the legislature for an emergency appropriation of $178 million to help it meet its obligation. The state honored its moral pledge but the comptroller commented: "There is no doubt that the UDC demonstrates a basic fault in the way this public authority has been authorized."[93]

But the UDC crisis was only the beginning. Throughout 1975 fiscal conditions worsened as the state failed to balance its budget and struggled to find a way to help New York City avoid default. The city's difficulties and the problems of the UDC led, in turn, to the closing of the bond market to other municipalities in New York State, to other state public authorities, and ultimately to the full-faith-and-credit obligations of the state itself. Short-term notes, issued to take advantage of interest rates, could not be refinanced with long-term bonds. By the end of 1975, the Carey administration was piecing together desperate month-by-month solutions to avoid default by the Housing Finance Agency, the Dormitory Authority, the Medical Care Facilities Corporation, and the Environmental Facilities Corporation. [94]

A final solution was found in March of 1976, and was based on a highly complex financing package devised by Governor Carey's budget director, Peter Goldmark. An absolute limit of $2.6 billion was placed on all future moral obligation borrowing by public authorities, "just enough to redeem hundreds of millions of dollars' worth of short-term notes coming due each month, as well as to complete the construction of all the housing, dormitories, hospitals and other facilities the agencies had under way."[95] A new agency, the Public Authority Control Board, with members appointed by the governor and the legislative leaders, would decide which authority projects should be completed. And, as a condition of obtaining major financial participation in this plan by the Teacher's Retirement System, controlled by state comptroller Arthur Levitt, the legislature passed a bill bringing to an end the use of moral obligation borrowing in New York State.

The Fiscal Issue in Politics

The nature and extent of state borrowing was a political battleground almost from the very beginning of the Rockefeller governorship. Arthur Levitt, the state's Democratic comptroller, attacked Rockefeller's first fiscal policy, pay-as-you-go financing, on several grounds. Levitt claimed that it was better to finance capital projects over the long term, so that the cost of these projects would be paid by the citizens who actually benefited from them. Payment of total capital costs out of general fund revenues in one or two fiscal years placed too great a burden on current taxpayers for facilities that would be used long into the future. Second, the comptroller said, Rockefeller's financing was not really pay-as-you-go. The governor, the comptroller claimed, was keeping borrowing costs out of the general fund by greatly expanding the use of Public Authority borrowing. In doing so, Levitt continued, Rockefeller was increasing the ultimate cost of the facilities to the citizens of the state and bypassing the intent, if not the letter, of the constitutional referendum requirement for borrowing.

These themes, first sounded by Levitt, were taken up by Robert

Morgenthau, the Democratic gubernatorial candidate in 1962.[96] But the comptroller's first major assault on the governor's use of public authorities and lease-purchase agreements with municipalities came in June of 1963, as Rockefeller prepared to seek the 1964 presidential nomination. In an appearance on the NBC television program "Citizen Union Searchlight," Levitt claimed that Rockefeller's use of these devices had "caused concern" among the bond rating companies and could lead to the loss of New York's AAA bond rating. Predicting new taxes in 1964, the comptroller argued that indirect borrowing led to the earmarking of revenues that would otherwise go into the general fund (thus placing a needless strain on the state budget), that such borrowing cost the state more, and that constitutional safeguards were being bypassed.[97] Furthermore, Levitt pointed out, the voters had already approved major bond issues by the regular process for State University and mental hygiene facilities; Rockefeller was able to finance these facilities without recourse to the Dormitory Authority and Housing Finance Agency. The only advantage of the governor's doing so and of the bill he pushed through the 1963 legislative session allowing cities of more than 75,000 people to borrow to build facilities that would be leased back to the state, the comptroller concluded, was to enable him "to say he is not borrowing."[98]

Rockefeller replied to Levitt's attack three days later. Calling it a politically motivated act directed from the Kennedy White House, the governor denied that the borrowing vehicles he had created to finance state capital projects were either unconstitutional or more expensive than conventional borrowing. The Housing Finance Agency, the State University Construction Fund, the Mental Hygiene Facilities Improvement Fund, and the Job Development Authority were created, the governor said, to cut red tape, thus expediting construction, and, by relying on user fees, to avoid heavy investment of tax revenues in these policy areas. In an inflationary period, speed in construction avoided increased costs and more than made up for minimally higher agency borrowing costs. And financing through user fees, Rockefeller said, "took two billion dollars' worth of public works off the backs of the taxpayers."[99]

The governor offered a fuller defense as an addendum to his 1964 budget message. Public authorities, he said, were long established in New York State. All capital programs of public authorities, Rockefeller pointed out, were self-liquidating. User fees were assigned to meet bond costs. Thus HFA borrowing to finance middle-income housing was paid for through repayment by private developers who owned and operated the housing, and bonds issued by that agency for mental health facilities were repaid by patient fees collected in the Mental Hygiene Facilities Improvement Fund. Similarly, $1 billion in State University construction was to be repaid by tuition and fees, and the State Atomic Research and Development Authority borrowing to "encourage atomic industry in the state" was to be repaid through rents paid for the facilities by private corporations. State Job Development Authority bonds were to be similarly repaid from rents paid by businesses newly attracted to the state or induced to expand by low-cost loans.[100]

Democratic critics responded by saying that earmarking revenues in this manner in effect deflected them from the General Fund. Furthermore, the self-liquidating aspects of some of the programs, they said, was something of an illusion. With regard to State University construction, for example, tuition was imposed for the first time in the state system in 1963 to back the bonds. All students in good standing, however, were given Scholar Incentive aid (a minimum of $100 a year) to help them pay this tuition, and this aid was paid from the General Fund. The result was indirect General Fund backing for authority borrowing for State University construction. It was administratively less complex, fiscally less expensive, more in tune with the state constitution, and simpler for the voter to understand, the Democrats said, to use direct borrowing, already authorized, for this purpose.[101]

Rockefeller's critics were especially concerned about the use of lease-purchase agreements with authorities and municipalities as a device for budget balancing. In 1963, for example, the state sold twelve State University buildings then under construction to the State University Construction Fund for $67.26 million. Money was raised in the bond market by the HFA to pay the state and to complete building construction. The state also agreed to pay a rental of $3.5 million for thirty years to lease back these buildings. The effect of this transaction was to remove about $29 million from the fiscal 1964 capital construction budget and thus help the governor close a $35 million budget gap.[102] The total cost of the buildings to the state, of course, increased by over 50 percent.

A further point was that, although public authority bonds were at first perceived to be a substitute for the issuance of state full-faith-and-credit obligations, by the late 1960s New York was massively engaged in both types of borrowing. One of Governor Rockefeller's justifications in 1963 for the use of high-interest-rate authority bonds was that the small increase in cost was worth paying to avoid the use of general obligations. This justification disappeared in the early 1970s, and the cumulative effect of both types of debt at the same time became a matter of concern. In 1974, lease-purchase obligations alone increased the per capita state debt by 86 percent, moving it from $188 to $350, and this figure did not include all moral obligation borrowing and other local borrowing with indirect state involvement.[103] In that year, the outstanding debt of the Housing Finance Agency alone, $4.874 billion, exceeded by over $1 billion the entire general obligation debt of New York State.[104]

The issue was complex. Rockefeller's methods were practical ones for getting needed facilities built quickly. He doubted that the voters would approve the massive bond issues necessary for these programs, and his points about the dollar costs of delay and the probable increased interest rates that would be attendant on massive state general obligation borrowing were valid. Moreover, in the area of housing and construction for independent colleges and hospitals the use of state moral obligation bonds permitted private nonprofit borrowers to obtain funds at a more favorable rate. In 1965, when the State University and most new mental health facilities were being built, these bonds were being sold at a rate of interest of approximately 3.5 percent.[105] Also, one may note that construction costs were lower in the 1960s than in the 1970s.

More troubling, however, was the question of whether moral obligation borrowing contravened the intent of the state constitution. The 1846 Constitutional Convention added a referendum requirement after injudicious borrowing in the 1820s and 1830s for public improvements and the support of private enterprise forced the state into an embarrassing fiscal position and caused it to levy a direct property tax to avoid default.[106] The fact that the referendum requirement served as a roadblock to innovative programs desired by an activist governor simply demonstrated that the provision worked as its drafters intended that it should. If this restriction was an intolerable impediment to proper policy formation, constitutional purists would argue, then the proper route was the removal of the referendum requirement by constitutional amendment.

As a practical matter, however, such an amendment was not possible. Given this circumstance, activists in various policy areas—higher education, mental health, public transportation, and so on—could easily find merit in one or the other program, financed through moral obligation borrowing or lease-purchase agreements. The real problems arose because of the injudicious use of these techniques. Once they became available, they were applied across the gamut of policy areas without regard for the overall fiscal problems that might arise in the future. To confuse the issue further, a survey of the use of moral obligation financing in the forty-eight states published in 1967 reported that constitutional limitations on state and local debt were not successful in restricting the issuance of obligations of this nature. Nor, for that matter, was there much difference between states having limitations and those that did not in the amount of debt issued.[107]

Moral obligation financing may be the best example of Rockefeller, the activist and innovative governor, pushing his powers and the resources of his state to their very limits. He defined large goals and set out to achieve them, not accepting as given the fiscal and constitutional limits he found in his path. Ways were found to cut red tape, to get things done. Problems were faced one by one, and imaginative solutions were found for each of them even if they required tax increases. In the end, however, there was too little consideration of the cumulative, long-range impact of these solutions upon the economy of the state, too little awareness that these innovations had within them the seeds of new difficulties that could threaten the very viability of state government in New York.

7

The Governor and
Urban Problems

"New York City is pie for the hayseeds.... Why should anybody be surprised because ex-Governor Odell comes down here to direct the Republican machine.... He, like all the other upstate Republicans, wants to get hold of New York City. New York is their pie.... We don't own our streets or our docks or our waterfront or anything else. The Republican legislature and Governor run the whole shootin' match."[1]

Speaking over a half century ago, George Washington Plunkett, sachem of Tammany Hall, had a point, and one that remains valid to this day. The politics and government of New York City, and indeed of all the cities and other local governments in the state, are intimately related to—some say even wholly determined by—decisions made at the state level. In law, cities, chartered by the state, are its creatures. This fact is of major importance. New York State's constitution, and legislation passed pursuant to it, demark the limits of the powers of local officials to govern, to tax, and to borrow. From a fiscal standpoint, the vast amount of state-raised revenue returned by New York to its localities gives the governor, the legislature, and state officials in Albany tremendous leverage over local decisions, even in policy areas traditionally of local concern.

The vast amount and complexity of legislation affecting cities made it difficult in specific instances for a city to determine whether it had the power to act. Politically, local officials often welcomed state intervention in their affairs. It gave them the opportunity to pass the buck to the state and thus relieved them of the responsibility for unpopular decisions.[2] Politics enter city–state relations in New York in another, more partisan way as well, and here again Mr. Plunkett's observations have stood the test of time. Cities, and especially New York City, have been the bastion of the Democratic party in the state, while the Republicans, who most often have controlled state government in Albany, have had their strongest base in suburban and rural areas.[3]

Most discussions of urban problems in New York soon become discussions of New York City's difficulties. This is natural, for New York, with its 8 million people and operating budget second in the United States only to that of the national government, is an overwhelming presence in the state. But New York State has sixty-two cities, ranging in size from New York to tiny Sherrill, which has fewer than 3,000 people. Some of these cities—Buffalo, Rochester, Syracuse, and Albany—are urban centers of national importance with social, political, and financial problems just as pressing as those of New York City, though on a smaller scale. Some less populous cities, such as Newburgh, with about 25,000 people, have all the problems faced by older municipalities in the eastern United States—loss of jobs and industry, deteriorating tax base, immigration of large numbers of unskilled minority group workers, and flight of the white middle class. The legal classification of "city" is itself misleading. New York has two "villages" that have larger populations than forty-seven of its "cities," and many suburban towns have displayed "urban" problems.[4]

Although the relationship between state and local affairs in New York has been a close one, it has not traditionally been the role of the governor to seek visible leadership in solving urban problems. Though both Democratic and Republican gubernatorial candidates had to cultivate an urban constituency to win elections, governors of both parties, especially Democrats, risked difficulty with the legislature if they appeared "too city oriented" once they got to Albany. Further, from the point of view of the governor, divisive and destructive fights between urban ethnic and interest groups were best left in the bailiwick of the cities' mayors. As one political scientist noted, "Few governors would risk the time, effort, or reputation for a genuine entry into big-city politics. ... Governors and big-city mayors were usually different breeds of men, catering to different kinds of constituencies. ... It was a rarity for a mayor to be elected governor; he usually came equipped with the wrong kind of record and organization. As a result of all this, governors came to deal with their cities on an arms-length basis."[5] (No New York City mayor has become governor of the state in modern times.) Further, political instinct was largely reinforced by the governmental division of labor.

State government dealt in matters—such as state parks, mental hygiene, highways, agriculture, and labor—that were not particularly specific to urban areas, and governors tended, perforce, to give most of their energies to these areas.

This political and governmental accommodation worked well enough when cities were rich centers of commerce and industry and were able, for the most part, to pay their bills from their own resources. But as a result of agricultural mechanization, the social trauma of the Depression, and the vast demands for labor of World War II, a great migration of the nation's poor and unskilled poured into the cities of the state, and the influx continued unabated into the 1960s. At the same time, federal initiatives (often unwittingly abetted by state policy) in highway construction and mortgage finance spurred the exodus of the middle class and industry from these same cities. The cities thus found themselves with populations that demanded more services but with diminishing resources to provide them. Burgeoning welfare rolls, deteriorating mass transit systems, educational problems, environmental pollution, narcotics addiction, housing shortages—the problems multiplied, but the tax base grew hardly at all.

When the disorders of the mid-1960s arrived, governors found themselves on the firing line. With the general increase in their powers and terms of office as the changes advocated by reformers began to take hold, their visibility in the states' political system increased and the things expected of them increased apace.[6] As the cities' own resources failed them, they increasingly turned to the state and federal governments for help. Expected to respond, the governors began to do so, not only to help solve problems that were spilling over urban borders into the hinterland but also to forestall the further development of an independent relationship between the national government and the cities that would circumscribe the states' role in the federal system. An urban governorship began to emerge.

In New York, the development of the urban governorship reflected the national trends. As early as 1961, at the National Governors' Conference, Governor Rockefeller sponsored a resolution calling upon the states to "assume leadership in the solution of urban and regional problems."[7] In fact, New York had a long tradition of state fiscal assistance to local governments, and in some policy areas, notably housing, an extensive history of involvement and concern. This involvement was renewed in the early 1960s, a time when major state initiatives were taken in other urban-related areas as well.

At a joint hearing of the House and Senate Subcommittees on

Intergovernmental Relations in June 1963, Governor Rockefeller restated his position, first offered at the Godkin Lectures at Harvard in 1962, that "state government is the logical leader of intergovernmental cooperation in the solution of urban and regional problems." He said further:

> The problems of urbanism have outrun individual local government boundaries, legal powers, and fiscal resources. And the national government is too remote to sense and to act responsively on the widely varying local or regional concerns and aspirations. The states—through their relations with local governments, their greater resources and powers, and their closeness to the people and the problems—can and should serve as the leaders in planning, and the catalysts in developing, cooperative action at the local-state-federal levels.[8]

In taking the lead in urban-related policy areas, however, Governor Rockefeller faced major difficulties. First, localities were resistant to "interference" by the state in local matters; they continued to fight the home-rule battle. Second, geographic and partisan battles were intensified by the tendency of New York's multiethnic citizenry to translate urban program proposals into racial terms. A recent study by Daniel Elazar, which ranked states according to their potential for intrastate political conflict, placed New York among the top three states in this category.[9] Such a political context made it difficult to institute an urban political agenda in the state. Nevertheless, this agenda became a priority for Rockefeller as he confronted the problems of the decade and a half during which he served.

Efforts of the Rockefeller administration to solve urban problems can be divided into three categories. Legally, there was an effort to amend the state constitution and laws affecting local governments to give counties, cities, towns, and villages more flexibility to work, both singly and together, to address the problems themselves. The success of these efforts was arguable. Second, state financial aid to localities was greatly increased. Thus local governments were becoming more fiscally dependent on the state while seeking more legal independence. Finally, the state became directly involved in certain problem areas that became matters of overarching concern.

Home Rule

The debate over the proper division of political power and legal authority over local affairs in New York extends back to the early history of the state. At the beginning of the nineteenth century, demands for home rule were closely linked to the malapportionment of the legislature, which worked to the disadvantage of New York City. At the 1821 Constitutional Convention, Martin Van Buren argued for the extension of the suffrage, only to arouse James Kent, who opposed giving the vote to "the motley assemblage of paupers, emigrants, journeymen, manufacturers, and those indefinable classes of inhabitants which a state and a city like ours is calculated to invite."[10] Later, after the Civil War, restrictions in state laws and constitutions concerning urban finance and self-government grew in response to the abuses of machine politics in large cities. These restrictions, in turn, brought on criticism by urban reformers.

In 1888, Frank J. Goodnow observed that since 1857 the state legislature had

> committed itself finally and definitely to the doctrine that it might change at will the city institutions, framing the municipal government and distributing the municipal powers as it saw fit. Since this date the largest city of the American continent has lain at the mercy of the State legislature; and the legislature has not scrupled to remodel and disarrange the governmental institutions of the city. Its charter has been subjected to a continual "tinkering" that has made the law uncertain, and a comprehension of its administration extremely difficult.[11]

The attempt of Goodnow and his municipal reform allies to reverse this governmental trend came to be known as the movement for "home rule." Since the inception of the movement, the definition of "home rule" has been somewhat elusive; one authority, Thomas H. Reed, called it more a state of mind than a tight legal concept.[12] In New York, the movement met with mixed success in its early stages. During the latter half of the nineteenth century, home rule advocates were successful on three occasions in imposing restrictions on state authority written into the constitution. What appeared to be the greatest single limitation on state activity became a part of the constitution of 1894. This provision required the legislature "to act in relation to the property, affairs, or government of any city only by general laws which shall in terms and in effect apply to all cities" except with the approval of the mayor, or, if he objected, upon repassage of the legislation.[13] Though restricting the state, the 1894 constitution did not provide a grant of power or sphere of autonomy to cities. This was done by a legislative act in 1913. The Home Rule Act of that year provided that "every city is granted power to regulate and control its property and local affairs and is granted all the rights, privileges and jurisdiction necessary and proper for carrying such power into execution," and empowered every city "subject to the Constitution and the general laws of this State" to conduct twenty-three specified kinds of programs, which seemed to run the gamut of municipal functions.[14]

In 1923, a constitutional amendment incorporated both prongs of what came to be called the *imperium in imperio* model of home rule into the state constitution. "A limited sphere of power [was] carved out in which local governments [were] autonomous, and, conversely, an attempt [was] made to preclude legislative intrusion into purely local concerns."[15] Municipalities were given legislative powers in nine specific areas, and the legislature was barred from local "property, affairs, or government" except when acting by general law. In a further revision in the 1938 constitution, the affirmative grant of power to cities was broadened to matters relating to their "property, affairs, or government" not inconsistent with general law, and state action in city matters was further limited by a clause permitting the legislature to enact special legislation relating to individual cities only when the mayor and the council, or the council alone by a two-thirds vote, request it in writing.[16]

The story of the period between 1894 and 1938 was not entirely one of expanding home rule. The 1894 constitution included restrictions on urban taxing and borrowing powers that were retained in later constitutional revisions. More important, however, has been the restrictive interpretation of constitutional and legislative home rule provisions made and sustained by the state judiciary. In New York, Dillon's rule prevails. Under this rule of law, cities are regarded as legal creatures of the state. In applying this rule the New York courts have almost universally interpreted home rule powers in ways that restricted local action.[17]

In the landmark case of *Adler* v. *Deegan*, for example, the court upheld a multiple-dwelling law, applicable only to cities with populations of over 800,000.[18] The court agreed with the social aim of this law, which was directed at hazardous conditions in the New York City tenements, but in upholding this form of legislative classification as "general" it undermined the constitutional home rule provision. In his decision, Chief Judge Crane of the Court of Appeals commented: "When the people put these words [property affairs or government of cities] in article XII of the Constitution, they put them there with a Court of Appeals definition, not that of Webster's dictionary."[19]

Judge Cardozo, in a concurring opinion, struck a blow against home rule with the enunciation of the "state concern" doctrine. He said that "if the subject be in a substantial degree a matter of state concern, the legislature may act, though intermingled with it are concerns of the locality."[20] This doctrine, of course, is very permissive for state action, since "state concern" can be found in almost any matter. Since this decision, the New York courts have consistently placed a narrow construction on the home rule powers of cities. The psychological impact of these decisions on local officials probably goes beyond the legal impact. One commentator has noted, for example, that "the uncertain limits of municipal power have had a stultifying effect on local initiative."[21]

The major initiative in the home rule area during the Rockefeller years was the constitutional amendment of 1963 and the home rule statute of 1964. The amendment had its roots in the work of the Temporary State Commission on the Constitutional Convention, chaired by Rockefeller in 1956 and 1957, before he became governor. The amendment, which extended home rule to towns and villages as well as cities (counties had been included in 1938), included a bill of rights of local government, a grant of power in ten specifically designated areas to augment the "property, affairs, and government" clause, and a clause mandating liberal construction of local powers. The home rule statute, also mandated in the amendment, was to be a vehicle further to augment "property, affairs, and government"; any power granted under it could be repealed by the legislature only by action in two consecutive years. In recommending the adoption of the home rule amendment to various meetings of local officials in 1962, Governor Rockefeller called it "a Magna Carta for local government" and "one of the most important developments in strengthening local government in this state's history."[22]

Despite these seeming steps forward, the 1963 amendment retained the "property, affairs, and government" language (the basis for restrictive judicial interpretation), and the 1964 statute included a provision that the legislature might adopt any law relating to local matters other than property, affairs, or government. An attempt at further constitutional liberalization failed when the 1967 constitution was defeated, and the courts showed little inclination to retreat from their application of Dillon's rule, despite the seeming intent of the 1963 and 1964 changes.[23]

As a practical matter, during the Rockefeller period the state legislature continued to enter into the affairs of cities and other local governments at its discretion. It did so, for example, in 1969 with the passage of a school decentralization law for New York City and again in 1971 when a vacancy decontrol measure applicable only to that city was passed over the protest of Mayor Lindsay and other city leaders. Although the reapportionment of the state legislature in the early 1960s took some of the sting from the charges that urban areas were underrepresented in Albany, cities continued to use the emotional appeal of home rule to oppose such measures as state-imposed pension costs and, again in New York City, attempts by the state to gain administrative input into the City University.[24]

Home rule, however, would not in itself solve the urban fiscal problems that appeared in the 1960s. While seeking greater freedom from state intervention in their affairs, localities increasingly turned to the state government for financial assistance. Like other cities throughout the nation in the 1960s, cities in New York, which largely depended on the real property tax, experienced difficulties in paying their bills. Between 1961 and 1971 in the state's cities other than New York City the cost of basic services rose 101.8 percent. In New York City the increase was 251.1 percent. In contrast, the fully taxable assessed valuation in these upstate cities rose only 26.8 percent during this period; in New York City the increase was 41.6 percent.

Although New York's cities frequently raised tax rates through the 1960s, the increase in real estate tax revenues came largely from the growth in assessed valuation, for two reasons. First, increasing rates was a highly visible action and one that local politicians were loath to take. They feared both voter anger and the loss of jobs and middle-class taxpayers to the suburbs, where realty taxes might be lower. Second, article VIII of the state constitution placed a ceiling on the taxes that cities might level on real estate to pay their current operating expenses. Many cities reached this ceiling by the late 1960s. In 1969 the state legislature passed a law allowing Buffalo, Rochester, and Yonkers to tax outside constitutional limits in order to pay for employee retirement and social security costs on the basis of the legal fiction that these were not "operating expenses." When, in the year after Governor Rockefeller left office, the state court of appeals declared this law unconstitutional, a crisis in local finance throughout New York was precipitated.[25]

The difficulties that the city of Buffalo has faced with the real estate tax, though perhaps more extreme than those of other cities in New York, illustrate the problems with this source of revenue. In 1974 the Penn Central and Erie & Lackawanna railroads were in bankruptcy and were being restructured under the federal Railroad Reorganization Act, and Buffalo could not collect $6 million in back taxes from these sources. Furthermore, economic problems and increased unemployment in the city made it impossible for many persons to pay their tax bills, and consequently Buffalo was unable to collect $3 million in real property taxes on private residences.[26]

The squeeze between revenues from local sources rising slowly (if at all) and rapidly increasing expenses, though a national trend, has perhaps been felt more heavily in New York's cities than in cities elsewhere because of the structure of local government in New York. In many states the costs of local governmental operations, such as mass transit, water supply, and park maintenance, are financed through special independent districts. In New York State, however, the costs of these services are largely carried by local governments of general jurisdiction, so the increases in these costs have been reflected in city budget figures. One study that compared New York City's budget with that of Chicago noted that "the people of Chicago get more services from Cook County and from the State of Illinois; [thus] the burdens and fiscal responsibilities of the city are shared more significantly by other layers of government. The result is that the municipal government does not feel as severely and directly the terrific impacts of an eroding tax base, of shrinking municipal resources, and of skyrocketing costs."[27]

The consequence of these fiscal pressures has been the increased dependence of New York's cities and other local governments on state and federal assistance. In 1973, an average of 29.0 percent of the budgets of the state's "Big Six" cities was state aid, up from 19.6 percent in 1958. Federal aid was up as well; it provided an average of 10.5 percent of the budgets of these cities, compared with 3.9 percent in 1959 (see Table 21).[28] Three recent studies of the geographic distribution of state aid have concluded that assistance to New York's urbanized areas, including cities and their suburbs, increased at a faster rate than aid to the rest of the state.[29] The case of New York City is exemplary. Between 1959 and 1972, state aid to New York City increased by 462 percent while state aid to the rest of the state increased by 290 percent.[30]

These statistics seem to belie the oft-heard charges that New York City is shortchanged by New York State in the various categories of local assistance. In 1959, that city received 22.2 percent of its general revenue from the state, which ranked it third among the Big Six cities.

Table 21.   Sources of Revenue for New York State's Big Six Cities, 1958 and 1973 (percentage)

City	Revenue from state 1958	Revenue from state 1973	Revenue from own sources 1958	Revenue from own sources 1973	Revenue from federal and other local governments[a] 1958	Revenue from federal and other local governments[a] 1973
Albany	14.7	13.0	83.9	61.2	1.4	25.8 (11.2)
Buffalo	19.5	41.2	74.0	41.2	6.4	17.5 (8.1)
New York City	22.2	43.2	76.5	51.8	1.3	4.9 (4.8)
Rochester	17.8	23.7	61.3	51.4	20.9	24.9 (9.4)
Syracuse	23.4	29.0	74.2	39.8	2.3	31.1 (17.4)
Yonkers	20.1	24.1	79.0	60.2	0.9	15.6 (11.9)

Sources: U.S. Department of Commerce, Bureau of the Census, *Compendium of City Government Finance, 1958–1959* (Washington, D.C.: Government Printing Office, 1960), Table 3; U.S. Department of Commerce, Bureau of the Census, *City Government Finances, 1973–1974* (Washington, D.C.: Government Printing Office, 1975), Table 5.

[a] Federal aid was not reported separately by the census in 1958/59, and therefore aid from the federal government and revenue from other local governments are presented together to preserve comparability. For 1973, federal aid alone appears in the table in parentheses.

By 1973, it was receiving over 43.2 percent, slightly better than Buffalo and extraordinarily better than the other major cities in the state (see Table 21).

The large increase in the percentage of state aid to New York City between 1959 and 1973 was tied closely to the tremendous increase in social service aid. Moreover, the redistribution of state aid was also tied to federal programs and influenced by them. In 1957 New York City received 65.5 percent of all state aid (excluding federal aid) for social services. By 1971 it was receiving 70.8 percent. Federal aid to New York City for the same group of services rose slightly, from 65.3 percent in 1957 to 69.1 percent in 1971.[31] Because of the increase in state aid to New York City for social services, every other category of the city's Local Assistance Fund registered a *proportional* decline between 1959 and 1972. State aid for city education took the most substantial drop. In some ways, therefore, the failure of New York City to achieve an even more dramatic increase in its share of total state aid resulted because grant formulas for education remained unfavorable to the city.[32] Generally, the change in the geographic distribution of state aid during the Rockefeller administration can be seen as a reflection of population movement, socioeconomic trends, and decisions at several levels of government.

Urban Lobbying

With the state an increasingly central factor in local finance in New York, it is not surprising that the executive and legislative branches in Albany were the focus of intense lobbying efforts by the full range of representatives of local governments and those interested in local government in New York. Traditionally, the interests of cities have been represented in the state capital by the New York State Conference of Mayors and Village Officials, although some large cities, notably New York City, maintained their own representatives in Albany even before Rockefeller became governor. Towns, counties, and school districts had their own associations, as did local public employees, whose organization and new militancy were a major factor in the fiscal pressures of the late 1960s.

As one of the first initiatives of his administration, in 1959, Governor Rockefeller, acting on the advice of Frank Moore (a former lieutenant governor and founder of the New York State Association of Towns), established an Office of Local Government (OLG) to provide a central focus for state–local relationships in New York. The OLG was given an executive director and an advisory board made up of the representatives of the various local jurisdictions in the state. Moore became chairman of the board.

Representatives of cities felt that Moore, who dominated the agency, was less sympathetic to their needs than to those of suburban towns and counties.[33] Indeed, these jurisdictions were much more likely to be Republican than were the state's cities, and thus they provided a natural "local government constituency" for a Republican governor. One indication of the administration's priorities among local governments was that Governor Rockefeller rarely addressed the annual meeting of the state Conference of Mayors, while he rarely missed an annual meeting of town or county executives during his tenure. In fact, during his first two terms he spoke at the state County Executives' Association meeting every year.

Generally, the objectives of cities during the Rockefeller period were increased state financial aid, reduction or elimination of costs mandated by the state, removal of factors in aid formulas that were viewed as discriminatory, adoption of legal and administrative changes that would make easier the incorporation of new cities, and avoidance of the transfer of functions and revenue sources to other levels of government that would undermine the cities' viability as general-purpose governments.[34] Some victories were won. In 1965, for example, the state agreed to pay the total land acquisition costs for arterial highways in cities. The previous 50 percent matching requirement had virtually blocked construction, since hard-pressed localities could not provide the funds from their own sources. Later in the 1960s, cities won the inclusion of a set of priorities based on need in the state Pure Waters Program.[35] Overall, however, during the Rockefeller period the continuing trend was toward an increased role for county government. This trend was reflected in the transfer of functions from cities, towns, and villages to counties, the increased administration of state programs through the counties, and the inclusion of counties in the per capita aid formula.[36]

Cities were thus fighting a difficult battle in Albany, and as the 1960s moved toward a close, their partisans came more and more to realize their overriding need to work together. Under the aegis of the state Conference of Mayors, the Big Six cities—New York, Buffalo, Albany, Rochester, Syracuse, and Yonkers—began to come together for a united lobbying effort.[37] Previously, partisan differences among the mayors had blocked united action, but when Lee Alexander, a Democrat, was elected in Syracuse, Rochester was the only city among the Big Six left with a Republican mayor (Stephen May), and therefore the potential for unification loomed large in 1970. A press conference in Albany in January, which was attended by all six mayors, attracted widespread attention. Donald Walsh, counsel to the conference, later developed a plan to have the mayors of each of the Big Six cities visit other cities in the state and speak before their councils, thus illustrating the commonality of city problems and the need to work together. The result of this plan was banner headlines throughout the state.

Meanwhile, the governor, under increasing municipal lobbying pressure, facing his fourth election campaign, and desiring to highlight his own lobbying campaign for federal revenue sharing through a dramatic gesture within the state, decided to meet many of the cities' demands. Late in February 1970, Rockefeller announced a plan of "state revenue sharing" under which the state shared 21 percent of its personal income tax revenues with its cities, counties, towns, and villages.[38] It was projected that this plan would produce $158 million for New York City in the 1971/72 fiscal year and $122 million for other

Rockefeller in consultation with Robert Wagner, former mayor of New York City (1970). Photo by Bob Wands. Rockefeller Family Archives.

local governments. In total, state revenue sharing and the other elements of the New York City financial package proposed by the governor and by legislative leaders Earl Brydges and Perry Duryea would produce, it was said, $495 million for that city in 1971/72. In announcing the state revenue-sharing program, Rockefeller thanked Mayor Lindsay and the other Big Six mayors for their "contribution in the achievement of this historic breakthrough." He said further: "Revenue sharing represents a major fiscal breakthrough in enabling our local governments to meet the demands placed on them by the sweeping changes they are experiencing."[39]

Ironically, the victories of 1970, won in scarcely the second year of the joint effort of the state's largest cities, marked the peak of their achievements in Albany. In 1971 the combination of a worsening fiscal situation and a recalcitrant legislature led to a reduction in the new state revenue-sharing program, slashes in a wide variety of social programs of importance to cities, and a denial to New York City of major new taxing authority.[40] Later, an attempt to form a united policy on the 1972/73 state budget with a newly organized group of suburban county executives failed when Governor Rockefeller was successful in splitting the largely Republican executives away from the largely Democratic mayors.

Timing was everything; without the pressure of a gubernatorial election in the offing, the Big Six cities found their joint leverage in the state's budgetary process to be minimal. Certainly, from inside the state budget division, their influence on appropriations seemed negligible.[41]

With the decreasing vitality of joint efforts more and more apparent, New York City returned to its practice, never really abandoned, of independently pressuring for its interests in the state capitol. In every year of the Rockefeller administration, New York City's mayor made a pilgrimage to Albany to ask the governor and legislature for additional state aid and taxing authority to balance the city's budget. The public relationship suggested the formal movements of the minuet. Annually, in public statements, mayors painted a grim picture of reduced services, personnel layoffs, and the general decline of the city if large infusions of new funds were not forthcoming. Rockefeller, in turn, released public statements pointing up the catastrophic state tax increases that would be needed to meet New York City's demands, stressing the need to balance the city's requirements against those of the rest of the state, and attacking the city for its profligate ways.

Though not commonly recalled, the politics of this relationship was as rough in the early 1960s as in the early 1970s. In 1962, for example, Mayor Wagner slashed $20 million for programs of medical care for the elderly, and blamed shortfalls in state aid. Rockefeller, citing $24 million in federal and state assistance provided for these programs in that year, commented: "The Mayor could have used this $20 million to render any type of care to any individuals that he may be concerned about, rather than buying Cadillacs and raising his own salary."[42]

Although portrayed in the press as a conflict of personalities—"Rockefeller against Wagner," "Rockefeller against Lindsay"—the tensions between the governor of the state and the mayor of New York City were inherent in the roles of these two chief executives. Rockefeller himself pointed this out in a radio interview in 1969:

> Frankly, it is always difficult for... the Mayor of the City of New York and the Governor of New York State.... There is a built-in conflict there because the Mayor has got a lot of problems and he's got a constant desire to get more support from Albany.... When he can't solve a problem here, because he doesn't have enough money or whatever the situation is, Albany is always there to either call upon or to involve in some way in the reason why the problem wasn't solved. So there is a natural difficulty.[43]

Nevertheless, personal differences can add to this "natural difficulty," as they did between Rockefeller and Lindsay. However blunt their public statements, the personal correspondence between Rockefeller and Wagner was always cordial. In 1965, when Wagner stepped down as mayor of New York City, the governor added his praise for the mayor to that of other city figures assembled for the annual Al Smith memorial dinner at the Waldorf-Astoria; he offered no such kudos at Lindsay's departure in 1973.[44]

One of the most dramatic clashes between Rockefeller and Lindsay came during a nine-day strike of New York City sanitation men in 1968. Lindsay refused to negotiate with the union while they struck, since their action was in violation of the state's Taylor law. After the City Health Department declared a state of emergency, the mayor asked the governor to call out the national guard to collect the garbage. Rockefeller refused, and finally negotiated a settlement. The *New York Times* hailed Lindsay for standing up to the unions and condemned Rockefeller for capitulating. This dispute deepened the animosity between the two men.[45]

The difficulties between Rockefeller and Lindsay reached a peak in early 1972. For the first time, one journalist said, "the Governor and Mayor finally stepped out of the shadows to do public battle after years of nebulous gibes." The clash came at a time when Mayor Lindsay was demanding more than $800 million in state aid, while Governor Rockefeller declined to increase aid to local governments and proposed a hold-the-line budget.

Rockefeller attacked the Lindsay administration, stating that "serious students of big-city government say the ordinary citizen actually had a better chance of being heard and getting help in the old days of the political machine—because there was a direct relationship between the people and the clubhouse, right down to the block level." The governor described the city as one "where housing can't be found, streets are unsafe, corruption undermines public trust, traffic is unbearable, garbage isn't picked up often enough and, worst of all, no one can ever seem to get anything changed for the better." Climaxing this scathing attack, Governor Rockefeller said that Mayor Lindsay was simply an "inept" administrator. The word "inept" was carefully chosen. If the governor had charged the mayor with "corruption," he would have been obligated to institute formal legal proceedings for his removal.[46]

Mayor Lindsay issued a strong retort to the governor's blistering attack. Lindsay claimed that the governor was uninformed about the management and productivity of the city. Then the mayor asked, rhetorically, why the state's "inept" fiscal management had left it three-quarters through its fiscal year without enough money to pay its bills. In addition, city commissioners defended their record of service delivery. Jerome Kretchmer, the environmental protection administrator, announced that garbage was "picked up here more often than it's picked up in any other major municipality in the country." Albert A. Walsh, housing and development administrator, said: "The Governor or his housing advisors should know and do know, I am sure, that the years 1970 and then 1971 were the biggest years in history for government-assisted housing in the City of New York."[47]

The effect of the ill feelings between Rockefeller and Lindsay eventually permeated the ranks of their subordinates and was noted later by Senator Jacob Javits. Javits asserted that Governor Rockefeller and Mayor Lindsay had let their political feud greatly influence state–city dealings. The senator said: "Lindsay really had to get along with the Governor, and the old idea that the way for a Mayor to do well was to make the state government the scapegoat was no longer valid." Javits argued further that comity in city–state relationships was also important because the state was the major conduit of federal financial aid to the city.[48]

One of the great problems that New York City faced in going to Albany for aid was the maintenance of credibility. On numerous occasions mayors cried wolf, failed to receive assistance, and then found the means to solve the problems. This caused them difficulty the next time they sought aid from the state. During the debates over the city's requests for assistance in 1972, for example, Assembly Speaker Perry Duryea recalled that in 1971 the state had denied the mayor $133 million in added taxing authority despite predictions that massive layoffs of city employees would result. The layoffs had not ensued. Small wonder, then, that one veteran of the state budget division commented, "The major area of fiscal dispute with New York City is determining the extent to which the city is overstating its needs. . . ."[49]

New York City's bargaining position with the state may also be undermined by the Byzantine nature of its politics. For New York City, the most important time in the appropriations process comes at the close of the state legislative session.[50] At that time, in the hope of obtaining more state money before the legislative session closes, city representatives meet privately with state officials. During the closing days of the 1971 legislative session, Mayor Lindsay rearranged expenditures in the city's budget and lowered his estimates for needed state aid in preparation for this time of "special access." Following the traditional script, Lindsay warned that without additional state funds the "brutal attrition" of city social programs would accelerate. Then, during the last-minute negotiations, Abraham Beame, at that time city comptroller and a mayoral hopeful, went to Albany and explained how Lindsay's estimates for needed increases in state aid could be drastically reduced. The result was an aid package far smaller than the one the mayor desired.[51]

State Housing Program

In New York, state action in areas of urban distress went beyond providing a legal framework and fiscal support for local efforts. In some key fields, the state sought to take the lead in solving urban problems. New York, of course, acted in a wide variety of policy areas that were either centrally or tangentially designed to meet the needs of its urban areas, not all of which can be discussed here. It is clear, however, that the four areas that are selected—housing, transportation, narcotics, and social welfare—were among the most important for cities during the decade and a half from 1958 to 1973, and they were certainly among the most controversial.

In 1959, aides of incoming Governor Rockefeller estimated that in order to provide adequate housing for the state's citizenry by 1975, construction of 125,000 units each year would be necessary. Studies disclosed, however, that during the 1950s only about 90,000 units had been built each year. To find a solution that would close this growing gap, Rockefeller appointed a task force on housing under the chairmanship of Otto L. Nelson, vice-president for housing of the New York Life Insurance Company and vice-president of the Regional Plan Association.

The concern of the Rockefeller administration reflected a long tradition of state involvement in urban housing problems in New York. The first known use of state policy to stimulate housing production occurred in New York under Governor Alfred E. Smith in 1920, when the legislature authorized New York City to grant all new residential construction exemption from local taxation for the following twelve years.[52] By 1928, New York City boasted 546,000 new housing units as a result of what later seemed to be the greatest housing boom ever experienced by any city in America. In 1926 the Limited Dividend Housing Law was enacted to provide state aid for the construction of cooperative apartments. The New York State Division of Housing, which was created to administer the program, became the first state agency to be charged with the responsibility of overseeing a publicly assisted housing program. In 1938 the state began a program of low-interest loans to local housing authorities for the construction of low-income housing. This approach yielded 55,000 low-income housing units by the mid-1950s, most of which were located in New York City.

Later, in 1955, the legislature enacted a major limited-profit housing program, commonly called Mitchell-Lama, to provide below-market-priced housing for individuals who were not poor. In return for limiting rents to the middle-income range and keeping profits at 6 percent, private developers were given tax abatements of up to 50 percent on their projects and were provided with low-interest state loans to finance 90 percent of the construction costs. The state also granted local governments the power of eminent domain so that land could be easily acquired on which to build the Mitchell-Lama projects.

Through its research, the Nelson committee discovered that

middle-income housing remained the major need in New York. The housing requirements of lower income groups were being met, at least in part, by federal, state, and local urban renewal efforts. Good housing for the upper class was available in the private marketplace. But New York's growing numbers of middle-class families, ineligible for low-income housing, could not find adequate accommodations.[53] It was felt that the unavailability of housing was accelerating the middle-class flight from the city.

As a preliminary answer to this problem, the committee devised a scheme to increase the impact of the $100 million the state had available under the Mitchell-Lama program by pooling it with $200 million in funds provided by insurance companies and banks to create a Limited Profit Housing Mortgage Company.[54] The ultimate aim was the construction of 20,000 to 35,000 housing units at relatively low rentals. Unfortunately, the Limited Profit Housing Corporation proved insufficiently attractive both to builders and to private-sector financial institutions. It also suffered from the reluctance, experienced throughout the middle-income housing program, of cities to offer long-term tax abatements, which would further limit their income as their expenses increased.

In June 1959, after the end of the legislative session, the Nelson committee issued its final report, which contained two additional major recommendations. One called for the establishment of a New York State Housing Finance Agency, which, as a substitute for direct state loans, would finance middle-income projects with private funds obtained through direct borrowing in the bond market. The second, which would require a constitutional amendment, suggested the establishment of a "little FHA," an insurance fund for middle-income projects.[55]

Governor Rockefeller decided to emphasize the first recommendation in his 1960 legislative program. Working with John M. Mitchell, then a well-known Wall Street bond attorney, his staff devised a Housing Finance Agency (HFA) that could issue tax-free, low-interest-rate bonds to be secured by housing and to be liquidated by rents or carrying charges. These bonds were not to be full-faith-and-credit and therefore did not require voter approval. The bill creating the HFA, which included $500 million in moral obligation borrowing authorization, had little difficulty in the legislature.[56] Thus the first of the moral obligation bonds came into being.

By 1970, considerable progress had been made in constructing middle-income housing units with agency financing, about 90 percent of them in New York City, and the legislature also had increased borrowing limits for this purpose. The HFA was solely a financing agency for these projects. The detailed administrative work on housing projects was done by the state Department of Housing and Community Renewal (DHCR). A study done in 1972 found that the state Mitchell-Lama program was more successful and less costly than similar New York City programs because of better management and supervision and larger-scale projects.[57] State officials, more distant from local pressures than those in the city, were more likely to require the necessary rent and carrying-charge increases to keep projects financially sound. In 1975, however, carrying-charge increases due to inflation and the increased costs of fuel oil at the largest state-financed project, Co-op City in New York City, led to a rent strike by 80 percent of the residents. Before the matter was settled, the HFA began foreclosure proceedings against apartment dwellers.

Governor Rockefeller was active in other ways in housing in the early 1960s. He reorganized the Division of Housing (making it the Division of Housing and Urban Renewal), pushed for antidiscrimination legislation, continued ongoing state programs in low-income housing, supported the continuation of rent control in New York City, and sought a larger state role in urban renewal programs.

By the mid-1960s, other problems made their appearance. State funds to subsidize housing were exhausted. Attempts to obtain voter approval of new issues failed. There were both bureaucratic and financial reasons for housing program difficulties. Governmental red tape signaled the death knell of many projects before they were begun. A private developer in New York City was required to obtain approvals from ten departments or agencies of city, state, or federal governments, and negative reactions at any of these decision-making points could halt processing indefinitely. As Robert McCabe, formerly of HUD, disclosed, "the average period for all renewal projects between loan and grant approval and the time when 75 percent of the development is complete . . . was twelve years; add to that some three years of survey and planning and two years to get the last one-fourth of planned development started and you have almost twenty years per project." Governor Rockefeller's own estimate placed the average time in New York from the planning of a project to its completion at ten years.[58]

Even if he could negotiate the bureaucratic maze, the private developer was confronted by rising costs caused by inflation, rising interest rates, and increases in construction union contract settlements. Despite incentives in the law, developers, disenchanted with difficulties in acquiring blocks of property, tight money, and tremendous labor and building costs, shied away from financing low-income and limited-profit housing projects. Furthermore, state agencies lacked the statutory authority either to initiate development or to expend funds to investigate the feasibility of proposed developments. Increasingly, private developers would not act, and the state could not act without them.

In 1968 the governor decided upon a dramatic new initiative to cut this red tape. In a speech in Washington, David Rockefeller, the governor's brother and chairman of the board of the Chase Manhattan Bank, called for the building of low- and middle-income housing on the basis of $4 worth of private capital to $1 worth of government aid. The governor read of the speech in the newspapers, called his brother on the telephone the next morning, and said, "David, I've got the twenty cents if you've got the eighty cents." Subsequently Governor Rockefeller in his 1968 annual message proposed a "non-profit New York State Urban Development Corporation" that "would have power, in cooperation with private enterprise and local government, to undertake the planning, development and construction of housing, light industrial, commercial, educational, recreational and cultural enterprises in our city core areas."[59] Rockefeller's earlier successes with public benefit corporations, notably the Housing Finance Agency, provided the base in experience for the proposed UDC. Unlike the HFA, which was purely a financing vehicle, however, the UDC was to be involved in its projects during every stage from planning to completion.

In a later special message to the legislature, Rockefeller outlined the proposed Urban Development Corporation's powers, powers that later led it to be called the "nation's most powerful state agency for physical construction of urban facilities." The corporation was given the power to override local zoning and building regulations, and condemn and acquire property. Its financing was to come from a complex combination of first-instance state appropriations, subsidies available under state and federal programs, and grants and loans from public and private sources. Its projects, except for industrial developments, were to be tax-exempt.[60] The agency was to have a governing board of nine members, four of whom were heads of state agencies and five of whom, including the chief executive, were appointed by the governor with Senate approval.

In the legislature, the UDC plan encountered opposition from upstate Republicans, who thought it too New York City oriented, and downstate suburban Republicans and city Democrats, who feared the threat that the agency's power to override local zoning posed to home rule. After some tough political bargaining and an initial setback in the Assembly, Rockefeller strong-armed his bill through largely intact.[61]

To head his new agency the governor recruited Edward J. Logue, who had acquired an admirable reputation in the field of urban development. In New England, he had run the New Haven urban renewal program under Mayor Chester Bowles and had designed the Boston Redevelopment Board. Interestingly, Logue had previously declined an offer of a housing post in the Lindsay administration after having been engaged in developing a large-scale urban renewal plan for New York City. In declining the post, he asserted that Lindsay's program was not adequately financed and that the agency did not have sufficient power. Logue was attracted by UDC's superagency structure; later it was disclosed that $176,000 in gifts and loans from Rockefeller helped induce him to take the New York State job.[62]

In creating the UDC in 1968, the legislature authorized $1 billion in self-liquidating bonds to finance construction of new towns and residential and industrial developments. By 1970 the agency had begun work on forty-two projects, and by 1972 it had constructed almost 30,000 housing units in thirty localities throughout the state. Throughout its early life, the UDC's most controversial power remained its authority to override local zoning ordinances, though as a matter of policy the agency acted only upon the approval of local governments. During the spring of 1972, however, the corporation announced plans to construct 100-unit garden apartments that would not conform to local zoning ordinances for persons of low and moderate incomes in nine towns in Westchester County. Edward Logue argued that these developments would relieve Westchester's housing shortage, which he predicted would worsen considerably as the decade proceeded even in spite of UDC's efforts.

Opposition to UDC's plan came swiftly. Residents from these communities formed a coalition called United Towns for Home Rule, headed by Stuart Greene of New Castle, to petition against the proposed developments. The purpose of this group was to oppose "the absolute and unfettered power of a state superagency to come uninvited into a community, to override its zoning and to unilaterally impose its will upon that community."[63] Local citizens voiced concern that low- and moderate-income families would impose unneces-

sary tax burdens on the towns. Beneath the surface of these comments about the financial problems attendant on UDC's plans were
local fears about the racial and ethnic identities of prospective ten-
ants. This solid joint effort to oppose UDC came as a shock to agency
officials, who said privately that the rationale behind the nine-town
approach was to avoid the possibility that one local supervisor would
successfully counter UDC's efforts and thus set an example that other
executives would be forced to emulate.[64]

During July, Rockefeller publicly announced his support of UDC's
activities in Westchester. Privately, he discussed with key aides the
possibility of going to Westchester to discuss the issue, but his associates strongly advised against such action. Yet, on July 19, Rockefeller arrived in Westchester. In an interview, the governor said that
he had made this decision because he believed that when you have a
"hot issue," going to where it exists and "telling it like it is" is the
best way of meeting the problem.[65] At the county meeting, Rockefeller claimed that UDC was not really the problem; the difficulty
was that young, low-income people could not obtain housing, and
home rule was not solving the problem. UDC, he argued, would
provide a solution.

But even lobbying by the governor could not counter local opposition. During the 1973 session, the legislature threatened to deny the
UDC $500 million in additional borrowing authority unless legislation
was passed to moderate the agency's power to override local zoning.
As Logue put it: "It was quite clear that, as somebody had warned
... [Rockefeller], 'you don't have to sign this bill, Nelson, but they
are going to catch Logue at the pass, they are not going to give him
any more bonds.'"[66] The governor, who through the 1972 election
had strongly backed UDC in a geographic stronghold of his own
party despite the opposition of virtually every local Republican
leader, reluctantly signed a bill giving villages and towns the right of
veto over UDC projects within thirty days of the announcement of the
proposal.

The overriding need of the UDC for more borrowing authority in
1973 was a harbinger of the corporation's financial difficulties. The
agency was designed to cut red tape and to expedite construction, but
this flexibility left it without the usual bureaucratic checks that would
have helped avoid financial difficulty. Its methods—building quickly,
taking risks on verbal promises of federal aid that might not be forthcoming, and assuming responsibility for projects that nobody else
would build—ultimately left the UDC holding large numbers of prop-

erties that could not generate the necessary revenues to meet the agency's debt to service commitments.[67]

On February 26, 1975, the UDC defaulted on $104.5 million in bond anticipation notes. The agency had been in financial trouble since 1973. The moratorium on federal housing subsidies, announced by President Nixon in that year, was a blow to the corporation, which had built projects on HUD's "administrative assurances." With other, more attractive investments available, the bond market became increasingly reluctant to buy the moral obligation investments of the UDC, especially when the corporation's independent auditors were writing equivocal statements in its annual reports. This reluctance was reinforced in 1974 when Governor Wilson signed a bill repealing the 1962 covenant on the bonds of the Port Authority of New York and New Jersey that barred the authority from using its surplus revenues for mass transit. Commenting on this action, Frank Smeal, vice-president of Morgan Guaranty Trust, said: "The inference was easily drawn that one who would revoke a legal obligation can have little regard for an annually maturing promise euphemistically referred to as a 'moral obligation.'"[68]

Despite the UDC's difficulties, partisans of Rockefeller and even some of his critics argued that, had he remained governor, default could have been avoided because of his contacts in the New York financial community.[69] It is highly questionable, however, whether such a great superstructure should have been built on the fragile web of the governor's personal connections. In any event, it was naive to assume that a government agency designed to undertake high-risk housing projects could long be successful without continuing government subsidies. This was the basic flaw in the UDC design.

A task force appointed by Rockefeller's successor, Malcolm Wilson, in September 1974 and chaired by Richard Dunham, his budget director, recommended a cutback of $400 million in UDC projects and a reduction of $400 million in agency bonding authority. Although Wilson did order a halt to UDC construction, he did little else to ameliorate the coming crisis.

Under the direction of Richard Ravitch, who was appointed chairman of the board of UDC by Governor Hugh Carey, with the creation of a new financing vehicle, the Project Finance Agency, and with a major infusion of state funds, the new Democratic administration was able in the spring of 1975 to bail out the UDC. After a difficult period, the UDC by 1978 was operating on a sound basis. It had a role, for example, in the successful effort to keep the American Stock Exchange in Manhattan. But, as Ravitch noted, in housing, as in other significant policy areas, "the major problem of the 1970s will be to find ways to pay for the solutions of the 1960s."[70]

Narcotics Addiction

Although many states reported problems arising from the rapid increase in the narcotics traffic during the 1960s, difficulties became especially acute in certain areas of New York. Vast amounts of illicit drugs entered the United States through New York City and a large proportion stayed there. Indeed, statistics indicate that over one-half of the drug addicts in the country resided in New York City and that one-half of the city's crimes were committed by drug addicts. By the late 1960s, the drug epidemic had begun to infiltrate even the city's most pristine suburbs. Residents of Scarsdale, for instance, complained bitterly about what they perceived to be a community narcotics problem as critical as that of the city. In city and suburb alike, the fear of addict-related crime became pervasive. Thus, although narcotics addiction did not become a significant electoral issue until 1966, these developments had earlier made it an important urban problem in New York State.

Governor Rockefeller's first efforts in the area of narcotics addiction were oriented toward offering the addict convicted of a crime the option of rehabilitative treatment in a special facility of a state hospital rather than a prison term. Under the Metcalf-Volker law of 1962, a special central narcotics office was established in the Department of Mental Hygiene, an advisory State Council on Drug Addiction was created, and a total of 550 beds was added to mental hospital facilities throughout the state to be used for in-patient care.[71] In speaking of his approach to this problem during 1962, Rockefeller termed the narcotics addict an "unfortunate victim" of a "dread disease," the proper subject for "human renewal." He said of the Metcalf-Volker law: "This is a humane, practical approach to make it possible for many unfortunate victims of addiction, in trouble with the law because of their helpless dependence on drugs, to be rehabilitated and saved as self-respecting, self-reliant members of society before it is too late for them."[72]

By 1966, however, Rockefeller had become convinced that his 1962 initiative was not working and that, despite his urgings, the federal government was not going to enter the area in a major way. In his State of the State address of that year, he said that the Metcalf-Volker approach proved inadequate because most addicted criminals chose short prison terms rather than the three-year treatment program and then returned to a life of crime. What was now needed, the governor argued, was a *compulsory* program of treatment, rehabilitation, and aftercare. In later hearings before the State Investigation Commission, Rockefeller's contentions about the effectiveness of the Metcalf-Volker Act were borne out. It was disclosed that 90 percent of those eligible for treatment did not apply, that 80 percent of those who submitted to treatment were rearrested, and that 90 percent of the 1,742 addicts treated from January 1, 1964, through June 30, 1965, absconded from the program.[73]

Within a few days, Governor Rockefeller and Mayor Lindsay had drafted a tentative proposal embodying the major recommendations set forth in the governor's State of the State address. The plan, released on February 24, was modeled after California's drug program, which provided a maximum of five years of compulsory treatment for addicts. The Rockefeller proposal, however, suggested a three-year maximum treatment period and also asked that the length of prison sentences be increased for those found guilty of selling drugs. The plan also called for the establishment of state rehabilitation centers and a Narcotics Addiction Control Commission (NACC) of five members, which was to be administered independently of the Department of Mental Hygiene. To finance the program, the governor asked for an initial appropriation of $75 million to cover construction costs and stated that he would request another $6 million in his supplementary budget later in the session.[74]

Citizens across the state, many important organizations, and most legislators voiced initial approval of the governor's plan. The New York Medical Society endorsed the program through its chairman and long-time Rockefeller adviser, Donald Louria. Frank Hogan, New York County district attorney, announced that the state district attorneys' association gave its "vigorous and enthusiastic support" to the governor's proposals. Later that year, the American Medical Association gave its approval. While the vast majority of legislators found it politically unwise to come out against the governor's plan lest they be accused of objecting to drug rehabilitation, some opposition surfaced. Senator Manfred Ohrenstein and Assemblyman Jerome Kretchmer, both Manhattan Democrats, argued that medical science had not found a way to cure addiction and that the Rockefeller program would be a failure and a colossal waste of money. These legislators called for a program of methadone maintenance. Harlem Assemblyman Percy Sutton declared: "The Governor calls this human renewal. I call it human removal." Criticism of the legislation also came from the New York Civil Liberties Union, which said it would challenge the constitutionality of a program for involuntary detention of persons not found guilty of crimes. Rockefeller replied that the addicts' rights were secured by judicial proceeding before commitment and jury trial after commitment if they desired. He also cited the 1962 Supreme Court decision that upheld the constitutionality of California's mandatory drug treatment program.[75]

Late in March, both the Senate and the Assembly overwhelmingly approved Rockefeller's new program to combat addiction. Reform Democrats, who favored a massive research program aimed at discovering a synthetic drug substitute, dissented. Although Rockefeller claimed that the new legislation would sponsor the "most comprehensive and best-funded drug program in the world," even those legislators who strongly supported the governor's antinarcotics effort did not exude such buoyant optimism. Indeed, Max Turshen, Democrat of Brooklyn, summed up feelings on both sides of the aisle when he said: "We haven't got the medical answer, so we've got to do the next best thing. We've got to keep these people off the streets."[76]

Rockefeller's plan was scheduled to take effect one year later, on April 1, 1967. Democrats charged that the entire program was simply a gubernatorial election-year ploy. Within a short time, Rockefeller's attention to New York's drug problem did prove politically wise. In campaigning for the governorship the following fall, Frank D. O'Connor, City Council president and Democratic gubernatorial nominee, took a strong stand in opposition to the governor's drug program.[77] O'Connor petitioned for the reinstatement of the Metcalf-Volker law, a position that worked to his disadvantage in the election, according to some political observers. Furthermore, in November after the election, President Lyndon B. Johnson signed into law three new anticrime bills, one of which instituted medical treatment for addicts. Rockefeller partisans subsequently claimed that the federal government was finally following New York's leadership in an area of national concern.

By the time the 1973 session of the legislature convened, the 1966 narcotics program administered by the Narcotics Addiction Control Commission was under fire from legislators and citizens alike. Opinion polls commissioned by the governor showed that, despite NACC's efforts, people in the state were still greatly concerned over the drug problem.[78] Responding to these findings in his State of the State address, Rockefeller unveiled new, hard-line tactics to deal with the state's narcotics problems. He proposed mandatory life sentences without the possibility of plea bargaining or parole for all drug users, dealers, and persons convicted of drug-related violent crimes. The governor also asked that bounties of $1,000 be paid to persons providing information on pushers who were ultimately convicted and that the provision in existing laws allowing less harsh penalties for youthful offenders be deleted.

The governor's new hard-line approach to the burgeoning drug problem resulted from his belief that the program of the Narcotics Addiction Control Commission was not solving the problem. Although he praised Howard Jones, chairman of NACC, in his 1973 speech, Rockefeller commented: "Our program was not achieving that goal, and I'm not only ready to admit it, I'm anxious to admit it."[79] The governor was repeatedly confronted with the drug problem by angry residents at his "town meetings" in black communities. Black clergymen charged that drugs were being openly sold on the streets of Harlem without police interference and demanded action. Support for this view from the sidewalks of the city came from several studies. An analysis by the State Investigation Commission revealed that during the period from September 5, 1972, to March 22, 1973, no jail term was imposed on over 59 percent of those sentenced for drug felonies.[80] Furthermore, the New York City Police Department Narcotics Division reported that in 1971, of 20,762 persons arrested for narcotics, 418, or 2 percent, went to prison, and in 1970, only 1 percent of those arrested received jail terms.[81] Underscoring the conclusions of these disclosures, State Supreme Court Justice Irwin Brownstein asserted: "The law already provides for severe penalties for drug pushers, but was not properly enforced."[82]

It must be said, however, that the NACC was designed to be a rehabilitative agency, not an enforcement agency. Its efforts were to be only an indirect deterrent to the selling of drugs; the accent was clearly on the user. (The commission's activities have since been broadened to include drug-related education programs and research.)

Assessment of the NACC has not all been negative. According to Anthony Cagliostro, director of the agency, an in-agency survey in 1973 indicated that over 67 percent of more than 70,000 persons in aftercare were constructively occupied and more than two-thirds of them were employed full- or part-time, earning an average of nearly

Rockefeller at a public hearing in Syracuse on his drug program. To the left of Rockefeller is Jackie Robinson; to the right, Milton Luger, director, Division for Youth (1970). Photo by Bob Wands. Rockefeller Family Archives.

$110 weekly. While 98 percent of those certified to the commission during its first year of operation had prior arrest records and 35 percent had been arrested five times or more, the rearrest rate of those persons in the NACC's program who were placed on aftercare status in the community hovered around only 7 percent. Finally, responding to the charge that the NACC, having spent over $1 billion—or more than $3.2 million to rehabilitate each addict—was not cost effective, Cagliostro maintained that this type of analysis could not be applied to drug addiction, a chronic relapsing condition.[83]

For a combination of reasons—political, moral, and emotional— Rockefeller decided to chart a new, tougher course. As he said in his address to the legislature: "What is needed now is a truly effective deterrent to the *pushing* of drugs so that innocent people will not fall victim to the pusher's tactics or be robbed, mugged, or murdered by him." The governor argued that "all the laws we now have on the books won't deter the pusher," and added: "The police are frustrated by suspended sentences and plea-bargaining in the courts for those they have arrested . . . and the judges, weighed down by calendars running months and years behind, hand out suspended sentences or go along with pleas of guilty to minor offenses that result in sentences of only six months to a year."[84]

Rockefeller's new plan aroused immediate controversy. It brought swift denunciations from some public officials who regarded it as being "too sweeping and simplistic." In a major speech, Mayor Lindsay attacked the governor's program as "impractical, unworkable and vindictive." He argued further that there were encouraging signs that the ongoing New York program was working effectively. Addict-related crime declined significantly in the first eight months of 1972, and the number of incarcerated criminals needing detoxification was decreasing. The *New York Times* editorialized that "Rockefeller's simplistic lock-em-up-for-life for everyone proposal is a gross disservice, making adoption of a responsible program less likely than ever."[85]

While the plan met with mixed reactions among some black New York City residents, who exhibited wariness lest the new laws provide excuses for "snatching brothers off the street," a coalition of Harlem leaders hailed it as a protection against "blood-thirsty, money-hungry, death-dealing animals." Senate Majority Leader Joseph Zaretzki of Manhattan stated that the governor's call for the severe handling of drug offenders was exactly the same as appeals he was getting in his home district. Furthermore, suburban counties such as Westchester were reported to be in favor of the proposal, and the Association of Towns of the State of New York also supported the plan.[86]

Although one should hesitate to infer a popular mandate from opinions extracted from the governor's incoming correspondence, it is worth noting that during the months of January and February, the time immediately following the announcement of his proposals, Rockefeller's mail was running almost 10 to 1 in favor of the harsh anti-drug measures. Moreover, and perhaps most important, legislative leaders of both parties initially voiced their approval of most aspects of Rockefeller's plan but withheld their full support until they had seen the proposals in bill form.

Hearings on the governor's new drug bills, held on January 29 and February 6, 1973, served to highlight a number of objections to the proposals but allowed the governor to defend his hard-line tactics. Although at first he refused to compromise, on April 12, 1973, Rockefeller submitted a new version of his original proposal that included some modification of penalties for drug sellers.[87] On April 27, 1973, the Senate passed the governor's proposal with further modifications by a vote of 41 to 14. The *New York Times* accused the Senate of having succumbed to "political hysteria over drug abuse" and called on the Assembly to reject the legislation.[88] Nonetheless, on May 3, the Assembly approved an amended bill by a vote of 80–65 with minority Democrats dissenting, and on May 7 the Senate passed the Assembly's version. One of the newest amendments instituted the controversial $1,000 bounty on a three-year trial basis. On May 8, 1973, Governor Rockefeller signed into law what he hailed as the "toughest anti-drug program in the country," calling on the police, district attorneys, and courts to "use these laws vigorously and effectively."

The drug program required the naming of approximately one hundred new judges to clear up the backlog of criminal cases in the courts and to handle the increased litigation anticipated from the new laws. Although Democrats first called the judicial appointments thus made available to Rockefeller "the biggest patronage bonanza in history," criticism was muted when the governor appointed a bipartisan screening panel to review the qualifications of potential judges. Later appointments were made from both major parties. Aside from the appointment of almost one hundred new judges, opportunities for patronage were seen to exist in the "hundreds of non–civil service jobs for assistants and stenographers assigned to the judges."[89]

By mid-August, the state had launched an intense advertising campaign to inform the public, specifically the drug community, about the new drug law and its harsh penalties. The campaign, which cost $500,000, included full-page newspaper advertisements, radio announcements, and television commercials that warned against "getting caught holding the bag." A hot line was set up so that people could call for information about the drug laws and be referred to treatment centers if they wished. With some help from former addicts, "drugmobiles" were sent to areas throughout New York City carrying information about treatment and the new laws.

Although the new drug law resulted in a reduction in blatant street dealing in narcotics during the first few weeks it was in effect and was at least partly responsible for a sharp decline in drug felony arrests, both of these trends were reversed in short order. By November of 1974, a *New York Times* survey showed that felony arrests were returning to previous levels. Although, on balance, law-enforcement officers felt that the law helped them combat crime, they were still critical of its "inflexibility" and its failure to distinguish between major drug dealers and young addicts. Frank Rogers, New York City special narcotics prosecutor, commented that the law discouraged "amateurs," who did not wish to gamble on life sentences, and it seemed to be encouraging the movement of some drug sales to neighboring states. One unanticipated by-product of the 1973 drug law, Rogers pointed out, was that it encouraged members of organized crime to turn against their associates in order to avoid indictment for offenses carrying fifteen- and twenty-five-year minimum sentences.[90]

During the first fourteen months of the law's enforcement, 209 persons were convicted of felonies carrying mandatory life sentences. Several of these convictions were appealed on the ground that the life-sentence provision violated the "cruel and unusual punishment" clause of the Eighth Amendment, but by late 1974 the justices of the Appellate Division of both the first and second judicial departments had rejected these contentions. Writing for a unanimous court in the first district, Justice J. Clarence Herlihy stated, "In our present-day society, the punishment fits the offense."[91]

As it turned out, Rockefeller got the best of the argument with his critics on the constitutionality of his hard-line drug proposals. In addition, many predictions made about the effects of the new laws were not fulfilled. Dealers were not driven to nearby states where laws were less stringent, shootouts between police and addicts fearful of life sentences did not occur, and judges did not set bail substantially higher. Although prosecutors were increasingly tough in pretrial maneuvering because of restricted plea bargaining, judges were more inclined to dismiss cases at preliminary hearings when there seemed to be little basis for a trial.[92] Finally, Rockefeller's own prediction of a tremendous increase in the number of addicts seeking drug treatment in the state's expanded rehabilitation program was not realized.

In the narcotics area the trend during the Rockefeller years, then, was from optional treatment through mandatory treatment to strict criminal law enforcement. His record in this area is one of the key pieces of data for those who cite the governor's career as reflecting a movement from left to right on the political spectrum. Probably, however, these policy changes were more the result of a pragmatic search for a solution than the reversal of an ideological position. Frustrated by the limited successes of early programs, sensitive to popular unhappiness over the drug issue, and distressed by the failures of the criminal justice system, Rockefeller sought and obtained the "toughest drug law in the nation." But this strategy, like the ones tried before it, did not solve the problem. The search for such a solution, if one is possible, still continues.

Transportation and the Metropolitan Transportation Authority

The history of transportation policy in New York during the Rockefeller administration is, as in other urban states, the story first of a gradual shifting of priorities from highways to mass transit and then of attempts to make mass transit organizationally and financially viable. In the early years the impulse was to respond to rural and suburban demands for more roads while doing just enough to stave off disaster in the mass transit sector. When, in the mid-1960s, the ultimate crisis finally arrived, New York City's heavy dependence on commuter and subway rail transport made it imperative for the state to accept a major role to keep these systems operating.

When Governor Rockefeller took office in 1959, he launched the state's largest highway-building program in its history. Between 1959 and 1967 the annual rate of highway construction in New York was more than triple that of the previous administration, and for three consecutive years, 1965, 1966, and 1967, New York led the nation in the dollar value of highway construction costs. This accelerated program of highway construction can be attributed to a variety of factors. First, the federal government greatly encouraged highway building by financing 90 percent of the construction of all interstate roads and

50 percent of the construction of other highways. Throughout this period, Washington spent fifty times more on highway construction than on mass transportation. Second, during the early 1960s New York's electorate expressed strong interest in building new roads, thus making it a politically safe position for the governor. Finally, economic considerations played an important role. One official of the Department of Transportation reported that emphasis on highway construction "was a political decision of the governor, who concluded that the condition of highways . . . was detrimental to the state's economic position."[93] Indeed, in arguing for increased state expenditures for highway construction in 1962, the governor predicted such economic benefits as the creation of new jobs in highway construction, the opening of new areas for development, and the opening of new markets and supplies of raw materials for business.[94]

When Rockefeller took office, he was strongly opposed to state government involvement in mass transit. He stated that his goal was "to preserve corporate life in mass transit operations," that is, to continue the system of private ownership.[95] But the suburban commuter lines were in deep financial trouble. Rockefeller responded with the Railroad Tax Relief Program, under which the state assumed 50 percent of rail taxes and, later, exempted railroads from property tax on the condition that they provide a minimum level of service. The state also set up a $100 million commuter car construction program under the auspices of the Port Authority and allowed railroads to lease these cars. Finally, in 1961, the Tri-State Transportation Committee was organized to deal with the area's transportation problems on a regional basis.

It soon became apparent, however, that these measures of expedience were not solving transportation problems. In 1962 the Hudson and Manhattan Railroad, which operated between New York City and Newark, New Jersey, went bankrupt, signaling the death of the tax relief program. To keep this line operating, New York and New Jersey authorized the Port Authority to build the World Trade Center on the condition that it also buy the railroad and run it. At about the same time, financial pressures on the New York City Transit Authority, which operated the subway system, grew in severity. In 1964 a strike by the Transport Workers Union was narrowly averted, but it became clear that increased labor costs would soon push the authority's operating deficit to intolerable limits.

The next blow came in January 1965 when the trustees of the New Haven Railroad, which had been in bankruptcy since 1961, recommended that commuter services be halted. Despite public pressure for the establishment of a public authority to operate the railroad, Rockefeller still clung to his position that the state should not operate commuter railroads. State and federal subsidies were obtained to keep the line going until the Interstate Commerce Commission made its absorption and operation a condition of the merger between the Pennsylvania Railroad and the New York Central.[96] The new Penn Central line fought this ruling, but ultimately paid $145.6 million for the assets of the New Haven line and took over its commuter functions in 1969.

Although Rockefeller was decidedly against state takeover in the case of the New Haven, he was pushed into state involvement by the course of events elsewhere. The Long Island Rail Road was on the verge of bankruptcy, which would have left 80,000 commuters without means of transportation to New York City. An ad hoc committee chaired by William Ronan strongly recommended that the LIRR be purchased from the Pennsylvania Railroad and that a Metropolitan Commuter Transportation Authority (MCTA) be created to coordinate and operate railroad, bus, air, and ferry services in New York City as well as Nassau, Suffolk, Westchester, Putnam, Rockland, Orange, and Dutchess counties. In endorsing the recommendations of his committee, Rockefeller stated that state takeover of the LIRR was "definitely not a prelude to taking over any other railroad."[97] Later he claimed: "We had this choice: take over the railroad as a state, which was totally against the policy that I was adhering to, or build highways." The highways would cost over $2 billion.[98] The governor's bills creating the MCTA, establishing a new car-leasing program for the New Haven, and authorizing the purchase of the Long Island were given strong support in the legislature and passed easily.

Later in 1965, William Ronan negotiated the state's purchase of the Long Island Rail Road for $65 million. An additional $800,000 was to be paid annually for the use of Pennsylvania Station and the East River tunnels. On January 20, 1966, the sale was completed. In announcing the transfer, Rockefeller, stated that the LIRR would become "the greatest commuter railroad in the nation in two months." The governor later regretted this statement, commenting that it was "almost my political undoing."[99]

By 1966 pressure had mounted for the integration of New York City's transit system into the state-operated system. A crippling transit strike in the early days of the Lindsay administration resulted in another expensive union contract settlement and underscored the urgency of the problem. One month after the strike, Mayor Lindsay proposed that a new public authority be created to operate all subways, bus lines, bridges, and tunnels in New York City. This proposal would involve the merging of all bridge and tunnel authorities into a new organization under the mayor's control. Robert Moses, chairman of the Triboro Bridge and Tunnel Authority, was vehemently opposed to Lindsay's plan. Lindsay pressed ahead in the legislature, although Rockefeller advised him that a plan for New York City alone that did not take into account commuter lines would not succeed. Later that spring, the mayor's plan failed to pass the legislature.

The next year, in a special message to the legislature, Governor Rockefeller set forth his own program to provide a broad base for restructuring the state's transportation system. In this message he recommended an interlocking directorate whose members would be drawn from existing transportation agencies to integrate transit facilities in New York City, a transportation bond issue to finance improvements for mass transit and highway construction throughout the state, and the creation of a state Department of Transportation to take over the transit functions of other state agencies.[100] For the New York City area, Governor Rockefeller proposed the establishment of a Metropolitan Transportation Authority to direct the operations, financing, coordination, and planning of city and commuter facilities.

The key to the financial success of the MTA plan was the use of surplus income from tolls on Triboro Bridge and Tunnel Authority facilities to meet mass transit operating deficits. After the MTA legislation was passed, TBTA bondholders, represented by the Chase Manhattan Bank, brought suit to block this use of the funds, claiming that the security of their investment was threatened. This suit was later settled out of court after a meeting between Governor Rockefeller and his brother David, chairman of the board of Chase Manhattan Bank. Both parties profited by the agreement.[101] The bondholders received an additional 0.25 percent interest and greater security. The state, at a cost of $12 million, obtained a new source of revenue for mass transit.

The $2.5 billion transportation bond issue that Rockefeller suggested was the largest ever floated by any state. The revenues from the bonds were to be divided between highways ($1.25 billion) and mass transportation ($1 billion). The remaining $0.25 billion was allocated for airports. The division of these revenues, which was personally determined by the governor, was designed to woo upstate legislators and the highway lobby as well as city legislators and officials.[102]

In contrast to Mayor Lindsay's plan, which covered facilities in New York City alone, Rockefeller's scheme was aimed at building a broad base of support. The bond issue would provide funds for mass transit in other large communities in the state as well as in New York City and for highways and aviation. Thus it earned the endorsement of legislators from all parts of the state. Under the same principle, a number of provisions desired by Mayor Lindsay were included as part of the bills.

On March 11, 1967, Robert Moses gave his support to the bills creating the MTA. It was reported that Moses' endorsement came in return for MTA authorization to the TBTA, which he headed, to construct two bridges spanning Long Island Sound. Opposition to the bridges came quickly from Nassau and Westchester legislators, but the governor countered by combining all the bills into one, thus preventing opponents from voting for only selected bills in the transportation package. (Later the governor postponed the final decision on the bridge construction for a year and then abandoned the projects entirely.)[103] The omnibus bill and the bond authorization passed the legislature by wide margins. On November 7, 1967, the state's voters overwhelmingly approved the new bond issue. Rockefeller appointed his chief aide, William Ronan, to head the new agency.

Plans for the improvement of transit operations in New York City began immediately. On February 28, 1968, Rockefeller and Ronan placed a total price tag of $2.9 billion on the plan for modernizing the city's transit system. In 1969, for the first time, the state made a direct financial grant for the city's subways, providing $99 million of the projected $1 billion needed for the construction of the new Second Avenue subway line, which began in October 1972.

By November 1, 1974, however, David Yunich, who succeeded William Ronan as head of the MTA, announced that the completion of the Second Avenue line would be delayed at least until 1986, and that projected costs for priority construction projects had risen from $1.2 billion in 1968 to $4.7 billion by 1981. Nonpriority projects in Brooklyn, Queens, and Manhattan were to be delayed for fifteen years from their originally scheduled completion dates. When asked by a reporter whether this action was "tantamount to cancellation" of these projects, Yunich commented: "I think when a project is put off that far, it is a polite way of saying not in our lifetime."[104]

Despite setbacks in subway construction, other railroad operations under the auspices of the MTA improved. In 1971 the MTA assumed responsibility for the commuter operations of the New Haven division of the Penn Central, and $80 million in improvements were planned. When the state purchased the run-down Long Island Rail Road through the MTA and promised to modernize it, critics said that the only change most commuters expected was the one at the Jamaica station. Improvement, however, surprised even the railroad's most vociferous critics. For instance, the railroad's on-time performance, which infuriated commuters in the mid-1960s, rose to about 94 percent, according to a standard set by the LIRR, which declares a train late if it is at least seven minutes overdue.[105] Trains were air-conditioned, and the railroad acquired almost eight hundred new Metropolitan cars.

There were still problems, however, in meeting transit operating costs. Between 1968 and 1973, subway and bus fares increased by 75 percent, from 20 cents to 35 cents; ridership declined; and the MTA's deficit grew from $44 million to $325 million. Operating deficits on the Long Island Rail Road also rose, doubling from 1970 to 1973.[106] It was no wonder that William Ronan called his mass transit operation "the biggest collection of losers ever assembled under one roof."

Unlike traditional public authorities, which are designed to be self-sustaining, the MTA, because of its financial problems, has become increasingly dependent on the city, the state, and the federal government for operating subsidies. These subsidies totaled almost $400 million in 1974. Critics were especially unhappy about back-door financing provided to the MTA by the state, when the state had little hope of receiving payment.[107] Usually, authorities are viewed as a trade-off. Some democratic control by elected officials is relinquished in return for a "businesslike" and "self-sustaining" operation that is not a burden on the taxpayers. In the case of the MTA, democratic control was indeed relinquished; William Ronan himself testified that the governor had little to say about the operation of the agency.[108] But, perhaps for reasons outside its control, the MTA did not become self-sustaining.

To meet transit operating deficits, on July 26, 1973, Governor Rockefeller proposed a new $3.5 billion transportation bond issue that would provide $2.1 billion for mass transit and $1.4 billion for highways. The governor and legislative leaders hoped that the allocation of a larger share of the proceeds of the bond issue to mass transit together with a provision for statewide operating subsidies would ensure its ratification by the state's voters. As some predicted, however, the distribution of funds in the bond issue contributed substantially to its defeat by pitting areas outside metropolitan New York City against the downstate area.[109]

Under Governor Rockefeller, New York State was a reluctant dragon in the area of public transportation. Looking backward, the governor summarized his efforts in this way:

> When I... took office in 1959, my attempt was... to preserve mass transportation in the hands of private enterprise. We cut the taxes in half. We did all kinds of things to help strengthen the private enterprise operation. Slowly, despite these actions, it deteriorated.
>
> First, the Long Island Railroad went into bankruptcy. And then the New Haven Railroad. Then the New York Pennsy [Penn Central] went into bankruptcy. The subway system in New York got beyond their capacity to operate. And so the State, rather than trying to support private enterprise in these areas, ended up having to take them over.[110]

When the state did act, it acted vigorously. A massive bond issue allowed the financing of capital improvements in both the subways and the commuter railroads, commuter rail service was upgraded, and for the first time the concept of the operating subsidy for mass transit gained ground. Reorganization downgraded highway programs and made them part of an integrated transportation program for the state. And a regional approach was taken to New York City's problems.

Nevertheless, when Rockefeller left office, capital programs had to be curtailed and the financial problems of mass transit remained virulent. Despite all of New York's innovation, the vast problems of mass transportation finance seemed beyond the reach of a solution at the state level.

Public Welfare

In the controversial policy area of public welfare, Nelson Rockefeller traveled a long road during his fifteen years as governor. He went from a stress on "enlightened care and assistance for needy individuals"[111] in his first term to an emphasis on cutting welfare costs in his last term. He moved from absolute opposition to a state residency requirement for the receipt of aid to advocacy of such a requirement, despite the fact that it was virtually certain that the U.S. Supreme Court would find it unconstitutional in short order. He presided over a vast increase in the public assistance rolls in the 1960s, only to

Rockefeller, Mayor John Lindsay, and Transportation Chairman William Ronan publicizing the transportation bond issue in 1971. This is recalled as the picture that killed the bond issue. Photo by Bob Wands. Rockefeller Family Archives.

devise legislative and administrative strategies to cut them back dramatically in the 1970s.

Some charged that Governor Rockefeller's changed positions on the welfare issue were taken simply out of political expediency. He moved to the right, it was said, to please an increasingly conservative statewide constituency and to carve out support for himself within the Republican party for a potential presidential bid. Rockefeller was a political man, and certainly his policy decisions had a political component. Nevertheless, changes in his attitude toward the welfare system were guided by two considerations, one ideological and the other financial. The governor had supported New York's generous public assistance and its liberal welfare policies because of his belief in "the dignity and worth of each individual in need," as he often said in his early years in office.[112] By the late 1960s, however, he was beginning to be concerned about "inherited dependency," the phenomenon of one generation on public assistance raising another that would be similarly dependent.[113] By 1971 Rockefeller had concluded: "Rather than encouraging human dignity, independence and individual responsibility, the system, as it is functioning, encourages permanent dependence on government." Although in his budget message of that year the governor insisted that "no one in our state will lack the minimum dollars necessary for a life of decency and purpose," this perception of the effects of the system was to guide his suggested policy changes.[114]

A second major consideration for Rockefeller was that the welfare system would "overload and break down our society," not only because it undermined the work ethic but also because of its sheer size and cost.[115] Between Rockefeller's first and last years as governor, the costs of public assistance in New York increased more than tenfold. By the late 1960s, the governor was a leading advocate of federal government assumption of welfare costs. The problem, he said, was national in scope, and the current system placed a disproportionate burden on states, such as New York, with generous systems of public assistance, which gained enormous numbers of low-skill minority-group workers as a result of the great internal migrations in the United States in the 1950s and 1960s. As it became evident that comprehensive federal action to assume welfare costs and programs was politically impossible, one option was for the governor to seek to control costs, insofar as he could, in his own bailiwick. When the fiscal crunch of the early 1970s came, political factors in the state increased the pressure to take this course, and it was taken.

During the early 1960s, welfare was not a major issue for Rockefeller. Some early reorganization was accomplished in the Department of Social Welfare, but not the main thrust of the reorganization suggested in 1960 by the governor's secretary, William Ronan. Traditionally, the commissioner of this department was appointed by the Board of Social Welfare with the governor's assent. Ronan had called for the direct appointment of the head of a new department of social services by the governor. The failure of this plan in the legislature left the commissioner of social welfare outside the governor's direct control, and limited the governor's role somewhat in this area of policy.[116]

As one scholar has concluded, New York's "state-supervised, locally administered" social welfare system during this period was in fact only loosely supervised by the state.[117] Rockefeller's position during the widely publicized Newburgh welfare controversy in 1961 illustrated well his attempt to adopt a stance "above the battle" in these years. In the late spring of 1961, the city manager of Newburgh, Joseph Mitchell, declared a crackdown on welfare recipients, arguing that cheating was widespread and the case load was draining the city's economic resources. (Later statistics indicated that there was no justifiable cause for alarm: only 2.9 percent of Newburgh's population was on welfare, and the city had not even established programs mandated by the state to encourage employment.) By June, a controversial thirteen-point program designed to clear the welfare rolls was adopted by the city council, and it immediately received national attention in newspapers and broadcasts. At the request of the Department of Social Welfare, Attorney General Louis Lefkowitz successfully enjoined Newburgh from continuing the program. In a later court action, twelve of the thirteen points of the Newburgh plan were ruled illegal. Although the state sought to stop Mitchell's program, the governor did not publicly criticize Newburgh's code. While the governor had the power to intervene, the judicial route was taken to curtail the plan.

Rockefeller's emerging concern with the cost of public assistance became evident when, in December 1964, he appointed a Citizen's Committee on Welfare Costs to explore reasons for the increase in the welfare case load while the economy was expanding. The report of this committee, chaired by Hugh Jones, chairman of the Social Welfare Board, called for a one-year residency requirement and an improvement in the quality of welfare caseworkers, but it was shelved after a flurry of activity. Despite these emerging financial concerns,

Rockefeller's move in 1966 to maximize New York's gains under the new federal Medicaid Act by raising the eligibility level in the state to $6,200 for a family of four demonstrated that his primary emphasis continued to be on providing a maximum level of program support.

At the 1967 Constitutional Convention, Rockefeller was in favor of a larger role for the state in welfare administration, but the new constitution, which provided for a state takeover of administration and costs, was defeated at the polls in 1968. At about the same time, the governor sponsored a meeting of business leaders at Columbia University's Arden House. The steering committee of this group, chaired by Joseph C. Wilson of the Xerox Corporation, ultimately recommended a guaranteed minimum income and negative income tax. Rockefeller was pleased with this result, which coincided with his lobbying on the national level for welfare reform, and he reconstituted the steering committee as the Governor's Steering Committee on Social Problems.

As New York's budgetary difficulties became more and more severe, Governor Rockefeller's public speeches increasingly emphasized the cost of welfare programs and the need for a major federal role. In 1969, for the first time, he proposed a number of strong measures designed to reduce the state's welfare case load and to slow the increase in welfare expenditures. He requested that the state cut local welfare allowances by 5 percent, reduce Medicaid fees by 20 percent, and further lower the eligibility level for Medicaid from $5,300 to $5,000 for a family of four. When asked at a press conference about these actions, Rockefeller said:

> Ten years ago, welfare costs were $168 million. This year they will be over a billion dollars. . . . Welfare costs are doubling now at the rate of every four years. This is beyond education costs, education costs doubling at the rate of every six years. This is beyond our capacity as State and local government, and, therefore, to meet the requests it has got to be done by larger Federal participation. I am for Federal standards and for phased-in Federal takeover of all welfare costs.[118]

The Republican legislature approved Rockefeller's proposals and instituted two additional hard-line measures. One required that able-bodied recipients report biweekly to state employment centers and accept any job offered, and another required that individuals living in the state for less than one year and collecting welfare payments prove that they had not come to the state to receive that money. Reactions to the initiatives by the governor and the legislature were predictable. Assembly Democratic Minority Leader Stanley Steingut called the program the most horrendous in the state's history. The *New York Times* assailed what it called the "heartless victimization of the poor."[119] Later in the year the U.S. Supreme Court struck down residency laws, with the exception of those involving a "compelling state interest."

The eased fiscal situation of 1970 (and the imminent gubernatorial election) allowed a partial restoration of the 1969 welfare cuts in 1970, but economic stringencies and legislative antipathy for public assistance programs reasserted themselves in 1971. In his budget message of that year, Rockefeller reluctantly offered the legislature a budget that included the state's portion of an estimated $1 billion in increased welfare costs. He said: "I am fully aware of the tremendous burden which an outmoded welfare system imposes on state and local resources, and I shall continue to work for Federal legislation to ease this pressure. I shall also take all possible steps to reduce welfare expenditures."[120] Then, late in March, he revealed a plan for total reorganization of the state welfare program.

In the area of employment, the governor's legislation began by redefining "employability" to include mothers with children six years of age or older who were receiving welfare assistance under the Aid for Families with Dependent Children (AFDC) provision—a group that had had the option of staying at home. Under the law, all employable welfare recipients were required to report twice monthly to the New York State Employment Service offices for job referrals, counseling, and training. If they did not appear, they would not receive their welfare checks. Furthermore, employable recipients who quit jobs or refused proffered jobs were to be removed from assistance rolls.[121]

Rockefeller's reforms also included an administrative restructuring that reduced the discretion of localities in program implementation, increased state participation, and augmented the gubernatorial role. The Social Welfare Board was severed from the department and became largely an advisory body, and the governor gained the power to appoint the commissioner of social services. Within the department, a Division of Operations was established to oversee more closely the local welfare districts. Local discretion in the critical area of determining eligibility and employability was circumscribed by the development of statewide law and regulations. Tightened administrative requirements included a new photographic identification card and, later, a detailed eleven-page application form for assistance.

Perhaps Rockefeller's most controversial reforms were the estab-

lishment of an emergency one-year residency requirement for public
assistance eligibility and the implementation of two demonstration
projects, Incentives for Independence and the Public Service Opportunities Project. Critics charged that the residency requirement was a
cynical step on the part of Rockefeller. He sought, they said, to force a
downturn in assistance rolls in the short run by doing something that
he knew had already been declared unconstitutional.[122] Incentives for
Independence, dubbed the "brownie point program," lowered the
basic welfare grant for a family of four to $2,400, but allowed increases
of benefits up to $3,900 to be earned by family members for participa-
tion in prescribed activities. The Public Service Opportunities Project
required work-eligible AFDC mothers for whom jobs could not be
found to work off their public assistance grants in public-sector jobs.

Despite Democratic objections that the governor had betrayed his
liberal principles and had introduced legislation that was "anti-
Negro, anti–Puerto Rican, and anti-poor people," most of his reforms
passed easily, with solid Republican backing, in early April 1971.[123]
The residency requirement, however, was not enacted until late in
May. At about the same time, the Office of the Welfare Inspector
General, a "watchdog office" outside of normal bureaucratic channels
charged with the responsibility for monitoring state and local welfare
administration, was brought into being. It was the first agency of its
type to be established in the country.

The story of why Rockefeller decided to establish this new office is a
dramatic one. He said, "I knew for a long time that something was
seriously wrong with welfare programs but every time I asked the
department, the social workers gave me a confusing answer." Then it
happened that he took a vacation at Caneel Bay in the Virgin Islands
in the summer of 1970. On the beach he encountered George F.
Berlinger, who was vice-chairman of the Board of Social Welfare.
Berlinger had previously made a number of random studies of the
welfare system which he said uncovered widespread ineligibility, a
finding that was disputed by George Wyman, commissioner of welfare. Berlinger was a layman; Wyman was a social worker. After their
discussion on the beach, Berlinger joined Rockefeller at his home that
evening. Later Rockefeller said, "This was the first time I got a clear
explanation of the problem." At the end of the evening, Rockefeller
asked Berlinger to draw up a report on his findings, and he did. After
returning to New York, Rockefeller submitted the report to Wyman.
Later, when the legislature approved the Office of Welfare Inspector
General at Rockefeller's urging, the governor selected Berlinger for

the post. At first Berlinger declined, but then he consented after Rockefeller argued that it was he that had prompted the governor's most recent initiatives in the area of welfare.[124]

Berlinger's studies over the following three years startled state officials and welfare administrators nationwide. Although a large portion of his work was done on more than 16,000 complaints received from private citizens, his spot studies of various welfare centers made headlines and initiated fierce battles with local welfare officials, particularly those in New York City. At the Yorkville and Gramercy welfare centers, Berlinger's staff recorded ineligibility rates averaging from 19 to 27 percent. In another study that sampled 10 percent from each category of assistance, Berlinger found the average ineligibility hovered at 37 percent, with a range of from 16.7 percent in AFDC to 48.7 percent in Aid to the Disabled. Berlinger's office also found, through a random sampling of Medicaid recipients, that 22 percent were totally ineligible and that the eligibility of another 49 percent was highly questionable. To be sure, Berlinger's findings were disputed consistently by city officials, who claimed that welfare ineligibility in New York City ran no higher than 3 or 4 percent, but later a city study of the Veterans' Center confirmed to some extent the results of Berlinger's spot checks. Here city welfare officials found that 3.2 percent were definitely eligible, 28 percent were ineligible, and 68.8 percent were of doubtful eligibility. Hence these findings added at least some support to Berlinger's charge that "confusion and disorganization weigh so heavily on the system that only the tip of the total problem can be seen—its full proportions being submerged in a sea of slovenly staff work, inadequate records and a pervasive attitude of unconcern."[125]

As an outgrowth of the statistics battle between city welfare officials and the Office of Welfare Inspector General came a number of significant reforms in the administration of welfare. An important one was the transfer of the responsibility for the quarterly audits of a sample of cases from the local Department of Social Services to the Office of Audit and Quality Control, established in the state Department of Social Services on July 1, 1972.[126] This office's first audit, covering the second half of 1972, disclosed a 17.6 percent ineligibility rate statewide. The disclosure of this fact prompted the governor to order, as of July 1, 1973, that the recertification process be "face to face," as recommended previously by the Office of Welfare Inspector General. The recertification interviews were to be conducted within the first ninety days after a person was placed on either AFDC or Home Relief and would continue at intervals of six to twelve months depending on the nature of the case. Despite foot dragging by New York City officials and a consequent threat by the state commissioner of social services to withhold city welfare funds, the recertification procedure was implemented. [127]

The establishment of the Office of Welfare Inspector General, however, meant more to the administration of welfare than just the prompting of band-aid reform measures. Practically speaking, it alerted New Yorkers to the possibility that federal aid to New York State could be curtailed under new statutes that required that ineligibility rates in all welfare categories be limited to 3.5 percent. Although no one can be certain that the high ineligibility rates uncovered by Berlinger's office were accurate, it seemed clear that the proportion of ineligibles receiving welfare checks was higher than 3.5 percent and might even approach four times that rate. Furthermore, as an administrative device in the guise of a watchdog agency, the Office of Welfare Inspector General also had a deterrent effect. Although the decrease of 200,000 from New York's welfare rolls in 1972 and 1973 reflected a national trend, it occurred after the first two years of the operation of this office, after a steady rise in the welfare rolls over almost a decade, and after the public was made aware that prosecution and fines for fraud were possible and had begun. Indeed, not only did Berlinger's office prompt local welfare agencies to establish antifraud units, but in Albany 348 persons asked to have their names dropped from the rolls following the fine and imprisonment of a nearby resident found guilty of welfare fraud. [128] Furthermore, other states have watched owig closely, and California, Pennsylvania, and Massachusetts have considered establishing similar agencies. Thus the office itself became something of an administrative model for monitoring the local administration of welfare by officials outside that bureaucracy.

The Office of Welfare Inspector General was never popular in New York City, which had about 70 percent of the welfare cases. It might be noted that not a single case involving fraud reported by the office was prosecuted in Manhattan, and few in other parts of the city. When the Democrats returned to power in Albany in 1975, the office was abolished. They argued that its functions were duplicated in the state Department of Social Services.

Governor Rockefeller's attempts at welfare reform met with mixed success. His one-year residency requirement was quickly declared unconstitutional, confirming the views of his early critics. The Incentives for Independence Program caused a major political uproar in the minority community, and, although ultimately upheld in the courts, was abandoned. The Public Service Opportunities project, similarly delayed by court action, had reached only the preliminary stages of implementation when Rockefeller left the governorship. During their first year in effect, the new employment requirements of state law provided jobs for 29,369 public assistance applicants and caused the removal of 53,430 from the rolls for failure to comply. In addition, 13,400 recipients of home relief were employed on public works projects in 1972. By 1973, however, the rate of job placements declined, and welfare rolls resumed their upward climb as the economy worsened and clients became accustomed to new regulations. Generally, Rockefeller's efforts won him the praise of some, such as management expert Peter Drucker, for his "attempt to bring order to the chaotic welfare situation," but they also earned him the undying enmity of the liberal and minority communities he had long cultivated. In their view, as black assemblyman Arthur Eve put it, Rockefeller was "attempting to make scapegoats of blacks and Puerto Ricans for all the economic and social problems of our state."[129]

Can State Government Solve Urban Problems?

In retrospect, it is evident that in each of the policy areas reviewed above, New York State under Nelson Rockefeller met with only mixed success. Rockefeller said that "urban problems were the most complex I had to deal with and New York City was the most frustrating because I could not make any headway." The difficulties in achieving change were enormous. The larger social environment was in constant flux, modifying the nature and magnitude of the problems for which solutions were being sought, and thus presenting elusive moving targets for policy makers. The larger economic environment changed too, altering the problems faced and the resources available for solution. (One example provides a good illustration: increased unemployment was reflected in lower mass transit ridership, which translated into greater fiscal problems for subways and commuter lines.) Entrenched bureaucrats committed to existing programs and established clientele were often hostile, or at best indifferent, to innovation. Finally, changing priorities at other levels of government affected the realistic options available at the state level.

In each of these policy areas new and innovative governmental structures were established under Rockefeller to meet emergent problems. In two cases, housing and transportation, the structure was the public benefit corporation. Both the MTA and the UDC represented attempts to solve difficult problems with massive infusions of new capital and a rational and integrated administrative structure unencumbered by the procedural and fiscal constraints faced by more conventional government agencies. For the MTA, the source of funds was full-faith-and-credit borrowing. For the UDC, it was the private bond market, tapped through the troublesome "moral obligation" device. Both agencies had substantial achievements. Commuter rail service was improved and considerable low-income housing was built. Nevertheless, in the months after Rockefeller stepped down, serious questions were raised about whether the achievements of these agencies were really worth their cost, a cost calculated in lost governmental accountability and state fiscal instability.

In the two areas of urban social policy under analysis, social welfare and drug abuse, early meliorative approaches gave way to more restrictive policies as the problems grew despite government efforts. Innovative administrative devices were evident here as well. In social welfare, a countervailing bureaucracy—the Office of Welfare Inspector General—was used to attempt to control burgeoning welfare costs and abuses and to make this policy area more responsive to gubernatorial control. The area of narcotics witnessed two dramatic policy shifts during the Rockefeller years. First, a separate agency was established and a massive compulsory treatment program instituted; when this tactic seemed not to work, the governor turned to a tough law-enforcement stance.

It is probably not useful to think of the social policy changes during the Rockefeller years on a liberal–conservative continuum, though they are often thought of in this way. The governor was a problem solver. When he thought that one solution did not work he turned to another, and he tried to do so quickly so that he could take potential issues away from political opponents. If there was an error in this approach, it was in the assumption that all problems could be solved. Indeed, such an attitude could well have contributed to the development within the state of a set of unrealistic expectations from government, something for which Rockefeller himself often denounced the national government in Washington.

New York State under Rockefeller showed considerable courage and initiative in entering a large number of extraordinarily difficult areas of urban policy. Though there were some meaningful achievements, in the end state efforts could do relatively little to alter what were urban manifestations of national social and economic trends. From New York's experience under Rockefeller, there thus emerges a very basic question: If a wealthy state with committed leadership cannot find solutions to its urban problems within its own resources and those of its localities, are these problems soluble on the state level?

8

Expanding Opportunities
for Higher Education

Nelson Rockefeller's platform for the 1958 New York gubernatorial campaign pledged "expansion of the opportunities for higher education in the state through further development of the State University and the community colleges and encouragement of the growth of the state's private colleges and universities." During the campaign, Rockefeller promised to "attack an array of problems in higher education to assure college education to every qualified student seeking it. This includes proper encouragement of private colleges, expansion of the State University, and expansion of the state scholarship and loan program."[1]

Indeed, Rockefeller's campaign statements had identified an area of very real need in New York State. Throughout the 1950s, New York remained a state with a net outflow of students, on both the undergraduate and the professional levels. The State University of New York (SUNY) had been established in 1949, but by the late 1950s New York found itself with an institution of questionable quality that had "sunk into a condition of psychological inertia."[2]

Difficulties with SUNY were only part of the problem. The backbone of New York's system of higher education, since the founding of King's College (later Columbia University) in 1754, was its private colleges and universities. In 1958 these institutions enrolled 240,000 students, 60 percent of the total in the state.[3] Pressed by increased costs incurred to meet the growing demands for more physical facilities, new programs, and higher faculty salaries, the private institutions turned increasingly to the public sector for aid. The federal government did provide some assistance, in the form of grants to

292

institutions for new programs and, to a limited extent, in direct aid to students. Often, however, federal assistance required matching funds and thus acted partly to enhance fiscal difficulties. As a result, there were widespread demands on New York State to supplement federal assistance through some form of state aid.

To be sure, New York had a long tradition of assistance to students through regents scholarships, but, although their number and dollar amounts had been adjusted from time to time, these scholarships still helped only a small percent of the state's graduating high school seniors in 1958 and fell far short of paying all college costs, as they had done in 1913 when the program was first established. Incremental changes in the regents scholarship program were possible, but the massive amounts of aid needed suggested that the methods for extending state assistance to college students required rethinking.

The problems abounded, but it was unclear whether the governor had the tools to find solutions to the state's difficulties in higher education. First, he was limited by the structure of educational policy making. In New York, the body with constitutional responsibility for education at all levels, elementary through doctoral, was the Board of Regents of the University of the State of New York.[4] The fifteen regents were elected by the legislature for fifteen-year overlapping terms, eleven from the state's eleven judicial districts and four at large.[5] Despite its name, the "university" that the regents headed was not a university in the American sense at all. Rather, it was more a department of government on the European model.

The regents appointed the commissioner of education, who served as the chief of the Education Department. The commissioner served at the pleasure of the regents and was answerable only to them. Further, he presided over a department that had a long and cherished tradition of independence from partisan politics. It was therefore not remarkable that incoming governors of New York were surprised at how little actual control they had over the Department of Education and its policies.

That is not to say that the governor was powerless in education. After all, like other departments of state governments, the Education Department was subject to the executive budget process, a fact that led one regent to comment, "We've never been autonomous. All our major decisions involve money."[6] Nevertheless, in his relations with the regents and the commissioner of education, the governor was dealing with people he did not appoint and could not remove. It was

a true bargaining situation, one in which, at least for higher education, the commissioner came to play the role of conduit between the
regents and the governor.

Governors in the past had either squabbled with the regents, as
Dewey had, or ignored them, as Harriman had. Rockefeller did
neither. He had a strong predilection for education. While he was no
less unhappy than his predecessors about the independence of the
regents in an area that absorbed such a large proportion of state
funds, he nonetheless developed effective working relations with
them. In his first term those relations might be characterized as cool,
but as the years passed they went from neutral to friendly. The
change came about partly because of personalities. The governor
usually met with the regents as a group only once a year, but he saw
the commissioner of education more frequently. Generally he and
Commissioner James Allen and, later Commissioner Ewald Nyquist
got on quite well together. Staff relations centered in the state budget
office, headed by T. Norman Hurd, who had been a professor at
Cornell University before becoming budget director. This relationship
between professionals was generally smooth, although there were
differences of opinion from time to time over the amount of spending
for education. (All of the regents were interviewed for this study.
Only one expressed hostility toward Rockefeller, and he admitted
that the cause was a partisan matter unrelated to education.)

If the administrative structure in higher education resisted gubernatorial direction to some degree, the underlying tensions in the policy area added to the complexity of the problems the governor faced.
The possibilities of conflict were not limited to the structural arrangements. The views of pressure groups regarding education were
well known. Increased government expenditures meant higher taxes,
so some might be expected to oppose appropriations for education.
Others concerned about state–church relations might be expected to
question aid to church-affiliated institutions. Even the matter of the
location of new educational facilities had political aspects, since a new
campus could bring prosperity to a moribund community. Maintaining tuition-free colleges in New York City had long been regarded as
vital to the interests of certain well-organized groups downstate. An
expanding state-financed system of higher education might well offer
a challenge to those groups. Thus the history of higher education in
the Rockefeller administration, with all of its potential political tensions, concerns more than simply educational issues. It opens an

unusual window on the complexities of state politics and pressure-group tactics.

The Public–Private Struggle

Throughout almost all of New York State's history, the private institutions of higher education were dominant. In 1784, at the first regular session of the New York State Legislature, Governor George Clinton called for the revival and encouragement of institutions of learning, which had virtually ceased during the War for Independence. As a result, a bill was passed to establish a university that would control all higher education in the state. This original act, which created the University of the State of New York,[7] made the Board of Regents directors of Columbia College (an arrangement that was soon changed) and gave them broad powers to charter colleges and disburse funds provided by the legislature. Later, however, the legislature began to incorporate colleges and to give each college its own board of trustees, as in the case of Columbia. As a result of the curtailment of their supervisory and financial powers, the role of the regents in higher education became largely advisory. By the mid-nineteenth century, higher education in the state had become almost completely private. The regents were virtually powerless to control it or direct its development.[8]

At every point at which the establishment of a state university similar to those in other states seemed possible in the nineteenth and early twentieth centuries, the opportunity was missed, often because of the active opposition or passive acquiescence of the regents, the governor, or the legislature. In 1862, for example, the federal Morrill Land-Grant College Act awarded New York scrip for 989,902 acres, one-tenth of the total for the entire country, for the establishment of agricultural and technical colleges. Most states used their land grants to establish state universities. In New York, maneuvering in the state senate by Ezra Cornell and Andrew D. White resulted in the awarding of all the scrip to Cornell University, an otherwise private institution established in 1867. The only proviso was that the university admit free one student from each assembly district each year.[9]

In 1913 the regents accepted a plan establishing 3,000 scholarships of $100 a year for four years, to be apportioned across the state and awarded on the basis of merit, with at least five given in each assembly district. These scholarships, awarded to individual students, were the first step in a state policy of indirect aid to private colleges, and were viewed at the time as an inexpensive alternative to a state university. Augustus Dowling, commissioner of education in 1913, commented that the scholarships would "forever set at rest the question of a state university for New York and at the same time provide for the people of the state all the benefits of a State University on a liberal basis and at a minimum cost."[10]

As late as 1938, the regents' official policy was to "avoid competition financially damaging to the nonpublicly owned colleges and universities in the state," a policy vigorously pursued by the Association of Colleges and Universities of the State of New York (ACUSNY).[11] And in 1944, in their Postwar Plan for Education in the State of New York, the regents expressed confidence that the private colleges could meet any needs that arose and suggested only an increase in the number of regents scholarships to cover 10 percent of high school graduates. To be sure, there was some public higher education in New York, such as teacher training institutions outside New York City, and the free municipal colleges in the city, which dated from 1842. Up to and through World War II, however, state resources donated to public higher education were minimal; in 1941/42, New York ranked forty-seventh among the states in gross support for higher education.[12]

A crisis developed in 1945, when it was projected that one-sixth of the half-million veterans returning to New York in the first six months of 1946 would want to enroll for some form of higher education in the summer or fall. These returning veterans would raise the number of new college students to approximately 100,000, doubling the enrollment of New York's institutions of higher education in a very short time. Syracuse University, which had enrolled 6,000 before World War II, had 7,000 in the spring of 1946 and 9,000 in the fall; Cornell had 6,000 before the war and 9,000 in the fall of 1946.[13]

A number of emergency steps were taken by the state and private institutions to meet the demand for places in two- and four-year colleges, but the regents, Governor Dewey, and the private colleges were firm in seeking to avoid a permanent commitment to public higher education. Writing retrospectively, J. Hillis Miller, associate commissioner for higher and professional education, and John Allen, director of the Division of Higher Education, commented that they "were resolved that the emergency should not be used as a means or as an opportunity to settle long-term questions of educational policy."[14] As one study noted: "Apparently with the concurrence of the

Governor [Dewey], policies which, in the cause of meeting an emergency, might have wrought permanent changes in educational patterns in the state were deliberately avoided."[15]

Nevertheless, the pressure for the establishment of a state university continued. The private colleges in New York could not cope with the combined demand of the returning veterans and the new high school graduates. Similar pressures in other states meant fewer opportunities for New Yorkers in the public universities of the Midwest. Demands for expanded public higher education also came from those who believed the private colleges were discriminating against certain applicants, particularly in the admission of Jews to medical schools. In late January 1946, a report by the staff of the mayor's Committee on Unity of New York City, chaired by Charles Evans Hughes, Jr., was leaked to the *New York Times*.[16] According to the report, prepared under the direction of Dan W. Dodson of New York University, nonsectarian colleges in New York discriminated against students from New York City, especially blacks, Catholics, and Jews. Backed by the United Parents Association, the New York Teachers Guild, and the American Jewish Committee, the study advocated the creation of a state university. The day after the newspaper account appeared, the Democratic minority leaders in Albany introduced legislation calling for the establishment of a state university.[17]

In his annual message three weeks previously, Governor Dewey had recommended examination of the need for a state university, but it was not until early February 1946 that he proposed a study commission in a special message.[18] In response, the legislature voted in April to create the Temporary Commission to Study the Need for a State University; in July, Dewey appointed Owen D. Young, former General Electric board chairman and a Democrat, as head of the commission. Dewey's fifteen other appointees were primarily leaders of New York's private colleges and included a classic pluralist balance among regions, religions, and economic groups. In addition, the president pro tem of the Senate appointed two senators and the speaker of the Assembly three assemblymen.

Various factions emerged within the commission, including those representing the interests of the governor, the regents and State Education Department, the private colleges, the Catholic colleges, and various minority groups, especially Jews.[19] Among the major issues were decentralization versus centralization, technical versus liberal arts education, the cost of a university system, and the nature of its governance. According to one account:

The regents, the State Education Department, and the representatives of New York's private colleges and universities were solidly opposed to any expansion of state-supported higher education except in technical or vocational schools. Downstate Democrats and representatives of minority groups ardently championed the state-university concept, and upstate Republicans—reflecting the traditional divisions in New York State politics—tended to support the regents.[20]

Governor Dewey was lukewarm to the idea of a state university, and with his representatives on the Young commission reluctant to go too far and with other interests pushing in their own special directions, the commission became stalemated.[21] President Harry Truman helped break the deadlock. Truman earlier had appointed his own Committee on Higher Education, headed by George Zook, president of the American Council on Education. The presidential committee's report came out a few weeks ahead of the New York commission's and stressed the need for rapid expansion of public higher education and for overcoming inequalities of educational opportunity on account of economic, racial, and religious discrimination by private colleges and universities. Dewey was thus in an unenviable position, for he would possibly have to defend a weak report in the 1948 presidential campaign against the Truman committee's bold and far-reaching proposals.

Confronted with this possibility, Dewey met with Republican leaders, some of whom were on the Young commission, including John Burton, director of the Budget Bureau. Burton became an energetic advocate of a state university on the commission and a leader in drafting a compromise plan that achieved unanimous approval. Under this plan, a state university was to be organized around the existing public teacher-training institutions; the commission felt that the geographically decentralized pattern, which would serve to bring the university to the students rather than vice versa, should be continued and expanded. Tuition at the university would be free, fees low, and scholarships available, thereby eliminating the economic barrier to higher education. Programs were to be broadened to include both vocational training at two-year institutes and graduate programs.

It was on this point that the commission faced its greatest opposition from private institutions, which naturally feared the possibility of competition. Accordingly, the commission assured the private colleges that the State University would supplement and not supplant them and that planning for higher education in the state would include the private sector.

In drawing up the legislation to implement the commission's report, Governor Dewey's counsel did not consult with the Education Department or the Board of Regents for fear they, with the private colleges, would try to block the bill. Dewey, who had for years been particularly annoyed by the independence of the regents and the Education Department, wanted legislation that would give them as little authority as possible in the administration of the university.[22] He insisted that the act provide for appointment of the university's board of trustees by the governor. Despite pressures from private institutions and the regents, the legislature passed an act creating the State University of New York, which Dewey signed into law on April 4, 1948.

Passage of the legislation establishing the State University did not terminate the conflict over control of public higher education in New York. Once appointed by Dewey, the trustees took the first steps to assume direction of the State University, but at a public hearing, President Everett Case of Colgate, representing the Associated Colleges and Universities of the State of New York, warned against "undue haste" on the part of the board. He suggested that the trustees delay assumption of their administrative responsibilities until 1950, though the law stipulated April 1, 1949.[23]

The regents also seemed determined to fight a rear-guard action. In 1949 they submitted legislation to reverse, at least partly, the State University Act of the previous year. Criticizing "dual control" of education and suggesting that the existing structure made political interference likely, Chancellor William Wallin and the regents pushed the Condon-Barrett Act, designed to limit the trustees' authority to new institutions, such as medical schools, liberal arts institutions, and community colleges, while the regents would control all existing institutions, most notably the teacher colleges. Chairman Oliver C. Carmichael of the trustees of the university declared such a change would "wreck" and "sabotage" the State University.[24]

The ensuing battle in the legislature pitted Governor Dewey, SUNY's trustees, and an ad hoc Committee to Save the State University against the chancellor and the regents. Surprisingly, the regents got little support from the private colleges, which were divided among themselves. The result of this "battle of the boards," as it was dubbed in the press, was another defeat for the regents. SUNY's trustees gained essentially the same control over the university as trustees had over private colleges, though they agreed to submit the university's budget and major questions of academic and admission policies to the regents for approval.

During its first decade, the State University made only modest progress. In 1949/50 its budget was $28.9 million and its full-time enrollment 25,525. By 1958/59 its budget was $44.1 million and its full-time enrollment 38,642.[25] SUNY suffered from lack of direction. Calling a collection of eleven teachers' colleges, seven professional colleges, and eleven two-year agricultural and technical institutes, all formerly autonomous, a university did not make them one. The trustees' mandate was vague. The board was charged with governing the new university and submitting plans for a permanent organization, but among its members there was considerable disagreement as to the functions SUNY should perform. Some individuals and interests wanted a holding company for the existing scattered institutions; others saw a university based on the Michigan or California model. Some viewed SUNY as a means for establishing new medical schools, a number saw it as a planning body without administrative authority, and still others hoped SUNY would become a dispensing foundation, parceling out tax dollars to private institutions.[26] Almost all agreed, however, that SUNY was to provide only those needed educational facilities unavailable at existing private institutions.

Among the achievements of the early 1950s was the addition of two liberal arts colleges and two medical schools to SUNY's ranks. The liberal arts colleges added were Champlain College and Triple Cities College (later Harpur College). But in 1953 Champlain was closed because the air force reclaimed the original army site on which it was located. By a formal agreement between SUNY's trustees and the private colleges, which feared competition, Harpur remained the only liberal arts college of SUNY for a decade. The medical schools added were those of Syracuse University and the Long Island College of Medicine, which became, respectively, the Upstate and Downstate Medical Centers. The need for medical education proved a significant positive force in the organization of SUNY.

Another important policy decision made in 1950 was the establishment of a system of eleven community colleges for each of the state's economic regions.[27] The community colleges, operating locally, were not officially part of SUNY. The state paid half the capital outlay for the construction and up to one-third of the operating cost. The local community provided two-thirds of the operating cost, although not more than one-third could come from tuition and fees.

As the 1950s progressed, SUNY's trustees discovered that the state government might officially be committed to a state university but did not want it to be too large or costly. Governor Dewey, always cautious about creating a large permanent state university, was reported to be "not unhappy" about the closing of Champlain College.[28] In 1954, when the Democrats came to power, little changed. In fact, Harriman, the new governor, accepted all of Dewey's nominees for the SUNY board of trustees. If anything, he was more restrictive than his predecessor had been in providing funds for the fledgling university.[29]

As the decade progressed, SUNY's facilities became increasingly overcrowded. Even when funds were available, bureaucratic delays stalled the construction of new buildings. A major $250 million bond issue was passed in 1957, but the university's trustees and administrators seemed unsure about what to do with the money. Too, SUNY suffered from a poor reputation for the quality of its offerings, especially in the teachers' colleges. Its acceptance of the limitation on expansion in the liberal arts indicated that the university had a second-rate image of itself.[30]

In 1957, enrollment in the nation's colleges and universities reached a seventh consecutive all-time high, but in New York, private college enrollments remained level. Major pressures were anticipated in the 1960s and thereafter, resulting from the first impact of the post–World War II baby boom on higher education and the renewed emphasis on education that followed the Soviet successes in the space race in 1958. The demands would be much greater than those of the late 1940s, and New York seemed to be entering the crisis period unprepared. On the eve of the Rockefeller governorship, as one analyst has noted,

> there was a vacuum, an abdication of responsibility for higher education which prevented any significant policy proposals or master plans... from being put foward.... There was no system at all; there was merely a weak and undistinguished group of public institutions lumped together in a State University on the one hand, and a diverse group of private institutions on the other, with questionable adequacy of resources for expansion or desire for coordination. There was no means, moreover, for a system to evolve or indeed for the parts of a potential system to come together... because the Regents were unwilling or unable to assume the responsibility. Neither mandatory legislation calling for a system (i.e., master planning requirements, etc.) nor even the will

to coordinate were present. Thus higher education in the spring of 1959 lacked focus and direction and was indeed hopelessly bogged down in the face of an impending crisis.[31]

The 1961/62 Watershed

Rockefeller entered the thicket of higher education cautiously. He was aware of the battles of the 1940s and had come to office on a platform of "fiscal integrity." While in his first annual message he called in general terms for "a clear plan and program of expansion which will meet [the] doubling of enrollment" in higher education, the new governor's budget provided for an increase in the State University's budget of only $2.6 million over the amount spent in Harriman's last year. At the installation of Thomas Hamilton as SUNY's new president in October of 1959, Rockefeller praised New York's public and private institutions for "serving magnificently" and recognized the state's responsibility "to help provide facilities for the steadily increasing number of young people graduating from high schools," but he also said that "we cannot give all the financial support which our State University may want or need."[32]

Upon Rockefeller's resignation the *New York Times* called the expansion of the State University his "proudest achievement."[33] Yet Rockefeller's alma mater, Dartmouth College, was an institution that had given its name to the Supreme Court case that established the principle of the independence of private colleges. The Rockefeller family had formerly supported the University of Chicago, Rockefeller University, and innumerable private women's colleges and black colleges throughout the South. If Rockefeller opted for the massive infusion of state resources into public higher education, it was not because of any personal predilection but because New York's private institutions could not meet the needs projected for the 1960s. And while Rockefeller built the State University and committed massive state resources in support of the City University, he also searched for and found ways to help the private institutions.

On December 21, 1959, Governor Rockefeller announced that he and the regents were establishing the Committee to Review Higher Education Needs and Facilities. The committee was to be chaired by Henry Heald, president of the Ford Foundation, and included only two other members, Marion Folsom of the Eastman Kodak Company, formerly secretary of the Department of Health, Education, and Welfare, and John Gardner, president of the Carnegie Corporation of

New York. This was scarcely a neutral group in the public college–private college debate; all three men were from the private sector, a fact that would later give their report added weight. The Heald committee, as it came to be called, was one of thirty groups appointed by the governor to study problems in the state. It was created largely at his initiative after conversations between the governor and James Allen, commissioner of education, established that such a study was needed and that the Education Department lacked the resources to do it. Allen suggested Heald to chair the committee.[34]

There were other sound reasons that a study on higher education be made by a blue-ribbon group outside the normal structure of state government. The assumption of leadership by the governor in the field of higher education was viewed with growing trepidation by some professional educators.[35] Assigning the task to the committee allowed Rockefeller to show personal concern without identifying the resulting plan too closely with himself, gave him flexibility in dealing with the committee's recommendations, and defused any automatic opposition that a "governor's plan" might attract. In addition, the committee could be used to educate the public about the problems and to mobilize support. Though the committee did not represent a broad coalition of groups, its prestige and air of independence were useful in the political arena.

The use of study committees, especially in the higher education policy area, was by no means novel. The Heald committee, however, was more effective than many of its predecessors. First, the governor had a clear commitment to act; he expected the committee to recommend a plan. This was not simply the commissioning of a study to avoid any other action. Unlike the earlier Young commission, which, with twenty-five members, was large, unwieldy, and faction-ridden, the Heald committee, with three members, was small and manageable. While the commission appointed by Dewey contained the usual balance among interest groups and included a majority of politicians, lawyers, and businessmen, the one appointed by Rockefeller had two foundation heads and one sometime cabinet officer–businessman *cum* Ph.D. The Young commission was a political battleground; the Heald committee left politics to the politicians, interest groups, and bureaucrats.

Once the committee was established, the governor and the regents charged it with reviewing available information and studies and with recommending ways in which the state could "(1) assure educational opportunities to those qualified for college study; (2) provide the undergraduate, graduate, and professional training necessary for the continued development of the State as a leading business, industrial, scientific, and cultural center; and (3) contribute its proper share of trained personnel to meet the nation's needs for education, health, and welfare services."[36]

Under Staff Director Sidney G. Tickton, a small full-time staff and seventy-five consultants prepared reports and position papers for committee analysis. Surprisingly, reaction from the state's private colleges was minimal; they seemed to underestimate the committee's importance.[37] While the study went forward, the governor worked at laying the political groundwork. In both his 1960 message to the legislature and his remarks at ground-breaking ceremonies at the new State University campus at Stony Brook on Long Island, he mentioned the hopes he had for the Heald committee report. Later, in the fall, he called higher education the "biggest remaining untackled area," and predicted that it would be the major issue before the legislature when it convened in January.[38]

On September 29, 1960, Rockefeller delivered a major address on higher education at Harpur College in Binghamton. Citing studies that predicted an "avalanche of enrollment," the governor stressed the need for more liberal arts institutions in the SUNY system (something long opposed by the private colleges) and for "fully adequate operating budgets for our public institutions of higher education" sufficient "to attract superior teachers and to maintain high standards of instruction."[39] Increasing his stake in the Heald committee report, Rockefeller once again spoke of his hopes for it:

> The Committee Report in November is not going to be one of those big, bulky studies that wind up by recommending four or five further studies. The Heald Committee Report will consist of clear, concise and definite recommendations as to how best to meet the already visible demand and need for a doubling and ultimately a tripling of our higher education facilities in New York. It will not be a hasty, crash program, but a well-thought-out, long-range program designed by the best minds in America and, when approved by the Legislature, put into practice with energy and determination. Such a program must be geared to educational excellence as well as the accommodation of a rapidly growing number of students.[40]

The report was all the governor expected it to be. One scholar called it "a blueprint for the further development of higher education in the state" that "was largely instrumental in transforming SUNY from an ill-coordinated collection of small colleges to one of the major systems of higher education in the country."[41] But the report did not focus solely on the state university; it also proposed major programs of aid to private institutions, an increase in scholarship support given to students, expansion of the New York City colleges, and a master planning process to cover all of higher education in New York State. It is worth quoting Donald Axelrod's summary of the report to illustrate its scope and breadth.

> Going beyond the timid estimates of the past, the Heald committee proposed doubling combined full- and part-time enrollments from 401,000 in public and private institutions in 1959 to 804,000 in 1970 and 1,102,000 in 1980. In view of the limited capacity of private institutions it foresaw a drop in their enrollments from 60 to 40 percent of the total by 1985. This of course implied a heavier burden for public institutions. The committee consequently stressed the urgency of expanding and strengthening SUNY. . . .
>
> The Heald committee regarded increased state aid for the New York City public colleges as essential and urged state representation on the New York City Board of Higher Education. In order to strengthen private colleges and universities, the committee recommended that state aid be given for each degree granted, with larger grants for graduate degrees. . . .
>
> As a basis for future development of the entire university, the committee proposed a comprehensive planning process whereby SUNY would prepare triennial master plans for review and approval by the Board of Regents. These would also take into account the activities of private institutions. . . .
>
> With regard to students, the committee recommended doubling the number of regents scholarships to reach 10 percent of each year's high school graduating class, year-round attendance, shortening the four-year period for a degree, and the use of statewide proficiency examinations to obtain credit toward degrees regardless of formal class attendance.[42]

After the Heald committee issued its report, Rockefeller took steps to implement many of its proposals. There seems little doubt that pushing for increased opportunity in education was one of Rockefeller's very top priorities, if not *the* top priority, for 1961. As he said to the legislature in his annual message, "Of all the important matters to be considered by your Honorable Bodies at this session of the Legislature, none is more urgent—none more vital to the future of freedom itself—than is the role of New York in higher education."[43] In his

television address following delivery of the message to the legislature, he made the same point about the pivotal role of higher education in the 1961 session. Between the annual message and the submission of his special message at the end of January, the governor
met with Republican legislative leaders and state officials James E.
Allen, Jr., Thomas Hamilton, and Henry Heald to formulate the
higher education program.[44]

The regents and SUNY trustees both made public a series of proposals. The regents proposed that the state give $18.2 million a year to
private colleges through a grant to students of $100 a semester, an
amount the colleges could then capture by raising tuition accordingly.
Accepting the recommendations of the Heald committee, the regents
also recommended that the number of regents scholarships be doubled in order to provide for 10 percent of the annual graduating high
school class. Increasing the maximum regents scholarship from $700
to $1,500 was also suggested.

The day after the regents unveiled their plans, the State University
trustees released theirs. The revised master plan for 1960 called for
$232 million in additional construction, including establishment of
two new four-year liberal arts colleges, the development of four
graduate centers, and an increase in the number of community colleges.

In an addendum, the trustees offered their comments on the Report
of the Committee on Higher Education. On the character of the State
University, the trustees and the committee were in substantial
agreement, differing only on matters of timing and numbers. As far
as the relation between the State University and the state government
was concerned, they were in accord, with both asking for an easing of
"handicapping procedural requirements."[45]

Later in the month the governor submitted his ideas on higher
education in a special message to the legislature. Citing the reports of
the Heald committee, the trustees, the regents, and the Association of
Colleges and Universities of the State of New York, he declared,
"There is general agreement as to the magnitude of the problem that
lies immediately ahead and as to a general outline of approach to this
matter."[46] Rockefeller was probably right that there was general
agreement on the magnitude, but the agreement, if any, on the approach was very general.

Rockefeller's plan was a combination of proposals advanced by the
Heald committee, the regents, and the trustees. From the Heald
committee, the governor took the recommendations to have SUNY and

the New York City colleges submit master plans to the regents and to establish two graduate centers (rather than the four urged by SUNY). Rockefeller recommended the continuation of SUNY's policy of broadening the liberal arts and sciences curricula in the teachers' colleges. The governor also said SUNY should be allowed to determine its own tuition policies, a move that would permit imposition of tuition there, as the Heald committee proposed. Finally, the governor praised New York City's Board of Higher Education for urging that the city colleges be combined in a city university, a move he approved.[47]

In early December the Association of Colleges and Universities of the State of New York (ACUSNY) held its annual meeting in Syracuse. While nearly half the membership of ACUSNY was composed of Catholic institutions, the leadership in the association was provided by the presidents of the nonsectarian private schools, notably from New York University, Pace, Hofstra, and Rochester. The association commended the Heald report and among the resolutions adopted were the following:

> That state planning include the maximum and effective use of all existing facilities, both private and public, including further consideration of contract possibilities with appropriate private institutions.
> That the state institute a system of tuition supplements for each full time state resident in attendance at private colleges, the amount varying according to the category of studies being pursued.
> [That] a matching grant system for capital construction of educational facilities in private institutions be established.[48]

The private colleges and universities were obviously most desirous of receiving state aid. Since they did not yet know what kind of program the governor would propose, however, they limited their resolution to favoring "tuition supplements," a phrase that could encompass any number of aid plans. On December 28 the Board of Regents endorsed the ACUSNY proposal for "tuition supplements."

Two weeks earlier, Catholic interests had issued a statement that set the tone for their position on aid to private schools during the coming months. The New York State Catholic Welfare Committee said:

> We urge that any program of State assistance to private institutions be so developed as to assure the full participation of all educational resources, including the many institutions under private and religious auspices. We

believe that no program should be inaugurated . . . unless it can function without discrimination for all institutions in the State. The present limitations of the New York Constitution would prevent such grants to colleges and universities under religious auspices, or in which religion is taught. Other constitutional and legal problems are inherent in such a program. Constitutional and statutory change must be considered in connection with such a proposal.[49]

The Catholic position was clear. The church would not support any aid program that would not include its institutions.

By the end of January, substantial opposition to aid to private colleges in the form of tuition grants was appearing. Jewish groups were especially opposed to public support to colleges under religious auspices. Although the governor had not yet made public his plan, it had leaked out that he was considering a "maintenance allowance" for each student resident in New York State of up to 60 percent of tuition charged with a ceiling of $600. At the time, the regents plan, calling for grants of $100 a student each semester to be used only for tuition at institutions that charged tuition, was the only one officially on the public agenda.

For reasons of personal conviction and political necessity, the governor's plans to expand public-sector efforts in higher education were closely linked to increased aid to the private colleges. The Heald committee had suggested direct aid to these institutions through a per capita grant based on the number of degrees awarded by them annually, but the Blaine amendment to the state constitution, which prohibited public aid to church-related institutions, blocked any plan that included assistance to sectarian colleges.

The governor was aware that opposition was forming. Strongly held views for and against aid to private colleges made higher education a dangerous political issue. As a result, he proceeded cautiously in developing his program. After considerable study, the governor's staff settled on some form of direct "tuition grant-in-aid" to the student as the best available strategy, since similar plans had previously withstood constitution testing. During December 1960 and January 1961, Robert MacCrate, counsel to the governor, worked on the details of several alternative plans before deciding on the one ultimately adopted.[50] Particular care was taken in naming the program, for Rockefeller realized that the name, as a symbol, could be important in building support for the plan. The name selected was Scholar Incentive. The purpose of this name was to provide an indication that awards would be made not to colleges but to students (scholars), only certain able students (scholars), and would be provided on a semester basis to encourage students to complete their degree programs (incentive). Governor Rockefeller sent his special message on higher education to the legislature on January 31. In his specific recommendation to the legislature the governor said:

> I recommend the establishment of a "New York State Scholar Incentive Program," to provide each full-time, tuition paying student attending an undergraduate college in the state, who is also resident of the State and who makes application, with an annual grant up to $200 to help him pay his tuition in excess of $500 annually.
>
> In addition, for graduate study, I recommend that to each full-time, tuition paying student who is a resident of the State and is enrolled in an approved graduate program leading to an advanced degree, a similar grant up to $400 be paid for students to the master's degree level; and, for students in graduate work above the master's degree level, I recommend a grant up to $800 per year.[51]

Some might question the governor's definition of every full-time undergraduate and graduate student in the state as a scholar. His program was actually wider in scope than the name suggested. But his motives for so naming and defining his program were political. The governor was aware of the difficulty involved in initiating a new policy and wanted to take account of both the opposition he knew was forming and his counsel's opinion that outright, across-the-board grants to colleges were unconstitutional. He also wanted to aid private colleges, if only indirectly.[52] In naming and defining his program he therefore used language that would both build public support and promote the assembling of a winning coalition in the legislature.

The Scholar Incentive Program was part of a $26 million higher education package that the governor presented to the legislature. Scholar Incentive in the first year was to cost about $6 million, and it would benefit about 160,000 students. It should be noted that, according to the governor's language, Scholar Incentive awards would benefit New York State students in both public and private colleges. In fact, however, the principal beneficiaries would be those in private institutions, because no award could be given to students paying less than $500 per year in tuition. If tuition was less than $700, the student would qualify only for the difference between the amount paid and $700. Thus at SUNY only medical students, who were charged $700 per year, would benefit; at CUNY, tuition was free. It was estimated by the *New York Times* that about 108,000 students at private colleges and universities would be eligible for awards.

At almost the same time that Governor Rockefeller announced his Scholar Incentive plan, Comptroller Arthur Levitt, a Democrat, released his own plan for aid to students. Levitt advocated a greatly expanded state scholarship program that would guarantee aid to all needy students among the top 50 percent of the state's high school graduates. Levitt's proposal explicitly included merit and need criteria, which the Rockefeller Scholar Incentive plan included only in name. Because of these criteria, Levitt's plan would avoid certain constitutional questions that Rockefeller's could not. Accordingly, it was politically appealing. On February 1, Levitt's plan was accepted and endorsed by state Democratic leaders Joseph Zaretzki and Anthony Travia.

By the end of the first week in February, the lines of support for and opposition to the Scholar Incentive plan had been drawn. The private colleges, in statements released by ACUSNY and the Commission on Independent Colleges, warmly endorsed the governor's plan. Edward J. Mortola, president of Pace College, speaking for the commission, described it as "characterized by vision, imagination, and a desire to preserve the traditional balance between public and private higher education."[53] Scholar Incentive also had the early and continuing support of a number of prominent Catholic educators. The state Catholic Welfare Committee also supported the governor, as did the state AFL-CIO.

Opposed to the governor's plan were a number of prominent Jewish, Protestant, educational, and civic and other interest groups and spokesmen. Among those indicating opposition to Scholar Incentive were the New York chapter of the American Jewish Committee, New York Board of Rabbis, Protestant Council of the City of New York, New York State Council of Churches, Public Education Association, United Parents Associations, New York State Teachers Association, National Association for the Advancement of Colored People, New York Civil Liberties Union, Liberal Party, and Americans for Democratic Action. The *New York Times* also published two editorials vigorously opposing the governor's plan. While each group had its own arguments for opposing the Scholar Incentive Program, all were agreed that the plan violated the separation of church and state. Some of the groups, in addition, opposed giving public money to private institutions on the across-the-board basis proposed by the governor.

This outpouring of opposition began to cause considerable difficulty in the legislature, where religious cleavages threatened to divide the Republican majority in the Assembly. As a consequence, the governor and his staff met with various interest groups in an effort to discover what changes in the original program would have to be made before it would be accepted.[54] The outcome of these discussions was that Rockefeller began to consider including both merit and means criteria in the program.[55] By February 11 a merit test had been tentatively devised that would permit awards only if the individual student were in the upper 80 percent of his college class. The governor's aides for education at first opposed the inclusion of the proposed merit test. They argued that because of the enormous variation in admissions and academic standards among the colleges and universities of the state, a figure of 80 percent was arbitrary and meaningless. They did, however, support the inclusion of a means test (which had not yet been designed) and a reduction of the $500 tuition requirement to $250.

By February 14 a revised bill had been prepared in the governor's office. The only merit test that was included was a general requirement that a recipient "give promise of satisfactory completion of the degree program." In addition, the tuition requirement was lowered to $100 a semester ($200 a year). The major importance of this adjustment was that students attending public as well as private institutions would be eligible for awards. Thus the new Scholar Incentive plan covered all students who paid at least $200 tuition, and it included community colleges and Harpur College of SUNY. Estimates now ran to 101,000 undergraduates and 20,000 graduate students who would be eligible for awards.

Scholar Incentive still faced difficulties. During the third week in February, Attorney General Louis Lefkowitz issued an informal advisory opinion on the program. He believed that Scholar Incentive would probably be unconstitutional unless some kind of means test were included. Thus the draft bill was still further delayed in the governor's office while a satisfactory means test could be devised. As a result of the means test, awards to undergraduate students would be scaled from $100 to $300 depending on need; graduate awards were similarly scaled. But the governor insisted on a requirement that no award could reduce tuition below $200, and that there be an eligibility time limit of eight semesters.[56]

After the governor made these changes, opposition to the Scholar Incentive Program by both religious groups and political leaders was withdrawn. The revised plan, sponsored by Earl Brydges, was approved by Republican members of the Senate at a closed conference on March 8, and was then immediately reported out for floor action by the Senate Finance Committee. The bill came to a vote in the Senate on March 10, and despite some concern by Majority Leader Walter Mahoney that a number of senators were anxious about what they regarded as excessive costs, the bill easily passed, 47–7. The bill also sped quickly through the Assembly with a minor change, and on March 15 final approval was given by both houses of the legislature.

The following day the *New York Times* carried an editorial critical of the Scholar Incentive Program, repeating many of the arguments previously given.[57] Despite these objections, Governor Rockefeller signed the bill on April 11, along with the other major aspects of his higher education package. These bills included measures expanding the SUNY system and its commitment to liberal arts education, establishing the City University as a unitary entity, easing the availability of student loan funds, and establishing a master planning process for higher education in New York State.[58]

A final episode in the development of the Scholar Incentive Program needs to be mentioned. On June 7, when machinery for administration of the program was being assembled, the regents suddenly announced that they intended to award Scholar Incentive money directly to the colleges and universities rather than to the students. Governor Rockefeller immediately issued a statement disagreeing with the regents. He said the language of the bill clearly indicated that the students were to be given the money. He feared awarding money directly to colleges and universities because of the constitutional prohibition against state aid to institutions with religious affiliations. A day later a spokesman for the governor announced that a "misunderstanding" had occurred between the regents and the governor, and the money would be sent to the students. Yet the matter was still not fully settled, for on June 24 a compromise plan was announced: checks would be made out to students but sent directly to the colleges. If tuition had already been paid, the check would be given to the student to spend as he pleased. The student would otherwise authorize the college to apply the money to his tuition bill. This episode illustrates quite clearly how a closely negotiated political compromise may be endangered by careless policy implementation.

The year 1961 was thus a watershed for higher education, both public and private, in New York. The growth of the State University in the next five years was phenomenal. In 1962 the entire university, excluding the community colleges, had awarded 13,530 degrees; by 1967 the number of degrees awarded more than doubled, reaching 28,416. In the 1967 academic year, SUNY had enrolled 138,027 full-time and 82,968 part-time students on fifty-nine campuses, thirty of them operated directly by the state. The total enrollment constituted the equivalent of almost 85,000 full-time students, and the university was projecting that it would meet the goals set for it by the governor and its own master plan—a doubling of the 1961 full-time equivalent enrollment by 1970—a year early. The budget of the university, $44.5 million in 1959, had by 1967 reached over $280 million.[59]

In order to provide the facilities to house this exploding enrollment, the governor turned to an innovative device that he was beginning to use in other areas of policy as well, the public benefit corporation. To avoid having to ask the legislature to appropriate money for the university's physical plant, in 1962 Rockefeller sponsored legislation to create the State University Construction Fund (SUCF). The SUCF was to carry out a projected $700 million capital program on State University campuses. The new agency's projects would be financed through borrowing in the private bond market and repaid through income from the imposition of student tuition. Charging tuition at the State University, necessary to implement this plan, became a major political issue. This public benefit corporation, headed by three trustees (one a trustee of the State University), would, the governor said, offer flexibility to university construction projects theretofore tied up in the red tape of the bureaucratic process. It could tap the expertise of both the public and private sectors and could have its projects carried out by both the state Department of Public Works and private contractors. The SUCF's focus would be on academic buildings; the New York State Dormitory Authority would continue to be responsible for the financing and construction of campus residential facilities. Its first priority, Rockefeller said, would be to expedite projects for which over $100 million in state funds had already been appropriated.[60]

By the end of 1967, the SUCF had completed 344 projects with a total value of $364 million.[61] But the growth of the State University's student body and physical plant was not only evidence of the increased commitment of the state to public higher education in the mid-1960s. In 1965, in connection with an agreement between Rockefeller and the Democratic legislative leadership leading to approval by the legislature of a statewide sales tax, the governor committed the state to a program of 50 percent support of the operating costs of the City University of New York. CUNY was already receiving considerable

The modernistic State University campus in Albany (c. 1970). Photo by Sheldon Toomer. New York State Department of Commerce.

state aid under a variety of programs, but aid increased from $37.7 million in 1965 to $61.8 million in 1967, and gave promise of rising at an accelerated rate in later years. State operating aid for community colleges was also growing by leaps and bounds; between 1965 and 1967 it went from $16 million to $29.9 million (see Table 22).

The Bundy Plan

Private college leaders in New York, looking around them, were troubled by what they saw. The new chancellor of SUNY, Samuel Gould, had developed a close relationship with the governor, and another high-level gubernatorial adviser, Frank Moore, chairman of the SUNY trustees, was a strong public-college advocate. Clearly the public colleges were capturing the preponderance of the resources

Table 22. New York State Higher Education Operating Costs, 1959–1973 (in millions of dollars)

Year	SUNY	CUNY	Community colleges	Regents scholarships and Scholar Incentive awards	Aid to private colleges and professional schools	Endowment of chairs	Total
1959	$ 63,870	$ 11,329	$ 3,450	$11,158	—	—	$ 87,807
1960	65,820	21,753	4,610	12,258	—	—	104,441
1961	81,314	24,075	8,690	25,044	—	—	136,123
1962	105,555	27,321	7,850	42,928	—	—	183,654
1963	124,855	29,821	9,500	44,455	—	—	208,631
1964	141,169	31,418	12,711	52,293	—	—	237,591
1965	177,772	41,900	16,000	66,230	—	$ 400	302,302
1966	225,238	49,150	23,000	69,915	—	600	367,903
1967	280,186	62,300	29,900	72,023	—	800	445,209
1968	342,252	80,481	34,400	69,403	—	1,000	528,036
1969	391,680	101,578	44,000	68,500	$20,117	1,000	626,875
1970	446,007	105,227	68,000	70,100	30,725	1,000	721,059
1971	475,804	121,820	91,700	73,680	33,075	800	796,879
1972	520,789	121,168	98,500	87,720	36,024	500	864,701
1973	556,359	144,600	112,400	88,700	69,628	500	972,187

Source: Compiled from New York State Executive Budgets, 1962–1974.

Note: This table includes operating costs only. Not included are capital costs of the Dormitory Authority or State University Construction Fund, or capital aid for CUNY and community colleges.

available for higher education in the state and the independents began to fear that "the growing wildflower... would ultimately take so much of the public nourishment... that their own growth would be stunted."[62] True, the private colleges had received about two-thirds of the regents scholarship and Scholar Incentive aid awarded between 1961 and 1967, a proportion that exceeded their percentage of total enrollment in the state, but this was not a systematic source of aid that could be counted on to meet mounting institutional deficits. Something more was needed.

During the early 1960s, Governor Rockefeller had consistently assured the representatives of the private colleges, when they pressed him about institutional aid, that he was aware of their problem and sympathetic to it. Their time would come, but first priority had to be given to building SUNY to provide the places needed for the vast numbers of students emerging from the state's high schools. By the mid-1960s, the state's private colleges began a lobbying effort. Such universities as Syracuse and New York University lent administrators to mobilize support in the public sector. Informal meetings were held with the regents, and the governor and his staff were informed of the financial problems facing private institutions. James M. Hester, president of New York University, officially suggested state assistance to private institutions at the June 1966 meeting of the regents.

These efforts reflected a consensus that had been reached by members of the Commission on Independent Colleges, the private institutions' subunit of ACUSNY, that their colleges were in real financial difficulty and that many of them could not continue much longer without state aid. Trustees of the numerous private colleges and universities were enlisted in independent efforts to bring their plight to public attention. These efforts were not without success; by the time of Hester's formal proposal to the regents, the problems of the institutions of private higher education were quite well known to the governor and his staff.[63]

The immediate result of the expressed need for assistance to private higher education and the general inadequacy of the available forms of assistance was Rockefeller's decision to establish an independent study commission to examine the problems of funding for private colleges and universities. The first public mention of such a commission was made by Governor Rockefeller on October 3, 1966, at the Golden Jubilee Dinner of St. Joseph's College for Women held at the Hotel Waldorf-Astoria in New York City. In the course of his address he said:

I am happy to announce here tonight that I shall invite the Board of Regents to join me in appointing a Select Committee on the Future of Private and Independent Higher Education.

This committee will be representative of the private and independent colleges and universities and of both lay and professional leadership. I shall expect this Committee to devote its best thinking and judgment to advise me and the Regents on an appropriate course of action for the State to adopt to meet the developments of the next decade.[64]

The selection of members of the committee involved the regents, the commissioner of education, and the governor and his staff. It was agreed that the committee would be a small body representing private and public institutions, with Catholic, Protestant, and Jewish representation, and would be drawn from educators who had no connection with institutions in New York State. The first choice for the chairmanship of the commission was James Bryant Conant, former president of Harvard University. But Conant refused to accept the chairmanship, citing his poor health, although he agreed to serve on the commission. McGeorge Bundy of the Ford Foundation was then approached for the chairmanship, and he accepted.[65]

On March 4, 1967, the governor formally announced that the committee would consist of McGeorge Bundy; James Bryant Conant; John Hannah, president of Michigan State University; Theodore Hesburgh, president of the University of Notre Dame; and Abram Sachar, president of Brandeis University. The only important groups omitted from the representation on the Bundy committee were the smaller colleges, but they did not choose to protest.

The governor announced that the committee would be asked to report by January 1, 1968, on the following questions: (1) How can the vital private institutions be strengthened in the decade ahead? (2) How can these private resources be appropriately related to expanding public institutions? (3) What further specific aid should the state provide to private institutions in the context of existing and potential federal, state, and local financing while preserving the full independence of these institutions? It should be pointed out that the 137 private institutions in New York had an enrollment in 1968 of 332,000, in contrast to the 328,000 enrollment at public institutions.[66]

The charge as presented by the governor was interpreted by the Bundy committee to mean that "the state has some responsibility for private higher education. This responsibility does not automatically imply an obligation to provide direct support to such institutions, but it does require that this possibility be considered in a time when there is general and genuine concern for their financial condition."[67] Thus the committee dealt with areas of need and methods of meeting those needs.

The Bundy committee also felt that its charge was to determine means to assist the private institutions as institutions: "The Governor and the Chancellor directed our attention to the private *institutions,* and not to the students or teachers within them. . . . It makes a real difference whether one is looking at the problem of helping qualified students through college or the problem of ensuring that there shall be colleges of quality for those students to get into."[68]

A careful examination of the charge to the committee leads one to ask how much real latitude the Bundy committee was given. Were the eventual recommendations of the committee substantially predetermined by its charge? The former associate commissioner for higher and professional education, Paul Bulger, felt sure that members of the committee would not have allowed themselves to be used merely as legitimizers or rubber stamps. As Commissioner Allen observed, however, the decision to assist the private institutions had, to a great degree, already been made. The problem for the committee, as stated fairly explicitly in the charge, was *how* the state could assist the private institutions while permitting them to retain their independence.

It should also be noted that there were certain political implications in the governor's charge. While Rockefeller wanted to aid private institutions, he was not irrevocably committed to the idea. If the Bundy committee reported that no aid was needed, the governor could drop the idea without political damage to himself or his administration. If the Bundy recommendations did call for aid, however, the governor would have an excellent opportunity, as he had earlier had with the Heald committee, to use the prestige of the committee to rally public support for the program he would present.

The Bundy committee began its study in March 1967 and undertook to complete its work within a year. Much of the research was done by a professional consulting firm. There was limited contact with the governor's staff during the deliberation of the committee, although a liaison position was established to act as a channel between it and the executive. Committee relations with the regents were more systematic, since the staff of the Bundy committee relied in large measure on data provided by the Education Department. In addition to the assistance received from governmental sources, the Bundy committee relied on information provided by various colleges and universities,

ACUSNY, and the Committee on Independent Colleges regarding their fiscal needs for the future.

One of the most important findings of the committee and its staff was that despite the various sources of information on higher education in the state, there were still relatively little hard data on the nature of actual fiscal problems of the private institutions. "Our studies reveal," they reported, "that few institutional administrators are aware of internal trends in student–faculty ratios, credit hours taught per faculty member, numbers of non-academic personnel, or other vital data affecting their financial condition." Furthermore, the available data were frequently poorly organized, and the information was lost in the maze of college and university bureaucracy. In a very broad and sweeping criticism, the committee reported that "in most cases projections of future requirements are either lacking altogether or are unsupported by detailed analysis."[69]

Despite these methodological difficulties, the Bundy committee made a number of recommendations in its final report, two of which were of particular significance. The first constituted a formula of aid to the institutions of the state, based on the number of degrees awarded annually and scaled according to the status of the degrees (i.e., bachelors', masters', and doctorates). The second set of proposals dealt with the abolition of the Blaine amendment as it applied to colleges and universities. The Blaine amendment, it will be recalled, prohibited state aid, direct or indirect, to educational institutions with religious affiliations.

In order to assess the need for direct aid to institutions, the committee examined the first five years' experience with the indirect approach employed in the Scholar Incentive Program. After this examination, the Bundy committee concluded that it should be continued, but also found that "our studies . . . do not give support to the view that aid to the student has materially aided the institutions or that increased aid to the student in the future would 'flow through' to the appreciable benefit of the institutions. If the aid is to be significant while still a modest amount in toto, it must be direct."[70]

As a consequence of this finding, the Bundy committee recommended that a special effort be made to replace the Blaine amendment with the traditional First Amendment protection in the area of higher education assistance. Although that proposal seemed at first to raise a difficult church–state problem, that was not really the case, for even the most severe critics of aid to church-supported schools were generally ready to acknowledge the difference between church-supported schools at the college level and the traditional church schools of the elementary and secondary levels. In point of fact, several members of the Board of Regents who had been outspoken critics of aid to church-supported elementary and secondary schools were willing to reach an accommodation on the Blaine amendment as it pertained to higher education.[71]

The Bundy committee faced the problem directly, regarding it as a matter that would require constitutional settlement. The committee said: "In our judgment it would be wrong, both as a matter of law and as a matter of policy, for us to recommend to the Governor and the Regents any measures designed to provide assistance to colleges or universities which fall under the language of this Article [article XI, section 3, the Blaine amendment] unless at the same time we are prepared to recommend an appropriate amendment to the Constitution insofar as it applies to the four-year colleges and universities."[72]

The governor's staff took a different position, which was approved by the regents. They decided not to tie a constitutional amendment repealing the Blaine amendment for the religious colleges and universities to legislation permitting aid to nonsectarian institutions. At the same time it was anticipated that several of the religious schools might be able to qualify for the aid formula if they could convince the State Education Department that they were not teaching doctrinal tenets and were not administered by a religious body. In fact, several of the schools that had religious affiliations were later able to qualify for aid, among them Yeshiva University, St. John Fisher College, Manhattanville College of the Sacred Heart, and Fordham University.

Difficulties of state–church relations, always a sensitive area, were averted for a number of reasons. The primary one was the desire of proponents of the Blaine repeal not to have their clause clouded with other issues. Moreover, certain church-related schools, such as Fordham, were willing to support the Bundy plan even if they themselves were excluded from its benefits. They hoped that they might qualify later, as indeed they did, as a result of changes made in their legal structures, relaxation of the rules defining a church-affiliated school, or the total repeal of the Blaine amendment.

The Bundy committee suggested that "aid to eligible private colleges and universities should be calculated on the basis of the number of earned degrees conferred annually, with differentials for the appropriate levels and types approximately proportional to average differences in cost. Such aid should be given directly to eligible institutions for general educational purposes upon receipt by the State Education Department of an acceptable count of degrees conferred and other evidences of eligibility."[73] The committee suggested that equal funds be provided for bachelors' and masters' degrees and six times that amount for doctoral degrees. Although merely a suggestion, this was the final formula that was accepted. The report also suggested $400 as a base figure. No rationale was offered for the $400 figure, and indeed, the report noted, "We recognize that Master of Arts is more costly than a one-year program, and that doctorates in the sciences are more costly as a rule than in the humanities. When appropriate cost comparison data are available it may be wise to refine the formula."[74]

When legislation was enacted, the $400 figure was accepted and the issue was settled without further refinement. Some individuals suggested that the committee had tried to divide the number of higher education students in the state into the number of dollars that it was estimated the governor was prepared to fit into the budget for aiding private institutions. That amount was $25 million.

In suggesting that the regents play a more active role in creating the master plan, the Bundy committee said:

> We find that for the most part the Regents have been too passive in the exercise of their regulatory functions with respect to higher education. The chartering of institutions and the registering of programs have often been perfunctory. The Regents have rarely revoked a charter. Sometimes charters have been granted to institutions so weak that they might better not have come into being. While the Regents have been commendably free of any tendency to inhibit the full development of the many superior colleges and universities in the state, they have on the other hand done little to weed out or upgrade the inferior ones.[75]

Rockefeller endorsed the Bundy plan on February 1, 1968, the day after the report had been publicly submitted. The governor stated that the Bundy proposals formed the basis for "realistic action" and were "a major viable solution" for keeping private institutions strong but not publicly controlled. He suggested that the program should begin with aid to schools not affiliated with churches since the constitution could not be revised before 1970.

The political lineup for and against the Bundy plan was much the same as the division over the Scholar Incentive Program in 1961: Jewish and "liberal" groups were opposed, Catholic groups and private colleges were in favor. On March 30 the regents announced general approval of the proposal to grant public funds to private colleges and universities in accordance with the Bundy formula. The regents said that they recognized that the private institutions were "in need of financial assistance to enable them to continue to play a vital role in education."[76]

The bill was drafted by Alton Marshall, the governor's secretary, but was not submitted to the legislature until near the close of the session. In the drafting of the bill, careful attention was given to ensuring that it would be constitutionally sound. Marshall insisted that provisions for planning and academic standards be included in the legislation to make certain that the state did not award money haphazardly. The inclusion of such provisions was important in the likely event of a court test of the bill's constitutionality.[77]

The pro-Bundy forces were well organized. They had even obtained the endorsement of the measure by Samuel Gould, chancellor of the State University of New York. Despite Gould's support, some opponents in the legislature argued that the money should be used instead to expand and improve the State University. Other opponents felt that the bill would convert private colleges into diploma mills, since there would be a financial incentive to graduate increasing numbers of students. Nevertheless, the bill passed the Assembly by 92 to 44. The coalition of assemblymen who were opposed to the Bundy proposal was composed of reform Democrats, who reflected the views of Jewish constituents in New York City and who formed the City University lobby, along with a few conservative Republicans who were opposed to spending money. In the Senate there was a similar division.

The measure that passed both houses of the legislature on the last day of the session retained the Bundy formula of $400 for each bachelor's or master's degree and $2,400 for each doctoral degree. It excluded from computation honorary degrees and any degree earned by a student for whom the state was already contributing directly to an institution. The state education commissioner was authorized to require institutions applying for aid to submit reports. It was signed into law by Rockefeller on June 20, 1968.

The next year there was an attempt to reopen the debate. Bills were introduced to postpone the funding and to restrict the formula to New York State students.[78] These efforts failed. During the first year, fifty-seven institutions received approximately $25 million in assistance. In 1970, sixty institutions received over $30 million (see Table 22).

The Bundy committee and its recommendations represent an important step for higher education in New York. From the committee's report came the first governmental acceptance of responsibility for direct aid to private higher education. The history of the Bundy committee is an example of intelligent and well-planned use of a committee by the governor to result in policy change within the state. No change, however, was made in the constitutional prohibition of state aid to religious schools.

New Problems Emerge

The implementation of the Bundy plan, though of help to the private colleges in New York in the late 1960s and early 1970s, did not redirect the major trends of the decade. In 1971, Bundy aid totaling over $33 million helped the independent colleges keep their cumulative deficit to $16.8 million, and by 1972 deficits declined to a total of $700,000. In 1973, recognizing that the value of the Bundy program had been diminished because of the impact of inflation, the governor and the legislature enriched the formula and brought total assistance to a level of about $60 million a year.[79]

But the gap in tuition between private colleges and the State University in 1972 remained close to $2,000 a year. Enrollment at SUNY continued to rise—it exceeded 150,000 full-time-equivalent students in 1973—and the proportion of state students in private institutions declined further. In addition, a study by the state Department of Education demonstrated that New York's Scholar Incentive Program, designed to aid the private institutions indirectly, was less and less effective in achieving this goal. In 1969/70, 48.9 percent of payments under the program went to private-college students, and these payments comprised 56.1 percent of all aid given under the program. Three years later, 39.3 percent of the students aided were at private colleges, and total aid to them had dropped to 35 percent of the amount awarded by the state. Although New York enriched the Scholar Incentive Program by 40 percent during this period, aid to private-college students rose only 5.6 percent, while aid to students at SUNY rose 7.1 percent. Clearly, the widening gap between public and private tuition charges was channeling increasing numbers of New York high school graduates to public campuses.[80]

Difficulties in higher education in the late 1960s and early 1970s were felt at public as well as private institutions. At SUNY, enrollments began to level off, state budgets got tighter and funds thus more difficult to obtain, and inflation began to take its toll. The turnaround in SUNY income from state funds was dramatic. Between 1969 and 1970, the university, following the pattern of previous years, gained an increase in its state purposes budget of $50 million, or 13.8 percent. Between 1970 and 1971 the increase, just under $30 million (6.3 percent), was significantly less than the rate of inflation (see Table 22). Leveling enrollment projections also resulted in dramatic alterations in construction plans. In 1971 the State University Construction Fund cut from its plans 539 projects valued at about $1 billion.[81]

At the City University (CUNY), the institution of open enrollment for all graduates of New York City's high schools, the pressure of a highly organized faculty for increased salaries and benefits, and other fiscal pressures caused burgeoning budgets. Under its 50 percent guarantee formula, the state in 1973 paid $132.3 million to support CUNY's general operation and $12.3 million to aid SEEK, a special program for disadvantaged students. Because of its ever increasing demands on the state treasury, the City University became a major tension point in city–state relations. As one authority has noted:

> Albany has long felt that the increasing inability of the city to pay its own way has not been met by any genuine attempts to invoke self-discipline and to limit spending. The City University of New York (CUNY), unlike the State University of New York (SUNY), does not charge its students tuition. Yet CUNY was permitted to expand its educational mission and its student population in ways that have evoked charges of undisciplined growth. Estimates in the 1961 City University Master Plan called for 117,000 undergraduate students by 1975; the 1968 master plan called for 212,000 undergraduates by 1975; in 1972 a new master plan called for 228,000 undergraduates at CUNY by 1975. And the City University budget reached $500 million, half of which was paid by the state. Because of this rapid growth by the university and demands for an increased state subsidy for it, state officials showed dissatisfaction with the city's spending decisions in higher education.[82]

Concern about the growth of CUNY caused Governor Rockefeller to request that a special task force be set up in the Budget Division to examine the City University's budgetary process. It was customary for the mayor to write the governor a brief letter each year stating that the budget of the City University was so many millions and requesting a check for 50 percent of this amount. As a result of the task force study, changes in the 1965 legislation requiring the state to pay half of the City University's expenses were sought and obtained. Thereafter much more detailed information had to be furnished and expenditures justified, although not to the extent required of state agencies.[83] Later, in 1973, another commission appointed by the governor to examine problems in higher education and headed by Francis Keppel, a former United States commissioner of education, concluded that the City University should be even more heavily supported by the state, but the commission also said that CUNY should be required to impose tuition and that one-half of its directing board should be appointed by the governor. The tuition proposal was strongly opposed by almost every political leader in the city. After a major political battle, the governor did, however, win the right to appoint three of ten members of the new City University Board of Trustees (created to replace the twenty-one-member Board of Higher Education).[84] Later, as a result of the 1975 New York City fiscal crisis, tuition was finally imposed at CUNY.

Escalating costs of the community colleges in the early 1970s also caused the state to take action. Under a formula that provided that the state government pay one-third of the operating costs of these institutions, the level of state aid exceeded $112 million in 1973. Between 1969 and 1971, New York's assistance to community colleges had more than doubled; by 1973 it had risen another 50 percent from the 1971 level, to $112 million. State administrators were also concerned about the threat these institutions posed to the enrollment for the first two years in upstate private colleges, especially as the community colleges moved out of their original role as technical institutions and tended increasingly to emphasize an academic curriculum. Since, as in the case of the City University, the state lacked administrative control of the community colleges, its response to these trends was the carrot; it enriched its financial support to those institutions that placed certain limits on faculty salary increases (the major component of rising costs) and curriculum change.

With regard to the State University, there can be no doubt that Rockefeller was the principal force moving toward its development. Except for a substantial bloc in the legislature who were graduates of Brooklyn College and City College in New York, most of the legislators were graduates of private institutions. Constituent pressures, however, did play a role. Locating branches of the new State University in their districts had considerable appeal to upstate Republican legislators, and for that reason they supported the governor's plans for its expansion. By the middle of Rockefeller's administration, however, the size of the appropriations for the State University, which competed with funds for projects dear to the hearts of legislators, led to increasing reluctance to vote funds for the university. In the early years of the expansion, the governor had instructed the budget director to view requests from the State University favorably, but in the light of the legislature's growing disenchantment, the budget office became more critical.

Legislators had little direct interest in the operations of the State University until the student riots of 1968/69. Then there were charges in the legislature that the university was too permissive toward its students. The governor called a meeting of legislative leaders and representatives of the trustees. The legislators demanded that the State University control students and dismiss faculty members who were troublemakers. Rockefeller stood firm for academic freedom, however, pointing out that political intervention and attempts to administer the university from the statehouse would be disastrous. The legislators declared that they simply reflected the feelings of their communities and the political pressures that they were under because of the student riots. Rockefeller was successful in quieting the storm and getting the legislative leaders to agree that the problem should be left in the hands of the university administration.

The regents and the Department of Education found the Rockefeller administration easier to work with than preceding ones. Most of the conflict over higher education occurred between the Board of Regents and the Trustees of the State University of New York. During the early years of the Rockefeller administration there was considerable hostility on both sides. The regents felt that the trustees posed a challenge to their undisputed control of educational matters. Later, as the university grew, the regents became concerned about the impact on private education. At a public meeting called by the regents in 1970 to review planning for higher education, a vice-chancellor of the State University, in the presence of numerous heads of private colleges, declared, "Our goal is to put you out of business!" While the chancellor of the university himself disputed this statement, it confirmed the fears of many of the private school administrators who were present.[85]

The Rockefeller years were ones of explosive growth for higher education in New York. The state and city universities were created and expanded tremendously, direct aid to students increased by a factor of eight, indirect aid was offered to private colleges through State Dormitory Authority financing and construction of facilities, and a program of direct institutional aid to private colleges based on number of graduates was successfully implemented. These steps gave New York higher education facilities second to none in the nation. They made it possible for thousands of young men and women to go to college and for many to receive professional training in a wide variety of postgraduate areas. This would not have been possible except for the leadership that Governor Rockefeller gave to higher education.

Rockefeller, however, presided over the golden age of higher education in New York. In the years that followed his administration, inflation pushed operating costs of private institutions ever higher and led to increased tuition for students. At the same time, population projections based on the birth rate indicated a gradual long-term decline in student enrollment. The integration of public and private higher education programs proved ineffective. As competition for students intensified, there was concern about the decline in the educational quality of many colleges, both public and private. Moreover, it was charged that the expensive state and city universities had become larger than the state needed. Despite these problems, Rockefeller's contribution to higher education remained his greatest achievement, his foremost legacy to the people of New York.

9

The Quality of Life

New York's physical and cultural environment was one of its greatest assets. The state was fortunate in having vast areas of forest-covered mountains, numerous rivers and lakes, and miles of sandy beaches. From Lake Ontario and the St. Lawrence River on the north through the Finger Lakes to Long Island Sound on the south, the opportunities for water sports were unrivaled. Mountain areas provided opportunities for hiking and camping in the summer and skiing in the winter. Few New Yorkers lived many miles from some vacation area.

In cultural resources New York State was equally fortunate. New York City had library and museum facilities unmatched by those of any other American city. It was a world center for music, theater, and dance, and its cultural and artistic enterprises offered varied and wide opportunities for students and masters alike. While New York State's other large cities had fewer cultural resources, they equaled or exceeded those of other cities of their size in the United States. Rochester was a national center for the study and performance of music, and Buffalo's Knox-Albright museum had a leading modern art collection.

On the other hand, the growing population of the state after World War II posed threats to these advantages. As industry expanded and cities and villages grew, pollution of the lakes and streams became an ever increasing problem. As city dwellers sought suburban homes and summer cottages, developers used up land that was once rural. The automobile not only made it possible to reach areas of the state formerly inaccessible but attracted more people to the suburbs as longer commuting distances became feasible. To service this need, highways were built, posing an additional threat to the physical environment of the state.

Some of these problems were not new when Rockefeller took office in 1959. Fortunately, the state had been farsighted in attempting to preserve scenic areas by declaring in its constitution that some of them, particularly in the Adirondacks, should be kept "forever wild." Robert Moses and others had been successful in developing an extensive state park system that included miles of sandy beaches. State parks became crowded, however, and the demand for campsites far outstripped supply. Even the state's most unspoiled wilderness in the Adirondacks was threatened by plans of developers to build thousands of "second homes" there. The pressing need of New York City for additional electrical energy led to the proposal to build a power-generating plant on Storm King Mountain on the Hudson, in Rip van Winkle country. As the suburbs expanded outward on Long Island and up the Hudson Valley, the demand for expressways threatened to destroy some of the few remaining scenic areas in the metropolitan New York area.

In the cultural sphere there were problems as well. The larger cities were rich in resources, but smaller communities in rural areas offered few opportunities for the enjoyment of the arts. The state had done little to encourage cultural activities, and as the costs of maintaining symphony orchestras, art exhibits, and theaters multiplied, even those in New York City were placed under grave financial strain.

In the environmental area, water pollution control was the keystone to safeguarding the state's physical resources. If this problem could be solved, it would go a long way toward protecting the physical environment of the state.

Pure Waters Program

In a statement released in Albany on December 27, 1964, Governor Rockefeller estimated that $1 billion was needed for construction of new comprehensive Pure Waters Program to eliminate pollution. Rockefeller estimated that $1.7 billion was needed for construction of local sewage-treatment plants and intercepting sewers over the next six years. He declared, "Nearly two-thirds of all New Yorkers live in areas affected by water pollution, with 1,167 communities and 760 industrial sources pouring untreated waters and even raw sewage into the state's waterways.... Despite strict anti-pollution laws...

many of our communities throughout the state cannot meet the pollution problem by themselves."[1]

The greatest obstacle to local initiative, according to Rockefeller, was lack of sufficient funds. To remove this obstacle, he proposed a program of state leadership in federal-state-local sharing of costs of sewage-treatment-plant construction. The state would pay 30 percent of construction costs. He urged the federal government to eliminate discriminatory provisions in the federal law which set a ceiling of $625,000 on federal grants to any individual project and which channeled half of all grants to municipalities with fewer than 125,000 residents. With these changes the federal government could increase its share to a full 30 percent. The program also included state aid for research, encouragement of industry through tax incentives, and "vigorous enforcement" of the state's water-pollution laws.

In order to avoid delays until Congress appropriated the needed funds, the state offered to "prefinance" the federal government's rightful share. The money for the state share and for the prefinancing of the federal share was to come from a proposed bond issue, which if approved by the voters would be the largest one ever issued by New York State for any purpose. Submitted to the legislature on March 2, 1965, the bills embodying the program received final approval two months later by unanimous votes in both chambers. In the November election, the billion-dollar bond issue was approved by the voters by a 4-to-1 margin.

The water-pollution control program was unique in several respects. The bond issue was of unprecedented size, dwarfing previous ones. Moreover, it was approved without a single dissenting vote in the legislature, and the voters endorsed it by the largest margin of any bond issue in the history of the state. The program was proposed in opposition to a history of relative neglect by the states of their responsibility for water-pollution control and in an area in which the federal government was exercising growing authority. Finally, it was developed and implemented through the initiative of the governor. It made New York the leader among the states and suggested that states still had the power, if they wished to exercise it, to deal effectively with major issues. But if the problem was so critical, why did Rockefeller wait until 1965 to take action?

Serious efforts of New York State to prevent pollution of its streams and lakes started with the Water Pollution Control Act of 1949.[2] Throughout the nineteenth century, control of water pollution was considered a local responsibility. State action was limited to authorizing municipalities to enact their own sanitary regulations. Even after establishment of the state Board of Health in 1880, primary responsibility was left to the localities. Finally, in 1903, growing concern with the health hazards of pollution and the inability of municipalities to control it led to legislation prohibiting the discharge of substances into the waters of the state "in quantities injurious to the public health" without a permit from the health commissioner.

Conservationists, particularly those concerned with fish and wildlife, also obtained the passage of a series of laws in 1913 against water pollution, prohibiting discharges "in quantities injurious to fish life . . . or injurious to the propagation of fish." Despite the firm tone of the statutes, enforcement of which was assigned to the Health and Conservation departments, for the first half of the twentieth century pollution control was haphazard and little progress was made in implementing it. Divided and incomplete authority and lack of personnel were major factors in this record. Enforcement was difficult because legal evidence that "injury" had been done and that a particular defendant was responsible was elusive. Consequently, these early statutes were almost useless in preventing pollution.

The 1949 Water Pollution Control Act grew out of the concern of the Joint Legislative Committee on Interstate Cooperation over pollution of interstate streams. In 1946 this committee established the Special Committee on Pollution Abatement. Recommendations from this committee led to the 1949 comprehensive legislation, which unified administrative control of the state's water-pollution control program in a new agency, the Water Pollution Control Board, operating within the Health Department. Moreover, it charged the board with defining water-quality standards and defined "pollution" as the contravention of these standards. The board was to classify all waters of the state according to the "best usage" in the public interest, adopt standards of water purity for each classification, develop a pollution-abatement plan for each area of the state, and enforce the plans. Voluntary compliance was to be the first step, but abatement orders were to be supported by judicial action if necessary. The law also emphasized the importance of treatment-works construction and included provisions empowering the board to order municipalities to construct them.

It is important to note that these steps were to be taken in sequence, with classification coming first. This newly created program contained no deadline for the achievement of clean water for New York State, but it was hoped at the time that the classification of all waters and the establishment of water quality criteria for each grade of water would be completed in five years, and that pollution could be totally eliminated in some ten years. An indication of the board's progress can be obtained from figures given in a 1954 report. By the close of 1953, classification surveys had been completed or undertaken in fifty-four drainage basins, covering about one-third of the state's total area. Of these twenty-four surveys, fifteen had been published as required by law. Public hearings had been held to discuss all of these surveys. The board had adopted official classifications for eleven of the drainage basins involved. Of these, eight had had comprehensive plans developed and approved for them. For these eight basins, the board had initiated the cooperative stage of the enforcement provisions of the new law. Thus in the first four years of its operation a total of 2,115 square miles out of 47,654, or 4 percent of the state's area, had had plans for pollution abatement developed and compliance requested. Ten years later this figure had risen to only 52.2 percent.[3]

There is considerable evidence that industrial interests had an important influence on the final draft of the 1949 act. A March 1965 resolution of Associated Industries of New York State, Inc., read at the 1965 Federal State Conference on Hudson River Pollution, declared specifically, "Associated Industries worked closely with the Joint Legislative Committee on Interstate Cooperation in the formulation of the Water Pollution Control Law of 1949 which was unanimously adopted by the Legislature with public support from Associated Industries." Other observers gave added witness to industrial influence over the 1949 act, describing that influence as "strong" and in one case saying that the law was "largely written" by industry.[4]

In the years between 1949 and 1959, industries expanded and population increased, as did the amount of pollution. The board, however, was chronically short of funds and personnel. Every year the Joint Legislative Committee on Natural Resources made a plea for "sufficient funds" for the board to carry out its duties. Localities also questioned the legality of the law and the way the board was administering it. Some challenged in the courts the board's authority to issue classifications and abatement orders. By the mid-1950s, revised estimates gave fifteen years instead of five for completion of the classification work.[5]

There were two other factors of great importance to water pollution control in New York State. The first was the board's own attitude toward enforcement actions. From the start of its deliberations the special committee had stressed the need for stimulating voluntary compliance. On one occasion the committee declared, "Pollution abatement will be achieved, not by the mere passage of laws, effective though they may be in administrative and fiscal machinery, but by the willingness of pollution producers to correct these adverse conditions."[6]

Indeed, the law required the board to obtain voluntary compliance before issuing abatement orders. No time limit was set for this "cooperative phase." It was to continue as long as it was "productive of reasonable progress." Only when the board judged that "reasonable progress [was] not forthcoming," and that such progress was "not only possible but should have been obtained," was it to begin the arduous and time-consuming task of forcing compliance through abatement orders and, if necessary, court action. Even when the "enforcement phase" was reached (and by 1954 only one case had reached it), almost endless delays were possible. In 1965, Health Commissioner Hollis Ingraham declared that the Health Department's enforcement powers had been "hobbled by delaying devices in the law which enabled a polluter to hold us off for years."[7]

The second factor, which seriously damaged New York's control program, was that it was almost entirely regulatory. It was all stick and no carrot. The only financial aid to municipalities came in the form of planning grants of up to 2 percent of construction costs of treatment facilities. The Special Legislative Committee on Pollution Abatement was aware of the fiscal problems of municipalities, stating that abatement would "entail large financial expenditures on the part of both municipalities and industry."[8]

The recognition of "fiscal inability," however, did not lead to serious discussions of state aid. The prevailing philosophy was that "municipalities, industry, and other entities responsible for pollution of our waterways are responsible for the abatement of their pollution and should themselves bear the entire cost of needed improvements." Moreover, the fiscal difficulties of municipalities, as originally described by their representatives at public hearings held by the special committee, centered on constitutional and legal limitations on municipal debt. And indeed, the special committee found upon investigating these claims that "some municipalities would be unable to finance the construction of needed facilities within the debt margin available to them under present constitutional limitations." In other words, the problem arose from restrictions on municipalities, and therefore the solution, as seen by the special committee, consisted in removing or somehow bypassing these restrictions so as to allow the municipalities to generate needed funds themselves.

Faced with the prospect of large capital expenditures for treatment facilities, however, an increasing number of municipalities argued that more pressing needs, such as schools, made it impossible to divert funds for such construction. Moreover, construction of a municipal sewage-disposal plant frequently brought little benefit to the city providing the funds. Municipal raw sewage dumped into a river was carried downstream, and the downstream water user was the one who gained or lost by upstream treatment plants. Thus municipal officials found themselves expected to allocate funds to a function that conferred little direct benefit to anyone in their jurisdiction. Their reluctance to act was understandable.

When Governor Rockefeller took office in 1959, New York State water policy had reached a critical juncture. The Water Pollution Law of 1949 emphasized sewage-works construction, giving the Water Pollution Control Board authority to order municipalities to construct facilities to treat their sewage. But no state financial aid was available for this purpose, despite the repeated urging of individual municipalities and the New York State Conference of Mayors. Studies on the extent of the need for state aid had reached no conclusions on the obligation of the state to provide it or the form it should take. The thrust of legislative action from the enactment of the 1949 law was toward removing restrictions on the ability of municipalities to generate funds themselves within the state. Gubernatorial involvement was limited to recognition and approval of the efforts of legislative committees.

At the same time, the federal role in the water-pollution area was growing. After long years of debate and over presidential opposition, the Congress, under the leadership of John Blatnik of Minnesota, in 1956 enacted a bill providing grants-in-aid to local communities for sewage treatment plants. Though first designed to be funded at $100 million per year, as ultimately passed the program provided $50 million per year with a ten-year limit of $500 million. In a bid for support from less urbanized areas, and because of the belief that smaller towns and cities were experiencing the most difficulty in financing treatment works, the federal bill included a provision requiring at least 50 percent of the funds to go to municipalities with populations of 125,000 or less.

As a result of this legislation, by the end of 1957 a total of 1,292

treatment projects costing $575 million had been approved through-
out the country for federal grants totaling $110 million. Thus, for
every dollar of federal aid, over $4 was being raised by the state and
local governments. Twenty-five percent of the approved projects had
been completed and were in operation. Another 50 percent were
under construction. In a 1958 report, David Howells of the U.S. Public Health Service declared that there could be no question that federal
construction grants stimulated a large number of needed state works,
construction that would not have been undertaken without financial
aid.[9]

Overall statistics in the 1958 report, however, did not accurately
portray differences from state to state. Stimulation of construction
occurred "to the greatest extent in states with aggressive water pollution control programs and with construction needs reasonably in balance with the amount of federal funds available." Whether or not
New York State had an "aggressive" control program, it is clear that
its construction needs were not even close to being "reasonably in
balance" with available federal funds. With the ceiling for any one
project at first fixed at $250,000 and later raised to $600,000 and the
requirement that half of all funds be allotted to communities of less
than 125,000 population (and the limited amount of federal funds
appropriated), the federal grants program was too small to make a
real difference in urban New York State.

In a speech in 1962, Governor Rockefeller used a dramatic example
to illustrate how the federal program "grossly discriminated against
New York and other urban areas." A sewage-treatment facility
planned for New York City was to cost $140 million. Without the
$600,000 limit for a single project, this facility might have been eligible
for $42 million in federal aid, 30 percent of its cost. As it was, the city
could receive a maximum of $600,000, and in addition could compete
only for funds not reserved for smaller cities. Rockefeller claimed that
on this project alone, New York was shortchanged by $41.4 million.
He urged the removal of the dollar limitation on single projects and
allocation of funds to states on the basis of population.[10]

The administration of federal programs caused other difficulties in
New York as well. During the Eisenhower administration, efforts by
the president and Republicans in Congress to eliminate these grants
generated uncertainty as to their future. Municipal applicants on long
waiting lists for federal funds had excuses to postpone other action.
Then, beginning in 1961, the Kennedy administration and its congressional allies sought to extend the federal government's jurisdic-

tion to regulate water quality in both intrastate and interstate waterways. Governor Rockefeller's position was that more extensive federal enforcement efforts were not needed. Dr. Hollis Ingraham, New York State commissioner of health, testified at Governor Rockefeller's request before a subcommittee of the House Committee on Governmental Operations:

> With respect to pollution of interstate waters the Federal government now has all the authority it needs to bring about corrective action through cooperation with the water pollution regulatory agencies of the various states. Such actions should not be undertaken without advance consultation and concurrence of the State water pollution control regulatory agencies unless, after a reasonable opportunity to do so, there is clear failure on the part of the State regulatory agency to carry out its responsibilities.[11]

A corollary of Rockefeller's views on federal action was simply that the state must itself act effectively. In 1960 he had initiated a reorganization of the state's water agencies. He proposed "unification of responsibility" in a Water Resources Commission within the Conservation Department to achieve "strong program leadership" for a broad water resources policy. The Water Pollution Control Board was abolished. Its functions and powers were transferred to the Health Department. Basic planning and policy-making functions for water resources, including classification standards, were assigned to the Water Resources Commission, and administrative and enforcement responsibility to the Health Department.

Reorganization was only the beginning. There was still the issue of state aid. The Joint Committee on Natural Resources had stated the matter clearly: "Fiscal problems . . . still continue to impede the water pollution control program—and they will continue to do so until some final decision is made on whether some form of state aid is or is not to be provided for municipalities needing sewage works construction projects."[12] Intelligent decisions about whether and what kind of state aid should be given required accurate information. While the volume, type, and location of municipal sewage had been determined fairly accurately, data were lacking for industry, and accurate cost estimates were not available for either. Consequently, in December 1960 Rockefeller commissioned the Office for Local Government to conduct a study of sewage-works costs and financing and make recommendations for state action. It estimated the cost at more than $1 billion. This study came to be considered the real start of the state's program because it finally gave a realistic estimate of the costs involved.

Yet to many at the time it hardly seemed so. The estimate of more than $1 billion for one state was termed "a shocker" and met with considerable disbelief, especially since the Public Health estimates were much lower. Later, even the Office for Local Government's estimates proved to be too low. Omitted from the totals were costs of treatment for areas without any sewers at all, of suburban extensions, and of accelerating inflation.

Why these estimates should have been surprising to anyone is not clear. Several reports issued by other bodies gave figures comparable to these estimates. As one example, a joint report by the U.S. Departments of Commerce and Labor six years earlier had indicated that $25 billion would be needed nationally over a ten-year period for an effective attack on the water-pollution problem. [13]

It was clear from the Office of Local Government study, however, that the financial burdens on municipalities were going to be much greater than had been expected. Acting on these data, Rockefeller in 1962 introduced legislation for a comprehensive ten-year program of state aid for water-pollution control in New York State. Recognizing the restrictions on municipalities nearing their debt limits, Rockefeller proposed state aid for comprehensive sewage studies, operation and maintenance of sewage-treatment works, and sewage-plant construction.

Unfortunately, the legislature did not appropriate the necessary funds. Indeed, in 1964 Rockefeller himself recommended the continued postponement of the program's activation. Why, when the need in retrospect was so great, did the political leaders fail to act? The answer seems to be that time was needed to generate the necessary public support. Public apathy about water-pollution control was a problem.

One man closely identified with the program later said, in regard to the 1960/61 period, "There was not much public interest so we started slowly." When the Office for Local Government study made it clear that the cost of cleaning up New York's water was going to be far greater than had been thought, action without wide public support became even more difficult. As he said, "We were not ready for the big push, because the people were not ready for the big push." [14] It is clear that the extent of public support would be a key factor in the development of a new program.

The decision to push major antipollution legislation in the 1965 session of the state legislature apparently was made by Rockefeller in late 1964. Rockefeller himself attributed the impetus to his 1964 visit to California, where there was great public concern about lack of sufficient supplies of water to meet ever growing needs. It was vividly brought home to him that New York, unlike California, had sufficient water supplies if pollution could be overcome.[15] The Pure Waters Program was Rockefeller's plan to solve that problem.

The drought that began in 1962 also influenced his decision to act in 1965. The drought lasted several years, encompassed the entire Northeast, and was the most severe one in New York's history. By August 1965 the Federal Water Resources Council had called the drought the worst on record, and the president had declared the region a four-state disaster area. The connection between water supply and water pollution, which had not been widely recognized in past years, was much more deeply impressed on the public consciousness by the water shortage in New York City, while hundreds of millions of gallons of Hudson River water flowed past every day, polluted and undrinkable.

Another factor of a quite different character began to have considerable influence in arousing public opinion. The number of motorboat owners in New York State more than tripled between 1960 and 1964. As the use of small boats on inland waters increased, so did complaints about pollution. The complaints reflected growing middle-class concern about a threat to recreation. As one administrator put it, "When little old ladies in tennis shoes charged into Albany demanding that something be done about stinking rivers and lakes," public opinion at long last seemed ready to support a massive program.[16]

The governor gave William Ronan the task of developing a feasible approach. The program that was developed had three major aspects: (1) a comprehensive study of the efficiencies of present and future joint municipal action; (2) fiscal incentives, including direct construction and operation grants for municipalities and tax relief for industries constructing waste-treatment facilities; and (3) rigid enforcement of pollution-control laws. The key to the plan was the second of these goals. As Rockefeller himself put it, the major purpose was "to lift much of the crushing financial burden of building sewage treatment systems from the backs of our local communities." This decision to force a financial breakthrough lay at the heart of the Pure Waters Program.

Ronan assigned two staff members, Richard Wiebe and Edward Van Ness, to develop the project. These two relied on Robert Hennigan of the Office for Local Government, who had run the OLG's cost study, and Dr. Andrew Fleck, deputy commissioner of health. The only statement about the respective roles of the four was Dr. Fleck's joking comment: "Wiebe wrote it, Van Ness typed it, Hennigan and I were there to keep them honest."[17]

While it was agreed from the first that the state would provide massive financial assistance, there were other decisions to be made. One concerned the major cause of pollution. Apparently the group decided that water-pollution control was largely a municipal problem and that domestic sewage was the major concern. Domestic sewage was clearly a governmental responsibility and thus a less controversial point of attack; also, it was the "heavier load"; and if the "big area" (domestic sewage) were "tackled in a big way," the problem could be solved. Thus the decision was made to concentrate on municipal treatment plants.

These comments on domestic sewage as the biggest problem echo Dr. Ingraham's statements on "realities of New York's water situation" in the second in Governor Rockefeller's series of television broadcasts entitled "Executive Chamber." Speaking just a week before the announcement of the Pure Waters Program, Ingraham said, "By far the greatest cause of water pollution—and the greatest problem for our state—is community sewage. . . . The really big water pollution problem is not industrial, but domestic sewage."[18]

It is not clear why domestic wastes were considered the "heavier load." If New York State was at all comparable to the nation as a whole, then all indicators showed industrial wastes to be by far the bigger problem. The president's Council on Environmental Quality reported that throughout the country the "more than 300,000 water-using factories in the United States discharge three to four times as much oxygen-demanding wastes as all the sewered population of the United States. Moreover, many of the wastes discharged by industry are toxic . . . [and] the output of industrial wastes is growing several times faster than the volume of sanitary sewage."[19] Concentrating on building municipal plants, however, combined with new enforcement procedures seemed to the governor's staff in New York to offer the best way of preventing pollution. Rockefeller said of newly established enforcement procedures, "We are applying this power firmly and evenly to community and industrial polluters alike." To be sure, many industrial establishments were tied in with municipal plants. In these cases municipal "sewage" contained large volumes of industrial wastes. A decision to concentrate on building municipal plants thus did include many that treated both municipal and industrial wastes.

Once the decision to aid municipal systems had been made, the next decision was which elements of the systems to aid. There were three basic parts to a sewage-treatment system. The collection system consisted of pipes that gathered wastes from individual units, such as homes, apartment houses, and office buildings, into a series of sewer lines. In the absence of a treatment plant, these lines usually led directly to outlets that dumped the wastes untreated into the nearest body of water. If there were treatment facilities, pipes called "interceptors" cut across the sewer lines and carried the sewage to the third element of the overall system, the treatment plant, where it was processed and then dumped into the nearest body of water. Property values were higher where collection systems existed; thus their construction was of immediate self-interest to residents. It was decided that this fact was a sufficient incentive to use municipal funds and that state funds were not needed for collection systems. Treatment facilities, however, were another matter. There was no municipal self-interest in constructing these facilities, since the sewage could be passed off to downstream cities. For this reason, it was agreed that aid for treatment-works construction should be provided. Interceptors, the pipes that picked up sewage from various outlets and carried it to a treatment plant, were considered "betwixt and between" collection systems and treatment facilities, but it was decided to give aid for them since their cost was very great.

In regard to industrial waste, one view held that industry should be actively encouraged to tie in to municipal systems. Another view held that it made no difference whether industry built its own plants or used municipal ones. Stricter enforcement would push them to take action. For those firms that chose to build their own plants, a financial incentive was offered in the form of a write-off on corporate income taxes for treatment-works construction and exemption from the property tax for land used for such facilities.

The next question was how much the state and the municipalities should provide. Finally it was decided that the localities would be more likely to support the program if they were paying less than half, and, accordingly, 40 percent was the amount fixed. It was also decided that the federal government was not providing nearly enough funds and that it was time to press vigorously for more. Consequently, the Pure Waters Program called for state financing of 30 percent of project costs and federal financing of 30 percent (much more than was then available). Furthermore, the proposed federal share would be "prefinanced" with state money if Congress was slow to vote sufficient appropriations.

The prefinancing idea was a mix of practical problem solving and ingenious political maneuvering. As a practical idea it was designed to solve two problems: an inflationary price system and the lag in federal appropriations. In order to avoid the increased costs caused by any delay in construction due to the lack of federal aid, New York decided to advance the federal government's "rightful share," hoping to be repaid later, when appropriations were made. The idea had been used with some success earlier in the interstate highway program and seemed appropriate to this new area.

As an ingenious political maneuver, however, it was also attractive. At the time, the federal government was providing 30 percent of project costs, or $600,000, whichever was less. For New York State's construction needs, that amount just about covered planning costs. With this new state program, New York showed itself willing to fulfill its responsibilities and even, if needed, those it felt were the national government's. This seizure of the initiative put strong pressure on the federal government to act. That it had *some* effect is suggested by the fact that in November 1966 Congress endorsed the principle of retroactive payments, while of course appropriating none. Moreover, prefinancing the federal share eliminated the excuses that many municipalities gave for not moving rapidly in the construction of treatment plants.[20]

With the Pure Waters Program ready, the next step was to assure its acceptance by the legislature. Rockefeller met with the state's newspaper editors to explain the program and used one of the Sunday broadcasts in his own television series ("Executive Chamber") to promote the plan. In meetings with legislative leaders he sought their support for the coming session in Albany. There seems to have been general agreement that it was a good program. New York City at first was hostile, because it felt that it would not receive a fair share of the funds. After conferences between state and city officials, however, the city was persuaded to support the program because it realized that even money spent upstate was clearly important for the water supply of a city that was downstream from everybody else. The result of these efforts was a unanimous approval of the program by the state legislature, on condition that the electorate endorse the bond issue in the November election.

There was no organized campaign with a schedule of events to get voter approval for the bond issue. Rather, Rockefeller and other state officials accepted speaking engagements they would otherwise have declined and appeared at congressional committee hearings they would otherwise not have attended. The *New York Times* reported that Rockefeller made twenty-four speeches in support of the referendum.[21] Finally, on November 2, 1965, the New York electorate approved the Pure Waters bond issue by an overwhelming 4-to-1 margin.

On September 1, 1965, the new enforcement procedures went into effect. On September 29, Assistant Commissioner of Health Hennigan reported that enforcement proceedings had started against some thirty-four municipalities and industries, which he said indicated the change in attitudes and scope of the state program: "More legal action . . . has been taken in the past two months than took place in the previous sixteen years."[22]

Since 1965 a number of legislative proposals have been enacted as aids in control efforts. In 1967 Rockefeller proposed and the legislature approved the establishment of a public corporation, the Pure Waters Authority, to help municipalities that were having difficulty raising their share of construction costs. Given the power to sell its own bonds, the authority could contract with municipalities to design and construct municipal sewage systems. In 1970 a major administrative reorganization took the old Conservation Department and the pollution-control agencies from the Health Department and combined them in a new Department of Environmental Conservation. This reorganization was intended to bring all matters of environmental quality into one agency and to give added impetus to already existing programs by creating a new agency to handle them.

The years since the enactment of the Pure Waters Program have seen much activity. The logjam caused by municipal fiscal problems was broken. By July 1, 1974, 317 sewage-treatment projects costing $1,033,863,979 had been completed or were far enough along in construction to be in operation, and forty more projects with an estimated cost of $2,327,179,938 were under construction. State grants for these projects totaled $1,003,903,398.[23] By mid-1975 news reports attributed the improved quality of beach water in the New York metropolitan area and the return of certain species of fish to the Hudson to massive investments in municipal sewage-treatment plants. Later concern about PCBs, a problem unanticipated in the 1960s, caused major accomplishments in this area to be undervalued.

Prefinancing costs borne by the state and local governments had skyrocketed, however. Although the federal government after 1966 was committed to financing up to 55 percent of the construction costs, the actual amount made available by Congress through December 1973 was only about 13 percent. The state government had prefinanced approximately $530 million of the federal government's share of the projects' costs, and localities had prefinanced about $770 million, bringing the total prefinancing to almost $1.3 bullion.[24]

The two most obvious conclusions about policy making in the field of water-pollution control are that the initiative shifted from the state alone to a federal-state cooperative effort and that within New York State that initiative passed from the legislative to the executive branch. Whereas before 1959 the legislature was the locus of policy making, by 1965 it was clear that the initiative had been seized by the governor. Speeches and appearances before congressional committees gave the New York governor a leading voice on the subject of water pollution, not only in the state but in the nation as a whole. Although federal entry to the field was belated, the pace of federal activities has accelerated since 1966. From a temporary assertion of authority over pollution of interstate waters the national government came to permanent assertion of authority over all navigable waters, with a grants program disbursing hundreds of millions of dollars annually. Rockefeller by astute strategy managed to help push the federal government into assuming a much larger financial role than it had done in the past.

Adirondack Park Legislation

On May 22, 1973, after five years of study, controversy, and intense political negotiations, Governor Rockefeller signed into law a bill that made the Adirondack Park the largest area in the United States to come under comprehensive land-use control. Commenting on the new legislation that authorized New York State to regulate the development of almost six million acres of land in the park, the governor stated that such regulatory measures "are of historic national significance, for regional and statewide land-use planning is a number one environmental priority facing our nation today."[25]

The Adirondack Project is a mountainous area of some six million acres (20 percent of the state's land area) in upstate New York. About 2.3 million acres, owned by the state, were designated a "preserve" in 1885. Under the terms of an 1894 amendment to the state constitution, this portion of the area was to be kept "forever wild," and timber cutting, road building, and development of any kind were prohibited. There had been considerable development, however, on some 3.7 million acres of privately owned property intermingled with state land, which made that land difficult to maintain "forever wild."

In 1967 Laurance Rockefeller, the governor's brother and chairman of the State Park Advisory Council, recommended that the federal government make a section of the Adirondack Park into a national park. The governor called the recommendation "a most interesting and imaginative one that would receive careful study."

Conservationists generally, as well as the state Conservation Department, were cool to the proposal, however, fearing that more intensive development as a national park would endanger the wilderness area. In the face of this dispute, Rockefeller, as he did on so many occasions, appointed a fact-finding body. On September 19, 1968, he created the Temporary Study Commission on the Future of the Adirondacks. The eleven-member group was to "identify the problems of the Adirondacks in broad, long range terms." It was to address itself to such questions, among others, as state policy toward acquisition of additional lands and measures that might be taken to ensure that the development on private land was appropriate.[26]

On January 3, 1971, the commission released its report, which was based on extensive field surveys and mapping throughout the Adirondacks. The core recommendation of the study called for the "creation of an independent agency with the power to regulate the use and development of all land, public and private, in the 6-million-acre Adirondack Park, and where it is necessary, override the zoning decisions of local communities and the land-use plans of private property-holders." The governor hailed the commission's efforts as "an outstanding public service" and termed the report "a landmark in the environmental history of the state."

Underlying the commission's recommendations was a sense of urgency concerning the need to check unregulated development. Noting that 60 percent of the Adirondack area was privately owned and that, since only 10 percent had been zoned as to use, restaurants, campsites, motels, and housing developments were rapidly multiplying, the commission predicted that if this development were permitted to go on unchecked, the whole area would be ruined within a generation.

On May 8, 1971, Governor Rockefeller presented the state legislature with a series of bills designed to implement some of the proposals made by the temporary study commission.[27] The bills created an Adirondack Park Agency (APA), composed of the director of the

Office of Planning Services, the commissioner of environmental conservation, and seven members to be appointed by the governor with the consent of the Senate. The agency was required to submit to the governor and the state legislature a master plan for the management of state or public lands of the park by June 1, 1972, and a program of land-use controls for private lands on or before January 1, 1973. For the time being, the agency was empowered to review and approve land developments that exceeded more than five acres or more than five lots within the park. This measure, the governor stated, would provide interim safeguards against improvident uses of lands within the park that would threaten its future value. With some minor changes the legislature accepted the governor's proposal, and the measures were signed into law on June 25, 1971.[28]

During May 1972, the Adirondack Park Agency released the first draft of its master plan for regulating the state-owned lands in the park. It emphasized that these lands should be less developed than the private lands but proposed using some state land for recreation. Specifically, the plan divided state-owned land into four broad categories: wild forest, 1,150,300 acres; wilderness, 997,960 acres; primitive area, 75,670 acres; and canoe area, 18,000 acres. The plan also designated smaller areas as Intensive Use and Special Management areas, Wild and Scenic and Recreational Rivers areas, and Major Travel Corridors. The plan did not permit any new uses for state-owned land within the park and curtailed or limited some existing uses in keeping with the physical and biological characteristics of the land.[29]

The park agency scheduled a series of public hearings throughout the state on the temporary study commission's recommendations. The hearings were not legally required, but they were held because the commission "felt that all of the citizens of the state as actual owners of this valuable resource should have an opportunity to express themselves on the proposed plan." Since the agency recommendations on state lands did not require legislative approval, Environmental Conservation Commissioner Henry Diamond, the agency chairman, admitted that these regulations were "the easier side of our job." On July 26, 1972, Governor Rockefeller approved the master plan for the development of the state-owned lands in the Adirondack Park.

In the spring of 1972, while the Adirondack Park Agency was drawing up plans to regulate land use in the state-owned area of the park, developers began efforts to establish additional housing developments on privately owned lands within the park. The Horizon Corporation, a major land developer in the Southwest, bought from the Northern Lumber Company 22,500 acres of land near the town of Colton, in St. Lawrence County, which it intended to subdivide into small lots for second homes. The public reaction to this proposal was mixed. Richard Grover, staff director of the St. Lawrence County Planning Board, was vehemently opposed to the Horizon development plans. Although his office had no legal authority to stop the development, it could be halted by the Adirondack Park Agency and the Department of Environmental Conservation. On the other hand, Franklin P. Little, publisher of the *Ogdensburg Journal*, called for Grover's resignation because of his opposition to development. Little wrote that the Horizon Corporation "would take over what is now wasteland, producing nothing, and make it into a multimillion-dollar source of new income, new business, new employment, and new taxes for St. Lawrence County."[30]

In November 1972, another plan to build a large housing development in the Adirondacks was announced. The Ton-Da-Lay Project proposed to create a 20,000-person community of second-home owners on an 18,500-acre tract of land at Altamount, in Franklin County, a community of only 5,000 people. The local chamber of commerce supported the plan, claiming that Ton-Da-Lay would upgrade the area's local tax base and would be important to the town's survival. Although the town's planning board also approved the project in early November, Henry L. Diamond said that the final decision on Ton-Da-Lay would be "weighed very carefully" because of the precedent it would set for other developments. Both projects soon suffered setbacks at the hands of the Adirondack Park Agency.

On December 21, 1972, the APA released its preliminary plan to regulate the development of private land in the Adirondacks, which comprised "some of the most sensitive and critical land in the state." The plan would block large housing developments such as those proposed by the Horizon Corporation and Ton-Da-Lay. It would place more than half of the 3.7 million acres of privately owned park acreage under "very stringent" land-use controls.[31] While housing developments would still be permitted in the counties in which the Horizon and Ton-Da-Lay projects had been proposed, by limiting the number of principal buildings to not more than ten per square mile the plan ensured that those projects would have to be considerably smaller than the 20,000- to 25,000-person second-home developments anticipated by the two companies.

Specifically, the agency's plan provided for six categories of private land-use areas with intensity guidelines regulating the maximum number of principal buildings per square mile. Existing hamlets were little affected, but new development for industry and housing was made difficult. A review and permit system was devised by which the Adirondack Park Agency would negotiate with local governments to reconcile their interests with recommendations of the park agency.

Public opposition to the regulation of private land use in the Adirondacks was aired at public hearings held throughout the state between January 8 and January 20, 1973. There was extensive criticism of the plan. Some argued that Adirondack residents had had little voice in formulating the plan and that at least one year's reprieve from legislative action on the proposal was needed. Density guidelines proposed by the APA also came under attack. Some argued that they were far too restrictive, claiming that some areas, such as those designated as Resource Management, would be better suited for higher population densities. Opponents of the plan also argued that it would erode the tax base of the Adirondack communities, cause catastrophic losses of property values, and eventually stifle development to the point where young people would have to leave the area to make a living. The review and permit system also came under attack as the generator of an expensive new state bureaucracy.

On March 9, 1973, the Adirondack Park Agency issued its final plan for the use of private lands in the park. The new plan, although not substantively different from the older version, allowed for a maximum population of about 2 million in the park, compared with a maximum of 1.2 million people recommended in the earlier draft—an increase of more than 65 percent. Consequently, the "intensity guidelines" establishing the maximum number of principal buildings per square mile for each major land-use category were increased somewhat. Two weeks later, on March 21, Governor Rockefeller sent a bill implementing the park agency's plan for the use of private land to the state legislature for approval.

At almost the same time, however, in response to local criticism, the state legislature approved a bill that would delay legislative consideration of the plan until June 1, 1974. Though ostensibly for a year, the delay actually would have been for much longer because the bill passed by the legislature required a comprehensive analysis of the plan's potential impact on land values and property taxes in the Adirondack region before it could be put into effect. Commenting on the proposed one-year delay, Rockefeller said, "When someone doesn't like something he is always saying we are pushing too fast and they haven't had time to read it. Why, I'm busy and I've read it. This subject has been around for years."[32] Later, when vetoing the bill, the governor said, "Its inevitable impact would be to create a dangerous time-gap during which irreversible damage can be done to the Adirondacks."[33]

Finally, on May 22, 1973, the state legislature approved, with a few modifications, the agency's proposal. The slightly modified version of the original bill included virtually all the major features of the park agency's original proposals over which conflict had developed. A fourth Adirondack resident was added to the nine-member park agency, however, and the agency was enlarged to include the state commerce commissioner. Also, a review board chosen by the county legislators in the Adirondacks was set up to monitor the activities of the park agency, but it was to have no veto power. Upon signing the bill making the Adirondack Park the largest area in the country to come under comprehensive land-use control, Governor Rockefeller said, "Many other states have undertaken regional land-use planning to protect environmentally sensitive areas. What distinguished our regional planning for the Adirondacks is its scope and its timing. Comprehensive planning is almost always a response to environmental or economic damage. But here in New York State, we have established regional planning for the Adirondacks before, rather than after, serious damage was done."[34]

However attractive comprehensive planning was to Governor Rockefeller, it did not please residents of towns and villages in the Adirondacks. In 1975, dilatory agency zoning procedures resulted in mass meetings in the region. Bills were introduced in the state legislature to abolish the APA and transfer its functions to the Department of Environmental Conservation. Though this effort failed, as did two major lawsuits challenging the constitutionality of the APA's mandate, ensuing pressures did cause the agency to become somewhat more responsive to local concerns.[35] In general, Governor Carey reaffirmed the state's commitment to preservation values, but tension remained between this statewide perspective and local desires for more freedom for property development.

Parks and Recreation

One of Rockefeller's earliest concerns as governor was the expansion of the state park system. He had not been long in office when he directed the commissioner of conservation, Harold G. Wilm, to survey the needs of the state and develop a program in consultation with the chairman of the Council of State Parks, Robert Moses. The group would collaborate, the governor instructed, with a nationwide study undertaken by the National Recreation Resources Commission headed by his brother Laurance Rockefeller.

On March 14, 1960, the governor sent a special message to the legislature based on the Wilm-Moses report. It noted that "the state is short of almost every kind of public, outdoor recreational facility to meet the needs of our present population."[36] Rockefeller observed that in the preceding season, 107,000 persons had been unable to secure accommodations at the thirty-eight state campsites and estimated that 67,000 new acres would be required for new campsites by 1965. Consequently, he recommended that a $75 million bond issue for acquisition of parklands be submitted to the voters at the November elections.

The bond issue was supported by Robert Moses, most newspapers, and many citizen groups, and was overwhelmingly approved by the voters in November 1960 by a 4–1 margin. Its success led the governor to seek another $25 million in 1962, in response, he said, to "demand by localities."[37] The planned division of this fund provided a precursor to the strategy Rockefeller was to use to build statewide support for later, larger bond issues in other policy areas. Approximately $15 million was earmarked for new state parks and the remainder for counties, towns, villages, and cities, whose costs would be reimbursed by the state to the extent of 75 percent. Under the proposal, New York City would qualify for $5 million by appropriating $1,675,000 in matching funds. Endorsed by Robert Morgenthau, Rockefeller's Democratic opponent for governor in 1962, the bond issue passed by a vote of 1,702,281 to 594,335 in November 1962.

Immediately following the 1962 election a major controversy erupted between the governor and Robert Moses, the long-time chairman of the Council of State Parks. Moses held four other state posts: he was president of the Long Island State Park Commission, chairman of the State Park Authority, president of the Jones Beach State Parkway Authority, and president of the Bethpage Park Authority. He also held three New York City positions: chairman of the Triboro Bridge and Tunnel Authority, president of the New York World's Fair Corporation, and special representative of the mayor in federal-state highway programs.

State employees were required by law to retire at age sixty-five, but the State Retirement System granted extensions at the request of the governor. In 1962 Moses was seventy-four years old. Governors Harriman and Rockefeller had both arranged extensions so that he could continue to hold his state posts. But Rockefeller became increasingly reluctant and thought that Moses should reduce his state commitments, especially after he became president of the New York World's Fair, a major task. Finally, on the eve of Robert Moses' seventy-fourth birthday, the governor suggested that he resign the chairmanship of the Council of State Parks and that Laurance Rockefeller, who had been vice-chairman, succeed him. Moses had agreed previously to this move but apparently was under the impression that it would take place at some time in the indefinite future.[38] He reacted as he had before when mayors or governors had sought to curb his wide-ranging authority: he threatened to resign from all his state positions with a "public explanation" of his reasons. Rockefeller was well aware of the public esteem in which Moses was held and thought a public quarrel might well have political repercussions. Moreover, he appreciated Moses' long public service, although he was difficult to work with. Consequently, the governor urged Moses to retain his other state posts but asked that an "orderly transition of leadership" take place in the chairmanship of the Council of State Parks. The massive parks development program was about to begin. It would take years to accomplish, and the chairmanship of the council should be held by an individual who could give it his full attention.

Moses, however, presented Rockefeller with an ultimatum: either extend his term as chairman of the council or he would resign all his state positions. Thus Rockefeller had the choice of complete surrender or of accepting Moses' resignations. He chose the latter. Moses issued a statement to the press in which he charged that the governor had asked that he resign in order that he might appoint his brother Laurance to the post. In Albany, Rockefeller stated that he had suggested that Moses resign "because of the growing load on him from other positions." Rockefeller praised the services of Moses but rejected his "invidious references to my brother Laurance." The governor pointed out that his brother was the vice-chairman of the Council of State Parks and had been connected with the park system since Governor Lehman appointed him to the Palisades Interstate Park Commission in 1939.[39] Indeed, although the original plan to expand the parks council in 1959 came from the report prepared by Wilm and Moses, the idea for a bond issue to acquire parklands was Laurance Rockefeller's.

The governor stated that in his opinion Laurance Rockefeller, not Moses, would be best suited to head the development program. The *New York Times* in an editorial regretted the resignations of Moses but noted that his attack on the brother of the governor was unfortunate, for Laurance Rockefeller was not a "Johnny-come-lately in the park field."

Oddly enough in view of the heat engendered by this quarrel, Moses ten years later in private conversation expressed the opinion that Rockefeller had been one of the great governors of the state—not equal, of course, to Al Smith, his hero, but much better than some of the governors under whom he had served. Rockefeller seemed equally without bitterness, and in private conversation spoke warmly of Moses' service to the state.[40]

Under the leadership of Laurance Rockefeller, the Rockefeller administration initiated the next step in its program for parks in New York.The $100 million land-acquisition program financed from the two bond issues yielded approximately 360,000 acres in undeveloped land. The problem then was to develop it for use as parks. To this end, on June 28, 1965, the governor signed a bill providing for a $400 million, ten-year program of park and recreation development throughout the state.[41] In the proposal submitted to the voters in November 1966, $200 million was authorized in state bonds, to be matched by another $200 million in state, local, and federal funds. The bill also instructed the Conservation Department to act for the state in order to take full advantage of money available under the Federal Land and Water Conservation Fund Act, and provided for the repayment of the state bonds from fees paid by users of the recreational facilities.

The $200 million Outdoor Recreation Development Bond Issue was approved by the voters in November 1966. Therefore, by 1967 the state had provided for $300 million in bond issues, some of which was to be matched by federal and local funds, for the acquisition and development of parklands in New York State. With the unqualified support of the governor, New York pursued an aggressive and ambitious program of park development. By 1973, the end of the Rockefeller administration, the state maintained 133 parks and 35 historic sites serving nearly 50 million people annually and had been making substantial progress in the development of the 360,000 acres of undeveloped land purchased via the $100 million bond issues of the early 1960s.[42]

The Storm King Controversy

The overriding problem in the environmental area was to determine when the economic advantages of a proposal outweighed environmental considerations. Governor Rockefeller was keenly aware of the need to maintain a balance between these conflicting claims.[43] Although he had an abiding interest in parks and recreational areas and the need to preserve the scenic areas of the state, he also realized that on occasion there had to be some compromise between conservation efforts and what appeared to be important economic gains. Three controversies during his administration illustrate his pragmatic approach to this problem.

The first concerned the proposal of the Consolidated Edison Company in 1962 to build a giant hydroelectric plant on Storm King Mountain near Cornwall in the Hudson Highlands. Con Ed relied on steam-generating plants to supply New York City and neighboring communities with electric power. These plants, old and high-cost operations, were incapable of developing sufficient supply during periods of peak demand for power. Moreover, they were major sources of air pollution in New York City.

Con Ed proposed to draw water from the Hudson River into a reservoir on top of Storm King Mountain and to generate electricity as the water returned to the river. With this new plant the company argued that it could dramatically increase its capacity to meet peak power needs of New York City. Unfortunately, the new plant would be located in a scenic area of the Highlands, and thus conflict was inevitable between those who saw the economic advantages of the plan and those who wished to protect a scenic area.

Initial reactions of Cornwall residents and officials ranged from silence to enthusiasm.[44] When Con Ed informed Mayor Michael "Doc" Donahue of Cornwall-on-the-Hudson of their plans, he could barely contain his euphoria over having a major tax-producing industry dropped into his lap. Donahue was concerned over the loss of the village reservoir, which had been given to Cornwall by one of its wealthy families, but Con Ed said that it would finance its replacement. Some local leaders vied with the mayor in claiming credit for bringing Con Ed to town, and there was some discussion about the possibility of eliminating all local taxes on residential property.

The Palisades Interstate Park Commission and its chairman, Laurance Rockefeller, as well as William Osborn, president of the Hudson River Conservation Society, however, expressed displeasure over the location of the plant's transmission lines. Osborn's concern was personal; the lines would destroy the view from his window. Consequently, in January 1963 Con Ed announced that it would install a submerged cable in place of the overhead power lines at an additional cost to the company of $6 million. The company also offered to build a waterfront park, as well as a new water system, for Cornwall at an estimated cost of $3 million.

In March 1963 Con Ed filed application with the Federal Power Commission for a license to construct the power plant on Storm King Mountain. Various company officials began briefing key public leaders, including Governor Rockefeller, to win their support for the project. At first Rockefeller's position was ambivalent, but when his brother Laurance succeeded in negotiating changes in the transmission lines, he was gradually won over to full support. Later he characterized the project as "an imaginative, large-scale attempt to relieve the power shortage." Rockefeller knew that power shortages and brownouts were developing, particularly in the New York City metropolitan area, and that they would hamper industry and change life-styles. To be sure, consumption of energy per person in New York City was less than in suburban areas, but the total energy needs were tremendous and growing rapidly, especially because of the greater use of air conditioning and electricity for heating. Proposals to build nuclear plants in densely populated areas met with fierce local opposition. The topography of the region for the most part was flat, and the possibility of developing hydroelectric power was limited to the Hudson Highlands. Exotic plans to use seawater or solar power required more engineering expertise. Thus the alternatives were limited and unlikely to solve the energy crisis in the near future.

Rockefeller, however, also felt that, once the state took steps to reduce the environmental impact of Storm King, the federal government, particularly the Federal Power Commission (FPC), would have the major responsibility for deciding whether to permit the construction. Consequently, he played a relatively minor role in the controversy, which was fought at much greater length before federal regulatory agencies and in the federal courts. Nevertheless, the story in brief illustrates some of the difficulties of deciding upon a balance between use and conservation of natural resources. Ultimately the controversy led to a Rockefeller proposal for arbitrating future disputes of this nature.

As opposition to the Cornwall plant surfaced, Mayor Donahue responded by charging that opponents cared more about the view from their windows than about the local school, police, and fire services, which would benefit from the plant taxes. Nonetheless, during the latter part of 1963 a small group of about twelve opponents established a valleywide organization called the Hudson Preservation Conference to spearhead the attack on the proposal. Shortly thereafter,

New York State's Joint Legislative Committee on Natural Resources voted to request the Federal Power Commission not to grant a license for the Storm King project until the state legislature could study it.

In June 1964 the hearing examiner of the FPC approved Con Ed's license. The proceedings of the hearing were sent to the full commission for oral argument and a final decision. Almost one year later, in March 1965, after it was disclosed that large numbers of fish had been killed at the Con Ed nuclear plant at Indian Point, the FPC approved by a three-to-one vote a revised application that gave greater protection to marine life. The majority opinion stated that the Storm King plan was "far superior to existing alternatives," was cheaper and cleaner, and would damage neither the landscape nor the environment. In part, the commissioners decided: "The undisputed proof shows that the Cornwall project would produce savings in the cost of electricity of over $12 million each year as compared with a modern steam plant, the only practical alternative source suggested. It will not alter the existing environment in any conspicuous or unsightly way, and, if anything, will enhance public recreation in the area."[45]

The lone dissenter, Charles Ross, said that his position "was based on the way the Commission had treated Scenic Hudson and had reached its decision, not on the merits of the plan." Nonetheless, environmentalists took the decision to the United States Court of Appeals, whose three-member panel unanimously overturned the FPC ruling in December 1965, stating that the FPC had "failed to compile a record . . . sufficient to support its decision . . . and failed to make a thorough study of possible alternatives to the Storm King project." The court ordered the commission to give further consideration to the environmental impact of the proposed facility.

Three years later, by mid-1968, two significant events occurred in the Storm King controversy. First, Con Ed revised its plan in response to continuing environmentalist objections to the project and decided to build the Storm King plant largely underground. And at the request of the FPC, a three-year study was completed on the effect the proposed plant would have on marine life in the area. The study concluded that "the effect of losses [of fish] by the operation of the plant probably would be minimal."[46]

Nevertheless, the controversy continued. Again the Federal Power Commission approved the project, and again the federal courts intervened, and again there were appeals to higher courts. Finally, in March 1973, the New York Court of Appeals ruled that as far as the state was concerned, the plant could be built, but further litigation in the federal courts continued to block construction.

Rockefeller realized that similar controversies would arise in the future. In his annual message to the legislature in 1972 he said, "One of the principal reasons for the state's electrical power shortage is the absence of a regulatory procedure for determining where and under what conditions power plants should be built in order to provide for necessary power while insuring necessary protection of the environment from abuse."[47] The legislature responded by creating the State Board on Electric Generation Siting and the Environment. In his memorandum approving the legislation, Rockefeller noted that the power shortage could "be ascribed in part to the past failure of the utility industry to plan adequately," but that delays in construction could also be attributed to "multiple requirements for approval and permits from a host of governmental agencies."

Under this law, public utilities would be required to obtain "a certificate of environment compatibility and public need" from the new five-member board, which would consist of the chairman of the public service commission, the commissioners of environmental conservation, health, and commerce, and one ad hoc member from the judicial district in which the facility would be built. The ad hoc member would be appointed by the governor. The act required extensive hearings before an examiner, but the board would decide to grant or refuse the application by a majority of three members. In certain cases the board could override local zoning regulations if they were found to be unreasonably restrictive. Judicial review was provided through the appellate divisions of the Supreme Court and ultimately by the Court of Appeals. But no other state court would have jurisdiction, nor could any other agency or municipality require any additional approval for the construction. This legislation, of course, would not apply to cases involving the Federal Power Commission, the Army Corps of Engineers, or the federal courts. The new board was intended to bring the entire process under one roof. Instead of multiple hearings before many government agencies, henceforth there would be one agency and one set of hearings.

Despite the noble intentions of the 1972 legislation, the creation of the Siting Board failed to expedite the construction of power plants in New York State. Between 1972 and 1979, seven applications for the building of power plants were submitted, but only one was approved, creating what one environmentalist called a "de facto moratorium" on such construction in the state. Under the new system there was only one set of hearings but they went on for years. In one case the files of hearings covered 120 running feet of shelf space.

A crisis in the supply of electricity in New York was avoided only because economic difficulties in the state greatly reduced the levels of demand previously projected for the mid-1970s. In 1978, when the legislation creating the Siting Board automatically came before the legislature for reconsideration, the search was renewed for a procedure that would satisfy environmental concerns and at the same time allow the expeditious construction of generating facilities.[48]

The Hudson River Expressway

In May 1965, at the time environmentalists began marshaling their arguments against the Storm King project, another state plan aroused considerable opposition. It was disclosed that a six-lane highway was being planned along the east bank of the Hudson River extending from the vicinity of Beacon or Wicopee on Interstate Route 503 south to the northern city line of New York. The bill authorizing construction of the expressway easily received legislative approval, and Governor Rockefeller signed it into law on May 28, 1965. Although critics later charged that the bill was "pushed through the legislature under highly undemocratic procedures," one political observer commented that "while the legislature's procedures were hardly commendable, they were not all that unusual."[49]

It was long recognized that traffic congestion plagued the towns and cities north of New York City, particularly in Westchester County. When the New York State Thruway was under construction on the west side of the Hudson during the 1950s, state planners predicted traffic congestion on the road and urged the construction of a parallel north–south commercial expressway on the east side of the Hudson. A commercial expressway, they argued, would also help reduce congestion on Route 9, which formed the main streets of a number of villages north of New York City. Increased traffic from the General Motors plant in Tarrytown made congestion on Route 9 in that area particularly bad. On June 1, 1962, the trustees of the Village of Tarrytown proposed a bypass to relieve congestion on Route 9 and asked the Department of Public Works to expedite a feasibility study. Three years later, on April 29, 1965, the mayors of other villages along the route, in a petition to Governor Rockefeller, urged the construction of bypasses on existing highways to ease traffic flow along the

Hudson corridor. The proposed Hudson River Expressway would give them much more than they had requested.

Initial reaction to the plan in the four towns most affected was mixed. Tarrytown officials were vehemently opposed to the expressway, arguing that it would substantially reduce property tax revenues as well as ruin the town's planning program. Ossining officials, however, endorsed the road as a solution to its severe problem of traffic congestion. Environmental groups, such as the Scenic Hudson, the Sierra Club, the Hudson River Fisherman's Association, and the Citizens Committee of the Hudson Valley, were opposed to the expressway. These groups argued that the proposed road would ruin the scenic value of the area and would impair accessibility to the shoreline of the Hudson River.[50]

As a result of mounting public opposition, Rockefeller decided to restrict the road to the northernmost 10.4 miles slated for construction, thus dropping the largest segment of the proposed highway. Under this revised plan, the expressway would begin in Croton and extend south, terminating at the New York State Thruway at Tarrytown. This change had been recommended by the Regional Plan Association in its Policy Statement on the Proposed East Hudson Expressway, released on July 19, 1965.

The association's policy statement also said that while the need for an expressway was not a "pressing one," there existed a "long-range need" for the road, which would "provide a continuous freeway route for commercial as well as passenger traffic" through "an important development corridor that lacks freeway access." Though it would provide "a magnificent view for motorists," the study said, the road would also "make the riverfront less attractive for those living in the areas." In the early part of 1966, the state sweetened the expressway proposal by combining it with a plan to build a four-mile riverfront park with beaches, boats, bicycle and hiking paths, fishing piers, a golf course, a restaurant, and parking for 2,000 cars. The Rockefeller family proposed to donate some 165 acres that they owned along the river to the county for community recreational purposes. This property was estimated to be worth between $6 and $8 million.

In the meantime, the federal government had become involved in the dispute. In 1965 President Lyndon Johnson, in proposing the creation of a new agency to preserve the natural beauty of the Potomac, had expressed the hope that similar agencies might be created by state and local governments to protect other urban rivers. During the next year a number of bills were introduced in Congress to establish a Hudson National Scenic Riverway, which would include the area through which the proposed expressway would be built and also include Storm King on the western bank. While Rockefeller was vitally concerned with protecting the Hudson, he was equally opposed to putting the valley under federal control. Accordingly, he quickly established a Hudson River Valley Commission to indicate that the state was not defaulting on its responsibility.[51] The governor favored a plan for collective action by the federal government, New Jersey, and New York. Since most of the Hudson Valley lay in New York, he thought that the controlling voice in any agency should be that of New York. Secretary of the Interior Stewart Udall countered with a proposal for a three-man commission—one federal, one from New Jersey, and one from New York—charged with preparing a master plan for the preservation of the valley and with authority to override local zoning laws under some conditions.

At about this time, Congressman Richard Ottinger (Democrat) of Westchester, who was opposed to the expressway, succeeded in getting legislation through Congress that gave the secretary of the interior responsibility for reviewing all federally related projects within the "Hudson Riverway" for a period of three years to ensure that they did not have an adverse effect on natural resources.[52] Since the expressway would be built with the assistance of federal highway funds and on land fill along the Hudson, it would be a federally related project involving the Corps of Engineers and the Department of Transportation. Secretary Udall had already indicated his opposition to the expressway. Rockefeller unsuccessfully fought the legislation, which he termed "a federal power grab."

Over the following year and a half the expressway plan lay dormant. Then, in 1968, Secretary Udall appointed, in succession, two Hudson River task forces composed of federal officials to examine the expressway proposal under the 1966 legislation. Both reported favorably on the plan, maintaining that it would provide not less but more accessibility to the shoreline of the Hudson as well as increased recreational opportunities. The second report, which was much more detailed than the first, countered every criticism advanced by expressway opponents.[53]

On December 11, 1968, Secretary Udall wrote to the Corps of Engineers reversing his opposition to the construction of the expressway, citing the two studies as the reason for his change of position. On January 27, 1969, the Corps of Engineers approved the necessary dredging and fill for the expressway.

Nevertheless, the expressway encountered other problems. The Sierra Club, the Village of Tarrytown, and the Citizens Committee of the Hudson Valley appealed to the courts to enjoin the corps from releasing the permit. Although a federal district court denied the motion on February 27, 1969, the plaintiffs took the case to the U.S. Court of Appeals in Manhattan, which ordered the district court to hold a trial on the issues raised by the expressway's opponents.

In an ingenious approach, the attorney for the opponents argued that the issuance of the dredge-and-fill permit violated the 1899 Rivers and Harbors Act, which stated that "it shall not be lawful to construct or commence the construction of any bridge, dam, dike, or causeway over or in any navigable river of the United States until the consent of Congress to the building of such structures shall have been obtained." The original intention of the act was to prevent the Corps of Engineers from performing favors for selected localities. Opponents of the expressway argued that the road's embankment was a "dike" and therefore required congressional approval, not a dredge-and-fill permit. Despite state efforts to show that the embankment was not a dike "that controlled water flow," the district court judge ruled that the corps permit violated the Rivers and Harbors Act.

The state joined with the federal government in an appeal to the Second Circuit Court of Appeals, which ruled that the proposed expressway did need the approval of Congress, and the expressway was again halted. Finally, on November 2, 1971, the $2.5 billion transportation bond issue including funds for the expressway was overwhelmingly defeated by the state's voters. Two weeks later, on November 20, Rockefeller announced at a conservationists' workshop in Tarrytown that the expressway was a "dead issue."[54]

The Rye–Oyster Bay Bridge

In March 1967, while the controversies over Storm King and the Hudson River Expressway raged, Governor Rockefeller announced a proposal for the construction of two bridges across Long Island Sound.[55] One bridge would link Rye and Port Chester with Oyster Bay, while another would join Port Jefferson with Bridgeport, Connecticut. Rockefeller's plan was based on a study by William J. Ronan that evaluated several proposals for bridges linking Long Island with Westchester and Connecticut. These projects had long been favored by Robert Moses. In the absence of bridges over Long Island Sound, traffic from the eastern end of the island bound for Connecticut had to go through New York City, thus increasing congestion on the city's highways.

Two months later, the legislature, as part of an omnibus transportation bill supported by both parties and passed by large majorities, authorized the Metropolitan Transportation Authority to construct the two bridges. The Connecticut legislature failed to act on the Port Jefferson bridge, however, and therefore what had been a plan to build two bridges became a plan to build one from Rye to Oyster Bay, which would be entirely in New York State.

Rockefeller's announcement of the proposed bridge generated immediate opposition from local groups. The Rye City Council, the Rye Planning Commission, the Citizens Committee for the Preservation of Rye, and H. Clay Johnson, the mayor, were adamantly against the bridge. The Oyster Bay Civic Association and the Joint Committee on Community Rights were equally opposed. During 1968, opponents of the bridge in Oyster Bay succeeded in having 3,117 acres of town-owned wetlands in the area of the proposed bridge's landfall transferred to the U.S. Department of the Interior as a wildlife preserve on the condition that it be kept forever wild; otherwise, ownership would revert to the town.

Support for the bridge came from business groups, building trades unions, trucking firms, and companies engaged in heavy construction. Principal advocates of the proposed bridge were the Nassau-Suffolk Regional Planning Board, the Tri-State Regional Planning Commission, Suffolk County Executive John V. N. Klein, and the Long Island Association of Commerce and Industry. The Long Island Association argued that "heavy vehicular congestion on both the Throgs Neck and Whitestone Bridges and the Long Island Expressway is strangling economic growth on the island." Without the bridge, the association added, "Long Island will be seriously impeded in attracting the new industry that will be urgently needed to provide services and jobs for an estimated three million people in Nassau and Suffolk counties by 1980."[56] Countering objections that the bridge would be ecologically damaging, the association said, "Everyone knows that bumper-to-bumper traffic such as exists today on the Long Island Expressway causes fantastic air pollution." William Ronan added, "If prior generations had given such undue consideration to the minimal effects upon the environment of putting bridge piers in the East River, the Brooklyn Bridge wouldn't have been built—and we would not be celebrating the seventh-fifth anniversary of New York City's consolidation."

Town residents based their objections to the bridge on traffic, noise, pollution, and, particularly, what they argued would be the inevitable destruction of their communities by the bridge and its approach ramps. The Regional Plan Association of New York claimed that the bridge would "proliferate commercial sprawl in Long Island, Westchester, and southwestern Connecticut," "would weaken urban centers" in the area, and would violate Long Island Sound as a major open space and unique recreational resource of the New York region.

Rockefeller replied, "I am aware of the fact that nobody wants any more bridges, roads or anything built in their area. However, Long Island, with its growth, must get an independent passing out to Westchester and Connecticut without going to New York [City]."[57] Amusingly, later during the 1970 campaign, Rockefeller was so busy shaking hands that he inadvertently signed an antibridge petition drawn up by the Committee to Save Long Island Sound, a Long Island organization with headquarters in Locust Valley.

Nevertheless, local opposition increased, and in 1971 the state legislature passed a bill stripping the Metropolitan Transportation Authority of power to build the Rye–Oyster Bay Bridge. Rockefeller vetoed the measure, arguing that numerous studies, including those by the Tri-State Transportation Commission, had shown "important benefits that would accrue by linking Long Island with Westchester County." To withdraw the power from the MTA "would be contrary to sound long-range transportation planning for this state."[58]

Events during 1972 and 1973 foreshadowed the demise of the proposal. In April 1972, the New York State Legislature again voted to deprive the MTA of the power to build the bridge, and again the governor vetoed the measure. In 1973, the Department of the Interior blocked Rockefeller's proposal to place the approach roads to the bridge through the wildlife sanctuary ceded by Oyster Bay to the department. Rockefeller was reportedly quite angry that the decision had been made by a "lower echelon department member." An aide to the governor stated that Rockefeller "could cope with the fact if the secretary [of the interior] had ruled, but a second in command burns the governor." When asked if he would still build the bridge in spite of the department's ruling, Rockefeller replied, "Yep." When asked how, the governor said, "That's up to me. You'll find out as the scenario unfolds."

Finally, in 1973, the legislature again passed a bill depriving the

MTA of its power to build the bridge. This time the governor surrendered and signed the bill, saying, "It is clear that the people want to take a more careful look at decisions which affect the face of their land."[59] There were a number of reasons for his action. Local opposition was intense and increasing rather than declining. Unfortunately for the governor, the opposition came from staunch Republican strongholds on Long Island and threatened other programs in which he had an interest. At this point, Rockefeller apparently decided that the political price had become too great.

Council on the Arts

Just as environmental programs focused on the quality of life in New York, so did efforts to enrich the cultural resources available throughout the state. In the past, state government had been concerned only with the physical environment. Under Rockefeller's administration, the state added a new dimension.

The Rockefeller family had long had an interest in the arts, and soon after Nelson became governor, he commissioned a private consulting firm to make a survey of cultural resources and activity in New York State. In the following year, 1960, in his annual message to the legislature he recommended "the creation of an Advisory Council on the Arts to be composed of private citizens who have distinguished themselves in several fields of cultural activity." "The United States," he said, "is in the process of a tremendous surge of public interest in art, music, the drama, and other forms of cultural expression. New York State must make a contribution to this cultural advance commensurate with its unequalled cultural resources." The proper role of the state, the governor thought, was "to act as a catalytic agency to stimulate and encourage participation in the performing and fine arts generally . . . [but] the State should not in any way act in a manner which might limit the freedom of artistic expression so vital to the well-being of the arts."[60]

There was little support for the project in the legislature, especially among upstate Republicans. On the other hand, neither was there great opposition. Rather, the legislature's attitude could be described as one of indifference. As Rockefeller later said, "The only way that I could get many of the legislators to take the bill seriously was to ask that it be tried as a temporary commission on a two-year basis—and, finally, to ask some vote for it as a personal favor." The governor said, "I discovered that while I could not carry a tune, I could persuade a legislature. Thus, in 1960, my second year as governor, a New York State Council on the Arts was enacted [sic] at my request."[61]

The legislation as passed and signed by the governor declared it "to be a policy of the State to join with private patrons and with institutions and professional organizations concerned with the arts to insure that the role of the arts in the life of our communities will continue to grow and will play an ever more significant part in the welfare and educational experience of our citizens and in maintaining the paramount position of this state in the nation and in the world as a cultural center."[62] The act provided for fifteen council members to be appointed by the governor with staggered terms, beginning April 1, 1960. Rockefeller named as chairman Seymour M. Knox, president of the Buffalo Fine Arts Academy, chairman of the Council of the University of Buffalo, and a trustee of the Yale Arts Gallery, and as director Laurance Roberts, formerly director of the American Academy in Rome. Although a few other states had provided funds before 1960 to support museums of fine arts or had given occasional support to state symphony orchestras, New York was the first state with a comprehensive program. Michigan soon followed, creating a cultural commission later in 1960, as did many other states in the next decade.

As a first step, Laurance Roberts, director of the new council, was instructed to do a survey of the state's cultural institutions. The study found that "the arts tended to be concentrated in a few metropolitan areas. They were unavailable on a high level of quality to a broad geographic cross section of our population." In addition, the study found that there was "no cultural institution in New York State . . . that [was] self-supporting." The council recommended the appropriation of funds primarily to finance traveling theatrical companies and exhibitions, as well as to provide professional service to small museums needing assistance for preservation, repair, and restoration of their collections. The governor persuaded the legislature to appropriate $450,000 in 1961 for the work of the council.

In January 1961 Laurance Roberts returned to Italy and John Mac-Fadyen succeeded him as director of the council. During the next year MacFadyen traveled extensively around the state, conferring with various groups concerned with the arts. In many communities these groups later transformed themselves into more permanent associations, thus marking the beginnings of the Community Arts Council movement. The effort of the state council during its first year could be characterized as an initiative "to bring the best in the performing arts to as many communities in the state as possible" and to become familiar with "the many detailed and specific problems of the high-quality amateur and semi-professional groups which already exist." By October 1961 the governor was able to write: "All reports on the Arts Council program have been excellent and I think we have inaugurated an enterprise which will have widespread repercussions not only in our own state but outside as well."[63] A few months later, on March 27, 1962, Governor Rockefeller approved a bill that continued the council for five more years. Three years later he persuaded the legislature to make the council a permanent agency of the state government.[64] In April 1964 John MacFadyen was succeeded by John B. Hightower, who served as director until 1972, when he was succeeded by Eric Larrabee.

Originally the council offered what were, in effect, grants to certain well-known professional performing arts groups to help them underwrite the cost of tours to some of the state's smaller communities. Later, instead of offering aid to the touring groups, it channeled money directly to local arts organizations, which in turn chose the touring companies they wished to invite and used council money to help pay them. Thus the choice among touring groups was broadened and the initiative was shifted to the communities. The evidence of public acceptance of the program was overwhelming. The number of performances supported by the council rose from 107 in 1962/63 to 224 in 1963/64. The number of communities served increased from fifty-three to eighty-eight, and the number of performing organizations on tour grew from nine to fifty-seven.[65]

Gradually over the years the council expanded the scope of its programs. It undertook restoration of paintings and artistic objects through its Cultural Resources Fund. It encouraged composers of music by arranging performances of contemporary productions at which the composers would be present. It arranged artists' exhibitions in college campus galleries. It offered financial assistance to arts service organizations, which planned programs, served as information centers, and publicized art events. Art exhibitions were sponsored at numerous points in the state. In 1970/71, for example, 22 exhibitions traveled to 112 institutions in 67 communities and enlisted the cooperation of numerous colleges, elementary and secondary schools, and libraries.

A program to enhance cultural opportunities in urban areas was started, aimed especially at ghetto neighborhoods. In 1966, with a special appropriation from the legislature, a Museum Aid Program was started, and later, in 1970, it was expanded under the Aid to Cultural Organizations Act. This legislation was intended to aid local museums and historical societies. As the council undertakings grew, various other forms of art were included. For example, a cooperative poetry program was begun to stimulate interest in poetry in colleges as well as communities in various parts of the state. Summer arts festivals were begun, and experiments in filmmaking were tried. Consultants were provided to organizations requesting them. In 1970 some 200 consultants served 174 organizations with technical advice. This program was the first of its kind in the United States.[66]

State appropriations for the Council on the Arts grew steadily, from $450,000 for the fiscal year 1961/62 to $2.25 million in 1969/70. The fiscal year 1970/71 was a critical one in the life of cultural institutions in the state. Many of them faced rapidly increasing costs and declining revenues. Rockefeller, in his annual budget message to the legislature in 1970, urged an emergency appropriation of $18 million.[67] Later he sent an "arts letter" to some 2,000 trustees of major arts organizations in the state suggesting that they urge their legislators to support his request. The legislature did appropriate slightly more than $20 million—$18 million as an emergency grant and $2 million for normal expenses.

The next year, 1971, the state legislature, faced with deficits, cut the council's total appropriation to $14.5 million. The popularity of the council's programs was immediately evident from the flood of protests that descended on Albany. Some of the money was restored the following year and the budget was increased to $16 million, where it remained until Rockefeller resigned.

While the programs that the council sponsored met with wide popular support, its administrative procedures were subject to criticism on several occasions. The staff, with the aid of anonymous panels of outside consultants, reviewed applications for grants to determine their artistic worth and financial soundness. Recommendations from the staff and the consultants were submitted to the council, which could either approve or disapprove the proposed grant. Organizations receiving aid had to obtain as much support from nonstate sources as they had obtained in the previous year. Once the council approved it, the grant had to work its way through the cumbersome state fiscal procedures before the funds actually reached the organization to which they had been granted. All of this took time and occasioned complaints. Part of the difficulty was apparently inherent in the state's fiscal procedures, but some of it may have arisen because the council staff was composed of people who knew and understood artistic problems but were not skilled in management and administration. This was the major conclusion of a study done in 1970 by the state Budget Office.[68] The study reported that the council lacked administrative controls in budgeting, internal accounting, and personnel management. Staff duties were not clearly defined. An administrative reorganization was recommended, but several years later the same complaints were aired in public, although clearance through the state fiscal authorities seemed to account for much of the delay in transferring funds from the council to cultural groups.

Besides the Council on the Arts, several other state activities in support of cultural projects were begun or expanded during the Rockefeller administration. In 1966 the legislature established the State Historical Trust at the governor's suggestion to identify and acquire historic sites, through purchase or gift.[69] In previous years the state had occasionally acquired historic areas, but this was the first time that a substantial amount of money—$20 million—had been made available and an agency created to operate the program. The next year, federal legislation under the Historic Preservation Act made federal-state cooperation and funding possible.

In 1966 the legislature created the Natural Beauty Commission, again at the governor's request, to coordinate state agency preservation of areas of scenic attraction and to advise local governments to the same end.[70] The commission was also to promote aesthetic considerations in state construction projects.

Two other cultural undertakings were closely associated with Governor Rockefeller. When Lincoln Center was built in New York City in the mid-1960s, the state contributed $15 million for the New York State Theatre, which was part of the theater and opera complex.[71] The second was the Saratoga Springs Center for the Performing Arts.[72] The Rockefeller family contributed $4 million for the amphitheater, one of the largest in the world. Eugene Ormandy called it "the greatest and most beautiful I have ever seen or participated in."[73] This was the summer home for the New York City Ballet and the Philadelphia Orchestra.

No project sponsored by Governor Rockefeller during his sixteen years in office generated so much popular support as did these cultural programs. His files include hundreds of letters from all over the state expressing appreciation and pointing out what even small sums have done to make possible cultural events that could not have been initiated without state financial support. While the amount of money expended in these endeavors was only a tiny part of the total state budget, it had a major impact on the quality of life in communities large and small across the state. Moreover, the success of New York's programming led to the establishment of similar undertakings by all the other forty-nine states and the federal government.

On the whole, however, Rockefeller's experience with projects that had an environmental impact was a mixed bag. The Adirondack Park legislation and the arts program were solely the result of his initiative and persistence. They were hailed by environmentalists and art patrons alike as outstanding achievements. The Pure Waters Program came into being more slowly, and, to a certain extent, Rockefeller was nudged into it. Once involved, however, he proceeded with a vigor to create a program that led the nation.

With regard to the Hudson River Expressway and the Oyster Bay bridge, Rockefeller, balancing economic needs against environmental concerns, concluded that highway communications could be improved with little damage to the environment. To his surprise, he was bitterly attacked by conservation groups, and this he found particularly painful. While he did not play an important role in the Storm King controversy, the environmental groups that had opposed him in the highway debates criticized him on the same grounds on this project.

These episodes clearly illustrate the constraints on gubernatorial power. Among them was the changing public attitude toward large-scale projects and the increasing strength of the environmental movement. Moreover, in the political dynamics of the situation, opposition was particularly effective because it developed in staunch Republican areas. And, unlike social issues, these two projects had little appeal to city-based Democrats. These disputes also pointed to the difficulties that politicians will continue to have in trying to make capital improvements while preserving the natural environment. Indeed, there is no doubt that this dilemma will continue to plague leaders of all parties in the years ahead.

10

The Governor
and Washington

Two decades ago, few commentators on a governor's administrative record would have devoted much space to what the chief executive did or tried to do in dealing with Washington. This was considered a relatively unimportant aspect of a governor's job.[1] No doubt national elections, changes in federal policies, and the condition of the national economy vitally affected state politics, but these broad national forces were beyond the reach of any incumbent governor. Most likely, he would be assessed historically as the victim, beneficiary, or reactor to these trends.

Events of the 1960s, however, changed all this. "It is not too much to say," observed David Davis and James Sundquist, "that federalism, as it had been known in the preceding seventeen decades of the American Republic, had been revolutionized."[2] The enormous transformation in the relations among governments left no level of government untouched.

At the vital center of these changes in the federal system was state government, which in the 1950s and 1960s began to reverse a long decline. And at the vital center of state government was the governor. It was he who was caught between growing public demand for services, escalating expenditures, and public protests against taxes. It was he who faced rising expectations by both voters and the national government regarding what the states should be doing.[3]

The federalism of the 1960s turned states into clients of the national government and governors into lobbyists. Effective intercession in Washington, however, was far more complicated that a one-shot impassioned plea before a congressional committee. It required subtlety, tact, effective utilization of all available resources, sustained penetration, and many allies. It also required information, knowledge of the federal establishment, strategies, a keen sense of timing, and patience. A governor was not likely to be successful if his Washington activity was limited to a hit-and-miss pattern: a press release, a recrimination, a single or partisan appeal.

Special access to the president, to the extent it existed, had to be used sparingly lest its effectiveness be quickly dissipated. A state's congressmen could help—subject, of course, to partisan considerations, their own constituencies, seniority, and committee memberships. Fellow governors often were divided by partisan issues and the wide range of differences among the states. Other interest groups might be helpful, but typically their concerns varied with each issue, requiring constant alliance building.

Nelson Rockefeller brought to the governorship of New York a compelling belief in the viability of state government. He nurtured a profound appreciation of the potential role the states could play in an increasingly urbanized society. In Rockefeller's opinion, they were not only the keystone of American political life but also the fundamental benchmark against which the viability of a federal form of government could be measured. The success of the American federal system thus depended in large measure on the performance of the states themselves. In the Godkin Lecture Series at Harvard University in 1962 Rockefeller declared, "If state inaction creates a vacuum, the federal government, under the pressure of public opinion, will fill it."[4] He said, "The time is upon us now to assert again the older and more vital tradition—to call upon our states to be active where they have been passive—progressive where they have been timid—creative where they have been merely cautious. In a word, it is time for the states to—*lead*."[5]

Yet as time passed, what Rockefeller did, his goals and objectives, options and strategies, became increasingly intertwined with what happened or failed to happen in Washington. Why did his position change? How did national policies become such a determining influence upon the governor's agenda for the state? What actions did Rockefeller take not only to change the course of national domestic policy but to produce the most favorable results for the people of New York State? These are difficult questions, and the answers, to the extent that they can be found, are complex and still controversial. Rockefeller's successes and failures should be viewed, therefore, in the context of the formidable tasks he undertook as well as the environment in which he acted.

Relations with Presidents

Nelson Rockefeller had a keen appreciation of the decisive role that the White House played in determining national domestic policies, establishing the agenda for congressional action, and shaping the direction of intergovernmental relations. Consequently, he paid considerable attention to cultivating personal contacts with the men who held the office of the president, from Eisenhower to Nixon.

Rockefeller became governor during the last two years of the Eisenhower era. He had known the general since World War II. Notwithstanding their differences while Rockefeller served on Eisenhower's White House staff,[6] their relations continued to be cordial. After Rockefeller's election as governor in late 1958, they frequently corresponded. The governor's abiding interest in civil defense and fallout shelters culminated in a White House conference on the problem and later national legislation to deal with it. Rockefeller visited Eisenhower from time to time, attended White House functions, and was consulted on several speeches of major domestic importance. Their relationship was warm and personal, as is illustrated by the governor's response to a birthday message from Eisenhower to him: "Your friendship and understanding are deeply appreciated and mean more to me than I can say."[7] Association between the president and the governor continued long after Eisenhower left the White House.

The governor's relations with John Kennedy, though not unfriendly, were overshadowed by partisan politics. In a conversation with Ben Bradlee of the *Washington Post,* Kennedy said, "Nobody ever had any doubt . . . [Rockefeller] could beat me in 1960. I knew that."[8] The possibility that Rockefeller would be Kennedy's Republican opponent in the 1964 presidential election kept the relationship between the two men a formal one. That possibility died with Kennedy, however, when his assassination in November 1963 brought Lyndon Johnson to the presidency.

Lyndon Johnson and Nelson Rockefeller had both gone to Washington in the 1940s, Johnson as a freshman congressman and Rockefeller as a young administrator. Their paths crossed frequently over the next twenty-five years, encouraged by their mutual regard for Sam Rayburn, speaker of the House of Representatives. This early friendship blossomed into respect and deep affection for each other during President Johnson's five years in the White House. Soon after Johnson became president, Rockefeller took the opportunity to establish personal relations, writing him, "Americans of all parties are

Rockefeller lobbying for the states with President Johnson (1966). Wide World Photos.

grateful to you for the sure, skilled hand with which you steered the Ship of State through a shattering, perilous period."[9]

During the next five years there were frequent communications and many personal meetings between the two. The governor brought to the attention of the president and his staff his concern about civil rights, education, water pollution, and narcotics addiction, citing New York legislation that possibly could be useful in developing national programs. Relations between the two became more personal as time passed, and the governor's signature on correspondence became simply "Nelson." Invitations to dinners at the White House flowed in a continuous stream to Albany, and usually they were accepted. Brief personal notes to the president for birthdays and congratulations on speeches were interspersed with more formal letters regarding legislation. When Johnson began his second term in 1964, the governor wired, "Congratulations on your sweeping victory." He attended the president's inauguration and later conferred with him on legislation in which they were mutually interested.

Recognizing the governor's experience and interest in federalism, President Johnson appointed Rockefeller to the bipartisan Advisory Commission on Intergovernmental Relations. This appointment pleased Rockefeller, for the ACIR became an increasingly important instrumentality to him in focusing national attention on such issues as the modernization of federal grant-in-aid procedures, welfare reform, revenue sharing, and the larger problems of fiscal and programmatic balance in the American federal system. Rockefeller generally applauded President Johnson's Great Society programs. He supported federal leadership in outlawing racial discrimination, increasing educational opportunity, ensuring health care for the aged and indigent, improving the environment, and cleansing rivers and the air. In turn, Johnson consulted with Rockefeller concerning dealings with other governors, particularly as White House relations with the chief executives of the states tended to deteriorate in the late 1960s.

Nonetheless, Rockefeller expressed both public and private concern over federal methods in achieving domestic goals—the downgrading of state governments, the proliferation of narrow grants-in-aid, and the inattentiveness to administrative planning and fiscal implications of Great Society programs. Also, Rockefeller did not permit his fondness for President Johnson to detract from his negative view of national policies, particularly during Johnson's last eighteen months in office. Then, in Rockefeller's view and that of many other observers, the president failed to readjust domestic spending to the enormous budgetary strain of the Vietnam war. To Rockefeller, the "guns and butter" strategy of federal spending precipitated an inflationary momentum that had severe economic consequences, particularly for state and local governments. Rockefeller's prophecy proved accurate, and, in fact, New York State incurred the disastrous consequences of the inflation-recession combination from 1969 through 1971. Later, in his defense of President Nixon's domestic policies, the governor would often allude to the economic problems Nixon inherited in 1969, which severely constrained the president's options.

Rockefeller's personal esteem for President Johnson and his impressive legislative record may be gleaned from a letter written to the president in the final days of his administration. "I cannot allow your term to end without trying to tell you how much I admire your stewardship of the office . . . your human concern, your ability, and your extraordinary record with Congress in the field particularly of social legislation . . . and I rejoice with you at the accolades that are yours today and will be even greater as the years go by."[10] Party differences did not seem to come between these two prominent chief executives. At least, they never allowed partisan feelings to interfere with their personal regard for each other. The governor supported Johnson on the Vietnam war and the aims of his domestic program, and this support made the beleaguered president all the more appreciative of and responsive to the governor's advice.

The ongoing rivalry between the governor and President Nixon over control of the direction of the Republican party and their pursuit of the presidential office left deep scars on both men. Whatever cordial relations existed between Rockefeller and Nixon were harmed appreciably by events of the 1960 presidential election. Not only did the governor decline Mr. Nixon's offer to be his vice-presidential running mate, but he also openly disagreed with him over party policy. The celebrated confrontation between the two in resolving the problems of the 1960 Republican platform led to what became known as the "Compact of Fifth Avenue."[11] Four years later Nixon helped isolate the governor nationally from party regulars, faulting him as a "party divider" and a "spoilsport" for his failure to provide complete support to the 1964 GOP presidential candidate, Barry Goldwater. The governor's presidential aspirations were undercut, in part, by Mr. Nixon's opposition.

During the next four years their relations failed to improve. Rockefeller did little to help Nixon during his period of wandering in the political desert between 1962 and 1968, and in fact resisted his involvement in the gubernatorial and congressional races in New York in 1966.[12] Political ambitions conflicted again in 1968, and this time the outcome was the nomination and election of Richard Nixon as president. Now the two men dealt with one another from different vantage points—a Republican president and the Republican governor of the nation's most populous state. A mutual need for each other developed, and with it came a steady improvement in relations. The long-standing animosity between them was subordinated to the mutual recognition that each was a successful professional politician.

Soon after the 1968 election, Rockefeller met with President-elect Nixon to discuss cabinet choices, White House staffing, and a domestic agenda. As the senior and leading spokesman among state and local officials, Rockefeller could not be ignored by the new Republican administration. Indeed, from the president's perspective, the New York governor had to play a vital supportive role if Nixon was to be more than a single-term president. Several prominent New Yorkers associated with the Rockefeller administration assumed key cabinet and subcabinet positions, the most important being Henry Kissinger, the architect of the president's foreign policy. President Nixon also appointed several governors who were allies of Rockefeller to leading positions in his administration—George Romney of Michigan, John Volpe of Massachusetts, and John H. Chaffee of Rhode Island.

In his dealings with presidents, Rockefeller was particularly careful to distinguish between the man and his policies. He sought to avoid personalities and sought rather to deal with issues and problems. He praised President Nixon's foreign policies. He chided the Democratic-controlled Congress for its unwillingness to move on the president's domestic agenda for partisan reasons. He rallied state and national constituencies in support of the president's programs for grant reform, revenue sharing, and welfare reorganization.

Rockefeller had a high personal stake in the success of President Nixon's domestic programs. From 1969 on, New York's burgeoning need for revenues required a strong national economy and a balanced fiscal federalism. President Nixon, leader of his party and of the nation, occupied the preeminent position to help achieve these goals.

Thus, hardly a month passed during the president's first sixteen months in office during which the two men did not meet, in Washington or elsewhere, to discuss domestic legislation and New York State's problems. There were numerous invitations to White House functions and, with the exception of prayer breakfasts, Rockefeller accepted when his schedule permitted. The ultimate turn-about in their relations was most amply manifested in Rockefeller's role in President Nixon's reelection in 1972. Lauding the president for his capacity to "think anew" and "act anew" on foreign and do-mestic policies, Rockefeller delivered the principal nominating speech for Nixon at the 1972 Republican Convention. There he listed the policy areas in which President Nixon had made great strides forward. Rock-efeller served as the New York State chairman of the president's reelection campaign, with the result that Nixon carried the state by more than one million votes, or 59 percent of the overall vote. Rock-efeller also operated as a surrogate speaker for the president's cam-paign and appeared in this capacity in states across the continent.

Finally, in Richard Nixon's time of crisis, his deepening involve-ment in the Watergate cover-up, and the impeachment proceedings against him, Rockefeller refrained from condemning him. Rather, he addressed the situation in terms of its "personal tragedy," with deep sorrow and regret for those involved. It was a measure of the new relationship he had developed with Nixon in his first term, but it was also good politics. He did not want to antagonize the right wing of his party. Later, during the hearings on his nomination for the vice-presidency, Rockefeller was attacked for not being more openly criti-cal of the Watergate abuses. He responded that, in being circumspect, he was trying to avoid harmful consequences to New York in its dealings with Washington. [13]

Rockefeller dealt frequently with cabinet and subcabinet officials on a personal basis, regardless of administration. His previous experi-ences at HEW and the White House made him familiar with the importance of the bureaucracy. The governor realized that to deal effectively with the federal government, he had to persuade the lead-ers of federal departments and agencies of New York's needs. These men controlled federal regulations, guidelines, and grant disburse-ment, and consequently were often the critical decision makers.

The governor maintained close contact with members of the White House staff and Office of Management and Budget who had domestic policy responsibilities. He personally appeared before the president's Urban Affairs Council, argued the New York State case before its successor, the Domestic Council, and even pleaded for revenue shar-ing with the president's budget advisers. These were all access points that, when fully exploited, kept issues alive and policy alternatives before decision makers.

At times Rockefeller's high-level intercession in behalf of what he perceived to be New York's interests became controversial. This was the case, for example, in 1972, when he sought, through conversations with President Nixon and correspondence with Attorney General John Mitchell, to encourage the awarding of contracts to Grumman Industries on Long Island for the F-14 fighter aircraft and the NASA space shuttle project. When asked during the hearings in the Senate on his confirmation as vice-president whether this was "a proper use of political influence," Rockefeller replied that, as a practical matter, political factors were involved in these decisions and said, "I have always felt... [it] was my responsibility to put [forward]... the interests of the contractors in New York State who were legitimate contractors, and whose receipt of the contract would be to their interest, to the State's interest, in the sense it gave more employment.... I though I was doing my duty for my constituents."[14]

The Governor and Congress

Like many a chief executive, Rockefeller often grew impatient with legislative bodies, whether in New York or in Washington. Perhaps none of the possible resources available for dealing with Washington proved more exasperating, however, than the state's congressional delegation.[15]

When unified across party lines, a state's congressional delegation can be a powerful resource for any governor. On the other hand, a delegation that is uncohesive, fragmented, and torn by partisan, ideological, and personal differences can undercut the overall interests of a state and mute the governor's efforts to be heard in the Washington community. Some delegations, with members united by a dominant economic interest or predominantly from districts of the same socioeconomic composition or party allegiance, have proven highly effective in augmenting state claims through the legislative process. Traditionally these delegations have been those of the smaller, less populous southern and western states. Other states, such as New York, tend to be a microcosm of politics nationally. They have wide income variations, many ethnic groups, rural and urban divisions, and highly diversified manufacturing and service economies. This diversity leads to divisions in the state congressional delegation. But no other large delegation has been so fragmented as that of New York.

Shortly after becoming governor, Rockefeller helped organize a bipartisan steering committee for the New York State congressional delegation.[16] Chaired by Emanuel Celler, a Brooklyn Democrat and senior congressman from New York, the steering committee was instituted as a communications device for informing members of pending legislation considered to be important to New York State. Because of the delegation's bipartisan composition, Rockefeller was careful from the outset to call upon it in matters where partisanship could be held to a minimum and where the state's overall interest could unite Republicans and Democrats. Rockefeller seemed pleased with the initial results of these organizing efforts, for he wrote Senator Jacob Javits in late 1959 that the steering committee had "definitely served a useful purpose, and it is my hope that it will continue in the next session."[17] It did, and it remained intact over the next fifteen years.

In later years Rockefeller continued to try to deal with the New York delegation as a whole, using Celler and Javits as the key contact men. Increasingly this approach proved to be unwieldy and rather ineffectual, as the governor later acknowledged. Nevertheless, Rockefeller never lost hope that it might be productive in the long run. He often sent round-robin letters to delegation members on issues deemed to be of major significance to the state: civil rights, interstate compacts, reimbursement for the New York Thruway, water pollution, welfare reform, revenue sharing. These letters would detail the state's experience, outline its current and projected needs, and conclude by indicating how a particular piece of federal legislation or pending administrative decision affected the state.

At least once a year, usually at the beginning of a congressional session, the governor would sponsor a dinner for the delegation, at which he would outline what the state was trying to accomplish and how the delegation could help. The governor's staff prepared a position book for this meeting which specified important pending legislation and appropriations and outlined an agenda for congressional action. As one long-time member of the Rockefeller staff observed, "In the beginning years we were hopeful that the delegation meeting would produce results; however, after several years, we conducted them merely to protect our flank. We did not want the delegation to fault the governor for his lack of leadership, cooperation, or providing direction."[18]

The key New York House member, from the governor's perspective, was Emanuel Celler. First elected to Congress in 1923, Celler not only was chairman of the powerful Judiciary Committee but was also among the most senior members of Congress. The governor and the congressman developed a personal and professional relationship that went beyond partisan politics to the essential issues that bound them, aiding New York City and New York State, the interdependency of which both acknowledged. Rockefeller wrote to Celler at least twice a month over a ten-year period. His correspondence fell into three categories: (*a*) opposition to or support for pending congressional legislation, (*b*) appropriations requests seeking maximum benefits for New York, and (*c*) delegation assistance in retaining existing or new federally funded facilities within the state.

Apparently Celler tried to be as obliging as he could be to the governor's requests. He would seek the support of individual delegation members, generate legislative revisions favorable to the state, and even trade votes with non–New Yorkers. As a well-respected senior member of his party, Celler had contacts beyond the delegation and spoke with authority in the Democratic party's inner circle in the House. The Brooklyn congressman also introduced legislation requested by the governor and at times openly intervened at the White House and before executive departments and agencies when administrative decisions affected the state. Rockefeller, in turn, was extremely accommodating to constituent requests forwarded from Celler's office to state officials.

In the Senate, Rockefeller relied principally on Jacob Javits. Elected to the Senate in 1956 after four terms in the House, Javits established a reputation on Capitol Hill as a hard-working and energetic legislator. The governor and Javits communicated frequently on improving social service programs. As ranking minority member of the Senate Labor and Public Welfare Committee, Javits was acutely aware of the state's problems in the health, education, employment, and welfare areas. The senator had some success in raising in Congress several major issues of concern to New York: welfare overburden, grant allocation formulas that impeded the state's participation in federal programs commensurate with its needs, and inflexibility in federal grant programs generally.[19] Javits and Rockefeller joined forces against a federal cutback in Medicaid funds and an amendment to the Social Security Act that froze federal contributions to welfare programs. This protest against punitive federal action was successful. The freeze was postponed a year and eventually lifted altogether.

Senator Javits also assisted Rockefeller in seeking other legislation to meet New York's problems. He advocated federal tax credits for state income taxes, revenue sharing with preference to high-tax-effort urban states, and the overhaul of federal grant-in-aid programs to make them more responsive to the needs of large industrial states. The two men also advocated greater federal involvement in civil

At the Republican State Convention after Rockefeller's nomination for a fourth term. Left to right: Senator Jacob Javits, Happy Rockefeller, and the governor (1970). Photo by Bob Wands. Wide World Photos.

rights, welfare, and mass transit. Indeed, their views on most issues were so alike that personal correspondence was not often required. This unique relationship between a state's senator and incumbent governor was perhaps best illustrated by Rockefeller's warm note to Javits in 1971, shortly after his reelection: "One of the most satisfying aspects of these past years has been working closely with you. I look forward to our continued close association."

Four other senators served New York during Rockefeller's governorship: Kenneth Keating (1959–1964), Robert Kennedy (1965–1968), Charles Goodell (1968–1970), and James Buckley (1971–1976).[20] Like Javits, Keating established himself in the liberal wing of the GOP and hence the two senators rarely disagreed with each other in their Senate voting. Rockefeller persuaded Keating to abandon a safe seat in the House to run for the Senate and later appointed him to the New York Court of Appeals upon his defeat in 1964. Nevertheless, the governor still relied more upon Javits or Celler in his communications with the delegation. Since Keating served only during Rockefeller's first two terms in office, he was not a party to the governor's most intense efforts to involve the federal government in New York's problems.

For obvious partisan reasons, the relations between the governor and Senator Robert Kennedy were cool. Upon entering New York politics, Kennedy sought to unite warring factions of the Democratic party by attacking the governor on all fronts. Such a strategy enabled Kennedy to gain recognition as the chief Democratic spokesman in the state, but it had the short-term effect of straining relations between the two men.

Kennedy's charges leveled at the governor started at the beginning of his Senate service. To Rockefeller's call for federal grant modernization, Kennedy responded that the present system was adequate for New York's needs. The problem, according to the senator, was that New York had not been taking full advantage of existing grants and programs. He used as an example the state's laggard behavior in the mental health field. Responding to the senator's charges both by letter and in a television interview, the governor noted that the senator, a newcomer to New York politics, was perhaps uninformed about New York's mental health program, which his brother, President Kennedy, had used as a model for a national plan that he had sent to Congress.[21]

In a detailed letter to Kennedy explaining New York's problems with existing federal aid formulas, Rockefeller closed with a conciliatory appeal. "It is my sincere hope," he said, "that there can be a return to this nonpartisan position among the state government, New York's Congressional representatives and the Federal Government in support of these important matters of human concern."[22] Kennedy's charges continued. The governor remained aloof, attempting to defuse or rebut them with detailed press releases. Rockefeller would not be provoked into engaging in personal attacks against the senator. His aim was to unite the state's delegation, not to divide it further. The irony of their brief but embattled relationship was the fact that the governor and senator agreed on the substantive issues more often than they disagreed. Partisan differences and the pursuit by both men of a national constituency made reconciliation all but impossible during Kennedy's thirty months in the Senate.

Kennedy's tragic death by an assassin's bullet left the governor with the responsibility of filling the vacancy. His first choice, New York Mayor John Lindsay, then a Republican, turned down the opportunity. The governor next consulted with House Minority Leader Gerald Ford concerning which of the state's Republican congressmen would be closest to the party's inner circle and the most productive appointment for New York. The answer was Charles Goodell, Jr., the five-term Chautauqua County legislator. Goodell had a rather conservative voting stance in the House, but Rockefeller felt he would overcome it in the Senate because he would be representing a much broader, more liberal constituency.

After Goodell was appointed, more appeals flowed from Washington to Albany than the reverse as the new senator and his staff sought Rockefeller's aid in responding to constituent requests. Goodell became a strong advocate of increasing authorizations and appropriations under the Federal Water Pollution Control Act. Since New York, between 1963 and 1968, had committed $150 million to prefinance the federal share of water-pollution control in addition to the state's share, this was a primary goal of the governor. Rockefeller also praised Goodell publicly for his decision to vote against the 1969 Tax Reform Act, legislation to reduce taxes which the governor thought was irresponsible as fiscal pressure on states and localities mounted.[23]

Goodell soon embraced an issue that he strongly felt would produce a more liberal constituency, opposition to the Vietnam war. This stance nearly cost him his party's renomination in 1970 and probably cost him the election. Rebellious GOP county chairmen were livid about Goodell's rapid change of image. Rockefeller expended considerable political credit in obtaining the renomination for Goodell, only to endure criticism for not fully supporting him in the general election. Goodell ran last in a three-way race, with the Conservative party candidate, James Buckley, winning the seat. Buckley marked out his own areas in the Senate—conservation, pollution control, and national defense—and, as a junior senator, was not a major resource in aiding the governor's lobbying efforts.

Why the New York delegation failed to unify or develop a sense of "real estate" is a complex story. Much of the explanation was partisan. As Table 23 indicates, the Democrats obtained a clear numerical majority within the delegation in 1965 and retained it thereafter. This date coincided with the Eighty-ninth Congress, which produced the Great Society programs and the virtual explosion in new categorical grant programs. New York City Democrats constituted between 60 and 80 percent within the Democratic majority in the state delegation. For years the city's Democratic members had been split along ideological and personal lines. To some extent, therefore, problems within the state delegation were an outgrowth of feuds among Democratic factions that spilled over to the group as a whole, and made agreement on major issues almost impossible. There was also rapid turnover among members and a noncareerist orientation because of the greater attraction of state and city and opportunities in the practice of law and in business. Consequently, New York congressmen rarely remained in Congress long enough to obtain important committee posts through seniority.

Table 23. New York State's Congressional Delegation, 1959–1974 (congressmen and U.S. senators)

Congress	Years	Democrats	Republicans	Total
86th	1959/60	19	26	45
87th	1961/62	22	23	45
88th	1963/64	20	23	43
89th	1965/66	28	15	43
90th	1967/68	27	16	43
91st	1969/70	26	17	43
92d	1971/72	24	19	43
93d	1973/74	22	17	39

Source: *Congressional Directory.*

Note: Reapportionment resulted in the state's loss of two seats in 1963 and four more in 1973.

The reluctance of Democratic members to support anything the governor wanted could be expected in light of their party's plight in New York State. Aside from Robert Kennedy, a newcomer to the state, the regular Democratic party organization had failed to support a single winning candidate for senator, governor, or mayor since 1957 (until Abraham Beame was elected New York City mayor in 1973). Indeed, opposition to the governor became one of the few points upon which factions could unite. Open cooperation with the governor by delegation Democrats, even on the most bipartisan of issues, proved a political risk. It was notable that sometimes congressmen who were the governor's most outspoken critics wrote him privately indicating support or sympathy. From 1966 on, cooperation among delegation members, even of the same party, was further subjected to concern over reapportionment. Since the state's population as a percentage of the overall national population declined in both the 1960 and 1970 censuses, New York relinquished two congressional seats in 1963 and another four in 1973. Regular redistricting of congressional boundaries by the state legislature exacerbated tensions among delegation members, who were fearful that districts would be merged and two incumbents would be forced to run against each other.

During Rockefeller's first two terms (1959–1966), the congressional delegation weighed more prominently in his strategic approaches to Washington than in later years. This change reflected both the increased urgency of federal action for New York in the late 1960s and the governor's sustained attention to Washington matters in his third and fourth terms. From at least 1969 on, the frustration of working through the delegation as a whole had taken its toll on the governor's patience. Rockefeller had an overriding need for immediate federal action, and thus, though he kept the state delegation informed, more and more he sought direct contact with the congressional hierarchy and powerful committee chairmen.

No other state or local official could make the claim, as Rockefeller could, that he had testified before every major House and Senate committee in the execution of his duties. The governor testified, at one time or another, on transportation, social security, domestic expenditures, foreign policy, taxes, intergovernmental relations, grant reform, education, crime control, and revenue sharing, and this list is not exhaustive. The numerous roles in which he delivered congressional testimony were also revealing. At various times he appeared as governor of New York, member of the Advisory Commission on Intergovernmental Relations, chairman of the Governors' Conference

Human Resources Committee, and president-appointed fact finder on the United States' Latin American policy. Indeed, these roles often overlapped. Addressing one House investigatory committee on grant consolidation plans, the governor began, "I am delighted, Mr. Chairman, to have this chance to be here to represent the Governors of the fifty states, as chairman of the National Governors' Conference Committee on Human Resources, and, also, to be here as a Governor of one of the States and a member of the Advisory Commission on Intergovernmental Relations."[24]

The governor, of course, was no novice to Capitol Hill.[25] What endeared him to several committee chairmen was the fact that he was a lively witness, always prepared, properly deferential to members, informative, and combative under probing. Most often his knowledge of the issue at hand went far beyond its relation to New York State. Instead of reading a lengthy prepared statement (a procedure that upsets many a committee member), he would make summary comments, allowing ample time for a question-and-answer dialogue, which both he and members enjoyed. Rockefeller's appearance typically meant media coverage for the committee and its work. It also meant, on most occasions, a large attendance at committee meetings.

Rockefeller employed a variety of tactics in arguing his case. He stressed the human-interest aspect, presented short case histories of frustration with federal policies, and emphasized the headaches and problems of being a state chief executive. Often Rockefeller would intersperse his testimony with visual aids—charts, graphs, and diagrams—to support his arguments and provide a sense of trends. Central to his presentation was a spirit of collaborative action: here is a problem, this is how it developed, and these are various constructive alternatives that might be pursued by all government levels in dealing with it.

According to the Rockefeller staff, probably no greater example of the governor's forthrightness in taking his views to Washington can be found than his testimony on the federal 1971 water-pollution control amendments. This far-reaching legislation set as a national policy the termination of all pollutants into navigable waters by 1985. The legislation had sailed through the Senate with a vote of 85 to 0, and it was expected to meet little resistance in the House. After all, the year 1971 found ecological interests at high tide, with nearly every legislator seeking some political benefit from riding the crest of this national movement. In short, Congress was not likely to be receptive to the view that what they were doing was unfeasible and unreasonable.

Against this background, Rockefeller, before the House Public Works Committee, attacked the language and federal commitment contained in this legislation. The governor did not take issue with the intent of the bill. No state at the time had made a greater commitment to water-pollution control than had New York, as evidenced by its Pure Waters Program.[26] But using a literal interpretation of "pollutants" as related to their discharge into navigable waters, Rockefeller challenged the standards in the federal legislation: "We have figured for New York State the cost of eliminating all discharges into any navigable waters by 1985 would be $239 billion. Projecting that on a national scene, the cost of a strict interpretation of this bill would be between $2 and $3 trillion in the United States."[27] Rockefeller charged that the legislation would have severe unintended consequences that bordered on irresponsible action. It set goals that, if taken literally, were fiscally impossible to achieve. It allowed for administrative exceptions that amounted to a cruel deception upon the public and those who sought to achieve the goals. Not only did Rockefeller argue that a zero pollutant discharge goal by 1985 could not be achieved, but he also pointed out that the program represented another example of the national government's raising expectations without providing commensurate funds to attain its stated goals. The consequence was that the states and the governors were left holding the bag.

Despite Rockefeller's efforts, the legislation passed essentially unchanged. A Brookings Institution study in 1975 showed that, as he had predicted, the program was underfunded, and, even then, appropriated funds were impounded.

The governor's sense of humor was widely appreciated by his congressional audience. Members of the House Public Works Committee will long remember the governor's heated exchange with the outspoken New York City congresswoman, Bella Abzug. Rockefeller asserted before the committee that billions of dollars would be required to meet the goal of zero pollutants in navigable waters by 1985. These estimates were based on studies by Rockefeller's conservation advisers and the director of the state's water-pollution program. Congresswoman Abzug challenged the governor's "figures" and berated him for employing scare tactics. Her strident cross-examination of the governor caused alarm among some committee members, who sought to intercede. Rockefeller patiently awaited an opportunity to respond to the rotund and notoriously abrasive Manhattan legislator, and then said, "The distinguished Representative from New York has questioned my figures. My concern is that in challenging my figures, she has none to substitute, except a very beautiful figure of her own."[28] The governor's response quickly defused a rather tense situation and allowed the committee chairman to end the day's hearings on the upswing.

In case after case, Rockefeller's appearances before Congress were warmly received. What impact this reservoir of congressional goodwill had for New York State or the states generally is difficult to ascertain. When many congressional committees were chaired by rural state representatives, Rockefeller often served as a balancer, a spokesman for the larger, urbanized states of the North. When urban congressmen sought to bypass the states and develop direct federal relationships with cities, Rockefeller presented state government as a viable alternative.

Other Governors

During his fifteen years in office, Nelson Rockefeller's relations with his peers, the governors of other states, became an increasingly important resource in dealing with Washington. These relations were developed on several levels: (*a*) through individual, informal contact; (*b*) through the formal national organization of all governors, the National Governors' Conference; (*c*) through the partisan affiliate of the National Governors' Conference, the Republican Governors' Association; and (*d*) through formal and informal groupings of state governments in regional associations. Each of these gubernatorial associations emerged as a resource for Rockefeller's use in dealing with Washington.

By 1967/68, Rockefeller had become senior among the governors of the states and something of a spokesman for the states. One governor noted in 1973, "On almost any major broad issue affecting state government, many of us look to Rocky." Similarly, Governor Linwood Holton of Virginia said, "Governors are very impressed by Nelson Rockefeller both personally and by his real grasp of issues";[29] and Richard Ogilvie, former governor of Illinois, commented, "When I first came into office, no governor and his staff were more helpful in providing ideas and assistance than Rockefeller."[30]

The personal rapport Rockefeller established with fellow state executives seemed to transcend political, sectional, and ideological differences. Among the more interesting relationships that developed between Rockefeller and fellow governors was the one that involved California. Although three thousand miles apart, New York and

California had much in common insofar as size, tax structure, budgets, and progressive traditions were concerned. Governor Edmund Brown, a Democrat, and Rockefeller, a Republican, exchanged numerous letters on such issues as housing, bond financing, water pollution, and antidiscrimination laws, and on such lesser matters as which state produced the better wine. When a testimonial dinner was given for Brown in 1966, Rockefeller wrote him a congratulatory letter that read in part, "You and I are, of course, on opposite sides of the political fence, but that does not prevent my saying . . . that I greatly enjoyed all the contacts I had with you."[31]

During his first two terms, Rockefeller had little enthusiasm for the National Governors' Conference (NGC). From his vantage point, the annual three-day gatherings of state chief executives afforded little time for dealing with the major issues of state government. These gatherings were largely social occasions. No real planning preceded the conferences. There were no working papers and no separate staff to follow up positions adopted. In the absence of a concrete agenda and backup staff, the conference was an organization of fifty prima donnas, divided by party rivalry, sectional and ideological cleavages, and personal ambitions.[32] The organization suffered from high membership turnover and little continuity in leadership. Voting rules and procedures operated as deterrents against dealing with highly visible major issues. By the early 1960s the NGC, which had met annually since 1908, was torn apart by the civil rights issue and was near dissolution.

As governor of the most populous state and a man with experience in Washington, Rockefeller was immediately welcomed to the governors' club. In 1960 he became a member of the conference's executive committee and assumed the chairmanship of its Civil Defense Committee through 1965. But he was not particularly vocal or even a conspicuous participant in the initial NGC meetings he attended. Besides serving on the Civil Defense Committee, he also had assignments on the State Planning and State–Urban Problems committees. These committees were largely ad hoc, were constantly being reorganized, and showed little continuity from one meeting to the next.

Between 1965 and 1966, Rockefeller's unhappiness with the NGC led him actively to support the Executive Committee's proposals for overhauling its entire structure. As a reaction to Great Society programs, which bypassed state governments, the governors established a separate Washington Office for Federal–State Relations in 1967. This office was to be "staffed, financed, and designed to serve the governors exclusively . . . to improve the effectiveness of the states, and particularly the governors, in dealing with problems arising out of federal–state relations."[33] This new direction in the governors' national operations and the prospect of a well-staffed and active Washington office to serve the conference, independent of the Council of State Governments, made Rockefeller more interested in taking an active role. He never became chairman of the conference, however, even though he was encouraged by others to assume the responsibility. An implicit rule within the NGC was that presidential contenders did not serve as chairmen lest the organization be compromised or torn apart by partisan bickering. Moreover, the governor's staff felt that too visible a role would be a political liability.

Once the Washington office was established, Rockefeller worked with NGC Chairman John Volpe (Republican, Massachusetts) in mapping out its operations. In 1967 Rockefeller was named head of the NGC's Health and Welfare Committee, which was later renamed the Human Resources Committee. He also served on the Governors' Federal–State Relations Committee, which was made up of other NGC committee chairmen and which planned strategies and tactics for the conference from 1967 to 1969.

Rockefeller's work within the NGC was primarily in the areas of bringing new issues to the fore, developing policy consensus around positions, and getting the governors to go on record as a group. This was a major contribution to the organization, particularly in light of its previous ineffectiveness. The governor's greatest successes were recorded at the NGC's annual meeting in 1969 at Colorado Springs. Rockefeller's resolutions were prominent on the governors' agenda and resulted in NGC support for federal welfare financing, a national health insurance program, and its endorsement, in emphatic terms, of federal revenue sharing with states and localities. Summarizing the governors' activities at this annual session, Rockefeller noted that "the Governors have moved ahead of the Washington scene in their perceptions of the needs and problems we face as a nation. It seems to me we have done more to grapple with national issues and take positions than any conference I have ever attended."[34]

In retrospect, however, the National Governors' Conference remained a disappointment to Rockefeller. He had harbored great hopes that the governors could subordinate their differences and unite as a kind of third force juxtaposed between Congress on the one hand and the president and executive establishment on the other. To Rockefeller, the immediate concern for state chief executives should have been to rectify the existing fiscal and programmatic imbalances in the American federal system. Such causes as grant-in-aid modernization, revenue sharing, welfare overhaul, and increased state involvement in intergovernmental programs seemingly could supersede partisanship. For the most part, however, this was not the case. After 1972, rapid gubernatorial turnover and a return to highly partisan issues once again debilitated the NGC, and Rockefeller's interest in it waned considerably.

Historically, Republican governors have played more important roles in their party's activities than the Democratic governors. Since the early 1930s, big-city mayors have been more conspicuous in Democratic party circles than governors, who typically have been split by the northern and southern factions within the party. Since the early 1950s, the Republican governors have been more closely identified with the progressive wing of the GOP as opposed to the more conservative congressional faction. The endorsement of New York Governor Thomas Dewey's "fair play amendment" at the 1952 GOP convention by eighteen of the twenty-three Republican governors not only helped disqualify the previously challenged delegates pledged to Ohio Senator Robert Taft but turned out to be one of the decisive factors that cost Taft his party's presidential nomination. It was the more progressive GOP governors who attempted unsuccessfully to block the nomination of Senator Barry Goldwater in 1964, and who led the successful fight to break the Goldwater faction's grip on the Republican National Committee in 1966. Thus the Republican governors typically composed a formidable bloc within the GOP, one to which party officials often paid considerable attention.

The Republican Governors' Association (RGA) was reconstituted in 1963, with Robert Smylie, a progressive westerner from Idaho, as its chairman. Between then and early 1967, Rockefeller's interest in the GOP governors tended to be more politically motivated than dedicated to forwarding policy and programs within his party. If the GOP governors could agree on a gubernatorial incumbent as the choice for their party's presidential nomination, that person would have an excellent opportunity for attaining that goal.[35] Obviously, Rockefeller hoped he would be the candidate. If he were not the choice, then he felt the governors should support another of their number whom they found more acceptable. Pennsylvania's William Scranton emerged as a less than unanimous choice among GOP governors in 1964, only to lose the GOP presidential nomination to Arizona Senator Barry Goldwater. Michigan Governor George Romney became Rockefeller's personal choice for the nomination in early 1967, only to fade as fellow Republican governors failed to rally to him.

Beyond the political machinations by individual governors to enhance their political careers, the Republican Governors' Association came to play an important role within the party. From early 1967 through 1970, the RGA dealt from a position of considerable strength. The Republican governors survived the 1964 Democratic landslide better than any other public official grouping within the GOP and won ten additional governorships in 1966 to return to their 1952 strength of control over twenty-five statehouses. In April 1967 the Republican Governors' Association was formally made a separately constituted unit within the Republican National Committee. By 1969, GOP governors had attained a postwar high of thirty-two governorships. In that year, Republicans controlled the governorships in nine of the ten most populous states, which contained nearly half of the nation's population.

Rockefeller was quick to capitalize on this shifting political balance within the GOP. He sensed an opportunity to strengthen the governors' role in party affairs and to lobby for more progressive stands within the party on public policies. In the spring of 1967, following a special meeting of Republican governors in Jackson Hole, Wyoming, Rockefeller became head of the Republican Governors' Association's Policy Committee. He decided to make something of this new assignment, though few had done so before him. The timing seemed right. The presidential nominating conventions were just over a year away. The Democrats had been in power for nearly eight years. The country was confronted with complex social problems and entangled in a difficult foreign war. The Republican party needed alternatives and options to take to the public.

Following the urban riots in the summer of 1968, one of Rockefeller's first actions was to wire President Johnson requesting that the national government consider remedial actions. Obtaining no immediate response, the Rockefeller-headed policy committee issued in August a "Nine Point Action Plan to Inaugurate a New Era of Creative State Leadership to Meet the National Crises of Social Injustice and Lawlessness." This plan, applauded by GOP governors, called for federal legislation authorizing the states to prefinance federal programs, speeding up and increasing federal funding for human resource programs, and establishing bloc grants and revenue sharing to assist the states in their fiscal difficulties. Much of this action plan was also adopted by the National Governors' Conference when Rockefeller brought it before the NGC's Federal–State Relations Committee, on which he served.

Following the action plan, Rockefeller published and disseminated two massive works for the Republican Governors' Association, one a statistical workbook and the other a handbook of suggested solutions for domestic problems. The first report was issued as a staff report for the RGA on December 8, 1967, and the second on June 14, 1968. Rockefeller never sought his fellow Republican governors' endorsement of these reports. They were controversial and the issues highly divisive. His objective was to air the most prominent issues of the day, getting party leaders and others to think of alternative strategies to solve national problems.

In addition, the New York governor, aided by Henry Kissinger, published five volumes on foreign policy under the aegis of the RGA. Rockefeller avoided labeling these volumes "position papers," knowing well that GOP governors would be annoyed. He termed them "working papers" and "background materials" for his party. He felt that the impact of these working papers was twofold. They allowed GOP governors to enhance their voice on national legislation and enabled them to exert some influence on the 1968 GOP platform and the positions taken by presidential candidates. Indeed, major segments of these materials found their way not only into the party platform but into the position papers disseminated by the Republican National Committee in the later campaign.[36] Rockefeller gained little credit for these contributions despite their significance for his party's successful presidential campaign that fall.

With the election of Republican Richard Nixon to the White House, the visibility of the RGA declined. Rockefeller's interest declined as well. He failed to attend the 1969 and 1971 RGA meetings. With massive Republican losses in the 1970 gubernatorial elections, the force of the RGA diminished further. In 1971 and 1972 Rockefeller again worked with fellow GOP governors, but the thrust of that effort was directed at lobbying the White House to move federal revenue sharing to the top of the president's domestic agenda.[37]

Like the National Governors' Conference, the Republican Governors' Association proved only partially helpful as a resource for Rockefeller in dealing with Washington. In light of the governor's output of energy and time, there were few demonstrable changes in national policies to show for the effort. Movement was slow and change gradual. Like the National Governors' Conference, the RGA was largely a disappointment.

The Advisory Commission on Intergovernmental Relations

Nelson Rockefeller was appointed to the Advisory Commission on Intergovernmental Relations (ACIR) by President Johnson on November 10, 1965. He resigned on May 21, 1970, at the beginning of his fourth campaign for election to the governorship. Only one governor served longer on the commission. ACIR members and staff were in agreement that much of the commission's visibility, prestige, and impressive work was attributable to Rockefeller's active participation. According to David B. Walker, assistant ACIR director, whose tenure spanned that of the agency's four executive directors: "Nelson Rockefeller attended the commission's meeting with his homework done and virtually dominated proceedings through his extraordinary command of information, forceful arguments, and overriding concern for solving problems. His ability to reconcile conflicting views and achieve compromise enabled the ACIR to take positions on new and controversial issues. The commission and American federalism benefited immeasurably from his leadership."[38]

The Advisory Commission on Intergovernmental Relations was established by Congress in 1959 as a permanent bipartisan body representing the executive and legislative branches of the federal, state, and local governments and the public. The ACIR provided a forum for the study of critical intergovernmental problems and developed policy recommendations. It was an anomolous federal creature with fourteen of its twenty-six members incumbent state and local government officials. As a body composed of public officials at all levels of government rather than an agency dominated or controlled by any one level, the ACIR had a diverse constituency.

The commission provided Rockefeller with a means to include mayors and county officials in a coalition to pressure Washington to overhaul the federal grant system and share more of its tax revenues with states and localities. Once the ACIR hammered out a consensus on specific policies, the governor often marketed these ACIR recommendations through other groups and institutions. Whether dealing with the National Governors' Conference, the Republican Governors' Association, fellow state or local officials, or the Congress, Rockefeller emphasized the ACIR's recommendations to support his arguments. With six members of Congress on the ACIR, three senators appointed by the president pro tem of the Senate, and three representatives appointed by the speaker of the House, the commission had built-in legislative access for its recommendations. This aided Rockefeller particularly in his dealings with the Intergovernmental Relations subcommittees of the House and the Senate Government Operations committees, which had responsibility for legislation in the intergovernmental area. House Subcommittee Chairman L. H. Fountain (Democrat, North Carolina) and his Senate counterpart, Edmund Muskie (Democrat, Maine), both ACIR members since 1959, frequently called upon the governor to testify on legislation before their committees. Thus Rockefeller's ACIR affiliation furthered his overall strategy of raising essential policy issues governing the direction of intergovernmental relations and forwarding concrete proposals for reform in this area.

Once Rockefeller became a firm advocate of federal revenue sharing, he found the commission to be a major instrument in keeping the policy alive and building consensus among state and local officials for its enactment. Just before he left the ACIR, the staff prepared a brief information report, "Overcoming Obstacles to Revenue Sharing," and in late 1970 the ACIR issued an information report entitled "Revenue Sharing—An Idea Whose Time Has Come." The commission's policy recommendations provided Rockefeller with considerable backup support for the positions he took. In most cases, these were policies Rockefeller had advocated long before formal ACIR ratification, but ACIR backing added a certain legitimacy to the governor's arguments. Rockefeller's interlocking memberships on the ACIR, NGC, and RGA enabled him to take policies he supported from one organization to gain adoption by another. He thus had a unique means of building consensus among public officials at all levels of government.[39]

Revenue Sharing: A Case Study in Washington Lobbying

Nelson Rockefeller's 1971 annual budget message to the legislature marked one of the darkest moments in his gubernatorial career. Gone were proposals for bold, innovative programs that had characterized previous messages. Instead, the governor opened his budget message with the depressing comment "We have reached a point at which the State alone can no longer meet its own needs and give adequate help to the schools and local governments." The 1970 economic recession, with its rising unemployment and declining business profits, was causing personal and corporate income taxes to decline. State revenues were estimated at one-quarter of a billion dollars less than they had been the previous year. Loss of employment led to increased welfare expenditures. The impact of inflation on state expenditures for personnel and materials was particularly severe.[40]

From 1968 through 1971, New York State expenditures increased more than 60 percent, from $4.6 billion to $7.5 billion. Expenditures for education in this period increased by more than $1 billion, welfare by $697 million, transportation by $306 million, and health care by $251 million. Rockefeller had resorted to large tax increases, short-term and long-term borrowing, transfers of funds from reserves, freezes and stretchouts in capital expenditures, and other fiscal maneuvers to match revenues with expenditures. In 1970 the state was compelled to cut back on programs, particularly aid to local governments, and to postpone increases in others.[41]

While the state government alone would not have an unmanageable fiscal problem, said Rockefeller in his 1971 budget message, New York had a history of helping local governments. Indeed, 63 cents of every dollar collected by the state went for local assistance, an increase from 54 cents a decade earlier. Local governments, especially New York City and other Big Six cities, were also in precarious fiscal straits, and a reduction in state aid would be disastrous. The answer was federal aid. "Too many of our problems," Rockefeller charged, "are at the local level and too much of the tax money is going to the national level and not coming back."

His efforts during 1971 were not his first to obtain increased federal aid for New York. Previous attempts had produced some results, but they were not commensurate with the state's need. Once the magnitude of New York's fiscal crisis became apparent, Rockefeller shifted from the view that general revenue sharing was one of several forms that increased federal aid to the states and localities might take to the conviction that the passage of this program should be made New York's primary objective in Washington. This shift resulted from the governor's reading of political realities in the nation's capital during the early 1970s.

Revenue sharing was not a new idea. Indeed, some form of it had been experimented with in the 1830s, the Kestenbaum commission considered the idea in the 1950s, and Congressman Melvin Laird (Republican, Wisconsin) introduced revenue-sharing legislation in Congress as early as 1958. Interest in the concept, however, grew in the 1960s for several reasons: (*a*) mounting expenditure pressures on state and local governments; (*b*) growing dissatisfaction with the existing method of distributing federal grants; (*c*) concern over growing federal influence on the states; and (*d*) belief, based on the moderately progressive federal tax structure, that surplus federal revenues would continue.

Walter Heller, shortly before his retirement as chairman of President Johnson's Council of Economic Advisers, formally proposed revenue sharing as an idea to be considered in 1964 in light of projected budget surpluses.[42] President Johnson, in turn, appointed a task force, headed by Joseph Pechman of the Brookings Institution, to study the possibility of setting aside a certain percentage of federal revenues for distribution to states and localities. The favorable recommendations of the task force were never made public. President Johnson lost interest in the plan because of escalating costs of the Vietnam war, rising inflation, and opposition from organized labor and other groups. Nonetheless, the concept gained favorable consideration from the Republican party and the National Governors' Conference, and it was advocated by both parties' presidential nominees in 1968.

Nelson Rockefeller was not an immediate convert to revenue sharing, at least in the form that was being discussed in the early 1960s. His coolness stemmed from a pragmatic political judgment. When a Democratic president turned down the idea and a Democratic-controlled Congress was not particularly receptive, he decided, the plan had little likelihood of being adopted.

Nevertheless, as the decade progressed, Rockefeller's position with respect to revenue sharing remained fluid. He kept his options open, geared to what he thought was attainable through legislative action at the federal level. He consistently supported the goal of a broadened fiscal mix and greater fiscal flexibility in federal aid to states and localities. Rockefeller's instinct was to push for major federal breakthroughs on all fronts, welfare takeover, revenue sharing, and grant reform, and to follow up the one that seemed most likely to be adopted. Two of these options failed to materialize, however. A coalition of opponents in Congress on the left and right defeated welfare reform. Congress also had little interest in the president's proposals for grant consolidation, block grants, and special revenue-sharing programs.

While Rockefeller supported general revenue-sharing as one of a number of alternatives, what finally made him focus on revenue sharing as his foremost objective was the state's fiscal condition in late 1970. On election day, November 3, 1970, at his Pocantico Hills home, with his fourth-term reelection bid assured by a landslide vote, Rockefeller began his systematic review of New York's finances in preparation for his 1971 budget message. T. Norman Hurd, the state's budget director, delivered the bad news to the governor, predicting a deficit of more than $1 billion between state revenues and expenditures. At that point, one of Rockefeller's aides quipped, "Well, Governor, you have two options—demand a recount of election returns or go all out for federal revenue sharing."[43]

During his campaign in 1968, Richard Nixon pledged to make revenue sharing a top priority if he was elected, and shortly after his inauguration he appointed a task force made up of governors, mayors, and county officials to study the concept. This task force endorsed the adoption of revenue sharing, and concluded that it should be based on four factors: an automatic annual appropriation of a set portion of federal income tax revenues; annual distribution to the fifty states, including a mandatory pass-through of funds from states to localities; aid to all general-purpose local governments; and no restriction as to use. In early February 1969, Rockefeller was invited to the White House to argue the case for revenue sharing before the newly formed Urban Affairs Council. One week later, President Nixon in his State of the Union message recommended "a start on sharing the revenue of the Federal Government, so that other levels of government where revenue increases lag behind will not be caught in a constant fiscal crisis."[44]

Much to the disappointment of Rockefeller and the other governors, however, when the president's specific proposal was released on August 13, 1969, it called for an allocation of only $500 million to the states in fiscal 1971 (this amount would be increased to roughly $5 billion by fiscal 1976). Nonetheless, Rockefeller applauded the president's plan and indicated that it was a step in the right direction. Three weeks later, President Nixon presented his plan and his "New Federalism" philosophy before the National Governors' Conference at Colorado Springs.[45] The governors required little prodding in expressing their unhappiness with a $500 million revenue-sharing base, which they felt was woefully inadequate. Undaunted by this rebuff from the governors, the president remained adamant about holding the line on a $500 million initial outlay for the program. "Dreams of unlimited billions being released once the war in Vietnam ends are just that—dreams," he stated in reference to those who had a much inflated estimate of what revenue sharing might provide.[46] Rockefeller criticized the president's plan. "It isn't good enough," he noted, "and we've got to put the money where the problems are—in the cities and the states."[47]

From 1969 through late 1970, revenue sharing made little headway in Congress. Despite support from the White House, large segments of Congress, and state and local officials, revenue sharing lacked a unified constituency. President Nixon supported it, but his welfare-reform proposal, the Family Assistance Plan, had assumed higher priority on his domestic agenda. Some of the president's economic advisers questioned whether the federal budget could support both welfare reform and revenue sharing. Wilbur Mills, chairman of the powerful House Ways and Means Committee, under whose jurisdiction revenue sharing fell, openly opposed the program. He not only denounced it from the steps of the White House but also said bluntly to the governors, "It is not any easier for Congress to raise money than state legislatures.... I would be willing to share part of the revenues if the states would share part of our deficit."[48] Mills's counterpart, Senator Russell Long (Democrat, Louisiana), chairman of the Senate Finance Committee, thought revenue sharing would be fiscally irresponsible at a time of rising federal deficits. The congressional appropriations committees were vehemently opposed, both on the fiscal merits of the revenue-sharing concept and on the procedural question of appropriating federal money through what they felt was a back-door raid on the federal treasury. The Democratic leadership and many rank-and-file members were not enamored of the idea of allowing a Republican president to gain the credit for enactment of what they regarded as a Democratic proposal. Thus the outlook for speedy congressional action on revenue sharing was bleak, and there was a strong likelihood that Congress would not even consider the idea.

More important at this juncture, perhaps, was the obvious lack of unity among governors, mayors, county officials, and state legislators. Many governors believed that the states should receive a predominant share of any revenue-sharing money and also some control over any amount passed through the states to local governments. Governors differed too on whether revenue sharing should be their most sought-after objective. The mayors and their congressional sympathizers viewed President Nixon's revenue-sharing plan as providing direct aid to the states and GOP governors but shortchanging the Democratic cities. These fears seemed all the more real in light of the governors' rhetoric and the fact that the president's proposal provided less than 30 percent of revenue-sharing funds to local governments.

Moreover, it became increasingly clear that support for the revenue-sharing concept was one thing, but agreement over details, allocation formulas, and specific legislation was another. Early negotiations between the National Governors' Conference and the two leading organizations of municipal officials, the United States Conference of Mayors and the National League of Cities, gave little promise of a broad-based coalition. Such a coalition required the participation of the other national associations representing state, county, and municipal officials, and related organizations of public officials. These Washington-based associations, called the PIGs, an acronym for "public-interest groups," included the Council of State Governments, the National Association of Counties, the National Legislative Conference, and the International City Managers Association.[49] The "Big Seven" PIG groups at this time were just beginning to negotiate seriously with each other and with administration officials over revenue sharing.

With a Republican administration in the White House and New York's fiscal picture growing desperate, Rockefeller became increasingly outspoken in support of revenue sharing. He appealed to New York State associations of elected officials to work through their national associations on behalf of revenue sharing and called upon fellow governors and mayors to reconcile their differences, lest their divisions deter Congress from moving.

The public-interest groups launched a massive campaign in the early spring of 1970 to gain public hearings on revenue sharing, only to be rebuffed by Chairman Mills, who commented that major legislation was already pending before his committee. Meanwhile, sizable cleavages had opened both among the public-interest groups and within each of the groups, especially among the governors. Therefore, by mid-1970 the president instructed White House staff members and Treasury officials to renew their efforts to bring the PIG groups together on specifics of a bill that they, the White House, and Congress might endorse. Led by the Nixon administration's chief negotiator, Murray Weidenbaum, who was then assistant secretary of the treasury for economic policy, the groups met continuously through late fall of 1970 and eventually agreed on basic principles of the legislation.

Governor Rockefeller was not a key participant in these preliminary negotiations. His impact was heavily felt from November 1970 on, however, both in directing pressure on the White House to increase the revenue-sharing base from $500 million to $10 billion and in sustaining the governors' interest in revenue sharing as their top priority. Rockefeller brought to the revenue-sharing campaign a certain leverage exercisable at the White House, an access and influence not possessed by other state and local public officials. In November and

December of 1970, Rockefeller met several times with President Nixon and personally lobbied for a $10 billion base figure for revenue sharing. After his November 18 meeting, Rockefeller indicated that New York State needed an increase of between $500 million and $1 billion in federal aid just "to hold the line at present levels of activity."[50] The governor later announced that Nixon was considering the whole question of funding revenue sharing at levels that ranged from $5 billion to as much as $20 billion. The president had pledged to make "meaningful recommendations to help states and localities solve their financial crisis."[51]

About the same time, in mid-December 1970, Rockefeller obtained from the Republican Governors' Association a unanimous resolution calling for a federal revenue-sharing program of at least $10 billion annually, to begin July 1, 1971. The governors then appointed a three-man delegation—Rockefeller, Louis Nunn (Kentucky), and Raymond Schaffer (Pennsylvania)—to convey their resolution personally to the president. The three met with President Nixon in early January 1971 and discovered that the White House was considering raising the initial base figure for the program from $500 million to $2.5 billion. The governors felt that this amount was still inadequate, and Rockefeller again insisted that his state needed a minimum of $500 million in new federal aid in the next year just to continue existing activities.

During a full day of meetings with the president, White House staff members, budget officials, and the vice president, Rockefeller emphasized that revenue sharing could be a potent national issue for the Republican party in the 1972 election. A much higher base figure supported by the GOP administration and an alliance of governors, state legislators, mayors, county officials, and city managers and opposed by the Democratic Congress could spell the difference in the upcoming election. Finally, a $5 billion base figure was chosen, a compromise between the Rockefeller-led advocacy of $10 billion and the president's budget advisers' recommendation of $2.5 billion. In late January 1971, President Nixon announced this new revenue-sharing plan in his State of the Union address.

Congress remained a formidable obstacle. Revenue sharing faced strong Democratic hostility. Two conservative committee chairmen, Mills and Long, had even opposed holding legislative hearings on the proposal. In dealing with Congress, Rockefeller first began building support for revenue sharing within his own state's congressional delegation. This was a sizable task in light of the delegation's Democratic majority and internal feuding. In his first news conference following his November 3, 1970, gubernatorial reelection, Rockefeller introduced the theme he would take to meetings with the state's county executives and with representatives of school boards, mayors, and town meetings—that a united effort would be required "to get more money back from Washington." Directing his comments to the state's congressional representatives, he said, "We have got to have the full cooperation of the entire delegation." He further urged the state's forty-one-member delegation and its two senators, the largest state delegation in the Congress, to begin "working for their constituents back home."[52]

In mid-November, Rockefeller convened a meeting of the state's congressional bloc at the St. Regis Hotel in New York City for a fiscal parley. Once again he set forth the New York case. The state had taxed itself to the limits of its capacity if it was to retain its industry and jobs. Two-thirds of the tax money collected in the state, or $23.5 billion, was sent to Washington, but New York received only $2.5 billion, or 11 cents on the dollar, in return. The state was discriminated against under existing federal aid formulas. New York would need an additional $500 million to $1 billion in federal aid to meet existing expenditure requirements in the next year. Even then, several members of the delegation were not impressed. Several of them left the meeting without waiting for its conclusion.

After considerable discussion, those delegation members still present endorsed a resolution to work for federal revenue sharing. One week later Rockefeller said that members of the Democratic-controlled New York congressional delegation "were the only ones who have the capacity to take the kind of action on a scale that will save New York City and New York State from destruction."[53] Within days, the governor followed this session with a meeting in Washington. There he exhorted the delegation to sponsor a $10 billion revenue-sharing proposal in Congress. In a blunt warning the governor stated, "I think the situation frankly is that we may well be facing a breakdown of public confidence in local government and a breakdown of our system."[54]

Rockefeller pledged to set up a new state office in Washington to work more closely with the delegation. The governor further indicated that his staff would draft model legislation to carry out his revenue-sharing program, and that he hoped it would be introduced by members of the New York delegation. The dean of the state's delegation, Representative Emanuel Celler, gave his enthusiastic approval to the governor's revenue-sharing campaign. He said, "The time for this idea has come and nobody can stop it."[55] Rockefeller's proposal, however, drew mixed reactions from other New York representatives.

The governor kept in touch with delegation members on a weekly basis. He dealt particularly with the two state representatives on the House Ways and Means Committee, Brooklyn Democrat Hugh Carey and upstate Republican Barber B. Conable, Jr. Carey had ties to the large bloc of urban Democrats in Congress. Conable, a long-time Rockefeller friend, was not only the most moderate Republican among the conservative Republican Ways and Means minority but also a strong revenue-sharing advocate. Once Ways and Means decided to develop a revenue-sharing bill, the legislation required months of closed-door hearings to assign formulas for allocating funds. On several occasions Conable was called from these sessions for an important telephone call, which invariably turned out to be from Nelson Rockefeller, wanting to find out what was happening and if he could help. The repetition of these calls eventually became a standard joke, so that every time Conable would leave to take an "urgent call," Mills and others would quip, "Nelson on the phone again?"

Rockefeller's acquaintances and personal friendships in Congress far transcended his own state's delegation. He and Wilbur Mills had known each other for two decades. Rockefeller also worked with House Minority Leader Gerald Ford to line up GOP support for revenue sharing, and even attempted to involve himself in the Democrats' selection of a new speaker and majority leader to replace retiring John McCormack. Rockefeller requested that New York Democrats and others withhold their votes from any candidate who would not support early enactment of a meaningful revenue-sharing program. The governor appeared before four congressional committees between 1971 and 1972 to argue personally the case for revenue sharing and to make converts wherever he could.

Rockefeller also stumped New York State, conducting town meetings, holding press conferences, and making special speaking appearances to highlight the state's problems with Washington. Whether speaking with public officials or citizen groups, the governor would characteristically conclude with a resounding plea for their assistance in getting Congress to move on revenue sharing. Some accused Rockefeller of deflecting pressures away from Albany to Washington, while conditioning taxpayers to the inevitability of future tax increases if Washington failed to act. Surely this was the case. The governor hoped, however, that if other governors and public officials followed his lead, a grass-roots appeal for revenue sharing would compel Congress to act. The target of Rockefeller's public appeals was Congress, but this lobbying also served to reinforce the White House's commitment to the program. Both were essential in moving revenue sharing forward.

In early 1971 Rockefeller created a New York State Citizens Committee for Revenue Sharing. The governor invited hundreds of New Yorkers from all walks of life to join this bipartisan statewide committee to stimulate public support for congressional approval of the program. To cap the New York campaign, the governor officially declared February 22, 1971, to be Revenue Sharing Day throughout the state. To dramatize the importance of revenue sharing to each county and citizen, Rockefeller's office released charts to newspapers throughout the state indicating how much each community would get under a $5 billion revenue-sharing program and the governor's $10 billion plan. In addition, Rockefeller assigned one of his key aides, Jim Cannon, to work full-time for revenue sharing. Cannon became Rockefeller's man in Washington and had a direct pipeline to the governor on all negotiations, strategies, and tactics. He worked with the New York State congressional delegation, House leaders, national citizens' groups, public-interest groups, and even Wilbur Mills and his staff. The fact that Cannon originally came from the South did not hurt his entrée with influential congressmen, many of whom were southern Democrats.

As 1970 neared its close, the *New York Times* noted, "Governor Rockefeller is winning political points with his campaign for federal revenue sharing even if it is still uncertain whether he will win any more federal cash for the state. This is the assessment of many politicians who have viewed with admiration the Governor's one man lobby for a $10 billion increase in federal aid."[56]

Rockefeller's activities in New York were closely coordinated with those by other governors and the campaign for revenue sharing directed by the White House. The National Governors' Conference had endorsed a policy resolution at its August 1970 meetings "to employ every means available toward the immediate and favorable enactment of revenue sharing." This mandate, together with agreement on basic revenue-sharing principles among the PIGs, gave rise in March 1971 to a National Citizens Committee for Revenue Sharing, composed of state and local officials, business leaders, professional groups, women's organizations, minority representatives, labor leaders, academics, and influential private citizens.[57] Some forty-five state organizations affiliated with the National Citizens Committee. Reflecting the impact of the grass-roots campaign, public support for revenue sharing continued to rise in public opinion polls.

President Nixon's new revenue-sharing plan became the major thrust of his January 22, 1971, State of the Union message. He made the strengthening of state and local governments a significant goal of his administration, stating, "I propose that the Congress make a $16 billion investment in renewing state and local government. Five billion of this will be in new and unrestricted funds to be used as the states and localities see fit." The president's final proposal was $5 billion a year in new money for general revenue sharing. The remaining $11 billion included $10 billion in existing grant programs and $1 billion of new money, which would be consolidated into special revenue-sharing funds for six broad programs.

Wilbur Mills continued to oppose Nixon's initiative. After meeting with the president in late January 1971, he indicated that he was willing to hold revenue-sharing hearings—"for the purpose of killing it."[58] Many Democrats in the House followed Mills's lead in expressing opposition, even using his argument that revenue sharing would separate the spending function from the revenue-raising responsibility. The U.S. Chamber of Commerce and the AFL-CIO, strange bedfellows, joined the opposition. The chamber was afraid of increased federal spending. The unions preferred decision making to be centralized in Washington, where they had more influence. They found support among liberals, who thought that specific social programs might be curtailed, and federal bureaucrats, who feared loss of power.

By early spring the president's new revenue-sharing bill had thirty-seven cosponsors in the Senate, but only four were Democrats. There were, in addition, 133 House cosponsors, of whom only eight were Democrats. The revenue-sharing issue seemed firmly drawn along partisan lines. Democratic leaders were more than ever disinclined to support what they now labeled a Republican proposal.

The policies of sponsorship were complicated. The Democrats argued that revenue sharing originally had been a proposal of President Johnson's staff. They were not about to permit Nixon to take credit for it. Moreover, Democrats in Congress were divided on the merits of the plan. The public-interest groups recruited scores of governors, mayors, and county officials to appear on Capitol Hill to manifest their unified support for revenue sharing in the spring of 1971. This mass lobbying strategy was in part successful, for, among other things, it divided the Democratic party. In the Senate, Democratic presidential hopefuls Edmund Muskie and Hubert Humphrey were attacked at meetings with Democratic mayors when they suggested various alternatives to revenue sharing. In the House, Wilbur Mills found himself under increasing pressure from urban Democrats on his own committee. They let him know that if some general relief for cities were not soon forthcoming, several congressmen might be in trouble with their own constituencies in the 1972 election. By late spring, both Humphrey and Muskie had introduced their own separate versions of a revenue-sharing bill. Several House Democrats, including Hugh Carey and Edward Koch of New York City, introduced a modified version of Rockefeller's $10 billion revenue-sharing proposal, and thirteen New York City Democrats joined them as co-sponsors.[59] In many respects, this bill was a precursor to the one to which Wilbur Mills finally agreed. But on June 2, 1971, when Mills convened hearings on the president's revenue-sharing bill, he still insisted that he did so only to kill the proposal and expose the weaknesses and dangers of the concept.

Whatever else may be said of Wilbur Mills, he remained close to the temper of the House and was aware that it had gradually moved toward support of revenue sharing. Moreover, he was not unsympathetic to the fiscal needs of large, older cities and impoverished rural areas or even of the high-tax-effort states that had fiscal problems. What Mills objected to primarily was the concept of indiscriminate sharing of federal tax revenues with all general-purpose governments, particularly when the federal government had been running deficits during most of the previous forty years.

During the second week of the Ways and Means hearings, Mills unexpectedly announced that his committee would consider a $3.5 billion, multiyear program of direct federal aid for cities and rural communities based on a "need factor." This change of heart was announced by the chairman before a meeting of Democratic leaders that included several mayors and governors. Mills's plan, which he did not call revenue sharing, involved an emergency aid program designed to meet urban needs until Congress could find a more satisfactory response to the fiscal problems of local governments.

Mills's fiscal assistance plan temporarily delighted big-city mayors. It raised hopes of a direct pipeline delivering millions of dollars from Washington to local governments. For Democrats, the idea had an obvious partisan appeal: it united the 1968 urban and rural presidential constituencies of both Hubert Humphrey and George Wallace. Among Ways and Means members there was little consensus on the details of the emergency plan.

Disturbed by this development, which threatened to sunder the fragile state-local coalition he had assembled, Governor Rockefeller flew to Washington to see Chairman Mills. On the plane returning to New York, where Mills was scheduled to speak, the governor persuaded him not to pursue the $3.5 billion plan. Rockefeller's argument, repeated publicly in his testimony before Ways and Means on July 16, was that such a national strategy would make cities into "federal reservations" and thus dependents of the federal government. The states would react negatively to this bypassing of state government, would reduce their aid to cities in proportion to federal money available under the program, and would "turn over to the federal government their responsibilities for cities which they are now attempting to carry."[60] Once this one-shot infusion of direct aid expired, the states would send the cities back to Washington for further assistance. If Mills was not at first convinced by Rockefeller's argument, he was by the time he discussed it with mayors and urban members of his committee who agreed with it.

The fact that Mills began to search for an alternative to revenue sharing constituted a significant breakthrough. Rockefeller now had an opportunity to use his staff resources in assisting and guiding Mills's search in the months ahead. The political aspect was even more important. Democrats controlled both houses of Congress and they had been understandably reluctant to support a revenue-sharing proposal of a Republican president. Now Muskie, Humphrey, Carey, Koch, and Mills, all Democrats, offered various forms of revenue sharing. It began to be respectable in Congress as a Democratic plan.

The governor's objective at this early stage of the legislative process was to get as many congressmen committed to revenue sharing as possible. Once they were committed, they could begin to worry about the details of the amount of the aid, its allocation, the aid formula, the duration of the program, and limitations on the use of the money. After a sufficiently strong alliance had formed in support of revenue sharing, Rockefeller hoped to obtain the maximum amount possible for New York State. To the governor, this meant that the states should get in aggregate at least half of the total revenue-sharing pie and that a combination of population and income tax effort should be central to the aid formula. The governor's insistence on state tax effort as a factor was not only for New York's advantage, but also because of his belief that the states that had heavily used their own resources to meet the problems of the 1960s should be rewarded more generously than low-tax-effort, non-income-tax states. Wilbur Mills shared this view, but in recognition of the needs of his own state, Arkansas, and other low-income states, he considered per capita income and poverty important factors to be included in the formula.

The governor sought a $10 billion revenue-sharing base for several reasons, the most obvious being the magnitude of New York's need. For the Democrats a $10 billion plan provided an alternative to the president's proposal of $5 billion. To be most effective politically, Rockefeller endorsed both plans. He wrote several letters to New York State delegation members requesting that they support both the president's $5 billion revenue-sharing legislation and the $10 billion program introduced by Carey and Koch. Rockefeller suspected that congressional pressure could reduce the $10 billion proposal by at least half. Thus the president's $5 billion figure could be a fall-back alternative. The governor also hoped that if a $5 billion legislative program emerged from Ways and Means, it could be amended on the House floor and raised to $10 billion. Rockefeller had assurances from New York members of both House and Senate that such amendments would be offered.[61]

One month before his appearance before Mills's committee, Rockefeller and four other governors testified before the Senate Subcommittee on Intergovernmental Relations on two alternative revenue-sharing proposals, Senator Edmund Muskie's Intergovernmental Revenue Bill (S. 1770) and the Humphrey-Reuss State and Local Government Modernization Bill (S. 241). The Muskie bill provided for the allocation of $6 billion in financial assistance to states and localities. It included a need formula that apportioned funds to the twenty-five largest cities and distributed $1 billion extra to the states in proportion to their income tax receipts. Rockefeller saw merit in the Muskie proposal, which was particularly helpful to New York State. For tactical reasons, however, he avoided endorsing any specific proposal. "I like any of these various proposals," he would say; "I am for the revenue-sharing program that can pass the House and Senate."[62] In fact, Rockefeller viewed the Muskie bill as a gadfly, which moved Mills toward a more comprehensive revenue-sharing plan and at the same time raised the issue of tax effort in allocating funds among the states.

In late June 1971, Mills and his committee began consideration of a revenue-sharing bill in executive session. For the next five months, the destiny of revenue-sharing was in the hands of Mills and the Ways and Means Committee meeting behind closed doors. Mills first sought technical assistance from his own Ways and Means staff and that of the Joint Committee on Internal Revenue Taxation. When, in early August, the committee still had not reached a consensus, Mills requested that the big seven public-interest groups have their representatives work with his staff in developing the legislation. The PIGs themselves were divided over two essential issues, division of funds among governments and the degree to which states should have control over funds given to local governments. Some consensus on these issues was essential to any compromise that would come out of the committee.

At one point in August, it appeared that Mills was considering dropping revenue sharing altogether. With the country in the throes of a recession, President Nixon asked for postponment of revenue sharing so that Congress could deal immediately with the New Economic Policy legislation that he announced on August 15. It seemed that Mills was now off the hook and that the president was backing away from revenue sharing, at least temporarily. Also, with Congress in recess during August, it seemed apparent that the congressional agenda would not allow enough time for consideration of revenue sharing by the year's end. According to Jim Cannon, "After the August recess, we had to start all over again on revenue sharing."[63]

Nonetheless, staff experts continued their work along the broad guidelines set by Mills. Much to Rockefeller's disappointment and that of the National Governors' Conference, Mills proposed that local governments get more than half the funds. They were to receive revenues in the range of $2.5 to $3.5 billion, with state governments getting $1.5 billion. Besides laboring to keep the PIG alliance intact and maintaining the White House allegiance to revenue sharing, Rockefeller and his staff focused on the amount of the state share and on keeping tax effort an essential factor in the allocation of funds. Still, the matter of state control over funds passed through to local governments remained the stumbling block both in committee and among the PIGs. Once again Rockefeller played the role of mediator, arguing with PIG officials that timing was essential.[64] Already there was little prospect for revenue sharing in 1971, and the following year the national elections might further jeopardize adoption of the legislation.

Finally, the public-interest groups endorsed the draft of the Mills bill. On November 30, 1971, Mills and nine Democratic cosponsors from Ways and Means introduced the Intergovernmental Fiscal Coordination bill of 1971 (H.R. 11950). Among other things, the bill (later substantially revised by the committee) provided for assistance to state government with a built-in incentive to use income taxes more fully to meet their revenue needs. With $3.5 billion for local governments and $1.5 billion for state governments, Mills's staff informed Rockefeller, New York would receive more than $300 million in new aid for 1972/73 and local governments in New York would get a comparable amount if the legislation was passed as drafted. At the request of Rockefeller and the NGC, Mills made the bill retroactive to January 1, 1972, instead of making the implementation date July 1, 1972, the beginning of the fiscal year.[65]

As the battle for revenue sharing continued, Rockefeller faced a fiscal crisis in his own state. His state budget called for $7.9 billion in expenditures and included only $7.5 billion in revenues. Even then, the governor's budget reflected a hold-the-line policy and included the planned layoff of 10,000 employees. Rockefeller's budget message to the legislature proposed closing the gap by including $400 million in anticipated new federal funds. The governor said, "I feel that the prospects are highly favorable for congressional approval of federal revenue-sharing with the states and a welfare reform program that will provide additional state-local funds."[66]

This risky move by Rockefeller, budgeting anticipated federal revenues to balance the state's 1972/73 budget, added to the pressure on Washington for revenue sharing. The governor made it clear to New York legislators and taxpayers alike that without $400 million in new federal funds there would have to be across-the-board tax increases. While this strategy placed the Nixon administration, the state's congressional delegation, and House Democratic leadership on notice that further tax increases in New York would be tied to their inactivity in an election year, Rockefeller was also vulnerable. His forthcoming budget included federal monies that had not yet been appropriated.

After taking this risk both to avoid new taxes and to add momentum to revenue sharing, Rockefeller invited Mills to come to New York personally to assure the state legislature that revenue-sharing action would be forthcoming. Mills, who harbored presidential ambitions at the time, seized the opportunity to gain visibility in a large northern state under Rockefeller's sponsorship. A back ailment, however, forced the chairman to cancel his December speaking engagement and return to Little Rock. Within hours of learning of

Mills's back trouble, Rockefeller had his own osteopath flown down to Arkansas in the governor's private plane to examine the chairman and offer assistance.

Mills's cancellation caused a problem for Rockefeller, because it could be interpreted by the legislature to mean that the powerful representative was not going to push for revenue sharing after all. With prior agreement by Mills, the Rockefeller staff drafted a strong letter for Mills to send to the governor stating that revenue sharing would be the first priority of Ways and Means when Congress resumed. On New Year's Day, 1972, Jim Cannon flew to Arkansas and Mills signed the letter without any changes. It stated: "I want to give you and the leaders of the New York State Legislature my assurance that H.R. 11950 will be my top priority as soon as Congress resumes. . . . I am confident we can bring a bill out of Committee promptly and to the House floor."[67] The governor was then able to circulate the letter as evidence that he could count on federal support. The state budget passed, and two months later Mills did address the New York legislature and assure it of forthcoming federal assistance.

As Ways and Means and the PIGs focused on the major issue—how much one state or local community would get as compared to others—various formulas relying on such data as population, per capita income, urbanization, poverty, and jurisdictional taxes had to be absorbed, fitted into computer models, and tested. Data suffered from age, time lags, and incompleteness. The PIGs fought among themselves over various allocations, and committee members complained when their districts received less than others. Rockefeller used New York's budget staff to feed the committee various weighted formulas and computer printouts and was thus an active participant in the allocation debates within the committee. He also helped build support among Republican Ways and Means members to ensure that the final committee vote reflected a clear majority on the eventual bill. Nonetheless, he failed to convince the ranking minority member on the committee, John Byrnes (Republican, Wisconsin), that Mills's approach incorporated a form of Byrnes's tax credit in the legislation. Byrnes remained unmoved throughout the passage of revenue sharing, even though six of the remaining eight Republicans on the committee voted favorably to report out the final Mills bill.

The State and Local Fiscal Assistance bill of 1972 (H.R. 14370), reported out of committee by a vote of 18–7, provided for a $5.3 billion first-year appropriation with a $30.2 billion total extended over a five-year period. The states would receive one-third, or $1.8 billion, in the first year, unrestricted as to use, in accordance with two formulas: one-half was to be awarded according to state income tax collections and the remainder according to combined general tax effort of state and local governments. The local governments' share, $3.5 billion in the first year, would be divided among the states with distribution to localities based on three equally weighted factors: general population, urbanized population (cities of 50,000 or over and the metropolitan areas surrounding them), and population inversely weighted for per capita income (the poverty index). The committee justified its allocation of a greater proportion of funds to local governments on several criteria: severity of fiscal need, taxing capacity, service needs (especially in urban areas), inflation, and lower-than-average increase in local revenues because of the sluggish economy.

The House formula with its five-factor combination reflected numerous trade-offs among committee members and was geared to the House of Representatives' population-based composition. The winners were the heavily urbanized states and those with high tax efforts. New York State would receive the most funds on a per capita basis both in the state's share and in that of local governments. In aggregate, New York State and its local governments stood to receive $643 million, compared to California's $612 million. In New York the state alone would receive $317 million, $13 million more than the total state and local share for Pennsylvania, the third highest beneficiary of the law. New York City alone was scheduled to receive more than forty states would. Thus, while Rockefeller was disappointed by the one-third to two-thirds distribution between states and local governments, he was delighted by the Ways and Means formula for apportioning funds among the states.[68] Indeed, under the committee formula, New York State would receive $115.5 million more than under the president's bill.

Though major differences existed between this version and what the administration preferred, the White House decided to back the Mills bill. The first fight came when Ways and Means sought a closed rule from the Rules Committee. Such a rule would prevent amendment of the revenue-sharing bill on the floor of the House. Though such rules were not uncommon, considerable opposition existed in this case, especially from Appropriations Committee members who believed that Mills, in combining both authorization and appropriation for revenue sharing in H.R. 14370, had willfully bypassed them. Through the minority leader, the White House obtained support from the five Republican members of the Rules Committee for a closed rule. Jim Cannon received assurances from James Delaney, a New York Democrat, and Rockefeller himself persuaded Claude Pepper (Democrat, Florida) and, through Hawaii's governor, John A. Burns, Spark Matsunaga (Democrat, Hawaii). A closed rule was obtained by an 8–7 vote. The rule, however, was challenged on the floor. For three weeks the outcome was uncertain, as the PIGs labored for the rule while the Chamber of Commerce, the AFL-CIO, and others worked against it. On June 14 the House leadership met with Governors Rockefeller and Marvin Mandel (Maryland), Mayors Moon Landrieu (New Orleans) and Henry Maier (Milwaukee), White House representatives, and PIG representatives for a bipartisan vote count in Speaker Carl Albert's office.[69] The revenue-sharing coalition concluded that it had enough votes to sustain the Rules Committee, and, on June 21, the House by a vote of 223 to 185 proved them right. The very next day, the revenue sharing bill passed by a much larger margin, 274–122. Only two members of the New York congressional delegation voted against the closed rule, the real test vote, and only one member against final passage. The delegation had, at last, pulled together on a major issue affecting the state.

Rockefeller's work had begun to pay off, but revenue sharing still faced the obstacle course of the Senate. In that body, where the less populous states had disproportionate strength, the House version faced political difficulty.

On June 29, 1972, the Senate Finance Committee began hearings on general revenue sharing. Time was crucial, for both parties had to convene their national conventions and the forthcoming campaign would bring business in the Ninety-second Congress to an early close. The time pressure therefore constituted a major element in the bargaining, negotiations, and compromise that ensued. The administration desired certain changes in the House bill to bring it into line with the president's proposals. Many senators disliked the emphasis in the House formula on the urban states; they felt that revenue-sharing funds should be more evenly distributed across the country. The state income tax feature in the House bill was strongly objected to by the nine non-income-tax states and their senators as well as by senators from those states with nominal income tax rates. The tax-incentive feature of the House formula was threatening to tear the fragile revenue-sharing coalition apart.

In a letter to Governor Rockefeller, Governor Winfield Dunn of Tennessee noted that New Yorkers would receive five times as much per capita aid as Tennesseeans under the states' portion according to the House formula and that failure to rectify this inequity "could cause division in our ranks, thereby lessening the chances of enacting revenue sharing this year."[70] Rockefeller had worked so hard to ensure that the governors and the mayors could present a united front that Dunn's letter came as a profound shock. He realized immediately that unless he could develop a compromise satisfactory to the Tennessee governor, his coalition would come apart. Any hesitancy in the testimony of the twelve governors scheduled to appear before the Senate Finance Committee on July 20 would be eagerly exploited by the opponents of revenue sharing, and lukewarm supporters would be given an excuse for delay.

When the NGC Executive Committee met in Washington on July 19, the day before the scheduled appearances of twelve governors before the Senate Finance Committee, Rockefeller pleaded for unity. "It was the eleventh hour," the governor said later. "In an election year, the time remaining for Senate action already is less than normal for such a major piece of legislation." He informed the governors, as he later did the Senate, that if they started amending the revenue-sharing bill, agreement between the House and Senate conferees would be unlikely.[71] Nevertheless, Governor Dunn stood fast, and stated that he would have to testify against the bill.

Rockefeller then persuaded President Nixon to invite the governors to breakfast at the White House the following morning. There Rockefeller proposed as a compromise that total state-local tax effort be substituted for income tax effort alone in the formula. Tennessee had low state taxes and high local taxes. By combining the two, Rockefeller overcame Dunn's objections. This also was a way of reconciling Representative Byrnes's insistence that progressive state income taxes be rewarded.

Rockefeller was jubilant that the governors and mayors had agreed on a common position. He said before the Senate committee: "I share the feeling with the other two governors who just spoke last on a 15 percent progressive income tax, so naturally we favor this. However, as they have said, were this to be based on state and local taxes, including the income taxes . . . , we would lose but we would still support the bill because it does give that emphasis of state and local tax effort."[72] In Rockefeller's opinion, it was the united front the governors had reached at the White House breakfast meeting—a front that transcended regional, economic, geographic, and party differences—that was the key factor in winning the support of the

Senate Finance Committee. This was the first time the governors had been able to remain united.[73]

Rockefeller later met with Russell Long and other Senate leaders regarding revenue sharing. Long expressed optimism about Senate action but indicated that the White House first wanted favorable action on the House-passed welfare-reform bill, a matter that had been before Long's committee for two years. Rockefeller immediately appealed to the White House to clarify scheduling priorities for the Senate leaders. Once this had been done, Majority Leader Mike Mansfield assured the governor that the Senate would not adjourn without acting on revenue sharing. Thus Rockefeller left Washington in late July confident that revenue sharing would soon be law.

He soon had another problem, however. Senator Long and several colleagues were bent on using revenue-sharing legislation to accomplish an additional goal, one that particularly concerned the senator: to terminate an open-ended program under which the federal government reimbursed the states for certain social service expenditures. Just before hearing the governors' testimony before the Finance Committee on July 20, Long stated for the record his alarm over the "runaway program of social services" matched by the federal government at a 75 percent rate.[74] The program was estimated in 1962 to cost $40 million a year, had risen to $746 million in 1971, doubled to $1.5 billion in 1972, and was projected to cost between $2.2 billion and $4.7 billion for 1973. Long said: "Now, this $4.7 billion is very near the $5.3 billion of revenue sharing provided in the House bill. We cannot afford to continue the present social services system if we are going to provide $5.3 billion a year, and more, in revenue-sharing funds under the bill before us today."[75] Long was thus signaling his desire for a trade-off, revenue sharing for a limitation on federal expenditures for social services. The administration supported this limitation. Social service costs constituted a drain on the federal treasury and had doubled nearly every year since 1969. Fiscal conservatives and antiwelfare legislators strongly favored this move, as did the president's budget advisers. Previous efforts in Congress to plug the open-ended funding of the program had failed. Long now had a chance to accomplish this.

Rockefeller immediately realized Long's strategy and its far-reaching consequences for New York, whose welfare load was the largest in the nation. California had been the first state, through sheer ingenuity and aggressiveness, to fashion its social services to HEW's definition of services eligible for matching funds on a 75–25 basis. Accordingly, California cashed in on nearly 30 percent of 1971 federal matching payments of nearly $750 million. New York followed the California practice, moving from $89 million in federal social service reimbursements in 1971 to $382 million in 1972, with a projected $618 million in 1973. Federal funds had eased somewhat the state's and New York City's welfare burden, and its repeal would be a budgetary disaster.

A further complication was the fact that the Senate Finance Committee, dominated by senators from the rural, low-income southern, southwestern, and Rocky Mountain regions, had their own notions about the revenue-sharing formula. The formula that the committee produced included just three factors: total population, state-local tax effort, and a "poverty index." These factors favored poorer rural states, especially those in the South. At the same time, the committee added funds to large cities and poorer rural areas to keep the mayors' support for the program. Under the Senate Finance Committee's formula, most states did better than under the House bill. Not only were allocations increased for thirty-four states, but thirteen of the sixteen states with senators on the Finance Committee were also gainers. To confuse the matter still further and to blunt the inevitable protest by urban states, the Senate version contained an extra $1 billion in social services to be allocated on a population basis, thus making it appear that urban states really did not lose under the Senate formula. At the same time, however, the existing open-ended appropriation was terminated. In aggregate, New York stood to lose $141 million, and in funds allocated to the state alone the difference between the House's $317.4 million and the Senate's $167.1 million was $150.3 million, a cut of nearly 50 percent. New York would be a major loser under the Senate formula.

Senator Abraham Ribicoff (Democrat, Connecticut), the only Finance Committee member from one of the ten most populous states, protested without success that populous states were being penalized. Revenue-sharing forces were able, however, to carry the five-year appropriation necessary to allow states and localities to plan ahead over the objections of the Senate Appropriations Committee and its chairman, John McClellan. On August 18, debate on the bill began on the Senate floor. Arguments by New York Senator Jacob Javits and other urban senators went unheeded. For all his efforts, Rockefeller could not change on the Senate floor what Long and his committee had drafted. Allocation politics were more powerful than any amount of lobbying or persuasion, for no senator would vote for less money for his state in order to help New York. Scores of amendments to change the Senate's formulas and increase social service funds went down to defeat by a majority coalition of senators whose own states benefited from the Senate formulas, and on September 12, 1972, the Senate voted 64 to 20 to approve its Finance Committee's version of the revenue-sharing bill, largely unchanged.

Faced with this result, and as one of revenue sharing's architects and key movers, Governor Rockefeller could not condemn what he had been so instrumental in developing. He therefore directed his efforts at obtaining the most favorable outcome possible when the conference committee met to resolve differences between the House and Senate versions of the bill.

Chairmen Mills and Long had met often in conference committees on tax, trade, social security, health care, and other issues. Both were deft bargainers and negotiators, highly skilled in reconciling differences and trading provisions in legislation about which one or the other felt strongly. Only two days after Senate passage, conferees began deliberation with formidable differences among them. Rockefeller's personal representative on revenue sharing, James Cannon, struck upon an idea that would restore some of New York's losses. Recognizing that the House bill and its five-factor version would not survive conference proceedings, and that under no circumstances would New York receive the $643 million allocated in it, Cannon settled on a middle-ground solution that allowed both chairmen to save face and New York to avoid the dire consequences of the Senate version. He suggested to Rockefeller that allocations to each state could be determined by both the House five-factor version and the Senate three-factor version and that each state could opt for the plan that maximized its share.[76] Since this selection process would undoubtedly lead to aggregate allocations in excess of the $5.3 billion appropriation, all shares could be reduced proportionately to stay within this limit. New York would, of course, select the House formula to recoup its losses, while Arkansas and Louisiana, as well as other states that fared better under the Senate version, could opt for it. Rockefeller conveyed this idea to Mills and others. This classic compromise was acceptable to the conferees, especially to Mills and Long, each of whom could claim victory. The Treasury Department later indicated that each state's share would have to be reduced by roughly 8.5 percent to stay within the budgeted limits to which both bodies had agreed.

At Mills's insistence, the conferees deleted much of the Senate's language on social services.[77] Instead of a $600 million limitation on specific family-planning and child-care services and a $1 billion bonus to be used for social services as found in the Senate bill, Mills obtained agreement on an overall $2.5 billion ceiling on federal matching grants for social services, with each state's percentage of funds geared to its population. In turn he conceded to the Senate conferees a broadening of categories for which local revenue-sharing funds could be used. Several additional compromises were struck concerning the expenditure of funds and reporting of their use.

With the dual-formula alternative, revenue sharing readily cleared both houses. It was passed on the next-to-last-day of the Ninety-second Congress, in the House by a vote of 281–86, in the Senate by 59–18. On October 20, 1972, at Philadelphia's Independence Hall, President Nixon signed the State and Local Fiscal Assistance Act of 1972 (P. L. 92-512) into law, and on December 6, 1972, fifty states and nearly 38,000 general-purpose units of local government received their first installments on revenue sharing from the Department of Treasury.

Conclusion

The story of the extended lobbying effort for revenue sharing is a lesson in the complexities of the federal system. As one group of many that made demands upon the national government, state leaders struggled to place their priorities high on the agenda of the president and Congress. This was a difficult objective to be achieved in an environment of limited resources, partisan conflict, and differing perspectives of constituent preferences. One clear moral of the revenue-sharing case was that the politics of federalism is distributive. In order to achieve something for New York, Rockefeller had to accept a program that gave him less than he would have liked, but that assured that every state would benefit substantially. No program that disproportionately benefited New York and other urban states could succeed in the Senate, where the less populous states had their strength.

Mayors and governors were natural enemies. To mayors it seemed logical that a direct relationship with Washington would result in a larger and more immediate impact upon urban problems. To governors state involvement was necessary not only to meet fiscal needs at that level but also to achieve an equitable distribution of resources.

Rockefeller was able to moderate these dichotomous perspectives by convincing both mayors and governors that the alternative was "something for everyone" or "nothing for anyone." The very nature of the goal, general-purpose aid for state and local governments with few strings attached, lent itself to this approach. Most other aid programs generated tremendous in-fighting—among the states, among the cities, and between the states and cities.

Much can be said for the importance of timing and of seizing on the personal ambitions of key political actors. President Nixon was planning to run for a second term and was publicly committed to returning power to the states and localities. He needed the support of state and local officials, and the revenue-sharing program offered him the opportunity to give something to each of them. Wilbur Mills, too, harbored presidential ambitions, and so allowed himself to be convinced of the program's value.

Just as individuals had interests, so did the major political parties. When state and local officials presented a bipartisan and united front and intensified their efforts, Democratic opponents to revenue sharing in Congress could not allow themselves to appear to be dogs in the manger. It was popular at the grass roots, where fiscal pressures were making taxpayers restive. There was a presidential election in the offing. To block action might be to give further ammunition to the incumbent Republican president. It was better, they concluded, to reclaim the idea as their own.

The time was ripe for revenue sharing. But it was one thing for the political opportunity to present itself and another for it to be seized. It was here that Governor Rockefeller's leadership and political skill became crucial. He recognized what might be done and did it. Revenue sharing was not without strong and well-placed opponents. Rockefeller was able to overcome them by creating a state-local alliance that transcended party lines and by holding it together when it seemed that it might split under the pressure of conflicting interests. As his staff generated modification after modification of original aid formulas in order to accommodate the unfolding political debate, the governor's personal lobbying effort maintained the momentum of the effort and, in the end, assured its success.

11

The Rockefeller Stewardship

"New York is a big, dynamic, high-powered state," William Ronan said, "and it wants a big, dynamic, high-powered man for its governor."[1] Nelson Rockefeller was such a man, a larger-than-life figure on the state's political scene for a decade and a half. For New York State, if not the nation, Rockefeller seemed to solve the dilemma of the democratic executive in America as defined by James Bryce almost a century ago: he was an effective chief administrator, and yet he was able to remain an attractive candidate to the electorate.[2]

Political observers often maintain that a politician's political stock declines as he continues in office because, whatever his programs may be, each of them will offend some people. Over time a coalition of disaffected minorities will emerge and he will find it more and more difficult to be reelected.[3] In other words, the longer a politician stays in office, the more enemies he makes, particularly if he is innovative in proposing programs. If this theory is true, how does one explain Rockefeller's reelection for four terms?

There are several answers. Rockefeller was one of the leaders in the establishment of high-technology politics and was the recipient of some of the most sophisticated public relations advice of any executive on the state level. In his campaigns he used public opinion polling, television advertising, and computer-based techniques for direct mail. Other candidates with more limited resources had to choose among these resources. Rockefeller could use all of them simultaneously. Here his skilled staff played a significant role.

Rockefeller was a repeated winner in a state that should have been Democratic, and he survived a period of national dominance by the Democratic party. One partial reason was that his liberal social programs left the Democrats without issues. He advocated increased financial support for housing, for schools, for the elderly, and for youth. What position could the Democrats take except "me too"? The programs cost Rockefeller support among conservative Republicans but less than it gained him in liberal circles.

Rockefeller's campaigns were always well financed. Indeed, his 1970 campaign chest held about $7 million, of which well over half was contributed by family members. The fact that he could always count on Rockefeller family resources gave his campaigns a stability and predictability that permitted careful advance planning. Moreover, Rockefeller's drive and personality made him an extraordinary campaigner and he was often fortunate in having his opponents divided. In his most difficult campaign, in 1966, the Liberal party, instead of uniting with the Democrats, ran its own candidate for governor.

Indeed, Rockefeller underwent a tremendous transformation following the 1966 campaign. He honestly believed that he would lose the election. His divorce and remarriage had hurt him, according to the polls. When he won, he felt that he had been elected on his merit, and that was the way he wanted to be elected. It was almost like a personal redemption. Suddenly he became confident that he was on top of his job, that he knew more about the governorship than any other person who had ever held the office, and that people recognized it.[4]

A strong, activist, aggressive executive has been the preferred model at every level of government in the United States since Franklin D. Roosevelt. An entire generation of political scientists argued for the chief executive as the center of energy in the political system. On the national level, one need only examine the reports of the President's Committee on Administrative Management in 1939 and the later reports of the two Hoover commissions to see how popular these views were. At the state level, reformers for decades advocated reorganization of government to center power in the governorship. Even in the large cities there was noticeable movement toward increasing mayoral powers.[5]

In 1960 Richard Neustadt argued the need for the chief executive to be conscious of his powers and personally to seek to maximize them.[6] Not until the escalation of the Vietnam war did most analysts have second thoughts about the growth of presidential power, and not until Watergate was there a serious questioning of established views about the chief executive. Indeed, in a widely read article published in

1970, Thomas Cronin demonstrated that political scientists had helped construct a presidency that was omniscient and omnipotent.[7]

In Nelson Rockefeller, New Yorkers found the kind of man for their governorship that the experts recommended, one who understood power and had the will to use it. Rockefeller inherited a political system that made the governor the key figure in public policy development. New York's constitution gave to its governor unparalleled formal resources, and Rockefeller himself had the ability to marshal extraordinary resources. He was a man of many worlds. His contacts ranged from bankers to labor leaders, from scientists to performing artists. Influence with a large number of elites enhanced his ability to govern. These sources supplied him with a constant flow of information from varied points of view. They aided in recruiting staff, and even more important, they permitted Rockefeller to act as a broker among groups that normally would not communicate with one another. Thus the governor could often use his strategic position for his policy ends.

The resource for which Nelson Rockefeller was best known, and the one that was most controversial while he was governor, was his great wealth. One of the primary consequences of Rockefeller's wealth on his behavior as governor may have been its effect on his style of decision, his conviction about the alterability of the environment.[8] One of the effects of wealth is that it eliminates barriers; it eases the way for its possessor and makes it simpler for him to work his will on others. A very rich man is not accustomed to constraints and limits; a very rich governor may not be receptive to arguments about factors that constrain and limit his policies.

Much has been written about the abuses of money in politics and about the dangers of wedding great political and great economic power. This was the dominant theme in the hearings concerning Nelson Rockefeller's nomination for the vice-presidency. Those most critical of Rockefeller argued that his interests and those of the dominant economic forces of American life were so inseparable that he should not be permitted to hold high national political office.

It is undeniable that Rockefeller's personal fortune was a major political asset, though he might never have been elected governor in 1958 if his opponent had not been almost as rich as he. Besides the great quantities of campaign funds that were available to Rockefeller from his own and his family's sources, the prerogatives of wealth constituted another resource that could be used with telling effect in the state political process. Few governors could afford to maintain a New

York City office for the state at their own expense. Few self-made politicians could fail to be impressed when the governor put his personal jet airplane at their disposal, or invited them to dine with the greats of American corporate and commercial life. It was not only that Nelson Rockefeller was rich, but that his very name was the symbol of wealth in America. When asked about the impact of his wealth upon his political career, one of the governor's comments was: "Well, I never suffered from a name recognition problem."⁹ On the other hand, the Rockefeller name in some circles aroused visions of the robber barons of the turn of the century. Sweeping denunciations of the Rockefellers in general and Nelson in particular were not uncommon.

In commenting on his wealth Rockefeller once said, "Minority and ethnic groups are in some ways more comfortable with a wealthy man because they are convinced that he would not use the office for personal gain."¹⁰ The issue, as he defined it, was not simply how much money he had, but how he chose to use it. Rockefeller's gifts and loans to associates and friends in government came under severe attack as corrupting, but the governor defended them as acts of friendship or as necessary to attract leading administrative talent to New York. Certainly, none of this spending has been linked to concrete decisions made by recipients for the personal advantage of the governor or his interests. Though some have claimed, for example, that Rockefeller's state financial decisions were intended to benefit the big New York City banks (and through them his own family), one former state banking commissioner wrote: "Never in the three years that I was in that office did he seek to influence or direct my course of action in the discharge of my statutory duties, although I have no doubt . . . that there were times when he was importuned to do so."¹¹

There were only two public scandals in the fifteen years of Rockefeller's administration. Considering the size of the New York State budget and the number of its employees, this was a remarkable record. Millions of dollars were spent to seek and get political office, and perhaps this spending was excessive, but Rockefeller violated no electoral rules or laws by his expenditures. There is no evidence that he made any decisions as governor to enhance his personal fortune or that of his family. Not all would agree with Rockefeller's judgments about what was best for New York, but few would deny that his actions were based on these judgments.

Rockefeller was an ambitious man, and his ambitions reinforced his natural activist orientation. One of his closest associates commented that he certainly wanted to succeed in public office, "because that is one thing that money cannot buy." Rockefeller wanted to be president. He thus sought to make a successful record as governor and to establish New York as a model for the nation. His presidential aspirations helped him with other politicians in the state as well, because they knew they were dealing with a man who was a national figure. Men who wanted to hitch their wagons to a rising star were attracted to his administration.

Like his wealth, Rockefeller's presidential ambitions are treated negatively in most accounts of his governorship. His ambition for the presidency, it is argued, underlay almost every major decision he made as governor; New York State's financial viability was sacrificed upon the altar of Rockefeller's desire for higher office.

Reasonable people can differ on the value of certain policies. Furthermore, Rockefeller, like other powerful executives, could at times be vindictive and ruthless. But to emphasize only the negative in assessing what drove Nelson Rockefeller is to be unfair to the man. Personal ambition is, after all, the engine of American politics. Rockefeller's motives were complex, but they did include a good deal of his vision for the state and compassion for its people.

A Test of Leadership

One test of Rockefeller's leadership was the extent to which he was responsible for developing major state programs. Scholars have long been interested in the relative impact of political, social, and economic factors on public policy in the state. The early research of V. O. Key and his students stressed the importance of political factors, especially party competition, in the determination of state policy, but studies published through the 1960s suggested the primacy of social and economic conditions rather than political structures and processes.[12] Though the office of the governorship was not central to most of these studies, one piece of research by Thomas K. Dye on the effect of executive fragmentation and formal gubernatorial powers concluded that "while states with fragmented executive structures pursue somewhat different policies than states with more streamlined executive branches, most of these policy differences are attributable to the impact of economic development rather than the structure of state executives," and that "there is little evidence that a governor's formal powers significantly affect policy outcomes in the fifty states."[13]

Responding to these findings, other analysts have suggested that, though social and economic factors may determine the outside limits of state governmental activity for the distribution of costs and benefits, within these limits political processes are crucial. A summary essay by Sarah McCally Morehouse stated flatly: "The political power of the governor is of great consequence and policy outcomes can be shaped by the type of political party he operates and the other resources he commands."[14] Comparative research has shown great gubernatorial influence on the level at which state agency budget requests are funded, and has also demonstrated that political factors have a primary impact on the redistributive effects of social policy decisions in the state.[15] Indeed, one scholarly article shows the governor's tenure potential to be one of the two statistically most significant political correlates of state policies that result in income redistribution.[16] Other research concludes that formal executive powers, when measured as they are actually used, became increasingly important in the 1970s in explaining state fiscal policy outcomes.[17]

Richard Hofferbert, one of the most innovative scholars in the field of the comparative study of state government, has highlighted the enormous difficulties in accurately measuring the governor's impact on policy:

> Ideally, if an analyst were investigating the influence of a governor on state policy, he would want to know the frequency with which the governor "had his own way," how often he got enacted the type of policies he desired. The data on which to base this estimate would include not only the legislative proposals the governor had recommended, but those he would have recommended had he not anticipated adverse legislative response. Further, the analyst would want some estimate of the relative importance the governor attached to all items in his program.[18]

How, then, can a study of one state, New York, and one governor, Nelson Rockefeller, inform this debate on the impact of the governor on state policy? Certainly such a study reinforces findings of the importance of political actors and processes. If tenure potential has been identified as a critical variable in assessing gubernatorial impact, Rockefeller was one of the few governors in recent memory to realize this potential. Although most state governors have longer tenure in office than their predecessors a century ago, few serve more than two terms. Thus most governors simply do not have the time to effect extensive policy changes. Each legislative year offers the opportunity for only a few major policy initiatives, and initiatives taken can hardly be fairly launched before the end of the gubernatorial term.

Rockefeller himself sought only a few major policy changes each year, but with reelection could follow them up more fully than most other governors. Initiatives for the State University taken in 1961, during Rockefeller's first term, could be supported by massive annual funding increases during the second and third terms, and they were. Rockefeller's personal commitment was a critical factor. Had the governorship been captured by Frank O'Connor in 1966, as it almost was, it is unlikely that this New York City Democrat, with his constituents served by the tuition-free City University and with independent colleges already bringing pressure for state aid, would have allowed SUNY's growth to continue apace.

Rockefeller was not committed to any ideology. Rather, he considered himself a practical problem solver, much more interested in defining problems and finding solutions around which he could unite support sufficient to ensure their enactment in legislation than in following either a strictly liberal or strictly conservative course. It has been suggested that he was liberally inclined at the beginning of his administration but became more conservative toward the end, both in response to changes in the New York electorate and because of his quest for the Republican presidential nomination. One prominent newspaper columnist, in expressing this view, asserted: "Events forced a change. As the voters became more conservative in 1968 and 1970, Rockefeller, the pragmatist, was influenced by the expectations of the voters." An examination of the record, however, gives little support to this explanation. Rockefeller's programs did not consistently follow either liberal or conservative ideology. Early fiscal policies were conservative, a description that would hardly fit later approaches to state financing. In the later years, "conservative" decisions on social programs were paralleled by "liberal" ones on highly contentious environmental issues.

When seeking a solution to a particular problem, Rockefeller did not wish to be told by his staff about the obstacles that he faced. A believer in the solubility of problems, the governor was not receptive to descriptions of legal or fiscal roadblocks to action. He was much more inclined to listen to the policy people on his staff who proposed solutions to problems than to budget officers who worried about the increased costs of government. Big problems, he thought, required big solutions. There were few cautious beginnings during the Rockefeller governorship, few pilot programs.

After an initial attempt to reorganize state government—an effort that failed—Rockefeller adopted the strategy of dealing with matters seriatim. He was a man of enthusiasms, who liked to shape the approach to a policy area and leave the detailed implementation to others. His involvement was intense until he considered the "conceptual problem" (one of his favorite terms) solved; then his attention turned elsewhere. Thus in the early 1960s the major emphasis was on higher education, in the mid-1960s on mass transportation and pure waters, and later in the decade on social problems, drug abuse, and welfare reform.

Knowing that he would ultimately have to depend on his staff for policy implementation, Rockefeller sought to surround himself with the best available people. He was fortunate in having a loyal, long-serving staff. New York State provided its governors with larger staffs than any other state. In addition, Rockefeller used his own financial resources to retain special assistants and to supplement the salaries of aides, a practice that later came into question. But staff loyalty was not based solely on Rockefeller's personal generosity. He offered not only the promise of action but action itself. Consequently, he kept people with brains interested. Other political executives—Lyndon Johnson, for example—had reputations for "using people up" and had difficulty retaining high-quality assistants despite the high status of their posts. Though Rockefeller was hard-driving—he kept his aides on tap seven days a week—his style with staff was not oppressive. He knew how to use his staff to research problems, perfect ideas, and develop policies. He expected his aides to be strong advocates, imaginative, and critical in testing ideas. Once he made a decision, however, he expected the staff to adhere to it.

Rockefeller supported his appointees to the full extent of his power. Though this practice encouraged staff loyalty and initiative, it sometimes led to embarrassing political situations. He had a tendency to adhere to a policy after it had become politically dangerous. Sometimes his tenacity worked. After three attempts to get the legislature to adopt no-fault automobile insurance, he succeeded. The same was true with the Adirondack land planning program. On the other hand, his early decisions in regard to the Attica rebellion and the Rye–Oyster Bay bridge were continued after it was evident that a change in direction was needed. In accepting criticism regarding delays in improving the Long Island Rail Road, Rockefeller showed unusual courage in taking public responsibility for unpopular stands.

Like all activist political executives, Rockefeller suffered from the defects of his virtues. He was not a "detail man." Once a program was launched, he often lost sight of it unless a problem arose. His desire for fast and highly visible results often caused him to select the more costly policy option, and to go forward with dramatic programs before all their implications were clear. This was evidently the case, for example, in his attempts to deal with the drug problem and the shortage of low- and middle-income housing in New York. Though Rockefeller took up problems one by one, when one looks back at his record it is the *cumulative impact* of his decisions on New York State that is perceived. Because of his long tenure, the overall result was a major reshaping of the scope and direction of state government.

During Rockefeller's governorship, state government grew, but so did state government everywhere during this period. The important thing is that government grew faster in New York than elsewhere, and that within the state different agencies grew at different rates. Because of his control of the executive budget process, the differential allocation of resources to state agencies largely reflected the governor's priorities. High-growth-rate departments, in addition to the State University, included Transportation and Environmental Conservation. The budgets of other agencies, such as Agriculture and Markets, Insurance, Health, and Labor, increased much more slowly. In real terms the budget for Veterans' Affairs declined. In the calculus of budgeting, political factors, of course, had considerable weight.

One major gubernatorial priority was state aid to localities. In New York, it has long been considered good administration to deliver as many services as possible on the local level, and good politics to return as large a percentage of state revenues as possible to local governments. (In order to get the political credit due them for this practice, state-level politicians require that local governments advise real-property owners of state local assistance payments on their tax bills.) During the Rockefeller administration this emphasis was continued, and increased local aid payments became a major achievement cited by Rockefeller in his reelection campaigns. But again, the change in the internal mix of aid payments reflected altering priorities. Though education aid grew, it grew less rapidly than general local assistance or aid for Medicaid and social welfare purposes. In sum, and despite mayoral complaints to the contrary, one cumulative result was vastly increased assistance to New York's urban centers.

Of course, the great growth of assistance to localities in some state programs was not entirely the result of gubernatorial priorities. Often, federal assistance provided the incentive for state action. Matching grants by the national government sometimes led directly to the creation of new state agencies, or made available resources to operate agencies that would otherwise of necessity have been supplied from the state's own revenues.

Though Rockefeller could not take credit for the availability of federal funds, he did seek to maximize the Empire State's share of the grant money that became available in ever increasing amounts as the 1960s progressed. Indeed, the aggressiveness of New York and a few other states sometimes led to the inclusion in federal formulas of limitations on the portion of the total aid that any one state could receive. New York's experience also showed that it did not pay to anticipate federal policy too much. Retroactive payments from the national government for early state initiatives in interstate highways and pure waters were very difficult to obtain.

Especially during Rockefeller's second and third terms, the congressional practice of funding programs considerably below their authorized levels caused the governor embarrassment, for he had made program commitments on the assumption of full federal funding. In some program areas—Medicaid, for example—an eagerness for federal dollars was one of the causes of New York's overextending itself. Ultimately, sharp programmatic cutbacks were necessary.

As the importance of federal assistance to New York grew, Rockefeller became a sharp critic of the administration of intergovernmental fiscal programs. As a leader of the Advisory Commission on Intergovernmental Relations and in numerous appearances before congressional committees, he fought against the proliferation of narrowly focused categorical grant programs and the red tape that accompanied them. When a Republican administration came to power in Washington in the late 1960s, Rockefeller seized the opportunity to argue for the consolidation of programs into a few functional areas, and for greater control of policy at the state level. Spurred on by an increasingly tight fiscal situation in New York, the governor became a leader in the fight for relatively unrestricted formula grants to states and localities. Though political necessity forced compromise on the details of the program, this fight was won with the passage of general revenue sharing in 1972.

Comparative research in state government stresses the limiting effect of economic factors on the level of state government activity, but a study of the Rockefeller administration demonstrates that at least one governor tested the limits of these constraints. Rockefeller sought and obtained eight tax increases during his fifteen years in office.

When he came to office, Rockefeller was convinced that New Yorkers desired more governmental services, and that they would accept higher taxation to obtain those services. During his administration, the tax burden rose to a higher level than in any other state, and the incidence of taxation shifted, with a greater share being borne by the individual taxpayer. Though avoidance of excessive taxation on business was an overt object of policy, in order to block an out-migration that would damage the state's economy, by the early 1970s it was clear that business was fleeing New York State, and especially New York City. Fears of the destructive effect on the tax base of further taxation spurred Rockefeller to renew his efforts for new sources of federal aid, efforts that reached their successful culmination with the enactment of revenue sharing in 1972.

At first a strong opponent of public borrowing in the tradition of New York Republicanism, by the middle of his second term Rockefeller had endorsed a billion-dollar bond issue for water purification. This issue won voter approval, as did similarly massive issues for transportation and the environment. Even during his first term, when he took a conservative stance on public borrowing, Rockefeller encouraged the development of the public benefit corporation and the concomitant "moral-obligation bond" technique for the financing of public projects through private-sector borrowing. Early public benefit corporations such as the Job Development Authority and Housing Finance Agency were attractive to Rockefeller because they permitted revenue-generating projects to be built quickly (in time to claim credit within the four-year election cycle), without the use of state tax funds. Furthermore, authority debt, though it involved a moral obligation of the state, did not, in law, commit New York's full faith and credit. Thus the 1846 state constitutional requirement that any state debt be authorized by a public referendum could be bypassed, and was.

Later the concept of the public benefit corporation was applied in other areas, notably public transportation (the Metropolitan Transportation Authority) and, after the failure of a $3.5 billion community development bond issue, low- and middle-income urban housing (the Urban Development Corporation). Other fiscal devices were used as well, when constitutional structures blocked gubernatorial goals. The lease-purchase idea facilitated the building of the Albany mall. Cash-based accounting—which allowed such budgetary practices as accelerated payments, rollovers, first-instance appropriations, and the like—eased any limitations that the constitutional requirement of a balanced budget may have placed on gubernatorial plans.

Rockefeller's fiscal practices were criticized in a limited way during his tenure, especially by the Democratic state comptroller, Arthur Levitt. Hostile comment reached a climax in 1975, with the default of the Urban Development Corporation during the severe New York State fiscal crisis of that year. Ultimately the state met its moral obligation, but, after a Moreland Commission investigation of the UDC, also took steps to limit the future borrowing power of the public benefit corporations Rockefeller had sponsored. Throughout this crisis, Rockefeller contended that he could have averted it. Certainly, much of what he undertook when governor gained added credibility in the financial markets because of his name and the economic power of his family, but one man's connections should not be relied upon to support a state's fiscal structure.

It is especially in the fiscal area that the cumulative effect of the Rockefeller years has been felt in New York. Certainly, alternatives to higher taxes, moral-obligation borrowing, and lease-back arrangements were available. Governors in adjacent states made it a priority to hold down taxes, and some were able to do so. Others were more selective in the number and ambitiousness of the policy directions they pursued. Indeed, in light of subsequent events, a major criticism of Rockefeller is that in his drive to find solutions to social problems he was unwilling to acknowledge the limiting effect of economic factors.

New York's experience showed the governor and the legislature that the bond-buying public eagerly welcomed agency bonds even though the full faith and credit of the state were not pledged. Thus the normal political and economic processes were not adequate to check unwise spending. Indeed, moral-obligation bonds were politically attractive because they provided a means of constructing educational and health facilities at little immediate pain to the taxpayer or the politician. If the expenditures were based solely on social need rather than revenue production, however, it was axiomatic that sooner or later the state would be called on to appropriate additional funds.

More than anything else, the projects for which he borrowed revealed Rockefeller's style as governor. He liked bricks and mortar, and was most comfortable with visible symbols of success. As one of his staff was reported to have said, "The governor likes to see holes in the ground." Rockefeller preferred to sit at the control of a machine rather than push a button. He was frequently pictured in a hard hat. In fact, on one occasion Rockefeller knocked down a building in downtown Albany and the next day the adjoining building collapsed. One need only contrast the constancy of Rockefeller's policies that produced measurable physical results with the variability of policies in social areas, where clear indicators of progress were elusive.

Especially in the politics of getting bond issues passed, Rockefeller showed himself to be an artful practitioner of what Theodore Lowi has called "distributive politics."[19] In this kind of politics, no interest loses, everyone gets a piece of the pie. Upstaters supported the transportation bond issue for more roads, downstaters for mass transit. The governor remained vague on the details of benefit distribution, allowing every participant who joined the coalition to maximize in his mind the benefits he might gain for his support. Thus a winning coalition could be put together by the governor with a minimum of concrete commitment.

It may be that an activist executive requires an arena that permits distributive politics. He needs bargaining chips, ways in which he can entice other powerful and independent actors in the political process to support his policy goals. Once politics becomes redistributive— once the process begins to produce clear-cut losers by visibly taking from one group and giving to another—coalitions against the activist executive become more likely. Indeed, Rockefeller's greatest achievements were in policy areas in which rewards were ample, visible, and widely distributed. The governor's major difficulties began later, when those who lost as a result of his policies—corporate and individual taxpayers—came to feel the loss and resist the expenditures.

Whereas Rockefeller's longevity in office allowed him to have a major impact on the state across a broad spectrum, it also caused him, more than most politicians, to be available during his later terms to feel the wrath of the opposition that developed over time to the positions that he had advocated. It may well be that the process of maintaining state service levels, or making painful redistributive decisions, demanded a different executive style. Since an executive's style is shaped early and rooted in the character of the man, it is very difficult for him to alter it.[20] It was clear, during his last years in office, that Rockefeller was less happy functioning in an atmosphere of constraints, trying to save money rather than spend it.

Comparative research has shown that New York under Rockefeller retained its position as one of the most innovative states in the federal system, one that was, in the words of Jack L. Walker, one of five "pioneer states."[21] When, in 1970, top state government executives working in eight major policy areas were asked to name the state with the "best agency carrying out the same type program," the Empire

State was one of only three states named in every policy area (California and Wisconsin were the others). New York was the preeminent model state in the areas of health, business regulation, and human relations, and close behind California in the reputation of its education department. These findings are even more remarkable when it is noted that no officials from the Northeast were included in the sample surveyed.[22]

In a number of policy areas, the governor's initiative, endorsement, or active political involvement was critical for the adoption of a policy, its revision, or its definition as a matter of state concern.[23] In such areas as the arts, civil rights, narcotics addiction, and urban housing, New York under gubernatorial guidance undertook roles that were innovative for state government at the time.

New York not only often led the other states but also, in a variety of notable ways, provided a model for the federal government in a number of programs. This fact offers further support for the view that a federal system allows the opportunity for experimentation. A state can try out a new program and if it is successful or politically attractive it can be adopted by the national government.

Certainly, New York State's reputation for being a leader in the federal system cannot be attributed entirely to Rockefeller. The much-acclaimed Education Department, for example, operated almost entirely independently of him. Though many new policy ideas originated in the governor's office, most, especially those concerning the improvement of ongoing programs, welled up from the operating levels of state government. Rockefeller did, however, establish an atmosphere of professionalism in state government through his improvement of civil service personnel policies. He also created a climate of receptivity to new ideas at the top in New York. Within his secretary's office, an elaborate annual search of departments and agencies for items to be included in the annual message was institutionalized. In many states, the dynamics of government are organized around budgeting, a process that inherently emphasizes constraints. In New York, the influence of the budgetary process came under Rockefeller to be balanced by methods of program development that rewarded, or at least recognized, the value of innovation.

The Altered Face of State Government

It is almost as difficult to sort out from other factors the effect of a governor on the living organism that is state government as it is to trace his independent impact on public policy. Governor Rockefeller's hand was most clearly evident in the organization and functioning of his own office. During the Rockefeller years, the influence of the Budget Division and counsel's office declined and that of the secretary's office grew. Early in the administration the establishment of program associates in the secretary's office created a new link between the governor and the operating agencies. A separate planning agency was established and, for a time, flourished. But of all the changes made by Rockefeller, those in the governor's office were the most mutable. They were largely the functions of the personality of the governor and his top aides. Though perhaps the enlarged secretary's office had within its design the capacity for survival, other governors will no doubt choose to organize things in different ways.

With regard to the larger corpus of state government, though Rockefeller set out in 1959 to reduce the number of departments and agencies, he was ultimately unsuccessful in attaining this goal. He did abolish and combine some state agencies, but social and political pressures led him to create new ones in other areas, such as environmental affairs and transportation. Moreover, his penchant for study groups resulted in greater use of temporary commissions than in any previous administration. Though a constitutional provision limiting the number of state departments to twenty remained in force throughout the Rockefeller years, an amendment of the early 1960s permitted the governor to reorganize freely, subject to legislative review, within this numerical constraint. This was an important power; a survey of governors published in 1968 found that the lack of the authority to reorganize significantly affected their ability to implement programs.[24] Rockefeller's use of this power resulted in thirty-one departments and agencies in 1973 that did not exist in 1959. With the inception of the Carey administration in 1974, the cycle began again. Rockefeller, the archfoe of administrative fragmentation in 1959, was accused of leaving a fragmented system behind him! The quest for an orderly organization chart for New York State was resumed with renewed zest by the incoming Democratic administration.

Given the values he espoused when he took office—a commitment to economy, efficiency, hierarchy, and symmetry in administration—the governmental system Rockefeller left behind taught a lesson. Administrative reorganization is not an end in itself. Structural disorder—for example, placing new functions in new agencies rather than in established ones where they might fit—might serve policy goals. Rockefeller reorganized for several reasons. In creating the Departments of Transportation and Environmental Conservation, he sought at once to symbolize a fundamental change in policy and actually redirect policy implementation. In restructuring the Departments of Parks and Mental Hygiene, he sought greater centralized control. In the case of the Alcoholic Beverage Control Board, he responded to public criticism with reorganization, whereas with the Human Rights and Public Service commissions, reorganization served largely to anticipate and defuse such criticism.

In almost all of these cases, symbolic action was about as important in mollifying the concerned constituencies as actual change. As with the establishment of study commissions, reorganization allowed the governor to act, to meet the problem, without a major fiscal commitment. From experience, Rockefeller learned that the redirection of policy implementation took time, and that it often required personnel changes at the top to assure that new organization names and structures did not mark the same old approach to problems. Effective reorganization required a judicious mixture of speed and patience: speed in designing changes and putting them in place (before opposing political alliances could form and block them) and patience in waiting for the results of change. Here was the fundamental clash in perspective between the politician and the bureaucrat. The latter could wait; the former, looking forward to the next election, could not.

More important than specific structural changes, the underlying thrust of Rockefeller's reorganization was to strengthen the hand of the governor in his dealings with the bureaucracy. Thus the chiefs of the Department of Social Services and the Public Service Commission came to serve at the governor's pleasure, and the center of power resistant to the governor in the Division of Parks was ultimately broken. Only the Education Department and the departments of the two independently elected statewide executives, the comptroller and the attorney general, were able to resist the insistent pressure over fifteen years for the consolidation of control over the executive branch. And in bureaucratic areas over which he could not gain direct control, Rockefeller established "countervailing bureaucracies," responsive to him, as a tool for indirect influence. These units included, for example, the offices of the welfare and education inspectors general, both of which worked in areas in which localities delivered the services but for which the state paid a large portion of the bills. Also in this category was the Scott commission, created to oversee the workings of the government of New York City.

Perhaps the most important development of the Rockefeller years on the structure of government in New York, however, was the movement of a sizable amount of the state's business outside of the direct aegis of state government. By 1973, measured by magnitude of expenditures, about one-third of New York State's public business was being performed by public benefit corporations created during the Rockefeller years. Such corporations were building hospitals and low-income housing, college dormitories and nursing homes. They were managing the New York metropolitan area's transportation system and developing the state's power resources. In addition to the fiscal issues they generated, these agencies caused concern because of the lack of democratic control over them; once appointed, authority chiefs were generally removable only for cause. Designers of these agencies envisioned the loss of democratic control as the necessary price for businesslike economy and efficiency. Too often, however, as in the case of the Metropolitan Transportation Authority and the Urban Development Corporation, control was relinquished without concomitant gains.

Governor Rockefeller's impact on the New York legislature as an institution, though clearly not so purposive as his effect on the executive branch, may be as long lasting. Over the years of his governorship, his ability to get what he "really wanted" in the legislature, regardless of its partisan stripe, became almost legendary. More than most executives, Rockefeller grasped that continued success in the legislature required that legislators perceive him as strong. With regard to legislative issues upon which he had taken a clear and highly visible stand, Rockefeller believed that he had to win, not only because of the substance of the issue but also because defeat would weaken him on matters that would arise later. Thus, for example, when beaten in the 1964 battle over liquor law reform during the regular session of the legislature, Rockefeller called it back into special session and won the adoption of much of his program.

It was in the legislature that distributive politics was most effective. At first hostile to patronage and partisan politics in the traditional manner of good-government advocates, Rockefeller soon learned that the quid pro quo was at the center of the legislative process. Ultimately he became a master at making "side payments"—administrative jobs, pet home-district projects, judicial appointments—in exchange for votes in support of major policy goals. Ordinarily the niceties of normal partisan politics were observed, but when Democratic votes were needed, the governor unfailingly traded for these as well. In this manner, he was able to have success with legislatures regardless of party control.

Certainly, Rockefeller's positive, activist style in the legislature reinforced the long-established expectation in New York that the governor would define the state's political agenda. One measure recently used by political scientists to gauge a governor's political effectiveness with the legislature is his ability to have his veto maintained once he employs it. This measure may be of questionable utility in New York, which has a tradition of not overriding the governor's veto; still, Rockefeller's veto was never overridden during the fifteen years of his administration.[25] His successor, Carey, was not so fortunate.

With all this said, it must also be noted that there were limits to Rockefeller's legislative effectiveness. Some were self-imposed. The governor did not concern himself with the selection of Republican legislative leaders or take the lead on such explosive substantive matters as abortion and divorce law reform. Some limits were imposed by others. There were battles—the Rye–Oyster Bay bridge controversy, for example—that Rockefeller lost. And, in his last two terms, the legislative leadership, both Republican and Democratic, took an increasingly independent role in reviewing and modifying the governor's executive budget.

Indeed, Rockefeller's overall effectiveness with the legislature may contribute to his successors' problems. Desirous of developing independent sources of advice and information when it came into power in 1964, the newly elected Democratic legislature began to hire a core of independent professional staff. For reasons of institutional pride and personal ambition, Republican legislative leaders reinforced this initiative when they returned to the majority and continued to enlarge the staff. Here again it is difficult to segregate Rockefeller's influence, since the movement toward professionalization of state legislatures was a national one. Certainly, however, some increment of the growth of legislative independence can be traced to a reaction against the governor's dominance of that institution. Thus Rockefeller in his later years had to deal with a much less tractable legislative institution, and this was one of the legacies he left to his successors.

The Limits of State Government

The era of the Rockefeller governorship in New York corresponded with a halcyon period for the states in the federal system. During the 1960s, state budget and employment roles burgeoned and a myriad of new tasks were undertaken. Sometimes the incentive for this growth came from the federal level, as grant-in-aid programs increased in numbers and magnitude as a result of the Creative Federalism of the

Johnson years and the New Federalism of the Nixon administration. Certainly, a series of decisions at the federal level, those of the Supreme Court concerning the reapportionment of state legislatures, helped redefine the parameters of state politics during this period. Often, however, the impetus for growth and change came from within those "great laboratories" of the federal system, the states themselves.

In academic circles, renewed attention to the complexities of federalism presaged and then accompanied the resurgence of the states. The work of Morton Grodzins and his students affirmed the historic and continuing importance of the states' role in the federal partnership.[26] Implicit in this research, which was in part a reaction to writing critical of the response of state government to the problems of the Depression and the post–World War II era, was the notion that the states were the appropriate and even the best level of government through which the domestic problems of the United States could be addressed. Summarizing this thesis, Daniel Elazar wrote in 1974: "Today there is simply no justification for thinking that the states and localities, either in principle or in practice, are less able to do the job than the federal government. In fact, there is some reason to believe that, even with their weaknesses, they will prove better able to restore public confidence in America's political institutions."[27]

New York under Rockefeller provided an example of a state government seeking an independent course. But if states are to be successful in performing new functions or taking over functions previously performed by the federal government, they must first have an adequate and professionally trained bureaucracy. New York, like California, Wisconsin, and a few other states, was fortunate in having such a bureaucracy for most functions. In addition, they also must have adequate financial resources.

Federal money had relatively less impact in New York than elsewhere over the 1958–1973 period. Federal aid formulas and limits often discriminated against the larger and wealthier states. As one consequence, throughout the Rockefeller period New York State remained a net loser from the redistributive effects of national taxing and spending policies, although its position was improving vis-à-vis other states. Certainly no state acted alone in addressing the major domestic problems of the 1960s—and New York was among the most aggressive in seeking federal financing and responding to federal incentives—but, more than most, the Empire State could be said to have relied on its own resources.

Social problems have no easy solutions, and certainly governmental efforts to address them should not be evaluated on the assumption that such solutions exist. As problems are addressed they take on new dimensions, which may be more significant and difficult to deal with than the problem as originally defined. To this mix must be added the unanticipated consequences of the original solution itself. The decisions of politicians, like those of Liddell Hart's generals, should be judged in the light of the information they have at the moment they make them. Policies, on the other hand, should be evaluated on their success or failure over time.

What was the result of Rockefeller's policies? Massive efforts were made across a large number of complex policy areas: higher education, mental hygiene, drug addiction, low- and middle-income housing, mass transportation, pure waters and land use planning. Of these problems, drug addiction was by far the least tractable. Neither a massive program of treatment and rehabilitation nor a later attempt at strict law enforcement resulted in amelioration of the problem. In the other areas there were major achievements, but Rockefeller's solutions contributed to later problems. A great state university was built to meet the peak needs of the 1960s, but competition from this new institution threatened the viability of New York's independent colleges as the pool of available college-bound students began to contract in the 1970s, and some argued that public higher education had grown much too fast in New York. Public authorities built tens of thousands of unit of housing, but their moral-obligation debt, along with that of similar agencies created to finance and build the State University, contributed to a frightening fiscal crisis in the state in 1975. A similarly structured authority and more state borrowing improved the quality of commuter rail service and other public transit in the metropolitan New York City area, but massive and growing operating deficits in the system remained. A great effort at water purification, begun in 1965 with considerable administrative daring—and still more borrowing for capital construction—began to succeed in the early 1970s as fish returned to the lower reaches of the Hudson River. But then, in 1976, it was discovered that a pollutant not controlled as a result of the Pure Waters Program made these fish dangerous for human consumption, and commercial fishing in the river was banned. Major changes in the direction of mental hygiene programs reduced the population of state institutions, but the release of disturbed patients into the community without adequate supervision was later attacked. Moreover, when state mental hospitals abandoned their former custodial role and denied admission to senile patients, a great new demand for nursing homes was created, a demand that later contributed to abuses in this field by greedy and unscrupulous operators. In reflecting on all of this, one might comment that progress did not ensure final solutions.

Nelson Rockefeller's penchant for problem solving defined his governorship. As one of his high-level aides recalled, "the tougher the sell, the better he liked it."[28] It was Rockefeller's style to move from issue to issue, from problem to problem. Timing was dictated by the phases of the political moon. Until the fiscal crunch of 1970, each legislative session had its dominant new program, each election campaign its claims of dramatic achievements. The process was incremental and disjointed, but the result was cumulative. This year's budget had to pay not only for this year's new program but also for those of last year and the year before that. And ultimately, when the national economy faltered, it became evident that the state had pushed itself to the limit of its means. Painful contraction was necessary, and it occurred.

New York's experience under Rockefeller is thus a lesson in the limits of the states' role in the federal system. A state must be highly selective in the issues it chooses to address with its own limited resources. Insofar as it attempts to take on the gamut of domestic problems that confront the American polity, over time it may risk the very economic viability that allows it to act at all. The need to be selective necessarily narrows the range of freedom within which a state may act; it may also cause politicians to seek low-cost symbolic outputs with which to satisfy their constituents in place of more expensive substantive policies.

A realization of the necessity of choice among issues also highlights the added danger of the approach of the activist executive in a situation of limited resources. States, indeed all governments, need energetic executives in order to function effectively. They also, however, require governors for whom the option *not to act* is viable. One of Nelson Rockefeller's characteristics as governor was his belief in the rightness of acting. His desire to transcend the constraints on state government resulted in many innovative measures, but it also led to action in times when the acceptance of constraint might have been a wiser course, and one that was equally viable politically.

Certainly, for his impact on New York State, Nelson Rockefeller was the most important governor since Alfred E. Smith. He had an unusual capacity to assess conflicting forces, a willingness to adapt policies to the realities of the situation, a good deal of administrative skill, a preference for attainable objectives, and an ability to combine a respect for the past with intelligent reform. Indeed, from the point of view of the resources that he aggregated and the length of time he used them, Rockefeller was the most powerful governor ever to serve in the Empire State. In the end, his career confirmed Woodrow Wilson's prescription for the chief executive, for as governor, Rockefeller proved extremely skillful in "the art of bringing the several parts of government into effective cooperation for the accomplishment of particular common objects."

After resigning as governor of New York on December 11, 1973, Rockefeller characteristically organized a study commission to consider the critical choices facing the nation. On December 19, 1974, he became vice-president of the United States, and served until January 1977. Returning to New York, he was not extensively involved in politics. He died of a heart attack on January 26, 1979.

In some ways, Rockefeller was an anachronism—old-fashioned, neither liberal nor conservative. Unlike Franklin D. Roosevelt, Rockefeller did not repudiate his class. He was disliked by conservatives, who regarded him as another FDR (and therefore denied him the Republican presidential nomination), and by liberals because he was never quite what they wanted him to be. Half a decade after he stepped down from the governorship, debate over the wisdom and social impact of Rockefeller's policies still raged unabated. In the end, what is most ironic is that Rockefeller's great achievement was inseparably bound up with his most telling failure. The achievement was the quality of leadership he offered, the unflinching way in which he caused the state to take up the preeminent problems of his era. The degree of success varied, but Rockefeller did not duck the problems. The failure was one of perspective. It resulted from Rockefeller's inability to accept the limits of his circumstances, and thus to anticipate the cumulative consequences of his decisions. Ultimately, it was the conservative, not the liberal, critique of Rockefeller that was most compelling. He achieved mightily, but tried to do too much too fast.

Notes

Preface

1. Woodrow Wilson, *Constitutional Government in the United States* (New York: Columbia University Press, 1917), p. 54.

2. Ibid., p. 68.

1. The Shaping of the New York Governorship

1. Rockefeller's service as governor actually exceeded that of Clinton, who spent much of his first several terms as a general, fighting the British. During this time his lieutenant governor, Pierre Van Cortlandt, was the effective chief executive of the state. See Jacob Judd, "Two Uncommon Men: George Clinton and Pierre Van Cortlandt," paper delivered at "The Genesis of the Empire State," a conference sponsored by the New York State Department of Parks, Senate House Historic Site, Kingston, July 30, 1977.

2. See, e.g., Myer Kutz, *Rockefeller Power* (New York: Simon & Schuster, 1974); Peter Collier and David Horowitz, *The Rockefellers: An American Dynasty* (New York: Holt, Rinehart & Winston, 1976), chaps. 19, 20, 22, 25; and Michael Kramer and Sam Roberts, *"I Never Wanted to Be Vice-President of Anything!": An Investigative Biography of Nelson Rockefeller* (New York: Basic Books, 1976).

3. Cited in William G. Colman, "The Changing Role of the States in the Federal System," *Proceedings of the Academy of Political Science* 31 (May 1974): 80.

4. See Daniel J. Elazar, *The American Partnership: Intergovernmental Cooperation in the Nineteenth Century* (Chicago: University of Chicago Press, 1962); and W. Brook Graves, *American Intergovernmental Relations: Their Origins, Historical Development, and Current Status* (New York: Scribner, 1964).

5. Roscoe C. Martin, *The Cities in the Federal System* (New York: Atherton, 1965). See also Robert H. Connery and Richard H. Leach, *The Federal Government and Metropolitan Areas* (Cambridge, Mass.: Harvard University Press, 1960).

6. One major study was the *Report of the Commission on Intergovernmental Relations* (Washington, D.C.: Government Printing Office, 1955).

7. See, e.g., Arthur W. McMahon, ed., *Federalism: Mature and Emergent* (Garden City, N.Y.: Doubleday, 1955); and James W. Fesler, *The Forty-eight States: Their Tasks as Policy Makers and Administrators* (New York: American Assembly, Columbia University, 1955).

8. For two interesting discussions of political culture, see Ira Sharkansky, *Regionalism in American Politics* (Indianapolis: Bobbs-Merrill, 1970); and Daniel J. Elazar, *American Federalism: A View from the States* (New York: Crowell, 1966).

9. See Joseph A. Schlesinger, "The Politics of the Executive," in *Politics in the American State: A Comparative Analysis*, 2d ed., ed. Herbert Jacob and Kenneth N. Vines (Boston: Little, Brown, 1971), pp. 210–237.

10. See Jack L. Walker, "The Diffusion of Innovations among the American States," *American Political Science Review* 63 (September 1969):800–899; and Virginia Gray, "Innovation in the States: A Diffusion Study," *American Political Science Review* 67 (December 1973):1174–1185.

11. Neal R. Peirce, *The Megastates of America: People, Politics, and Power in the Ten Great States* (New York: Norton, 1972).

12. Stanley Leiserson, "Measuring Population Diversity," *American Sociological Review* 34 (December 1969):850–862.

13. Donald M. Roper, "The Governorship in History," *Proceedings of the Academy of Political Science* 31 (May 1974):16–30.

14. These governor's councils were eliminated by the state constitutional convention of 1821. Similar councils still function in some New England states—Maine, for example.

15. Allan Nevins, *The American States during and after the Revolution, 1775–1789* (New York: Macmillan, 1924), p. 162. See also Bernard Mason, *The Road to Independence: The Revolutionary Movement in New York, 1773–1777* (Lexington: University of Kentucky Press, 1966), chap. 7; and Jackson Turner Main, *The Sovereign States, 1775–1783* (New York: Franklin Watts, New Viewpoints, 1973), pp. 172–175.

16. See Charles C. Thach, Jr., *The Creation of the Presidency, 1775–1789: A Study in Constitutional History*, Johns Hopkins University Studies, series 40, no. 4 (Baltimore: Johns Hopkins University Press, 1922), pp. 35, 41, 52, 87, 110. See also Nevins, *American States*, p. 161.

17. New York State Constitutional Convention Commission, *The Constitution and Government of the State of New York: An Appraisal* (Albany, 1915). See also Dwight Waldo, *The Administrative State: A Study of the Political Theory of American Public Administration* (New York: Ronald Press, 1948), pp. 36–37; and James Tracy Crown, "The Development of Democratic Government in the State of New York through Growth in the Power of the Executive since 1910," Ph.D. thesis, New York University, 1955.

18. Alfred E. Smith, *Up to Now: An Autobiography* (New York: Viking Press, 1929), pp. 137–150.

19. Robert A. Caro, *The Power Broker: Robert Moses and the Fall of New York* (New York: Knopf, 1974), chap. 7.

20. This research is vast. For a summary, see Ralph M. Stoghill, *Handbook of Leadership: A Survey of Theory and Research* (New York: Free Press, 1974). See also L. J. Edinger, "Comparative Analysis of Political Leadership," *Comparative Politics* 7 (January 1975):253–269.

21. Richard E. Neustadt, *Presidential Power: The Politics of Leadership* (New York: Wiley, 1960), p. 192.

22. James David Barber, *The Presidential Character: Predicting Performance in the White House*, 2d ed. (Englewood Cliffs, N.J.: Prentice-Hall, 1972), p. 445.

23. See Demetrios Caraley, *City Governments and Urban Problems* (Englewood Cliffs, N.J.: Prentice-Hall, 1977), chap. 9. For the impact of television, see Michael J. Robinson, "Television and American Politics: 1956–1976," *Public Interest*, no. 48 (Summer 1977), pp. 3–39.

24. For more detailed information on Nelson Rockefeller's early career, see Frank Gervasi, *The Real Rockefeller* (New York: Atheneum, 1964); Joe Alex Morris, *Nelson Rockefeller: A Biography* (New York: Harper & Row, 1960); James Desmond, *Nelson Rockefeller: A Political Biography* (New York: Macmillan, 1964); and, for an early account of the Rockefeller family, see Allan Nevins, *John D. Rockefeller: The Heroic Age of American Enterprise* (New York: Scribner, 1940).

25. Nelson A. Rockefeller, private interview, July 31, 1974.

26. Ruth B. Russell, *A History of the United Nations Charter: The Role of the United States, 1940–1945* (Washington, D.C.: Brookings Institution, 1958), pp. 693–698.

27. *New York Times*, December 17, 1954.

28. Rockefeller, private interview, January 23, 1976.

29. Ibid.

30. See, e.g., Rockefeller's testimony when he was undersecretary of HEW: U.S. Senate, Committee on Finance, *Hearings on the Amendment to the Social Security Act of 1954*, 83d Cong., 2d sess., 1954, pp. 151–221; and House, Committee on Ways and Means, *Hearings on the Amendments to the Social Security Act of 1954*, 83d Cong., 2d sess., 1954, pp. 117–185.

31. Rockefeller, private interview, July 31, 1974.

32. Ibid.

33. Ibid.

34. Rockefeller, private interview, September 5, 1973.

35. Gervasi, *Real Rockefeller*, p. 204.

36. New York Constitution, art. 19, sec. 2.

37. Rockefeller, private interview, September 5, 1973.

38. Ibid., January 23, 1976.

39. *New York Times*, January 13, 1958.

40. *New York Herald Tribune,* June 10, 1958.

41. *New York Times,* August 25, 1958.

42. See chap. 3.

43. Rockefeller, private interview, January 23, 1976.

2. *Party Leadership and Political Power*

1. See, e.g., Austin Ranney, "Parties in State Politics," in *Politics in the American States: A Comparative Analysis,* 2d ed., ed. Herbert Jacob and Kenneth N. Vines (Boston: Little, Brown, 1971), p. 65. Ranney ranks New York twenty-fifth and last among the two-party competitive states.

2. Neal R. Peirce, *The Megastates of America: People, Politics, and Power in the Ten Great States* (New York: Norton, 1972).

3. Statistics for this section were taken from *The New York Redbook,* an authorized publication of information about the government of the state of New York.

4. For a more detailed discussion of electoral trends in New York State, see Gerald Benjamin, "Patterns in New York State Politics," *Proceedings of the Academy of Political Science* 31 (May 1974):31–44.

5. Frank J. Munger, "New York," in *Explaining the Vote: Presidential Choices in the Nation and the States, 1968,* ed. David M. Kovenock et al. (Chapel Hill: Institute for Research in the Social Sciences, University of North Carolina, 1973), p. 70.

6. See Mark R. Levy and Michael S. Kramer, *The Ethnic Factor: How America's Minorities Decide Elections,* 2d ed. (New York: Simon & Schuster, 1972).

7. John J. Gargan, "Conservative Success in Liberal New York: Some Determinants of Conservative Party Support," in *The Future of Political Parties,* ed. Louis Maisel and Paul M. Sacks (Beverly Hills, Calif.: Sage, 1975), pp. 165–192.

8. "Mandate for Leadership," unpublished history of the 1970 Rockefeller campaign, 1971, Rockefeller Family Archives, Tarrytown, N.Y., chap. 1.

9. *Buffalo Evening News,* November 5, 1966; and *Newsday,* October 2, 1970.

10. Leo Egan, "Can Rockefeller Save the GOP in New York?" *Reporter,* October 30, 1958, p. 10.

11. Guy A. Graves to William Pfeiffer, April 30, 1962, Rockefeller Family Archives.

12. John H. Terry to Art Massolo, September 20, 1967, Rockefeller Family Archives.

13. Ira H. Freeman, "Along the Trail with Rockefeller," *New York Times Magazine,* September 30, 1962.

14. Tom Buckley, "The Three Men behind Rockefeller," *New York Times Magazine,* October 30, 1966. For a description of the 1966 campaign, see James Perry, *The New Politics* (New York: Potter, 1968).

15. Patrick Brosky, "Rockefeller's Efficient Organization," *Newsday*, October 2, 1970.

16. See Joe Alex Morris, *Nelson Rockefeller: A Biography* (New York: Harper & Row, 1960), p. 317.

17. *Schenectady Gazette*, September 10, 1970; *Binghamton Evening News*, October 6, 1970; and *New York Daily News*, October 23, 1970.

18. "Mandate for Leadership," chap. 12.

19. This account is based on Jack Tinker and Partners, *Media Report to the Governor on the 1966 Campaign*, 2 vols., n.d., Rockefeller Family Archives.

20. Perry, *New Politics*, p. 136.

21. "Mandate for Leadership," chap. 24.

22. Hugh Morrow, private interview, April 19, 1973.

23. Press release, Office of the Governor, Rockefeller Family Archives.

24. *Ogdensburg Journal*, September 27, 1962.

25. Morrow, private interview, April 19, 1973.

26. Perry, *New Politics*, chap. 6.

27. U.S. Senate, Committee on Rules and Administration, *Hearings on the Nomination of Nelson A. Rockefeller of New York to Be Vice President of the United States*, 93d Cong., 2d sess., September 23, 1974, p. 696.

28. Ibid., pp. 476–477.

29. Memorandums, John Wells to Rockefeller and Pfeiffer, May 17, 1966, and Wells to Pfeiffer, November 4, 1966, Rockefeller Family Archives.

30. "Mandate for Leadership," chap. 12.

31. *New York Times*, April 19, 1972.

32. In estimating the funds expended in New York gubernatorial races the usual caveats apply. Though reports of campaign expenses to the secretary of state's office are required by state law, no sanctions are applied for late filing or failure to file. Furthermore, these reports are retained for only three years, a circumstance that makes independent multiyear analysis impossible. In addition, the multiplicity of campaign organizations tends to obscure the exact amount spent. In this presentation, therefore, the quadrennial estimates of the *New York Times* are used for comparative purposes under the (dubious?) assumption that these figures, though not necessarily correct, reflect a constant error and therefore allow an accurate presentation of the *relative* position of state Democrats and Republicans. Other estimates are presented, where available, to show the range of estimated Republican spending.

33. *New York Times*, November 11, 1966.

34. Ibid., August 18, 1970.

35. Reports of the Governor's Club to the Secretary of State of New York, January 1–October 23, 1970, and November 24–December 31, 1970, Office of the Secretary of State, Albany.

36. *New York Times*, November 26, 1958; November 29, 1962; and November 30, 1966; Report of the Friends of the Rockefeller Team to the

Secretary of State of New York, October 26–November 29, 1970, Office of the Secretary of State, Albany.

37. The conception of the governor's tasks draws heavily on Richard E. Neustadt, *Presidential Power: The Politics of Leadership* (New York: Wiley, 1960).

38. For a discussion of the legislative leadership, see chap. 4.

39. Albert J. Abrams, secretary of the New York State Senate, private interview, July 12, 1971. Mr. Abrams noted that the position of the state chairman is analogous to that of the national party chairman. He is much more important when his party does not control the executive branch than when it does. See Cornelius P. Cotter and Bernard C. Hennessy, *Politics without Power: The National Party Committees* (New York: Atherton, 1964); and Warren Moscow, *Politics in the Empire State* (New York: Knopf, 1948).

40. *Albany Times-Union*, November 10, 1959. The State Executive Committee now has forty-one members since additional members at large have been added. The aim of this enlargement has been to make the committee more representative of the political forces in the state. Recently Puerto Rican and Labor members were added. (Conversation with Eunice Whittlesey, vice-chairman, Republican State Committee, September 23, 1972.)

41. *Binghamton Press*, April 29, 1959; *Troy Record*, April 10, 1959.

42. *Albany Times-Union*, September 24, 1959.

43. *New York Times*, February 4, 1959, and January 13, 1959.

44. Ibid., June 5, 1959.

45. *Albany Knickerbocker News*, July 10, 1959; *Watertown Times*, July 20, 1959.

46. *Newsday*, February 4, 1959, and April 25, 1959.

47. *New York Herald Tribune*, December 2, 1960.

48. *Kingston Freeman*, October 14, 1959.

49. *Buffalo Evening News*, May 26 and 27, 1960; *Albany Knickerbocker News*, June 10, 1960; *Elmira Star Gazette*, May 27, 1960.

50. *New York Herald Tribune*, May 25, 1960; *Long Island Star-Journal*, July 25, 1960.

51. *Binghamton Sun*, November 29, 1960.

52. Ibid.

53. *Utica Observer Dispatch*, November 29, 1960.

54. *New York Times*, March 21, 1960.

55. *Buffalo Courier Express*, January 26, 1963.

56. Ronald Steinberg, "County Chairmen Survey," mimeographed, 1970, p. 4. This sample, of course, does not take into account the views of the majority of the Republican county leaders who did not respond to the survey. It is in the very nature of patronage that county leaders will not be entirely satisfied with any administration. The demands on them for jobs will always exceed the supply. For the handling of patronage in the Harriman administration, see Daniel P. Moynihan and James Q. Wilson, "Patronage in New York State, 1955–1959," *American Political Science Review* 58 (June 1964):288–301.

57. *Syracuse Post-Standard*, July 20, 1965.

58. *New York Times*, March 12, 1972.

59. Martin Tolchin and Susan Tolchin, *To the Victor: Political Patronage from the Clubhouse to the White House* (New York: Random House, 1971), p. 96.

60. James Q. Wilson, "The Economy of Patronage," *Journal of Political Economy* 69 (August 1961):369–380.

61. Frank J. Sorauf, *Political Parties in the American System* (Boston: Little, Brown, 1964).

62. Richard Rosenbaum, private interview, June 21, 1973.

63. See Chapter 4 for a discussion of gifts and loans to staff members.

64. Carl Spad, private interview, May 2, 1973.

65. Tolchin and Tolchin, *To the Victor*, p. 94.

66. Spad, private interview, May 2, 1973.

67. Philip Weinberg, private interview, June 7, 1973.

68. Rosenbaum, private interview, June 21, 1973.

69. Ibid.

70. This account is based largely on two works: Theodore H. White, *The Making of the President*, 3 vols. (New York: Atheneum, 1961, 1965, and 1969), and Lewis Chester, Godfrey Hodgson, and Bruce Page, *An American Melodrama: The Presidential Campaign of 1968* (New York: Viking Press, 1969).

71. White, *Making of the President, 1960*, p. 81.

72. Chester, Hodgson, and Page, *American Melodrama*, pp. 391–393.

73. White, *Making of the President, 1964*, p. 82.

74. Nelson A. Rockefeller, private interview, January 23, 1976.

75. Joseph Schlesinger, "The Politics of the Executive," in *Politics in the American States*, ed. Jacob and Vines, p. 215.

3. *The Governor and the Legislature*

1. Matters were further complicated by the fact that Mahoney had been a contender for the GOP gubernatorial nomination in 1958. See chap. 2.

2. For information on the efforts of reapportionment, see Richard Lehne, *Reapportionment of the New York Legislature: Impact and Issues* (New York: National Municipal League, 1972).

3. Nelson A. Rockefeller, private interview, July 27, 1971.

4. See A. Lawrence Lowell, "The Influence of Party upon Legislation in England and America," Annual Report of the American Historical Association, 1901, cited in Duane Lockard, *The Politics of State and Local Government*, 2d ed. (New York: Macmillan, 1963), p. 280; and Warren Moscow, *Politics in the Empire State* (New York: Knopf, 1948), p. 170.

5. This phrase was used by Senator Harrison A. Williams, Jr., during Rockefeller's vice-presidential confirmation hearings and quoted in the *New York Times*, October 10, 1974.

6. *New York Times*, June 8, 1974.

7. Peter A. A. Berle, *Does the Citizen Stand a Chance?: The Politics of a State Legislature—New York* (New York: Barron's, 1974), p. 42.

8. *New York Times*, November 16, 1971, and July 11, 1972. See also U.S. House of Representatives, Committee on the Judiciary, *Hearings on the Nomination of Nelson A. Rockefeller of New York to be Vice President of the United States*, 93d Cong., 2d sess., September 24, 1974.

9. Citizens Conference on State Legislatures, *The Sometimes Governments: A Critical Study of the Fifty American Legislatures* (New York: Bantam Books, 1971), p. 156.

10. Eugene J. Gleason, Jr., and Joseph F. Zimmerman, "Executive Dominance in New York State," paper delivered at the Northeast Political Science Association annual meeting, Albany, November 9, 1974. The establishment of a "veto session" of the legislature was endorsed by Governor-elect Carey in November 1974.

11. Sarah P. McCally, "The Governor and His Legislative Party," in *The American Governor in Behavioral Perspective*, ed. Thad Beyle and J. Oliver Williams (New York: Harper & Row, 1972), pp. 151–170.

12. For a further discussion of patronage, see chap. 2.

13. Citizens Conference, *The Sometimes Governments*, p. 268.

14. Stuart K. Witt, "Modernization of the Legislature," *Proceedings of the Academy of Political Science*, 31 (May 1974):49–50.

15. Malcolm E. Jewell, "The Governor as a Legislative Leader," in *American Governor in Behavioral Perspective*, ed. Beyle and Williams, p. 133.

16. Albert J. Abrams, private interview, June 7, 1974.

17. Alan G. Hevesi, "Legislative Leadership in New York State," Ph.D. thesis, Columbia University, 1971, p. 25.

18. Ibid.

19. *New York Times*, March 27, 1964.

20. Hevesi, "Legislative Leadership," p. 115.

21. Rockefeller, private interview, July 27, 1971.

22. *New York Times*, May 18, 1966.

23. For a description of this trend in several states, see James A. Robinson, ed., *State Legislative Innovation* (New York: Praeger, 1973). See also Alan P. Balutis, "The Budgetary Process in New York State: The Role of the Legislative Staff," in *The Political Pursestrings: The Role of the Legislature in the Budgetary Process* (Beverly Hills, Calif.: Sage, 1975), pp. 139–172.

24. Albert J. Abrams, "New York Legislature Tries Harder," *State Government* 46 (Autumn 1973):256–259; Warren M. Anderson, "Institutionalizing Legislative Reform in the New York Senate," *State Government Administration*, July–August 1974; Anderson, private interview, May 27, 1975; Abrams, private interview, June 7, 1974.

25. Alan Rosenthal, *Legislative Performance in the States: Explorations of Committee Behavior* (New York: Free Press, 1974), p. 77.

26. Robert MacCrate, private interview, November 10, 1970; Michael Whiteman, private interview, October 8, 1974.

27. Charles Breitel, "Some Aspects of the Legislative Process," *New York State Bar Association Journal* 21 (July 1949):274–275.

28. Rockefeller, private interview, September 5, 1973.

29. Jewell, "Governor as a Legislative Leader," p. 128.

30. Nelson A. Rockefeller, *Public Papers of Nelson A. Rockefeller, 1965* (Albany: State of New York), p. 1378.

31. See Richard Lehne, *Legislating Reapportionment in New York* (New York: National Municipal League, 1971).

32. *New York Times*, March 17, 25, and 26, 1964.

33. Ibid., April 10, 1970.

34. U.S. Senate, Committee on Rules and Administration, *Hearings on the Nomination of Nelson A. Rockefeller of New York to be Vice President of the United States*, 93d Cong., 2d sess., September 1974, p. 114.

35. On the importance of a chief executive's public reputation, see Richard E. Neustadt, *Presidential Power: The Politics of Leadership* (New York: Wiley, 1960).

36. *New York Times*, March 25, 1964.

37. Ibid.

38. Ibid., April 17, 1974.

39. Ibid., April 11, 1968.

40. Albert J. Abrams, secretary of the Senate, "Senate Administration, 1974," interim report to Senate Majority Leader Warren M. Anderson, mimeographed, n.d.

41. Abrams, private interview, June 7, 1974; Whiteman, private interview, October 8, 1974.

42. *New York Times*, April 11, 1960, and July 3, 1970; Steven Rice, private interview, June 24, 1970.

43. For comparative data see Frank W. Prescott, "The Executive Veto in the American States," *Western Political Quarterly* 3 (January 1950):103; Illinois Legislative Council, "Executive Vetoes after Adjournment of the Legislature," bulletin no. 5-034 (Springfield, Ill., 1964), Appendix.

44. Samuel R. Solomon, "The Governor as Legislator," *National Municipal Review* 40 (November 1951):515–520.

45. MacCrate, private interview, November 10, 1970; Whiteman, private interview, October 8, 1974.

46. In 1917 four items in an appropriation bill were passed over the veto of Governor Whitman. See Samuel R. Solomon, "The Executive Veto in New York," Ph.D. thesis, Maxwell Graduate School of Citizenship and Public Affairs, Syracuse University, 1949, pp. 69–70. In 1976 the legislature overrode a veto by Governor Hugh Carey of the Stavisky-Goodman bill, a measure seeking to increase educational expenditures in New York City despite the constraints of the fiscal crisis. The override was fought bitterly by the governor and was a major blow to gubernatorial power in New York.

47. Whiteman, private interview, October 8, 1974.

48. William J. Keefe and and Morris S. Ogul, *American Legislative Process:*

Congress and the States, 3d ed. (Englewood Cliffs, N.J.: Prentice-Hall, 1973), pp. 380–381.

49. Wayne Francis, *Legislative Issues in the Fifty States* (Chicago: Rand McNally, 1967), p. 11.

50. *New York Times,* March 29, 1968.

51. Ibid., April 3, 1968.

52. Ibid., April 5, 1968.

53. Ibid., May 12, 1968.

54. Ibid., May 19, 1968.

55. Ibid., June 9, 1971.

56. Ibid., July 14, 1971.

57. Ibid., March 8, 1959.

4. The Executive Staff

1. Donald R. Sprengel, "Governors' Staffs: Background and Recruitment Patterns," in *The American Governor in Behavioral Perspective,* ed. Thad Beyle and J. Oliver Williams (New York: Harper & Row, 1972), pp. 106–108.

2. Alan J. Wyner, "Staffing the Governor's Office," in ibid., p. 120.

3. Ibid., p. 124.

4. U.S. Senate, Committee on Rules and Administration, *Report on the Nomination of Nelson A. Rockefeller of New York to Be Vice President of the United States,* 93d Cong., 2d sess., December 3, 1974, pp. 96–104 (hereafter cited as *Report*).

5. U.S. Senate, Committee on Rules and Administration, *Hearings on the Nomination of Nelson A. Rockefeller of New York to Be Vice President of the United States,* 93d Cong., 2d sess., November 13, 1974, p. 472 (hereafter cited as *Hearings*).

6. Senate, *Report,* p. 180.

7. U.S. House of Representatives, Committee on the Judiciary, *Report on the Confirmation of Nelson A. Rockefeller as Vice President of the United States,* 93d Cong., 2d sess., December 17, 1974, p. 25.

8. Ibid.

9. Senate, *Hearings,* September 29, 1974, p. 498.

10. Ibid., pp. 925–926.

11. Frederick C. Mosher, "The Executive Budget, Empire State Style," *Public Administration Review,* 12 (Spring 1952):79–80, as quoted in Donald G. Herzberg and Paul Tillett, *A Budget for New York State, 1956–1957* (University: University of Alabama for the Inter-University Case Program, 1962), pp. 3–4.

12. Robert Herman, private interview, August 11, 1970.

13. T. Norman Hurd, private interview, December 12, 1974.

14. Robert Kerker, private interview, December 31, 1975.

15. William Daniels and James E. Underwood, "Program Innovation and Program Output: The Role of Governor Rockefeller," paper delivered at the

1972 annual meeting of the American Political Science Association, Washington, D.C., September 5, 1972.

16. Alan L. Otten and Charles B. Seit, "Rockefeller's Triple-Threat Brain Trust," *Harper's Magazine* 227 (July 1963):77.

17. Steven Rice, private interview, September 19, 1974.

18. Donald Axelrod, private interview, October 28, 1970.

19. Richard Dunham, private interview, April 4, 1975. See also Allen Shick, *Budget Innovation in the States* (Washington, D.C.: Brookings Institution, 1971), pp. 117–128.

20. Daniels and Underwood, "Program Innovation."

21. Tracy Crown, "The Development of Democratic Government in the State of New York through Growth in the Power of the Executive Since 1910," Ph.D. thesis, New York University, 1955, p. 218.

22. Alan G. Hevesi, "Legislative Leadership in New York State," Ph.D. thesis, Columbia University, 1971, p. 216.

23. Michael Whiteman, private interview, October 8, 1974.

24. Ibid.

25. Steven Rice, private interview, September 19, 1974.

26. Whiteman, private interview, October 8, 1974.

27. Richard T. Johnson, *Managing the White House: An Intimate Study of the Presidency* (New York: Harper & Row, 1974), chap. 1.

28. Theodore Sorenson, *Kennedy* (New York: Harper & Row, 1965), p. 262.

29. *New York Times*, November 25, 1967.

30. Nelson A. Rockefeller, private interview, July 21, 1972.

31. Daniels and Underwood, "Program Innovation," p. 38.

32. Harvey Mansfield, Sr., "Government Commissions," in *International Encyclopedia of the Social Sciences* (New York: Macmillan, 1968), vol. 3, p. 12.

33. Claude Shostel, program assistant, private interview, August 19, 1970.

34. Hugh Morrow, private interview, April 20, 1973.

35. Rockefeller, private interview, July 21, 1972.

36. Ibid.

37. Morrow, private interview, April 20, 1973.

38. Senate, *Hearings*, p. 69.

39. Rockefeller, private interview, July 21, 1972.

40. Morrow, private interview, April 20, 1973.

41. Ron Maiorana, private interview, April 26, 1973.

42. Rockefeller, private interview, July 21, 1972.

43. Ibid.

44. John Moore, private interview, July 7, 1972.

45. Harold W. Case and Allen H. Lerman, eds., *Kennedy and the Press* (New York: Crowell, 1965), p. 239.

46. Bernard C. Hennessy, *Public Opinion*, 2d ed. (Belmont, Calif.: Wadsworth, 1970), p. 307.

47. Robert G. Lehnen, "Public Views of State Governors," in *American*

Governor in Behavioral Perspective, ed. Beyle and Williams, p. 265. In the 1970s, of course, trust in all governmental institutions measured by public opinion polls continued to decline.

48. Ibid., p. 269.

49. On the development of presidential press relations see Elmer Cornwell, *The President and the Press* (Bloomington: Indiana University Press, 1965).

50. Maiorana, private interview, April 26, 1973; Morrow, private interview, September 13, 1973.

51. Ibid.

52. American Institute for Political Communication, *The Federal Government–Daily Press Relationship* (Washington, D.C., 1966), p. 13.

53. *New York Daily News,* July 27, 1972.

54. Maiorana, private interview, April 26, 1973.

55. Richard Zander, private interview, July 1, 1972.

56. *New York Daily News,* July 27, 1972.

57. Rockefeller, private interview, July 21, 1972.

58. Telephone interviews with press officers in these states.

59. Nelson A. Rockefeller, *The Public Papers of Nelson A. Rockefeller, 1959* (Albany: State of New York) pp. 812–819, and *Public Papers, 1965,* pp. 1184–1195.

60. Joseph Persico, private interview, June 6, 1972.

61. See Joseph Persico, "The Rockefeller Speech Writing Operation: New York Gubernatorial Campaign, 1970," mimeographed, Rockefeller Family Archives, Tarrytown, N.Y.

62. Ibid.

63. Ibid.

64. For examples of these programs, see Rockefeller, *Public Papers, 1964,* p. 889; see also ibid., *1965,* pp. 1118–1126. For the use of media in campaigning, see chap. 2.

65. Morrow, private interview, September 13, 1973.

66. Ibid.

67. Political Surveys and Analyses, Inc., "Opinion Survey of New York on Several Key Issues," June 1969.

68. *New York Times,* December 10, 1972.

69. *Niagara Gazette,* November 25, 1972, and November 27, 1972.

70. Rockefeller to Brown, February 21, 1966, Rockefeller Family Archives.

71. See, e.g., *Troy Record,* November 14, 1972, and *Olean Times Herald,* November 27, 1972.

72. *Albany Times-Union,* March 13, 1969.

73. *New York Daily News,* December 31, 1972.

74. *New York Times,* January 4, 1973.

75. See Cornwell, *President and the Press,* p. 247.

76. Ibid. Rockefeller's mail can be compared with that of the governor of

Wisconsin; see David J. Olson, "Citizen Grievance Letters as a Gubernatorial Control Device in Wisconsin," *Journal of Politics* 31 (August 1969):741-755.

77. The attitudes of congressmen concerning their mail are discussed in Charles L. Clapp, *The Congressman: His Work as He Sees It* (Washington, D.C.: Brookings Institution, 1963).

5. *Administration, Reorganization, and Crisis Management*

1. Richard T. Johnson, *Managing the White House: An Intimate Study of the Presidency* (New York: Harper & Row, 1974), p. iv.

2. Cited in Robert A. Caro, *The Power Broker: Robert Moses and the Fall of New York* (New York: Knopf, 1974), pp. 260-261.

3. New York State Civil Service Commission, *Annual Report,* 1961 and 1972.

4. *Book of the States, 1958, 1972, 1975* (Lexington, Ky.: Council of State Governents).

5. Ibid.

6. The Taylor law is discussed in Raymond D. Horton, "Public Employee Labor Relations under the Taylor Law," *Proceedings of the Academy of Political Science* 31 (May 1974):161-174.

7. State of New York, Division of the Budget, *New York State Statistical Yearbook, 1974,* p. 98.

8. *Book of the States, 1972,* p. 185.

9. Edward Kresky, private interview, March 28, 1972.

10. *Attica: The Official Report of the New York State Special Commission on Attica* (New York: Bantam Books, 1972), p. 318.

11. U.S. Senate, Committee on Rules and Administration, *Hearings on the Nomination of Nelson A. Rockefeller of New York to Be Vice President of the United States,* 93d Cong., 2d sess., September 1974, p. 987.

12. T. Norman Hurd, private interview, June 23, 1975.

13. *New York Times,* August 30, 1975.

14. The situation is similar in the president's cabinet. See Richard F. Fenno, Jr., *The President's Cabinet: An Analysis of the Period from Wilson to Eisenhower* (Cambridge: Harvard University Press, 1959).

15. This account is based on a review of sample reports in the Rockefeller Family Archives for the period indicated.

16. For a discussion of the reasons for reorganization, see Frederick C. Mosher, "Organizational Change," in *Governmental Reorganizations: Cases and Commentary* (Indianapolis: Bobbs-Merrill, 1967), pp. 493-514.

17. Harold Seidman, *Politics, Position, and Power: The Dynamics of Federal Organization* (New York: Oxford University Press, 1970), p. 14.

18. Nelson A. Rockefeller, *Public Papers of Nelson A. Rockefeller, 1959* (Albany: State of New York), p. 31.

19. *New York Times,* August 22, 1958.

20. For the text of the report, see Rockefeller, *Public Papers, 1960,* pp. 1331–1394.

21. *New York Times,* January 17, 1960, and October 27, 1961.

22. For a full account of this controversy, see chap. 6.

23. State of New York, Division of the Budget, Department of Transportation Task Force, *Organization of the Department of Transportation,* August 1967.

24. Rockefeller, *Public Papers, 1969,* pp. 921–924.

25. *New York Times,* June 3, 1973.

26. Mosher, "Organizational Change," p. 574.

27. Patrick Bulgaro, private interview, July 1, 1970; Eugene Calahan, private interview, July 2, 1970.

28. Joseph Crook, private interview, July 8, 1970.

29. Robert Kerker, private interview, June 4, 1970.

30. *New York Times,* February 21, 1970.

31. Bulgaro, private interview, July 1, 1970; Calahan, private interview, July 2, 1970.

32. Ibid.

33. See Joint Commission on Mental Illness and Health, *Action for Mental Health* (New York, 1961), p. 12; *Albany Knickerbocker News,* August 1, 1960.

34. John Cumming, private interview, October 23, 1970; and Hyman M. Forstenzer, "New York's New Directions in Mental Health Services," *State Government* 37 (Autumn 1964):235–241.

35. Cumming, private interview, October 23, 1970; Paul Thomas, legislative liaison for the Department of Mental Hygiene, private interview, July 27, 1970; Hugo Gentilcore, private interview, November 18, 1970; Kerker, private interview, June 4, 1970.

36. Ibid.

37. State of New York, Department of Mental Hygiene, *Annual Report, 1959.*

38. Kerker, private interview, June 4, 1970; Barry Van Laer, private interview, July 21, 1970; *New York Times,* April 6, 1973.

39. Kerker, private interview, June 4, 1970.

40. Ibid.

41. State of New York, *Hearings of the Joint Legislative Committee on Mental and Physical Handicaps,* October 22, 1969, testimony of Jacob Schneider and Erwin Mauser.

42. State of New York, Department of Mental Hygiene, Division of Mental Health, *Budget Preamble—1969–70,* p. 8.

43. *New York Times,* October 29, 1974. But for the unanticipated effect of geriatric screening on nursing homes in the state, see above, p. 157.

44. See State of New York, *Hearings of the Joint Legislative Committee on Mental and Physical Handicaps.*

45. *New York Times,* October 29, 1974.

46. Ibid., November 8 and 17, 1974.

47. The creation of this structure is described in Caro, *Power Broker,* chap. 10.

48. The circumstances surrounding this charge are discussed in Caro, *Power Broker,* chap. 46. For a fuller discussion of environmental programs, see chap. 9.

49. Rockefeller, *Public Papers, 1972,* pp. 958–959.

50. *New York Times,* January 6, 1964. For a further discussion of this case, see chap. 2.

51. State of New York, Division of the Budget, *Management Survey of the State Liquor Authority,* December 1963, chap. 2.

52. Ibid., sec. 3, p. 13.

53. Thomas Ring, private interview, July 27, 1970. See also State of New York, Division of the Budget, *Management Survey of the State Liquor Authority,* sec. 3.

54. Rockefeller, *Public Papers, 1964,* p. 125.

55. *New York Times,* March 13, 1964.

56. A detailed account of the battle in the legislature is given in chap. 3.

57. Ring, private interview, July 27, 1970.

58. Vincent La Fleche, management analyst, private interview, June 10, 1970.

59. Ibid.

60. *New York Times,* February 7, 1967.

61. Ibid., March 4, 1967.

62. Ibid., March 16, 1967.

63. Ibid., March 17, 1967.

64. State of New York, Division of the Budget, *Management Survey of the State Commission for Human Rights,* Interim Summary Report, May 1, 1967.

65. *New York Times,* March 28, 1968.

66. Ibid., May 27, 1970.

67. Ibid., February 20, 1969, and October 7, 1969.

68. Rockefeller, *Public Papers, 1970,* p. 650.

69. *New York Times,* February 8, 1973.

70. Unless otherwise indicated, this account relies on *Attica: The Official Report of the New York State Special Commission on Attica* (New York: Bantam Books, 1972), also known as the McKay Commission Report. See also Gerald Benjamin and Stephen P. Rappaport, "Attica and Prison Reform," *Proceedings of the Academy of Political Science* 31 (May 1974):200–213.

71. U.S. House of Representatives, Committee on the Judiciary, *Hearings on the Nomination of Nelson A. Rockefeller of New York to Be Vice President of the United States,* 93d Cong., 2d sess., November 21, 1974, p. 164.

72. Thomas Malone, private interview, July 21, 1971.

73. State of New York, Division of the Budget, *New York State Executive Budget,* 1968 and 1972.

74. Allan Nevins, *Herbert H. Lehman and His Era* (New York: Scribner, 1963), pp. 121–122.

75. Tom Wicker, *A Time to Die* (New York: Quadrangle Books, 1975), p. 215.

76. For a highly critical account, see ibid., chap. 12.

77. *New York Times,* December 31, 1976.

78. Ibid., June 12, 1973.

6. *Fiscal Policies and Financial Programs*

1. William Safire, *The New Language of Politics: A Dictionary of Catchwords, Slogans, and Political Usage,* 2d ed. (New York: Macmillan, 1972), p. 625.

2. State of New York, Division of the Budget, Intergovernmental Relations Group, "Trends in Federal, State and Local Expenditures and Taxes," mimeographed, April 15, 1974, p. 2.

3. Seymour Sacks, "Financing the State," *Proceedings of the Academy of Political Science* 31 (May 1974):129.

4. Advisory Commission on Intergovernmental Relations, *Federal-State-Local Finances: Significant Features of Fiscal Federalism* (Washington, D.C.: Government Printing Office, 1977), p. 58.

5. Nelson A. Rockefeller, *Public Papers of Nelson A. Rockefeller, 1959* (Albany: State of New York), p. 1104.

6. Rockefeller, *Public Papers, 1961,* p. 998.

7. Rockefeller, *Public Papers, 1962,* p. 1314.

8. Ibid., p. 60.

9. New York State Constitutional Convention, *Report of the Special Study Commission on Taxation and Finance* (Albany, 1967), p. 44.

10. Rockefeller, *Public Papers, 1965,* pp. 56–57.

11. Rockefeller, *Public Papers, 1971,* p. 1132. The legislative politics of public finance are discussed in detail in chap. 3.

12. Ibid., p. 1623.

13. Michael P. McKeating, "New York's Tired Economy Is Going Flat," *Empire State Reports* 1 (September 1975):328.

14. Ibid.

15. Nelson A. Rockefeller, *The Future of Federalism* (Cambridge: Harvard University Press, 1962), p. 24; emphasis in the original.

16. Rockefeller, *Public Papers 1961,* p. 996.

17. Ibid., p. 41.

18. For a scathing Democratic critique of Rockefeller's budgetary practices during these years, see Jack E. Bronston, "Pay-As-You-Go: The Great Hoax," reprinted in U.S. House of Representatives, Committee on the Judiciary, *Hearings on the Nomination of Nelson A. Rockefeller of New York to Be Vice President of the United States,* 93d Cong., 2d sess., 1974, pp. 1094–1105.

19. Rockefeller, *Public Papers, 1967,* pp. 10, 11. For a full discussion, see chap. 10.

20. Rockefeller, *Public Papers 1968,* p. 11.

21. Rockefeller, *Public Papers, 1969,* p. 44.

22. Ibid., p. 47.

23. Rockefeller, *Public Papers, 1970,* pp. 55–56.

24. Rockefeller, *Public Papers, 1971,* p. 137.

25. Ibid., p. 1075.

26. Advisory Commission on Intergovernmental Relations, *Federal-State-Local Finances,* pp. 82–83.

27. Rockefeller, *Public Papers, 1962,* pp. 52–53.

28. Commission on the Quality, Cost, and Financing of Elementary and Secondary Education in New York State, *The Fleishmann Report,* (New York: Viking Press, 1973), vol. 2, pp. 150–51.

29. The Governor's Committee to Study Per Capita Aid, "Report to the Governor" (mimeo), December 1, 1970, p. 9.

30. Ibid.

31. See *Report of the Temporary State Commission on State and Local Finances,* 3 vols. (Albany, 1975), vol. 1.

32. Donna E. Shalala, "State Aid to Local Government," *Proceedings of the Academy of Political Science* 31 (May 1974):59.

33. Ibid.

34. *Book of the States, 1974–75* (Lexington, Ky.: Council of State Governments), pp. 388–389.

35. All figures are from State of New York, Budget Division, *Executive Budget, 1959* and *Executive Budget, 1974.*

36. For a further discussion of the Budget Division, see chap. 4.

37. State of New York, Budget Division, *Executive Budget, 1959* and *Executive Budget, 1974.*

38. Note that this figure includes only federal aid not appropriated in the state general purposes budget and presented in summary table 17 in annual budget documents. Revenue sharing funds and some other federal aid are appropriated and are thus excluded from this figure. Total federal aid to New York State in fiscal 1972/73 was $4.051 billion.

39. U.S. House of Representatives, Committee on Government Operations, *Hearings on Federal-State-Local Relations,* 85th Cong., 1st sess., 1957, p. 146.

40. U.S. Senate, Committee on Government Operations, Subcommittee on Intergovernmental Relations, *Hearings on the Intergovernmental Revenue Act of 1971,* 92d Cong., 1st sess., 1971, p. 216.

41. See Clay Richards and Carol Richards, "New York's Raid on the U.S. Treasury," *Empire State Reports* 1 (May 1975):201.

42. For a more general critique of the categorical grant program, see chap. 10.

43. U.S. Senate, *Hearings on the Intergovernmental Revenue Act,* p. 216.

44. See U.S. Congress, Joint Economic Committee, Subcommittee on Fiscal Policy, *Hearings on Revenue Sharing and Its Alternatives,* 90th Cong., 1st sess., 1967, pp. 269–283; *New York Times,* October 6, 1970.

45. Rockefeller recounted this story in several places. See, e.g., his address

before the American Political Science Association, New Orleans, September 5, 1973, pp. 12–13.

46. U.S. Senate, Committee on Government Operations, Subcommittee on Intergovernmental Relations, *Hearings on Creative Federalism*, 90th Cong., 1st sess., 1967, p. 549.

47. U.S. House of Representatives, Committee on Government Operations, Subcommittee on Intergovernmental Relations, *Hearings on Grant Consolidation and Intergovernmental Relations*, 91st Cong., 1st sess., 1969, p. 87.

48. Ibid., p. 89.

49. Advisory Commission on Intergovernmental Relations, *The Gap between Federal Aid Authorization and Appropriations for Major Agencies, FY 1966–1970* (Washington, D.C.: Government Printing Office, 1970), p. 4.

50. Terry Sanford, *Storm over the States* (New York: McGraw-Hill, 1967).

51. James L. Sundquist and David W. Davis, *Making Federalism Work: A Study of Program Coordination at the Community Level* (Washington, D.C.: Brookings Institution, 1969), chap. 7.

52. Rockefeller, *Public Papers, 1963*, p. 722.

53. State of New York, Budget Division, *Executive Budget, 1959*, and *Executive Budget, 1974*.

54. State of New York, Department of Audit and Control, Office of the State Comptroller, *Public Authorities in New York State* (Albany, December 31, 1974), p. 11.

55. Rudy Renko and Frank Mahoney, private interview, May 6, 1975.

56. Ibid.

57. Rockefeller, *Public Papers, 1959*, p. 1039.

58. Rockefeller, *Public Papers, 1961*, p. 55.

59. Rockefeller, *Public Papers, 1960*, p. 11.

60. Rockefeller, *Public Papers, 1961*, p. 1000.

61. Rockefeller, *Public Papers, 1963*, p. 1259.

62. State of New York, Department of Audit and Control, Office of the State Comptroller, *Annual Report of the Comptroller* (Albany, 1964), p. 24. (See Table 1.)

63. Rockefeller, *Public Papers, 1961*, p. 1003. For a further discussion of this $100 million special bond issue for parks, see chap. 9.

64. Rockefeller, *Public Papers, 1965*, p. 56.

65. Ibid., p. 1199.

66. Ibid., p. 13.

67. Ibid., p. 1201.

68. Rockefeller, *Public Papers, 1966*, p. 55.

69. Rockefeller, *Public Papers, 1967*, p. 802.

70. 268 N.Y. 52 (1935). Cited in W. Bernard Richland, "Constitutional City Home Rule in New York," *Columbia Law Review* 54 (March 1954):333.

71. See Robert A. Caro, *The Power Broker: Robert Moses and the Fall of New York* (New York: Knopf, 1974).

72. New York State Constitution, art. 7, sec. 11.

73. Ibid., art. 10, sec. 5, and art. 8, sec. 8.

74. State of New York, Department of Audit and Control, *Public Authorities in New York State*, pp. 52–56.

75. *New York Times*, August 1, 1960. For an example of a moral-obligation clause in state legislation establishing a public benefit corporation, see Bureau of Planning and Research, Office of the State Comptroller, *Comptroller's Special Report on the Public Debt of the State of New York, 1961–1971* (Albany, June 1971).

76. *New York Times*, March 25, 1960.

77. State of New York, Office of the Comptroller, "Debt-Like Commitments of the State of New York," in *Studies on Issues in Public Finances*, no. 2 (January 1973), p. 19, and memorandum, EJB to T. Norman Hurd, June 30, 1974, p. 2.

78. Rockefeller, *Public Papers, 1965*, p. 951.

79. Myer Kutz, *Rockefeller Power* (New York: Simon & Schuster, 1974), p. 91.

80. Eleanore Corruth, "What Price Glory on the Albany Mall," *Fortune* 84 (June 1971):94.

81. Rockefeller, *Public Papers, 1964*, p. 1213.

82. *New York Times*, January 26, 1975; Bureau of Planning and Research, *Comptroller's Special Report on the Public Debt*, p. 10.

83. *Moody's Bond Survey*, March 19, 1973, p. 1079.

84. Corruth, "What Price Glory," p. 94.

85. *New York Times*, January 26, 1975.

86. Ibid.

87. Corruth, "What Price Glory," p. 167. See also *New York Times*, July 2, 1976.

88. *New York Times*, June 24, 1976, and January 31, 1977.

89. Office of the Comptroller, *Studies on Issues in Public Finances*, no. 2, pp. 27–28.

90. Ibid., pp. 32–33.

91. Ibid., p. 35.

92. See State of New York, Office of the Comptroller, "Statewide Public Authorities: A Fourth Branch of Government," *Special Studies on Public Finance*, no. 1, November 1972.

93. *New York Times*, February 16, 1975. For further details on the UDC crises, see chap. 7.

94. *New York Times*, November 28, 1975; December 14, 1975; January 16, 1976; February 11, 1976.

95. *New York Times*, March 21, 1976. Other funds could be borrowed but would be secured only by the revenue flow from the projects and not by the moral obligation of the state.

96. *New York Times*, October 6, 1962.

97. Ibid., June 10, 1963.

98. Ibid.

99. Ibid., June 13, 1963.

100. Rockefeller, *Public Papers, 1964*, pp. 42–43.

101. *New York Times,* September 30, 1963.

102. Ibid., September 27, 1963.

103. State of New York, Office of the Comptroller, *Preliminary Annual Financial Report, 1974*, p. 16.

104. Memorandum, EJB to T. Norman Hurd, June 30, 1974, p. 3.

105. Rockefeller, *Public Papers, 1965*, p. 1367.

106. Finance Committee, *Report of the Temporary State Commission on the Constitutional Convention,* (Albany, 1967), p. 67.

107. William E. Mitchell, "The Effectiveness of Debt Limits on State and Local Borrowing," *The Bulletin,* no. 45, Graduate School of Business Administration, New York University, October 1967.

7. *The Governor and Urban Problems*

1. William L. Riordon, ed., *Plunkett of Tammany Hall* (New York: Dutton, 1963), pp. 21–22.

2. See Frank J. Macchiarola, "The State and the City," *Proceedings of the Academy of Political Science* 31 (May 1974):104–118.

3. See chap. 2 for a full discussion of political trends.

4. See Rinker Buck, "Asking Cities to Spend More and Get Less," *Empire State Report* 1 (May 1975):187.

5. John N. Kolesar, "The Governors and the Urban Areas," in *The American Governor in Behavioral Perspective,* ed. Thad Beyle and J. Oliver Williams (New York: Harper & Row, 1972), p. 240.

6. See J. Stephen Turett, "The Vulnerability of American Governors, 1900–1969," in ibid., pp. 17–30; and Robert G. Lehnen, "Public Views of State Governors," in ibid., pp. 258–269.

7. Nelson A. Rockefeller, *Public Papers of Nelson A. Rockefeller, 1961* (Albany: State of New York), p. 1290.

8. Rockefeller, *Public Papers 1963,* p. 722.

9. Daniel J. Elazar, *American Federalism: A View from the States* (New York: Crowell, 1972), pp. 194–195.

10. Quoted in W. Bernard Richland, "Constitutional City Home Rule in New York," *Columbia Law Review* 54 (March 1954):319.

11. See James Bryce, *The American Commonwealth* (New York: Macmillan, 1888), vol. 2.

12. See Kenneth E. Vanlandingham, "Municipal Home Rule in the United States," *William and Mary Law Review* 10 (Winter 1968):279.

13. Wallace S. Sayre and Herbert Kaufman, *Governing New York City: Politics in the Metropolis* (New York: Russell Sage Foundation, 1961), pp. 584–585.

14. Ibid., p. 585.

15. "Note: Home Rule and the New York Constitution," *Columbia Law Review* 66 (June 1966):1145–1163.

16. Sayre and Kaufman, *Governing New York City*, p. 585.

17. See John F. Dillon, *Commentaries on the Law of Municipal Corporations*, 5th ed. (Boston: Little, Brown, 1911). The contrary Cooley's rule, followed in a few states, holds that there is an inherent right of local self-government.

18. 251 N.Y. 467 (1929).

19. Quoted in "Note: Home Rule and the New York Constitution," p. 1150.

20. Ibid.

21. Ibid., p. 1154.

22. Rockefeller, *Public Papers, 1962*, pp. 1279, 1302.

23. See the following works by Frank Macchiarola: "Constitutional Statutory and Judicial Restraints on Local Finance in New York State," *New York Law Forum* 15 (Winter 1969):852–872; "The Theory and Practice of State and Local Government Relations in New York State," *Albany Law Review* 33 (Spring 1969):491–518; and "Municipal Home Rule in New York," *Syracuse Law Review* 22 (1971):736–747.

24. See Macchiarola, "The State and the City," p. 104.

25. See Buck, "Asking Cities to Spend More," p. 167.

26. *Empire State Report* 1 (February–March 1975).

27. *New York Times*, October 11, 1975.

28. Statistics for the "Big Six" cities are used for several reasons. They are the most important cities in the state and have attempted to act in political concert in recent years. In addition, they are the only jurisdictions in the state with dependent school districts, that is, they pay school costs out of the general municipal budget. In other regions, independent school districts tax separately for education; statistics for these regions are therefore not comparable with those for the "Big Six."

29. Jerry Wade, "Changes in the Distribution of State Aid Programs in New York State, 1959–1969," in *Local Government Finances in New York State, 1959–1969*, ed. Jesse Burkhead, Report to the New York State Temporary Commission on the Powers of Local Government, October 1971; Donna E. Shalala and Jerry Wade, *State Aid to New York City, 1961–1971*, Report to the New York City Commission on City-State Relations, June 1972; and Richard Lehne, *Reapportionment of the New York Legislature: Impact and Issues* (New York: National Municipal League, 1972); all cited in Donna E. Shalala, "State Aid to Local Government," *Proceedings of the Academy of Political Science* 31 (May 1974):99.

30. Shalala, "State Aid to Local Government," p. 97.

31. Seymour Sacks, "Financing the State," *Proceedings of the Academy of Political Science* 31 (May 1974):125–126.

32. Ibid., p. 126.

33. Donald Walsh, private interview, September 10, 1974.

34. This list of objectives has been compiled from a review of the New York State Council of Mayors annual programs for the period 1959–1973.

35. Walsh, private interview, September 10, 1974.

36. T. Norman Hurd, private interview, June 23, 1975.

37. Walsh, private interview, September 10, 1974.

38. New York State, Office of the Governor, press release, February 29, 1970; and Rockefeller, *Public Papers, 1970*, p. 1162.

39. Rockefeller, *Public Papers, 1970*, p. 1162.

40. See the case study on the politics of budgeting in chap. 3.

41. George von Frank, private interview, June 21, 1973.

42. Rockefeller, *Public Papers, 1962*, p. 771.

43. Rockefeller, *Public Papers, 1969*, p. 1506.

44. Rockefeller, *Public Papers, 1965*, p. 1012.

45. *New York Times*, February 18, 1968.

46. Ibid., January 19, 1972.

47. Ibid.

48. Ibid.

49. Von Frank, private interview, June 21, 1973.

50. Ibid.

51. *New York Times*, May 12, 1972.

52. Frank S. Kristof, "Housing," *Proceedings of the Academy of Political Science* 31 (May 1974):190.

53. Rockefeller, *Public Papers, 1960*, p. 1446.

54. Rockefeller, *Public Papers, 1959*, pp. 830–842.

55. Ibid., p. 1099.

56. For further discussion of the Housing Finance Agency, see chap. 6.

57. State of New York, Study Commission for New York City, "New York City's Mitchell-Lama Housing Program," 1973.

58. Robert E. McCabe, speech delivered at Lake Placid before the New York State Association of Housing and Urban Renewal Officials, June 16, 1970; see also Rockefeller, *Public Papers, 1968*, p. 191.

59. Rockefeller, *Public Papers, 1968*, p. 15.

60. Ibid., pp. 191–195; Kristof, "Housing," p. 195.

61. See chap. 3 for a description of political bargaining.

62. See U.S. Senate, Committee on Rules and Administration, *Hearings on the Nomination of Nelson A. Rockefeller of New York to Be Vice President of the United States*, 93d Cong., 2d sess., 1974, p. 996 (hereafter cited as *Hearings*).

63. *New York Times*, July 16, 1972.

64. Ibid., June 21, 1972.

65. Nelson A. Rockefeller, private interview, July 21, 1972.

66. U.S. Senate, *Hearings*, p. 997.

67. For further discussions of the UDC crisis, see Steven R. Weisman,

"Rockefeller's Pill: The UDC," *Washington Monthly* 7 (June 1975):35–44; and Timothy Clark, "The Rapid Rise and Fall of the UDC," *Empire State Report* 1 (April 1975):110, and "The UDC Crisis: Future Fallout in New York Bonds," *Empire State Report* 1 (May 1975):170. See also *New York Times* summary article on March 9, 1975.

68. Weisman, "Rockefeller's Pill," p. 43.

69. Hugh Morrow, private interview, April 2, 1975.

70. *New York Times*, March 28, 1975.

71. Rockefeller, *Public Papers, 1962*, p. 763.

72. Ibid., p. 1042.

73. *New York Times*, March 9, 1965.

74. Ibid., February 4, 1966.

75. Ibid., February 3 and 24, 1966.

76. Ibid., April 3 and 30, 1966.

77. Ibid., August 18, 1966.

78. Alan Chartock, "Narcotics Addiction: The Politics of Frustration," *Proceedings of the Academy of Political Science* 31 (May 1974):244.

79. *New York Times*, August 31, 1973.

80. Anthony Cagliostro, deputy director, Narcotics Addiction Control Commission, "Criminal Justice and the Treatment of Addicts: Co-options and Conflicts," speech delivered before the Sixth Annual Eagleville Conference on Alcoholism and Drugs, Eagleville, Pa., June 8, 1973.

81. *Attack* 5 (Fall–Winter 1972).

82. *New York Times*, February 4, 1973.

83. Anthony Cagliostro, private interview, June 22, 1973.

84. *New York Times*, January 4, 1973.

85. Ibid., January 23 and February 2, 1973. See also Chartock, "Narcotics Addiction," p. 246.

86. *New York Times*, January 23, 1973.

87. Ibid., April 28, 1973.

88. Ibid., May 13, 1973.

89. Ibid., August 2, 5, and 16, 1973.

90. Ibid., November 10, 1974.

91. Ibid., November 19 and 28, 1974.

92. Ibid., December 2, 1973.

93. John Mladinov, private interview, July 22, 1971.

94. Ibid. See also Rockefeller, *Public Papers, 1962*, p. 1126.

95. Nelson A. Rockefeller, speech delivered before the American Political Science Association (APSA) convention, New Orleans, September 5, 1973.

96. *New York Times*, April 28, 1966, and December 3, 1968.

97. *New York Times*, February 26, 1965.

98. Rockefeller, APSA speech and *Public Papers, 1965*, p. 1396.

99. Rockefeller, APSA speech.

100. For a further discussion of the creation of the Department of Transportation, see chap. 5.

101. See Robert A. Caro, *The Power Broker: Robert Moses and the Fall of New York* (New York: Knopf, 1974), chap. 49. See also U.S. Senate, *Hearings,* p. 499, and *New York Times,* October 10, 1974.

102. Rockefeller, private interview, July 21, 1971.

103. *New York Times,* March 23 and 29, 1967. For a further discussion of the bridge project, see chap. 9.

104. *New York Times,* November 1 and 12, 1974.

105. Ibid., June 3, 1974.

106. Joseph F. Zimmerman, "Public Transportation," *Proceedings of the Academy of Political Science* 31 (May 1974):220.

107. *New York Times,* April 6, 1975.

108. U.S. Senate, *Hearings,* p. 955.

109. Zimmerman, "Public Transportation," pp. 220, 223.

110. U.S. Senate, *Hearings,* p. 499.

111. Rockefeller, *Public Papers, 1960,* p. 1562.

112. Ibid.

113. Rockefeller, *Public Papers, 1968,* pp. 1298–1300.

114. Ibid., *1971,* pp. 91, 1116.

115. Ibid., p. 1116.

116. Ibid., *1960,* pp. 1380–1383.

117. Blanche Bernstein, "The State and Social Welfare," *Proceedings of the Academy of Political Science* 31 (May 1974):148–149.

118. Rockefeller, *Public Papers, 1969,* p. 1015.

119. *New York Times,* March 30, 1969.

120. Rockefeller, *Public Papers, 1971,* p. 91.

121. Bernstein, "State and Social Welfare," pp. 153–155.

122. See testimony of Arthur Eve, U.S. House of Representatives, Committee on the Judiciary, *Hearings on the Nomination of Nelson A. Rockefeller to Be Vice President of the United States,* 93d Cong., 2d sess., November 21, 22, 25, 27, and December 25, 1974 (hereafter cited as *Hearings*).

123. *New York Times,* March 29, 1971.

124. Rockefeller, private interview, August 17, 1971.

125. New York State, Office of Welfare Inspector General, "First Annual Report, 1971–72" (mimeo).

126. Bernstein, "State and Social Welfare," p. 154.

127. Ibid., p. 152.

128. George Berlinger, private interview, August 6, 1974.

129. Drucker's comments are in his introduction to Dan W. Lufkin, *Many Sovereign States: A Case for Strengthening State Government* (New York: McKay, 1975), p. 211. Eve is quoted in U.S. House of Representatives, *Hearings,* p. 296.

8. *Expanding Opportunities for Higher Education*

1. *New York Times,* October 5, 1958.

2. Calvin Tompkins, "Profile of Samuel Gould," *New Yorker,* November 18, 1967, p. 96.

3. Donald Axelrod, "Higher Education," *Proceedings of the Academy of Political Science* 31 (May 1974):131–145.

4. This institution was not the same as the State University of New York (SUNY).

5. The term of the regents was reduced to seven years in 1974. See Amy Plumer, "Whither the Board of Regents," *Empire State Report* 2 (December 1976):41.

6. Ibid., p. 40.

7. See above, n. 4.

8. For a history of higher education, see Frank C. Abbott, *Government Policy and Higher Education: A Study of the Regents of the University of the State of New York, 1784–1949* (Ithaca, N.Y.: Cornell University Press, 1958).

9. See Richard Scher, "The State and Private Colleges and Universities," Ph.D. thesis, Teachers College, Columbia University, 1972, p. 91.

10. Ibid., p. 97.

11. Ibid., p. 98.

12. Ibid., p. 103.

13. See John S. Allen, "New York Colleges Prepare for the Veterans," *Journal of Higher Education* 17 (May 1946):247–248, and "Higher Education in the State of New York," ibid. (October 1946):347–350.

14. Allen, "New York Colleges," pp. 247–248.

15. Abbott, *Government Policy and Higher Education,* p. 206.

16. *New York Times,* January 23 and 24, 1946. For a general treatment of the role of the Unity Committee in New York City at this time, see Gerald Benjamin, *Race Relations and the New York City Commission on Human Rights* (Ithaca, N.Y.: Cornell University Press, 1974), chap. 3.

17. *New York Times,* January 26, 1946.

18. Ibid., February 5, 1946.

19. Oliver C. Carmichael, Jr., *New York Establishes a State University: A Case Study in the Processes of Policy Formation* (Nashville: Vanderbilt University Press, 1955), p. 128.

20. Ibid., p. 116.

21. Ibid., pp. 215–218.

22. *New York Times,* November 24, 1948.

23. Ibid., February 26, 1949.

24. Ibid., April 1, 1949.

25. State of New York, Budget Division, *Executive Budget, 1949* and *Executive Budget, 1958.*

26. Alvin C. Eurich, "State University of New York: Ten Years Young," *Educational Record* 32 (January 1959):56–63.

27. "Trustees O.K. Master Plan for New York State University," *Journal of Education* 133 (March 1960):93.

28. Charles Foster, private interview, August 3, 1970.

29. Frank C. Moore, private interview, October 28, 1970. See also *New York Times,* December 17, 1954.

30. Tompkins, "Profile of Samuel Gould," pp. 100–102.

31. Scher, "State and Private Colleges," p. 178.

32. Nelson A. Rockefeller, *Public Papers of Nelson A. Rockefeller, 1959* (Albany: State of New York), p. 1160.

33. *New York Times,* December 12, 1973.

34. Moore, private interview, October 28, 1970.

35. Freda R. H. Martens, "Decision Making for Higher Education in New York State," Ph.D. thesis, Harvard University, 1966, p. 14.

36. Rockefeller, *Public Papers, 1959,* p. 1023. See also Scher, "State and Private Colleges," pp. 183–184.

37. Scher, "State and Private Colleges," pp. 186–187.

38. Rockefeller, *Public Papers, 1960,* p. 25.

39. Scher, "State and Private Colleges," p. 187; and Rockefeller, *Public Papers, 1960,* p. 1589.

40. Rockefeller, *Public Papers, 1960,* p. 1590.

41. Axelrod, "Higher Education," pp. 131–145.

42. Ibid., pp. 134–135.

43. Rockefeller, *Public Papers, 1961,* p. 6.

44. *New York Times,* January 16, 1961.

45. Trustees of the State University of New York, *Master Plan* (Albany, 1960).

46. Rockefeller, *Public Papers, 1961,* p. 43.

47. Ibid., pp. 43–53.

48. Robert MacCrate, memorandum on the development of the Scholar Incentive Program, December 11, 1963, pp. 1–2.

49. Ibid., p. 2.

50. Ibid.

51. Rockefeller, *Public Papers, 1961,* p. 42.

52. Lorne Woollatt, private interview, August 3, 1970.

53. *New York Times,* February 1, 1961.

54. Robert MacCrate, private interview, November 10, 1970.

55. James E. Allen, private interview, November 24, 1970.

56. MacCrate, memorandum, p. 7.

57. *New York Times,* March 16, 1961.

58. Rockefeller, *Public Papers, 1961,* p. 477.

59. See New York State, Budget Division, *Executive Budget, 1962,* and *Executive Budget, 1967.*

60. Rockefeller, *Public Papers, 1962,* pp. 1308–1309.

61. New York State Legislative Committee on Expenditure Review, *State University Construction Fund Program*, 1972, p. 81.

62. Scher, "State and Private Colleges," p. 479.

63. Paul G. Bulger, private interview, October 29, 1970.

64. Rockefeller, *Public Papers, 1966*, p. 1565.

65. Allen, private interview, November 24, 1970.

66. *New York Times*, March 5, 1967.

67. Select Committee on the Future of Private and Independent Higher Education in New York State, *New York State and Private Higher Education* (Albany, 1968), p. 13.

68. Ibid.

69. Ibid., p. 23.

70. Ibid., p. 46.

71. Max J. Rubin, private interview, November 2, 1970.

72. Select Committee, *New York State and Private Higher Education*, p. 47.

73. Ibid., p. 55.

74. Ibid., p. 56.

75. Ibid., p. 38.

76. *New York Times*, March 30, 1968.

77. Bulger, private interview, October 29, 1970.

78. Francis Horn, private interview, August 18, 1970.

79. See Axelrod, "Higher Education," p. 141.

80. *Report of the Select Legislative Committee on Higher Education* (1974), legislative document no. 6, pp. 30–31.

81. State University Construction Fund, *Questions and Answers* (Albany, 1975), p. 9.

82. Frank J. Macchiarola, "The State and the City," *Proceedings of the Academy of Political Science* 31 (May 1974):116.

83. T. Norman Hurd, private interview, June 25, 1975.

84. *New York Times*, May 27, 1973.

85. Hurd, private interview, June 25, 1975.

9. *The Quality of Life*

1. Nelson A. Rockefeller, *Public Papers of Nelson A. Rockefeller, 1964*, pp. 1, 198–201.

2. New York State Laws, 1949, chap. 666. See also J. Clarence Davies III, *The Politics of Pollution* (New York: Pegasus, 1970), p. 37; and Roscoe C. Martin, *Water for New York: A Study in the State Administration of Water Resources* (Syracuse, N.Y.: Syracuse University Press, 1960), p. 2.

3. State of New York, *Report of the Joint Legislative Committee on Natural Resources*, legislative document no. 72, 1954, pp. 159–63; and U.S. House of Representatives, Committee on Governmental Operations, *Hearings on Water Pollution Control and Abatement*, 88th Cong., 1st sess., May 21–June 5, 1963, p. 1557 (hereafter cited as *Hearings*).

4. Andrew C. Fleck, private interview, November 18, 1970. See also Harvey Lieber, "Politics of Air and Water Pollution in the New York Metropolitan Area," Ph.D. thesis, Columbia University, 1968.

5. *City of Utica* v. *Water Pollution Control Board*, 5 New York 2d 164, 156 N.E. 2d 301, 182 New York State 2d 584 (1959); and *New York Times*, January 23, 1959.

6. State of New York, Joint Legislative Committee on Interstate Cooperation, *Progress Report of the Special Committee on Pollution Abatement*, legislative document no. 59, 1948, pp. 57–58.

7. U.S. Department of Health, Education, and Welfare, *Proceedings of the Conference in the Matter of Pollution of the Interstate Waters of the Hudson River and Its Tributaries—New York and New Jersey*, 2 vols. (Washington, D.C.: Government Printing Office, 1965), vol. 1, p. 69 (hereafter cited as *Proceedings*).

8. Joint Legislative Committee on Interstate Cooperation, *Progress Report of the Special Committee*, p. 31.

9. State of New York, *Report of the Joint Legislative Committee on Natural Resources*, legislative document no. 22, 1959, pp. 231–233.

10. Rockefeller, *Public Papers, 1962*, pp. 1269–1270.

11. U.S. House of Representatives, *Hearings*, p. 1559.

12. State of New York, *Report of the Joint Legislative Committee on Natural Resources*, p. 202.

13. *New York Times*, March 23, 1965.

14. Richard Wiebe, private interview, July 10, 1970.

15. Nelson A. Rockefeller, private interview, August 17, 1971.

16. Fleck, private interviews, July 29 and November 18, 1970.

17. Ibid., July 29, 1970.

18. Rockefeller, *Public Papers, 1964*, p. 1109.

19. Council on Environmental Quality, *Environmental Quality: The First Annual Report* (Washington, D.C., 1970), p. 32.

20. Wiebe, private interview, July 10, 1970.

21. *New York Times*, July 15, 1965.

22.. U.S. Department of Health, Education, and Welfare, *Proceedings*, vol. 2, p. 438.

23. State of New York, Department of Environmental Conservation, *Pure Waters Progress in New York State*, July 1, 1974, Appendixes A, B, and C, pp. 23–27.

24. State of New York, Department of Audit and Control, Office of the State Comptroller, Division of Audits and Accounts, *Audit on the Pure Waters Program*, Managerial Survey, October 27, 1972; and Department of Environmental Conservation, Division of Pure Waters, *Quarterly Report of Status of Federal and State Grants for Construction of Municipal Sewage Treatment Works*, December 31, 1973.

25. *New York Times*, May 23, 1973.

26. Rockefeller, *Public Papers, 1968*, p. 1210.

27. Rockefeller, *Public Papers, 1971*, p. 251.

28. Ibid., p. 579.

29. *New York Times,* July 26, 1972.

30. Ibid., May 23, 1972.

31. *Albany Knickerbocker News,* December 21, 1972.

32. *New York Times,* March 15, 1973.

33. Ibid., April 28, 1973.

34. Ibid., May 23, 1973.

35. Ibid., August 23 and 25, 1976.

36. Rockefeller, *Public Papers, 1960,* pp. 152–53.

37. Rockefeller, *Public Papers, 1962,* p. 852.

38. Robert A. Caro, *The Power Broker: Robert Moses and the Fall of New York* (New York: Knopf, 1974), pp. 1074–1075.

39. *New York Times,* December 2, 1962.

40. Robert Moses, private interview, August 2, 1972; and Rockefeller, private interview, July 21, 1972.

41. Rockefeller, *Public Papers, 1965,* pp. 613–614.

42. See also chap. 5 for a discussion of parks.

43. U.S. Senate, Committee on Rules and Administration, *Hearings on the Nomination of Nelson A. Rockefeller to Be Vice President of the United States,* 93d Cong., 2d sess., September 23, 1974, p. 30.

44. Allan R. Talbot, *Power along the Hudson: The Storm King Controversy and the Birth of Environmentalism* (New York: Dutton, 1972), p. 77; see also Robert H. Boyle, *The Hudson River: A Natural and Unnatural History* (New York: Norton, 1969), pp. 153–74; and Myer Kutz, *Rockefeller Power* (New York: Simon & Schuster, 1974), pp. 157–171.

45. Talbot, *Power along the Hudson,* p. 121.

46. Nelson A. Rockefeller, *Our Environment Can Be Saved* (New York: Doubleday, 1970), p. 79.

47. Rockefeller, *Public Papers, 1972,* p. 152.

48. Steve Lawrence, "Only One Power Plant Has Been Approved in New York State since the Legislature Created the Siting Board in 1972," *Empire State Report* 1 (January–February 1978), pp. 14–17.

49. Talbot, *Power along the Hudson,* p. 168.

50. U.S. House of Representatives, Committee on Merchant Marine and Fisheries, Subcommittee on Fisheries and Wildlife Conservation, *Hearings on the Impact of the Hudson River Expressway,* 91st Cong., 1st sess., June 24–25, 1969, p. 123.

51. Rockefeller, *Public Papers, 1965,* pp. 1265–1266.

52. U.S. House of Representatives, *Hearings on the Impact of the Hudson River Expressway,* p. 123.

53. Ibid., pp. 53–54.

54. Rockefeller, *Public Papers, 1971,* pp. 1619–1621.

55. Rockefeller, *Public Papers, 1967,* pp. 892–893.

56. *New York Times,* May 9, 1973.

57. Marilyn Weigold, "Bridging Long Island Sound," *New York Affairs* 3, no. 3 (1975):57.

58. Rockefeller, *Public Papers, 1971,* p. 291.

59. *New York Times,* June 21, 1973.

60. Rockefeller, *Public Papers, 1960,* pp. 25, 428.

61. Rockefeller, *Our Environment* Can *Be Saved,* p. 125.

62. New York State Laws, 1960, chap. 313.

63. Rockefeller to MacNeil Mitchell, October 31, 1961, General File, Executive Chamber, Albany.

64. Rockefeller, *Public Papers, 1965,* pp. 591–592.

65. New York State Council on the Arts, *Annual Reports,* 1962/63, 1963/64.

66. Ibid., 1970/71.

67. Rockefeller, *Public Papers, 1970.*

68. State of New York, Division of the Budget, Organization and Management Unit, *Management Survey of the New York State Council on the Arts,* March 1971.

69. Rockefeller, *Public Papers, 1966,* pp. 495–496, 1172–1173.

70. Ibid., pp. 451–452.

71. Rockefeller, *Public Papers, 1964,* p. 1280.

72. Ibid., p. 1328; and Rockefeller, address delivered at groundbreaking for Center for the Performing Arts, Saratoga Springs, June 30, 1964.

73. *Albany Times-Union,* August 4, 1966.

10. *The Governor and Washington*

1. Coleman B. Ransone, Jr., *The Office of Governor in the United States* (University: University of Alabama Press, 1956). Ransone was one of the first writers to observe the growing importance of Washington relations to modern state and local government chief executives.

2. James L. Sundquist and David W. Davis, *Making Federalism Work* (Washington, D.C.: Brookings Institution, 1969), p. 7.

3. See Thad Beyle and J. Oliver Williams, eds., *The American Governor in Behavioral Perspective* (New York: Harper & Row, 1972).

4. Nelson A. Rockefeller, *The Future of Federalism* (Cambridge: Harvard University Press, 1962), p. 42.

5. Ibid., p. 55.

6. See chap. 1 for a description of Rockefeller's Washington experience.

7. Telegram, Rockefeller to Eisenhower, December 23, 1954, Rockefeller Family Archives, Tarrytown, N.Y.

8. Benjamin C. Bradlee, *Conversations with Kennedy* (New York: Norton, 1975), p. 121.

9. Rockefeller to Johnson, February 3, 1964, Rockefeller Family Archives. The following account is based on a review of the governor's correspondence with President Johnson.

10. Rockefeller to Johnson, January 7, 1969.

11. Nelson A. Rockefeller, private interview, January 23, 1976.

12. William Safire, *Before the Fall: An Inside View of the Pre-Watergate White House* (Garden City, N.Y.: Doubleday, 1975), p. 29.

13. Richard Reeves, *A Ford, Not a Lincoln* (New York: Harcourt Brace Jovanovich, 1975), p. 150.

14. U.S. Senate, Committee on Rules and Administration, *Hearings on the Nomination of Nelson A. Rockefeller of New York to Be Vice President of the United States*, 93d Cong., 2d sess., September 23, 1974, p. 143.

15. Donald Haider, "The New York City Congressional Delegation," *City Almanac* 7 (April 1973).

16. The number of congressmen from New York during the Rockefeller governorship declined from forty-three to thirty-nine because of changes resulting from the 1960 and 1970 censuses.

17. Rockefeller to Javits, September 29, 1959, Rockefeller Family Archives. The following account of the Javits–Rockefeller relationship is based on this correspondence. For a description of abortive moves by Javits for the governorship, see chap. 2.

18. Mary Kresky, private interview, May 24, 1973.

19. For a further discussion, see chap. 6.

20. For a fuller description of the relations of the governor with the state's United States senators, see chap. 2.

21. Nelson A. Rockefeller, *Public Papers of Nelson A. Rockefeller, 1965*, (Albany: State of New York), p. 1518.

22. Rockefeller to Kennedy, September 29, 1965, Rockefeller Family Archives.

23. Telegram, Rockefeller to Goodell, December 23, 1969, Rockefeller Family Archives.

24. U.S. House of Representatives, Committee on Governmental Operations, *Hearings on Grant Consolidation and Intergovernmental Cooperation*, 91st Cong., 1st sess., 1969, p. 86.

25. See chap. 1 for an account of Rockefeller's Washington experience.

26. See chap. 9 for a detailed examination of the Pure Waters Program.

27. U.S. House of Representatives, Committee on Public Works, *Hearings on Water Pollution Control Legislation*, 92d Cong., 1st sess., 1971, p. 481.

28. Ibid., p. 497.

29. Both quotations are from *Wall Street Journal*, December 4, 1973.

30. Richard Ogilvie, private interview, October 24, 1973.

31. Rockefeller to Brown, February 3, 1966.

32. See Glenn E. Brooks, *When Governors Convene: The Governors' Conference and National Politics* (Baltimore: Johns Hopkins University Press, 1961).

33. National Governors' Conference, *Official Papers—Special Interim Meeting* (White Sulphur Springs, W. Va., December 16–17, 1966).

34. *New York Times*, September 3, 1969.

35. See Stephen Hess and David S. Broder, *The Republican Establishment: The Present and Future of the GOP* (New York: Harper & Row, 1967), chap. 1.

36. See reports issued by the Republican National Committee, "The Restoration of Federalism in America," April 1967, and "New Directions for Urban America," May 1968.

37. See chap. 11 for an account of this effort.

38. David B. Walker, private interview, May 7, 1974.

39. U.S. Congress, Joint Committee on Government Operations, Subcommittees on Intergovernmental Relations and Human Resources, *Ten-Year Record of the Advisory Commission on Intergovernmental Relations*, 92nd Cong., 1st sess., 1971.

40. See chap. 6 for an account of fiscal affairs in New York.

41. Nelson A. Rockefeller, "Message Transmitting the Executive Budget and Recommending Appropriations for 1971–1972," *Public Papers, 1971*, pp. 64–67.

42. See Water W. Heller, *New Dimensions of Political Economy* (New York: Norton, 1967), and *General Revenue Sharing Proposals* (Washington, D.C.: American Enterprise Institute, 1971).

43. T. Norman Hurd, private interview, December 3, 1974.

44. *New York Times*, February 19, 1969.

45. For a discussion of the New Federalism, see Richard D. Nathan, *The Plot That Failed: Nixon and the Administrative Presidency* (New York: Wiley, 1975).

46. *Washington Post*, September 2, 1969.

47. Nelson A. Rockefeller, speech before the Brooklyn Chamber of Commerce, reported in the *New York Times*, September 12, 1969.

48. *New York Times*, April 25, 1969.

49. For a detailed discussion of lobbying by public interest groups, see Donald H. Haider, *When Governments Come to Washington: Governors, Mayors, and Intergovernmental Lobbying* (New York: Free Press, 1974).

50. *New York Times*, December 2, 1970.

51. Ibid., November 19, 1970.

52. Ibid., November 11, 1970.

53. Ibid., November 20, 1970.

54. Ibid., November 24, 1970.

55. Ibid.

56. Ibid., December 4, 1970.

57. See tesitmony by the National Citizens Committee for Revenue Sharing, U.S. House of Representatives, Committee on Ways and Means, *General Revenue Sharing Hearings of 1971*, 92d Cong., 1st sess., 1971, pt. 6, pp. 997–1028. See also Frank V. Fowlkes and Harry Lenhart, "Two Money Committees Wield Power Differently," *National Journal* 3 (April 10, 1971):779–807.

58. *New York Times*, January 27, 1971.

59. Ibid., May 27, 1971.

60. U.S. House of Representatives, *General Revenue Sharing Hearings of 1971*, pt. 5, p. 804; and *New York Times*, July 16, 1971.

61. Rockefeller to New York City congressional delegation, March 3, 1971, Rockefeller Family Archives.

62. U.S. Senate, Committee on Government Operations, Subcommittee on Intergovernmental Relations, *Intergovernmental Revenue Act Hearings of 1971*, 92d Cong., 1st sess., 1971, pp. 213–247.

63. James Cannon, private interview, February 8, 1973.

64. Kresky, private interview, June 7, 1973.

65. Ibid.

66. *New York Times*, January 17, 1972.

67. Mills to Rockefeller, January 1, 1971, Rockefeller Family Archives.

68. Kresky, private interview, June 7, 1973.

69. See Richard E. Thompson, *Revenue Sharing: A New Era in Federalism* (Washington, D.C.: Revenue Sharing Advisory Service, 1973), pp. 94–107.

70. Dunn to Rockefeller, July 11, 1972, Rockefeller Family Archives.

71. *New York Times*, July 21, 1972.

72. U.S. Senate, Committee on Finance, *Revenue Sharing Hearings of 1972*, 92d Cong., 2d sess., 1972, p. 132.

73. Rockefeller, private interview, July 2, 1972.

74. U.S. Senate, *Revenue Sharing Hearings of 1972*, p. 111.

75. Ibid., p. 113.

76. Cannon, private interview, February 8, 1973.

77. See Thompson, *Revenue Sharing*, 117–122; and Timothy B. Clark, John K. Inglehart, and William Lilley III, "Revenue Sharing Bill Authorizes Sweeping Innovation in Federal Aid System," *National Journal*, 4 (October 7, 1972):1553–1566.

11. *The Rockefeller Stewardship*

1. William J. Ronan, private interview, January 7, 1976.

2. James Bryce, *The American Commonwealth* (New York: Macmillan, 1888), vol. 1, chap. 8.

3. On this point see Anthony Downs, *An Economic Theory of Democracy* (New York: Harper & Row, 1957), pp. 60–61, and William H. Riker, "Arrow's Theory and Some Examples of the Paradox of Voting," in *Mathematical Applications in Political Science*, ed. John M. Claunch (Charlottesville: University of Virginia Press, 1964), p. 43.

4. Hugh Morrow, private interview, June 9, 1972.

5. President's Commission on Administrative Management, *Administrative Management in the Government of the United States* (Washington, D.C.: Government Printing Office, 1937); and Commission on Organization of the Executive Branch of the Government, *General Management of the Executive Branch* (Washington, D.C.: Government Printing Office, 1949).

6. Richard E. Neustadt, *Presidential Power: The Politics of Leadership* (New York: Wiley, 1960).

7. Thomas Cronin, "The Textbook Presidency and Political Science," *Congressional Record* 116 (October 5, 1970), S. 17102 15. See also Thomas Cronin, *The State of the Presidency* (Boston: Little, Brown, 1975), chap. 20.

8. On this point see Robert Coles, "The Children of Affluence," *Atlantic Monthly*, September 1977, p. 52.

9. Nelson A. Rockefeller, private interview, January 23, 1976.

10. Ibid.

11. Oren Root, *Persons and Persuasions* (New York: Norton, 1974), pp. 149–150.

12. V. O. Key, Jr., *American State Politics: An Introduction* (New York: Knopf, 1956); Duane Lockard, *New England State Politics* (Princeton: Princeton University Press, 1959); and Richard E. Dawson and James H. Robinson, "Inter-Party Competition, Economic Variables, and Welfare Policies in the American States," *Journal of Politics* 25 (1963):265–289.

13. Thomas K. Dye, "Executive Power and Public Policy in the United States," in *The American Governor in Behavioral Perspective*, ed. Thad Beyle and J. Oliver Williams (New York: Harper & Row, 1972), pp. 249, 253.

14. Sarah McCally Morehouse, "The Governor as Political Leader," in *Politics in the American States*, ed. Herbert Jacobs and Kenneth N. Vines, 3d ed. (Boston: Little, Brown, 1976), p. 219.

15. Ira Sharkansky, "Agency Requests, Gubernatorial Support, and Budget Success in State Legislatures," *American Political Science Review* 62 (December 1968):1220–1231; Brian R. Fry and Richard F. Winters, "The Politics of Redistribution," ibid. 64 (June 1970):508–522.

16. Bernard H. Booms and James R. Halldorson, "The Politics of Redistribution: A Reformulation," *American Political Science Review* 67 (September 1973):924–933.

17. Gerald Benjamin, "The Governor's Formal Powers and State Fiscal Policy," paper prepared for the National Endowment for the Humanities Seminar on Political Parties, University of Wisconsin, May 1977; see also Richard F. Winters, "Party Control and Policy Change," *American Journal of Political Science* 20 (November 1976):597–636.

18. Richard I. Hofferbert, *The Study of Public Policy* (Indianapolis: Bobbs-Merrill, 1974), p. 161.

19. Theodore Lowi, "American Business, Public Policy, Case Studies, and Political Theory," *World Politics* 16 (July 1964):667–715.

20. James David Barber, *The Presidential Character: Predicting Performance in the White House*, 2d ed. (Englewood Cliffs, N.J.: Prentice-Hall, 1972).

21. Jack L. Walker, "The Diffusion of Innovations among the American States," *American Political Science Review* 63 (September 1969):880–899.

22. Fred W. Grupp, Jr., and Alan R. Richards, "Variations in Elite Perceptions of American States as Referents for Public Policy Making," *American Political Science Review* 69 (September 1975):850–858.

23. Hundreds of laws were of course passed at each session of the legislature. Many of them concerned local matters; others might be called "private bills"; only a few affected major policy questions.

24. Thad Beyle, "The Governor's Formal Powers: A View from the Governor's Chair," *Public Administration Review* 28 (November–December 1968):540–545.

25. In 1976 the legislature voted to override the governor's veto for the first time in modern times when, over the objection of Governor Carey, it passed the Stavisky-Goodman bill, requiring the maintenance of the prior year's level of expenditures on the public schools in New York City. This fight developed out of the grave fiscal crisis that arose in the city in that year.

26. Morton Grodzins, *The American System: A New View of Government in the United States* (Chicago: Rand McNally, 1966); Daniel J. Elazar, ed., *Cooperation and Conflict: Readings in American Federalism* (Itasca, Ill.: Peacock, 1969).

27. Daniel J. Elazar, "The New Federalism: Can the States Be Trusted?" *Public Interest*, no. 35 (Spring 1974), p. 102.

28. Robert Douglass, private interview, February 6, 1976.

Index

Rockefeller of New York

Designed by Richard E. Rosenbaum.
Composed by The Composing Room of Michigan, Inc.,
in V.I.P. Palatino, 2 points leaded,
with display lines in Palatino Bold.
Printed offset by Vail-Ballou Press on
Warren's Olde Style, 60 pound basis.
Bound by Vail-Ballou Press
in Joanna book cloth
and stamped in All Purpose foil.